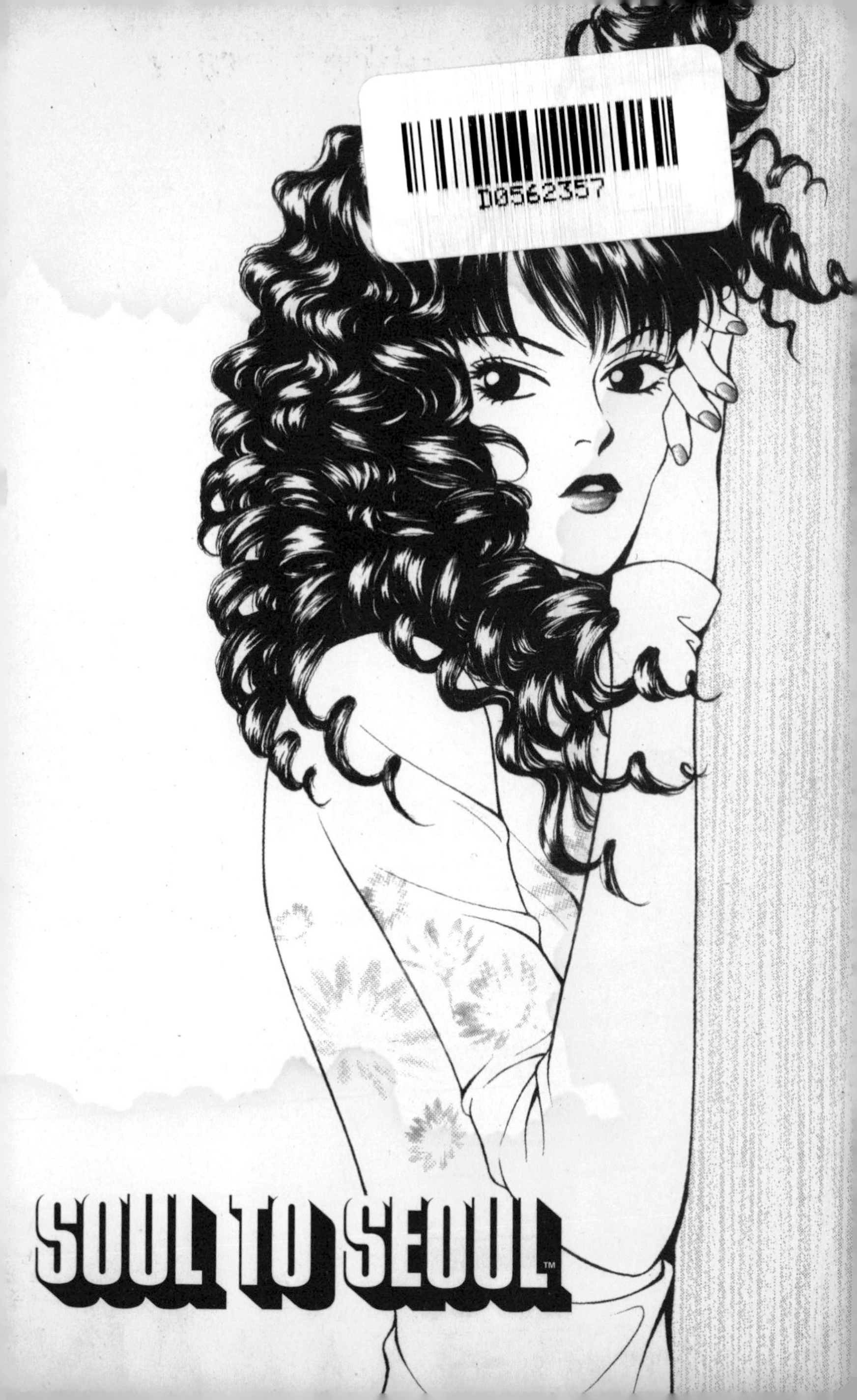
SOUL TO SEOUL™

Soul to Seoul Vol. 2
created by Kim Jea Eun

Translation - Ellen Choi
English Adaptation - Marc Goldsmith
Retouch and Lettering - Eva Han
Production Artist - Abelardo Bigting
Cover Design - Gary Shum

Editor - Julie Taylor
Digital Imaging Manager - Chris Buford
Pre-Press Manager - Antonio DePietro
Production Managers - Jennifer Miller and Mutsumi Miyazaki
Art Director - Matt Alford
Managing Editor - Jill Freshney
VP of Production - Ron Klamert
Editor-in-Chief - Mike Kiley
President and C.O.O. - John Parker
Publisher and C.E.O. - Stuart Levy

A **TOKYOPOP** Manga

TOKYOPOP Inc.
5900 Wilshire Blvd. Suite 2000
Los Angeles, CA 90036

E-mail: info@TOKYOPOP.com
Come visit us online at www.TOKYOPOP.com

ISBN: 1-59532-313-9

First TOKYOPOP printing: April 2005
10 9 8 7 6 5 4 3 2 1
Printed in the USA

SOUL TO SEOUL

Kim Jea Eun

HAMBURG // LONDON // LOS ANGELES // TOKYO

SOUL TO SEOUL™

Story So Far

Kai and Spike are best friends who share a common background: they are both half-Korean. Searching for identity in a world filled with intolerance, they feel uncomfortable even in their own homes because of their mixed heritage. Then they meet Sunil, a Korean foreign-exchange student, who leads them on a journey that is part self-discovery and all heart and soul....

From the Far East to the cool New York City streets, award-winning manga-ka Kim Jea-Eun has created a hot-blooded story filled with hip-hop flair, urban blight, and the power and passion of friendship.

Character Introductions

I've finally finished Vol. One! Since I was in the development stage, my art was going through a lot of changes. I'm hoping to be able to move onto Vol. Two with an improved and steady art style.

A Korean and white mix
Hobbies: Collecting army uniforms
Specialty: Lying, shooting
Wants to be: Gangster
Life motto: "Life is meaning-less, cruel and foolish, yet glamorous."

Kai Lee (Kangil Lee) 17 years old
177 cm / 67 kg / Blood type AB

A Korean immigrant
Hobbies: Swimming, dancing
Specialty: Tae Kwon Do
Wants to be: Traveler
Life motto: "It could be enjoyable to live in a place where you don't know anyone."

Sunil Sohn 17 years old
172 cm / 52 kg / Blood type O

Second-generation Korean American
Hobbies: Making dolls
Specialty: Screaming
Wants to be: Too young to decide that yet, don't you think?
Life motto: "I'm too young to think about that stuff..."

Gelda (Heesun Lee) 14 years old
158 cm / 48kg / Blood type A

Korean Adoptee
Hobbies: Read anything you can read
Specialty: Doing makeup
Wants to be: Punk rock musician
Life motto: "Any-thing you learn from pain is touching."

J.J. (Judas Jesus) 14 years old
163 cm / 51 kg / Blood type AB

A Korean and black mix
Hobbies: Working out
Specialty: Rap
Wants to be: A dad
Life motto: "Don't ever let them see you sweat."

Spike Washington. 17 years old
186cm/71 kg/ Blood type A

Exchange student from Korea
Hobbies: Hanging around
Specialty: Laughing at people
Wants to be: .....
Life motto: "I don't have a motto.."

Sangyul Choi 17 years old
165 cm / 58 kg / Blood type B

Soul to Seoul

CONTENTS

IN LIFE, THERE IS NO SUCH
THING AS A RESET BUTTON.
AND I DON'T EVER WANT IT
TO BE BORING.

THE GAME HAS ALREADY BEGUN.
BUT CAN I REALLY WIN IT ALL?

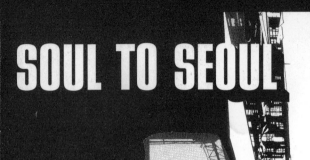

SOUL TO SEOUL™

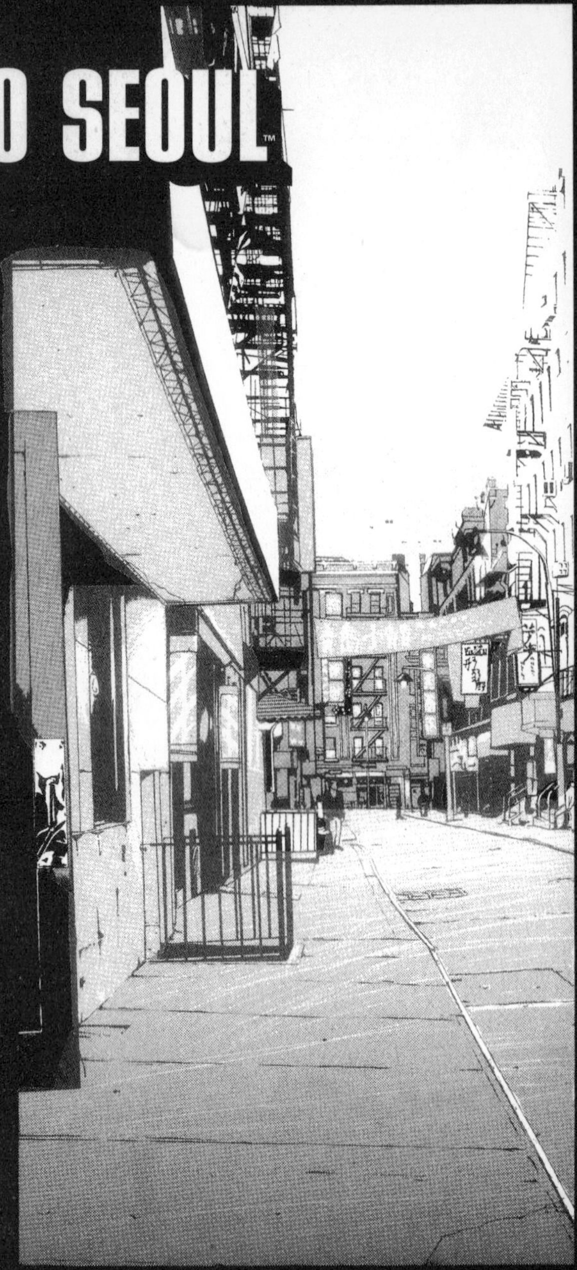

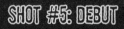

SHOT #5: DEBUT

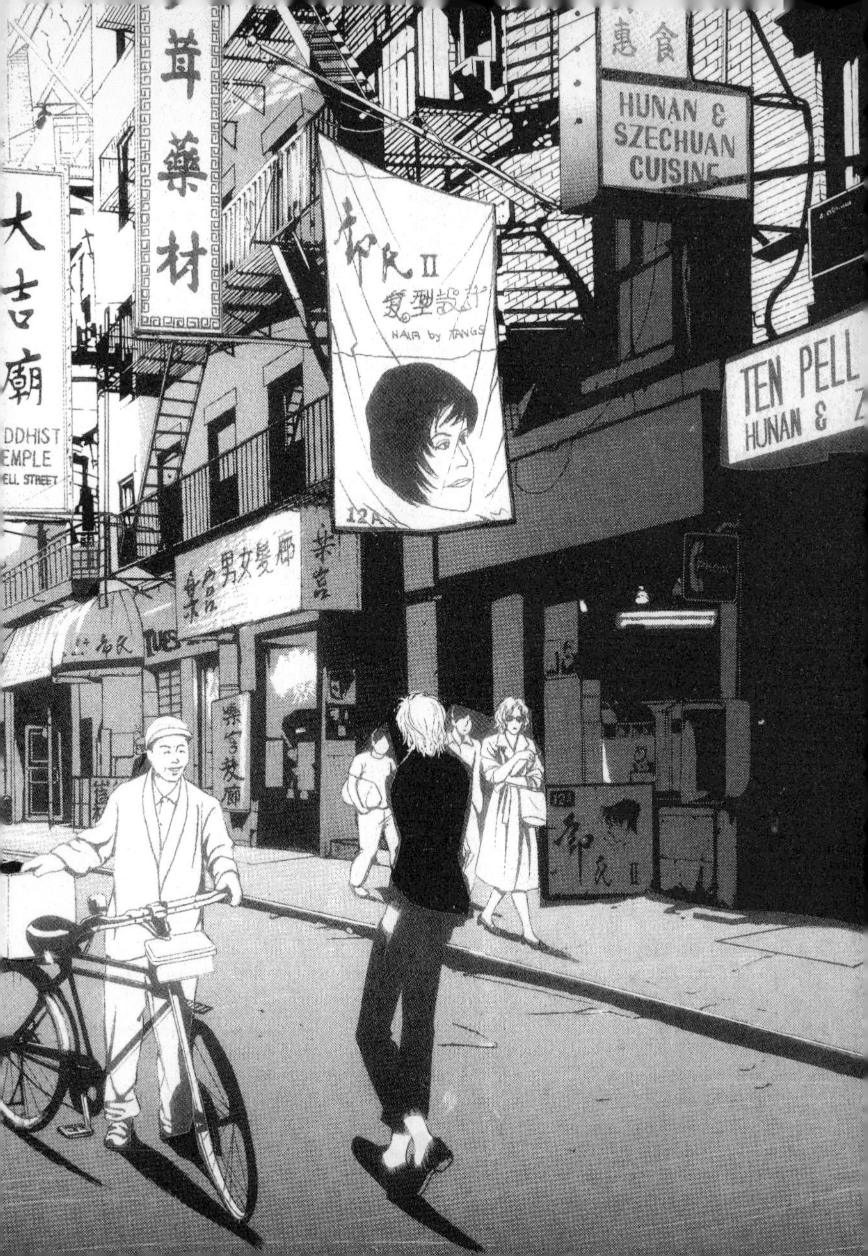

HUNAN & SZECHUAN CUISINE
茸藥材
大吉廟
HAIR by TANGS
12A
男女髮廊
TEN PELL
HUNAN &

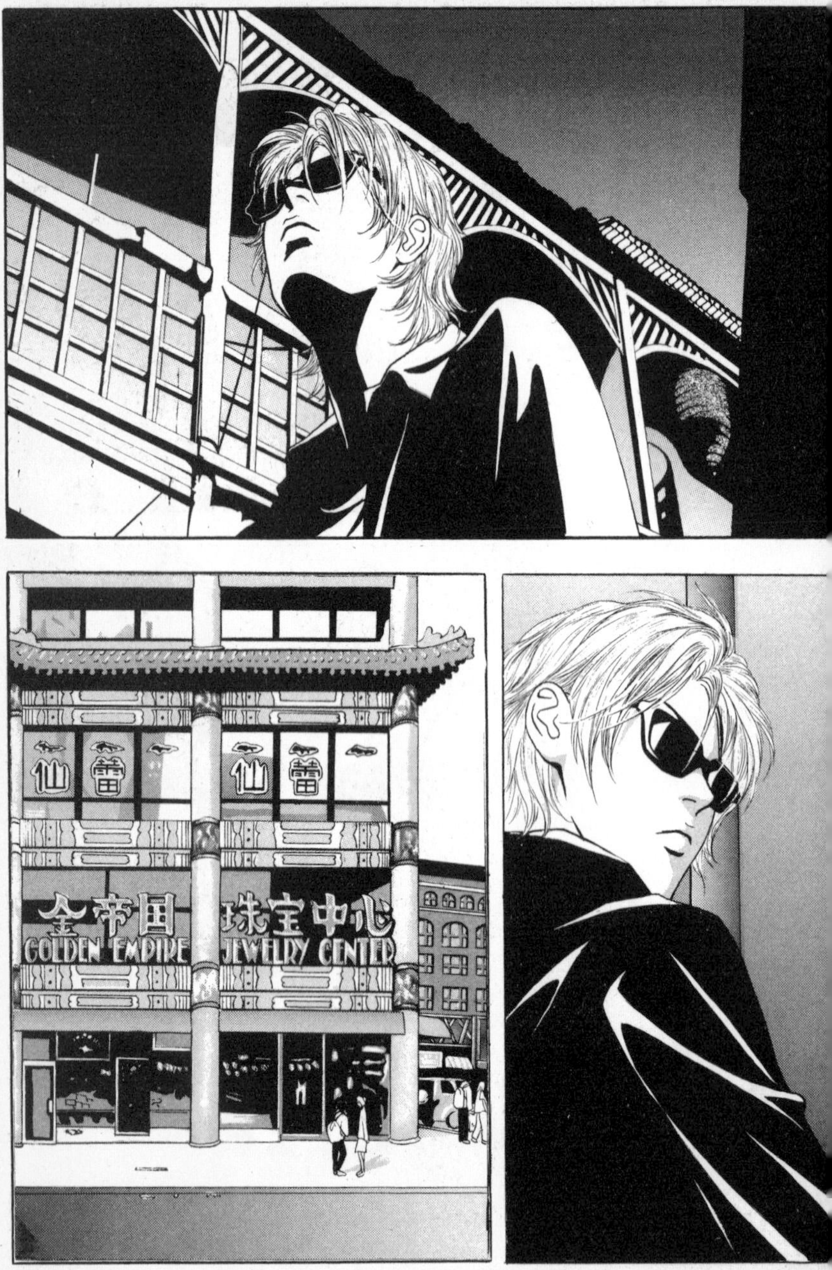

仙蕾
仙蕾
金帝国
珠宝中心
GOLDEN EMPIRE
JEWELRY CENTER

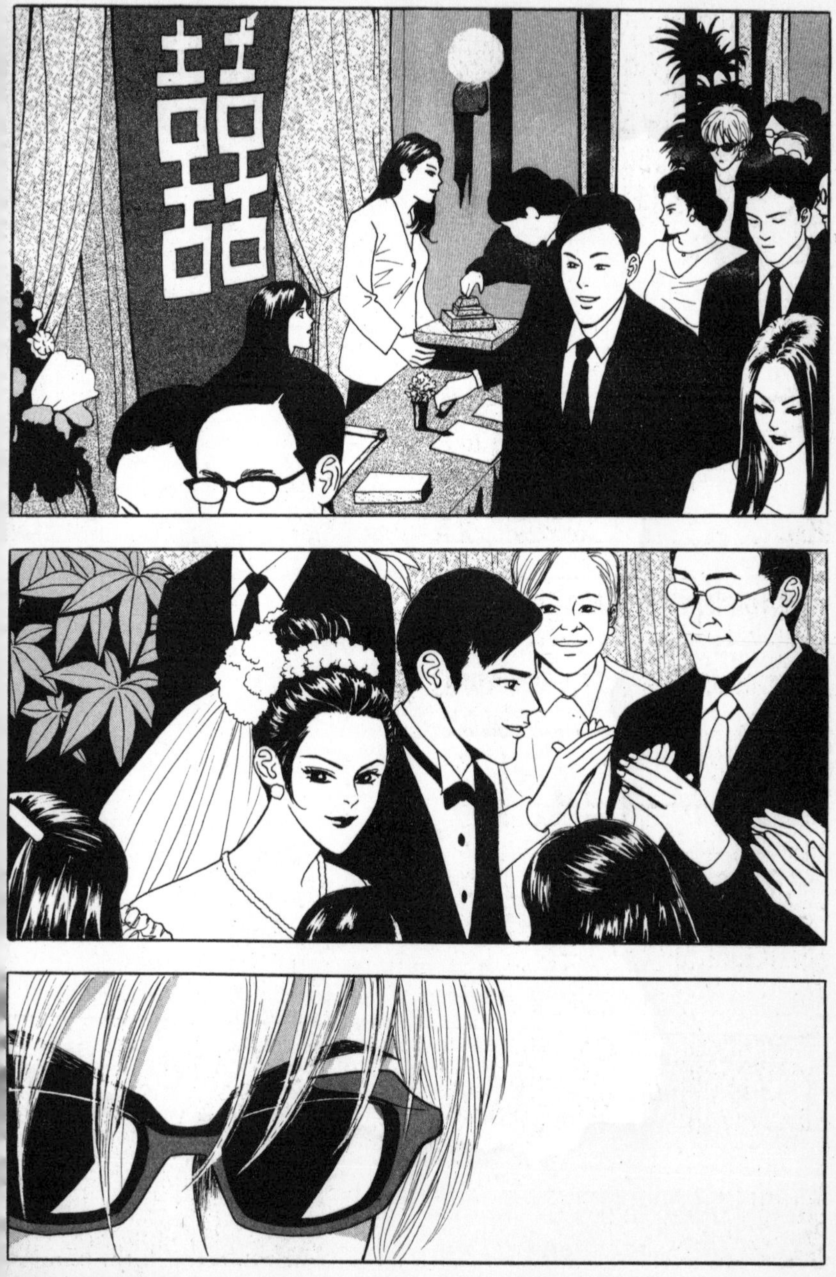
囍

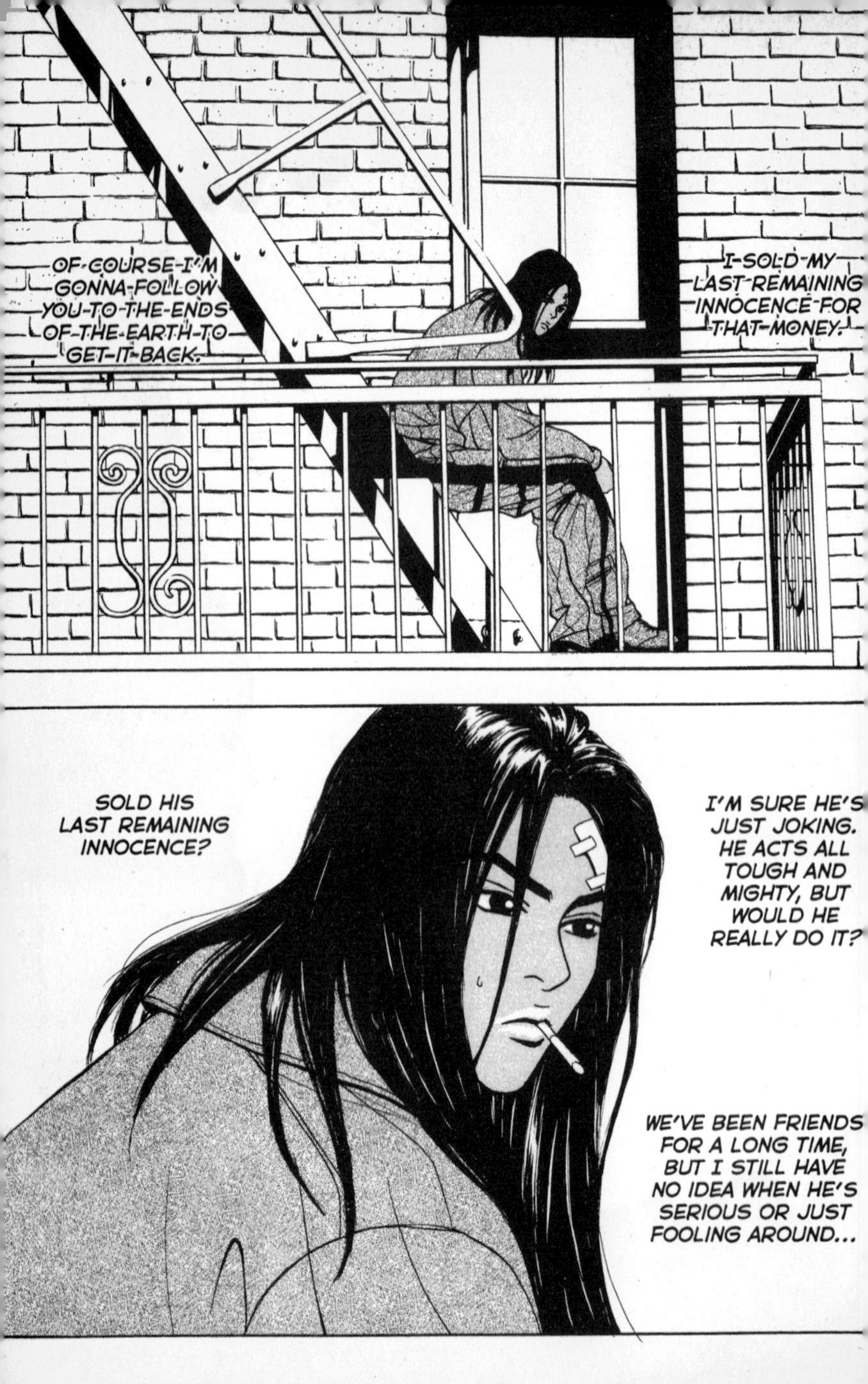
OF COURSE I'M GONNA FOLLOW YOU TO THE ENDS OF THE EARTH TO GET IT BACK.
I SOLD MY LAST REMAINING INNOCENCE FOR THAT MONEY.
SOLD HIS LAST REMAINING INNOCENCE?
I'M SURE HE'S JUST JOKING. HE ACTS ALL TOUGH AND MIGHTY, BUT WOULD HE REALLY DO IT?
WE'VE BEEN FRIENDS FOR A LONG TIME, BUT I STILL HAVE NO IDEA WHEN HE'S SERIOUS OR JUST FOOLING AROUND...

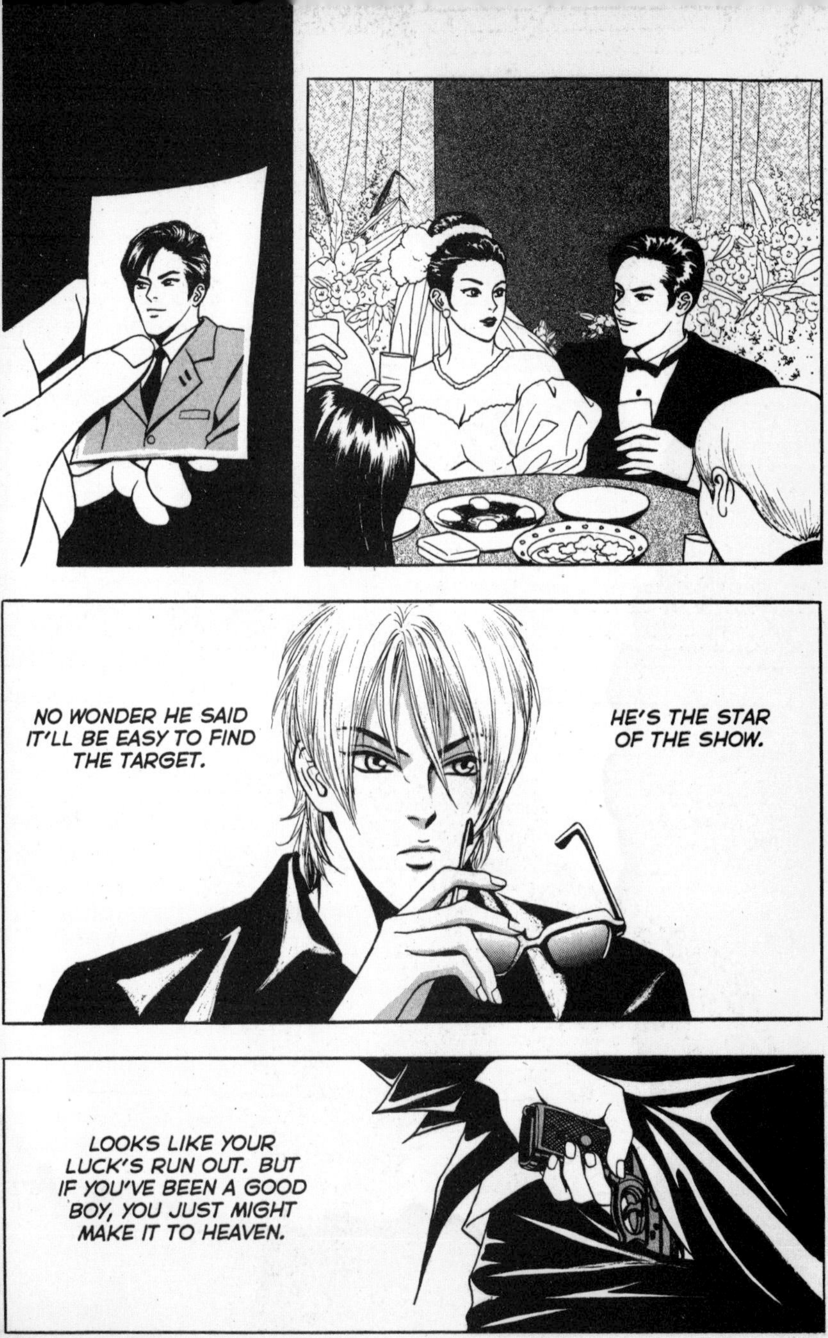
NO WONDER HE SAID IT'LL BE EASY TO FIND THE TARGET.
HE'S THE STAR OF THE SHOW.
LOOKS LIKE YOUR LUCK'S RUN OUT. BUT IF YOU'VE BEEN A GOOD BOY, YOU JUST MIGHT MAKE IT TO HEAVEN.

SANGYUL, YOU'RE ALONE? KAI STILL HASN'T COME BACK YET?

OH!

KAI?...OH, YOU MEAN KANGIL? IT'S BEEN AT LEAST THREE DAYS SINCE I'VE SEEN HIM.

I even cleaned up the room...

I hope she doesn't blame me for him not coming back.

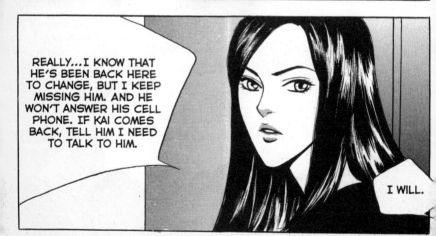

REALLY...I KNOW THAT HE'S BEEN BACK HERE TO CHANGE, BUT I KEEP MISSING HIM. AND HE WON'T ANSWER HIS CELL PHONE. IF KAI COMES BACK, TELL HIM I NEED TO TALK TO HIM.

I WILL.

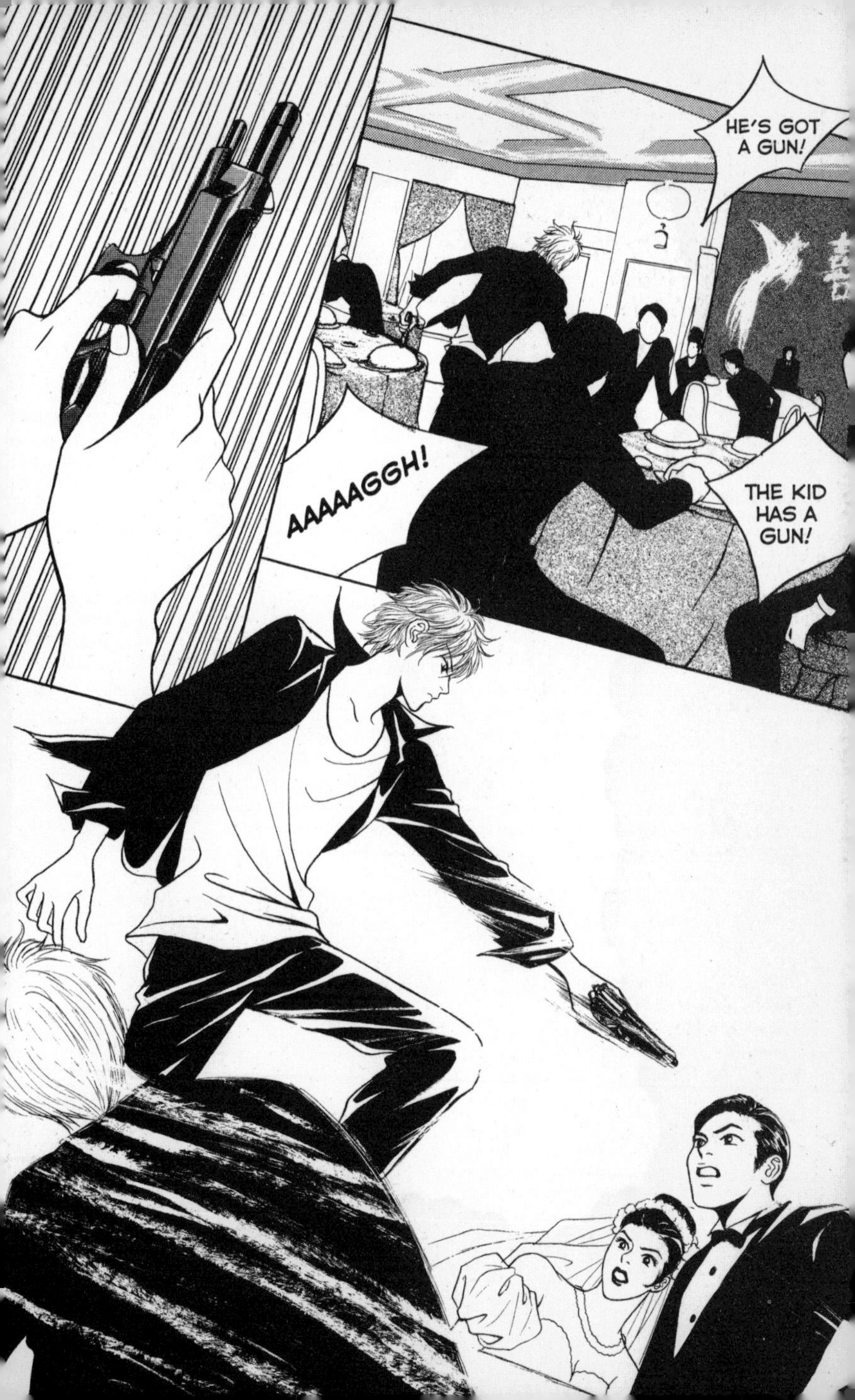
HE'S GOT A GUN!
AAAAAGGH!
THE KID HAS A GUN!

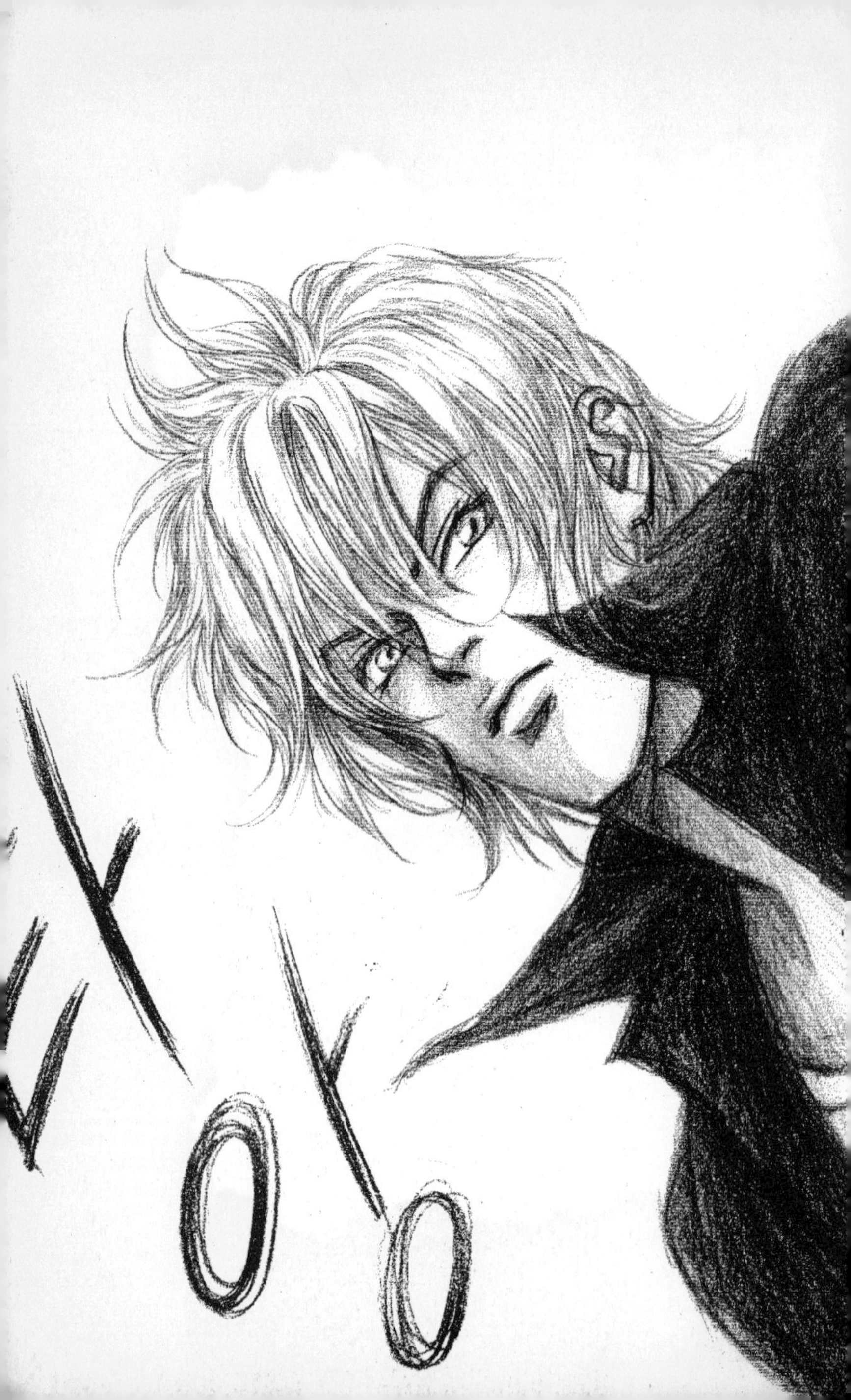

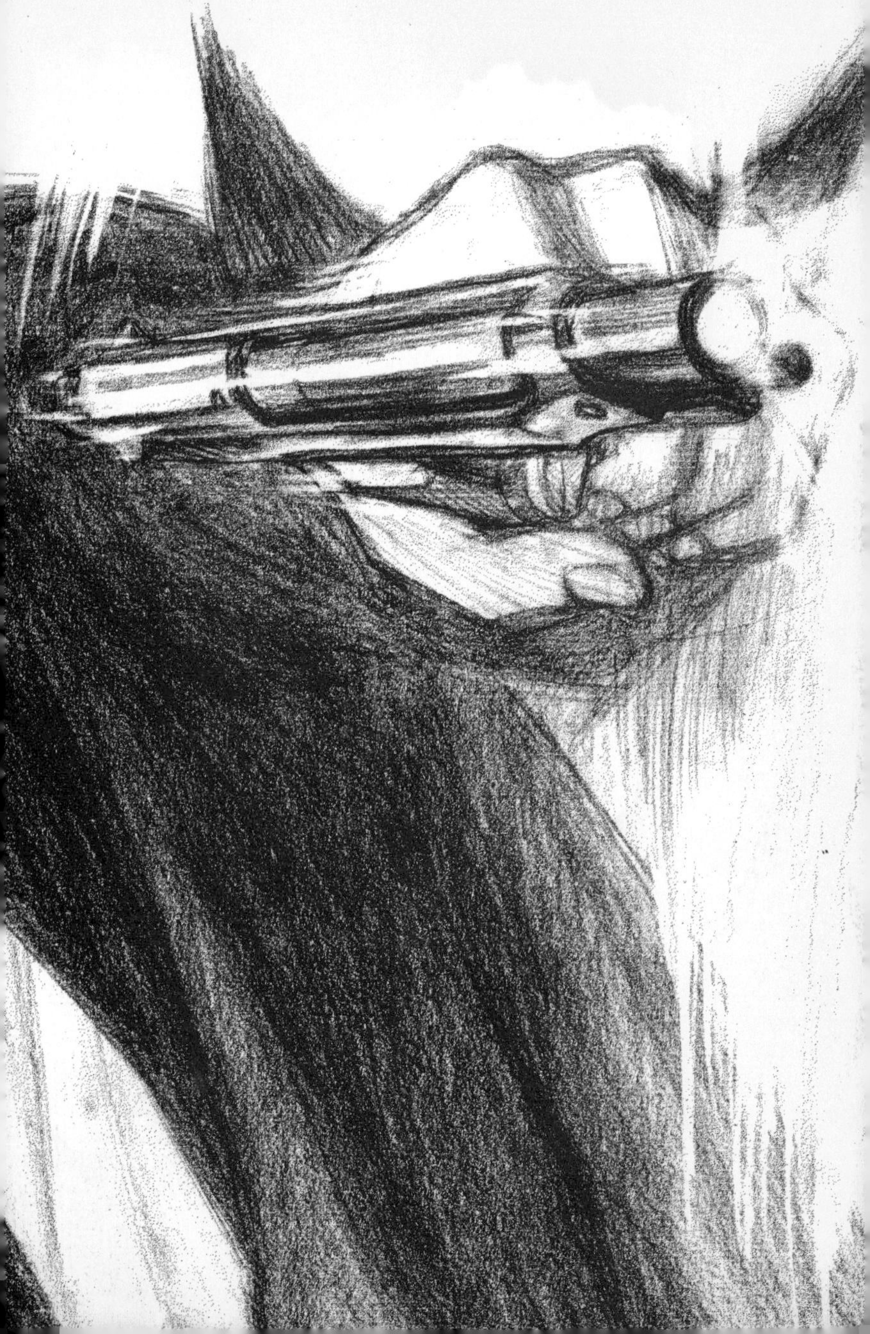

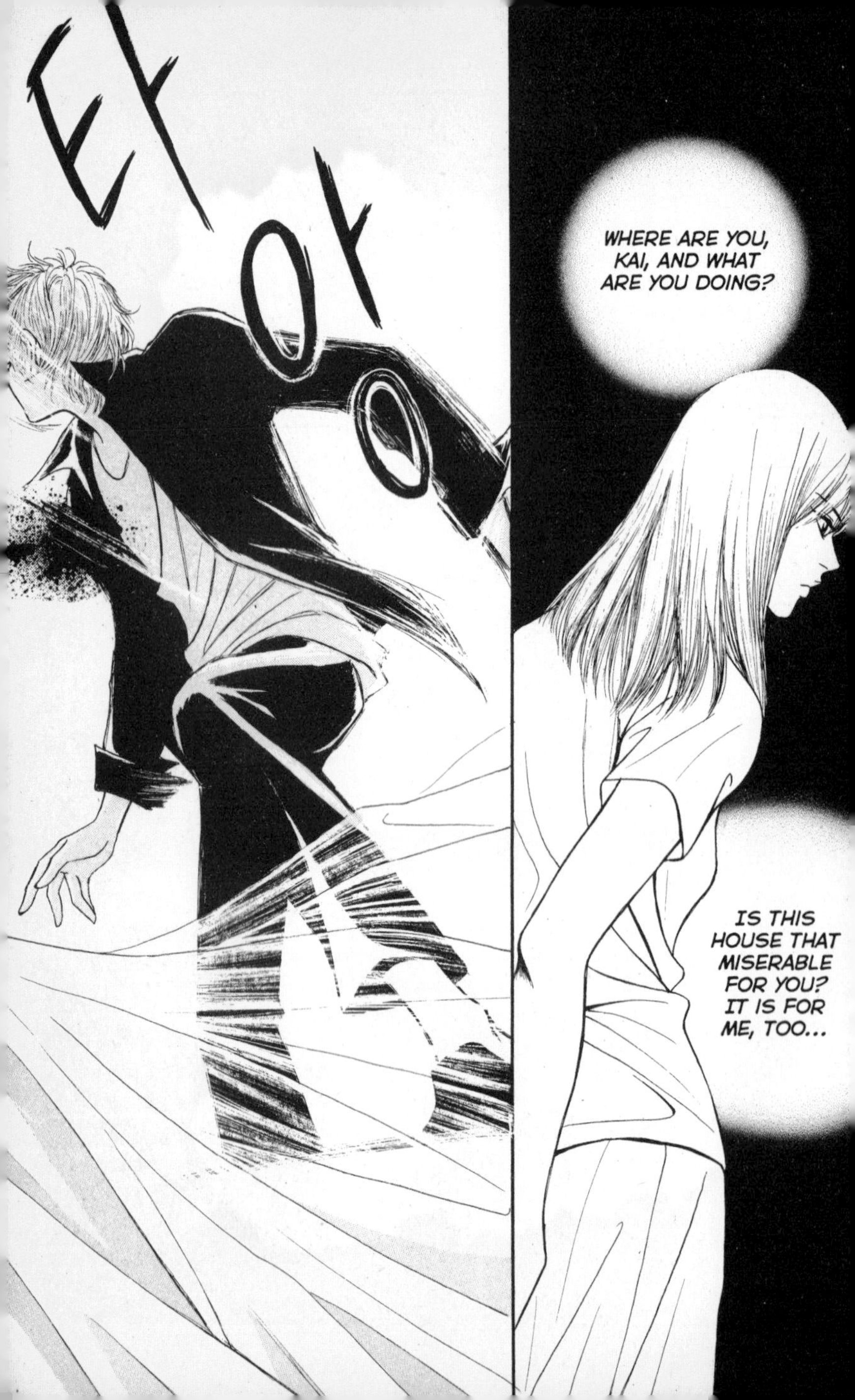
WHERE ARE YOU, KAI, AND WHAT ARE YOU DOING?
IS THIS HOUSE THAT MISERABLE FOR YOU? IT IS FOR ME, TOO...

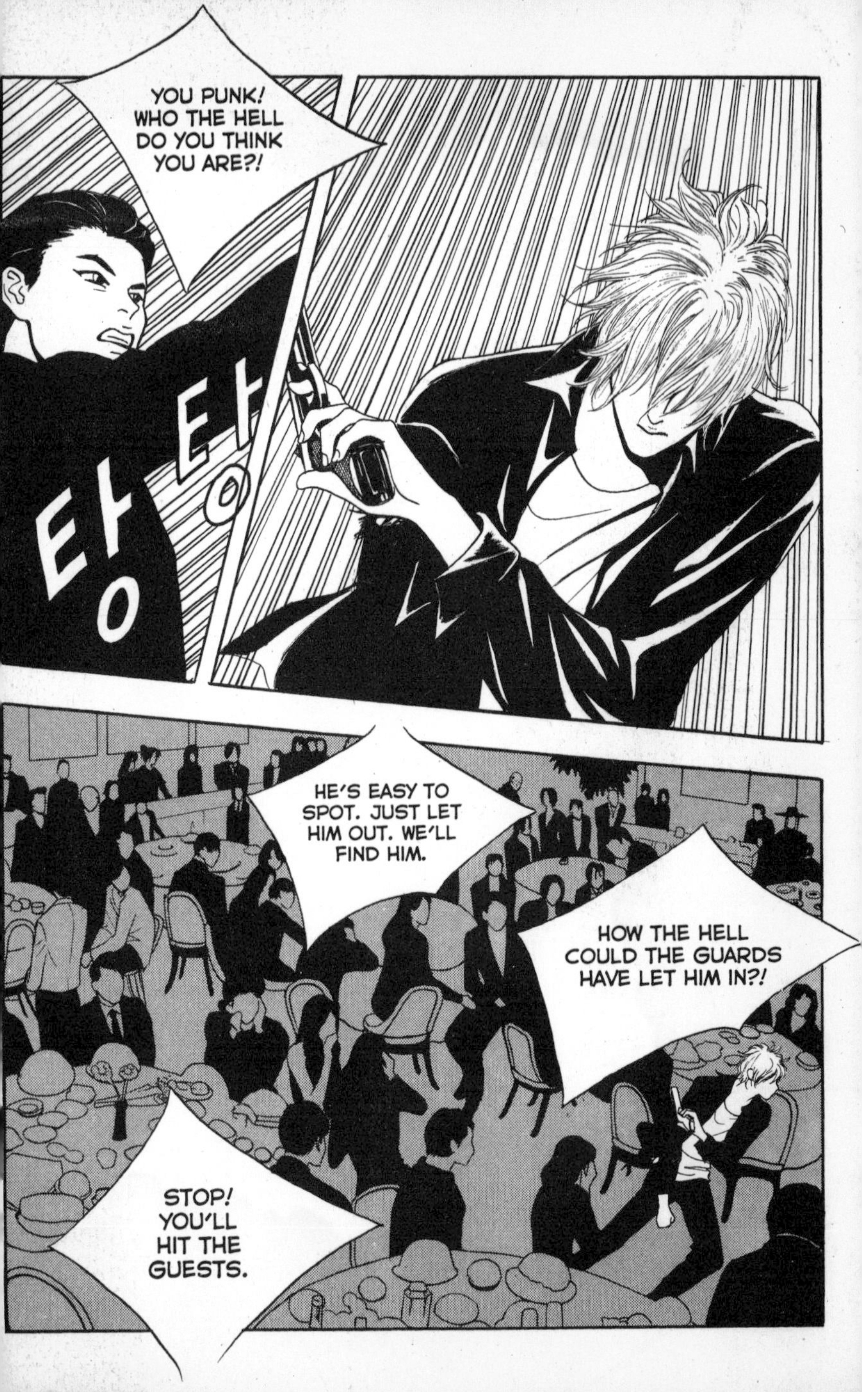
YOU PUNK! WHO THE HELL DO YOU THINK YOU ARE?!
탕
탕
HE'S EASY TO SPOT. JUST LET HIM OUT. WE'LL FIND HIM.
HOW THE HELL COULD THE GUARDS HAVE LET HIM IN?!
STOP! YOU'LL HIT THE GUESTS.

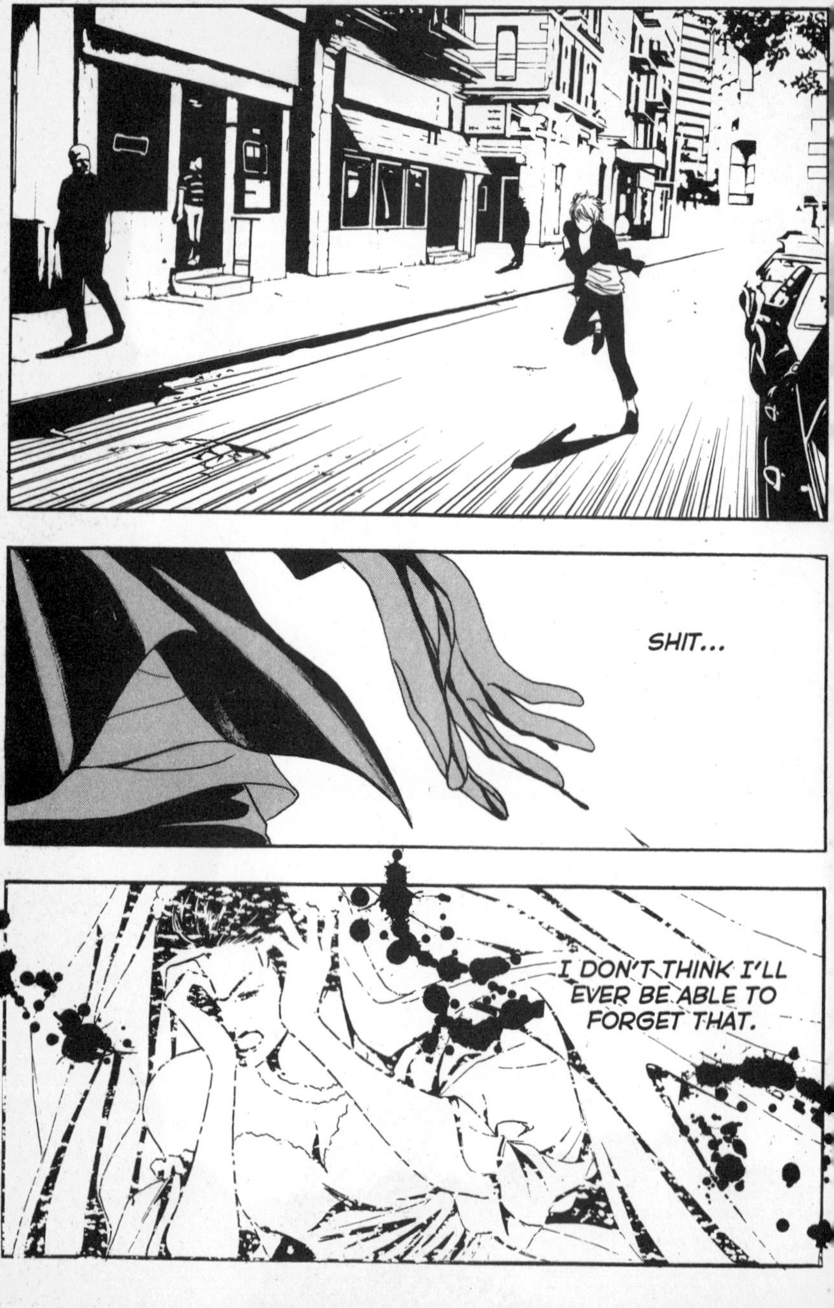
SHIT...
I DON'T THINK I'LL EVER BE ABLE TO FORGET THAT.

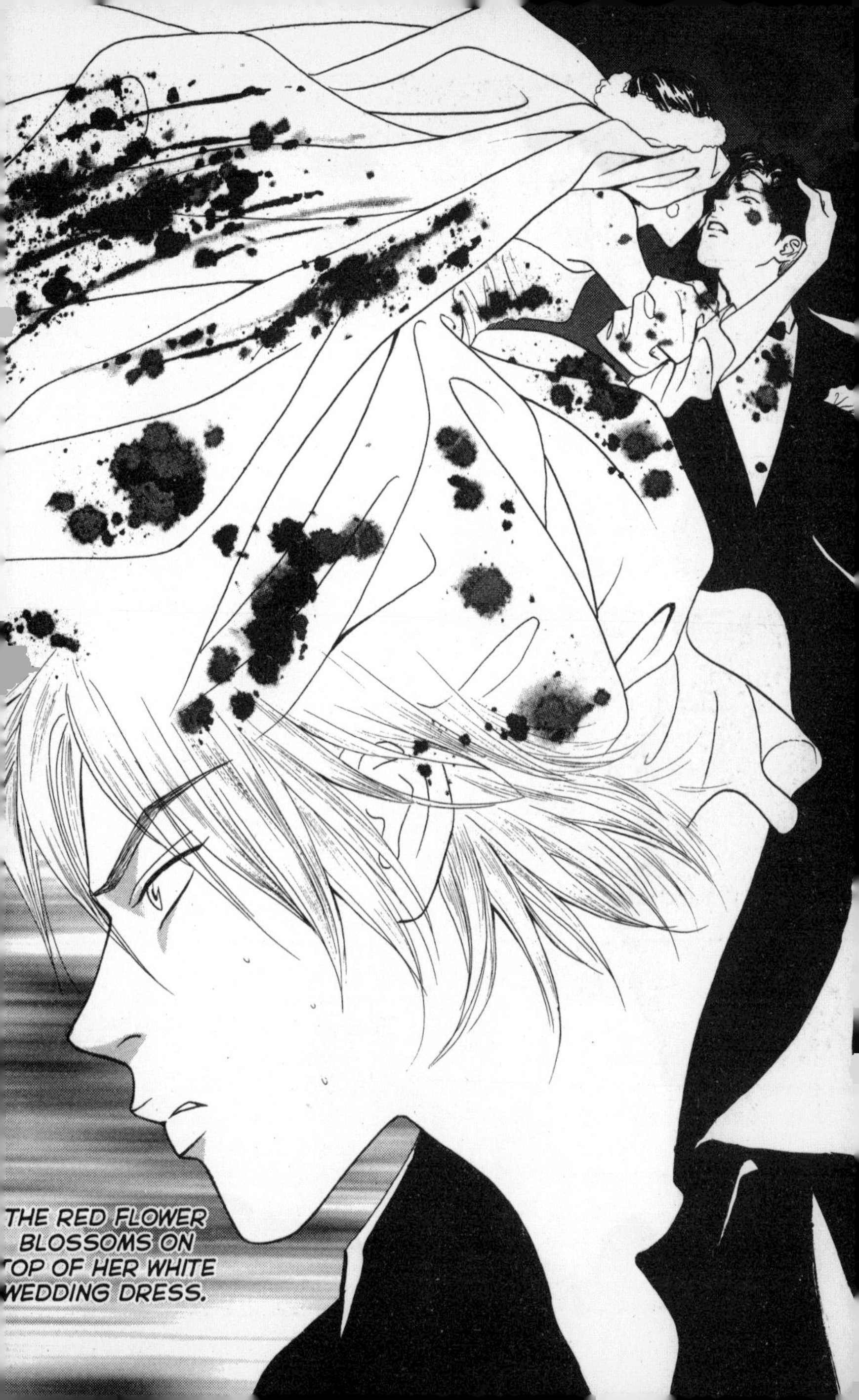
THE RED FLOWER BLOSSOMS ON TOP OF HER WHITE WEDDING DRESS.

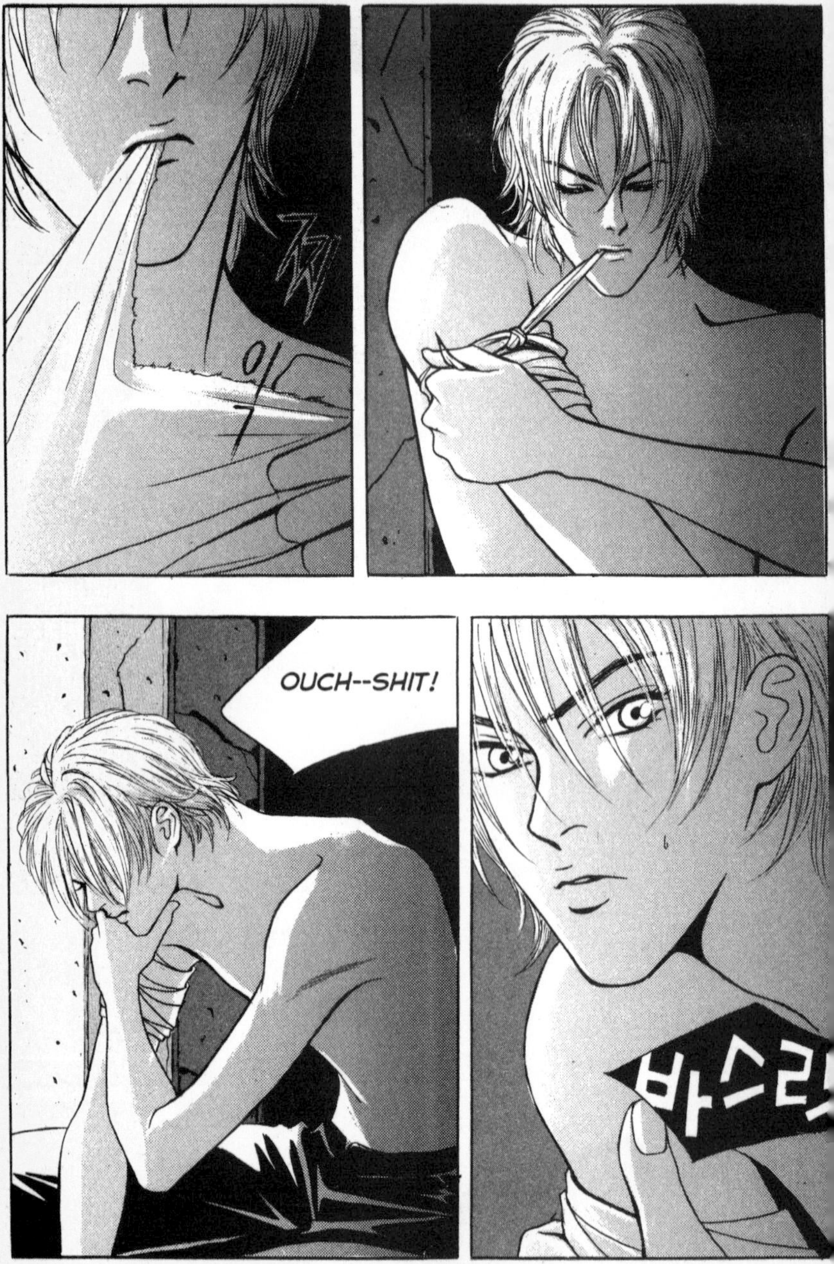
OUCH--SHIT!

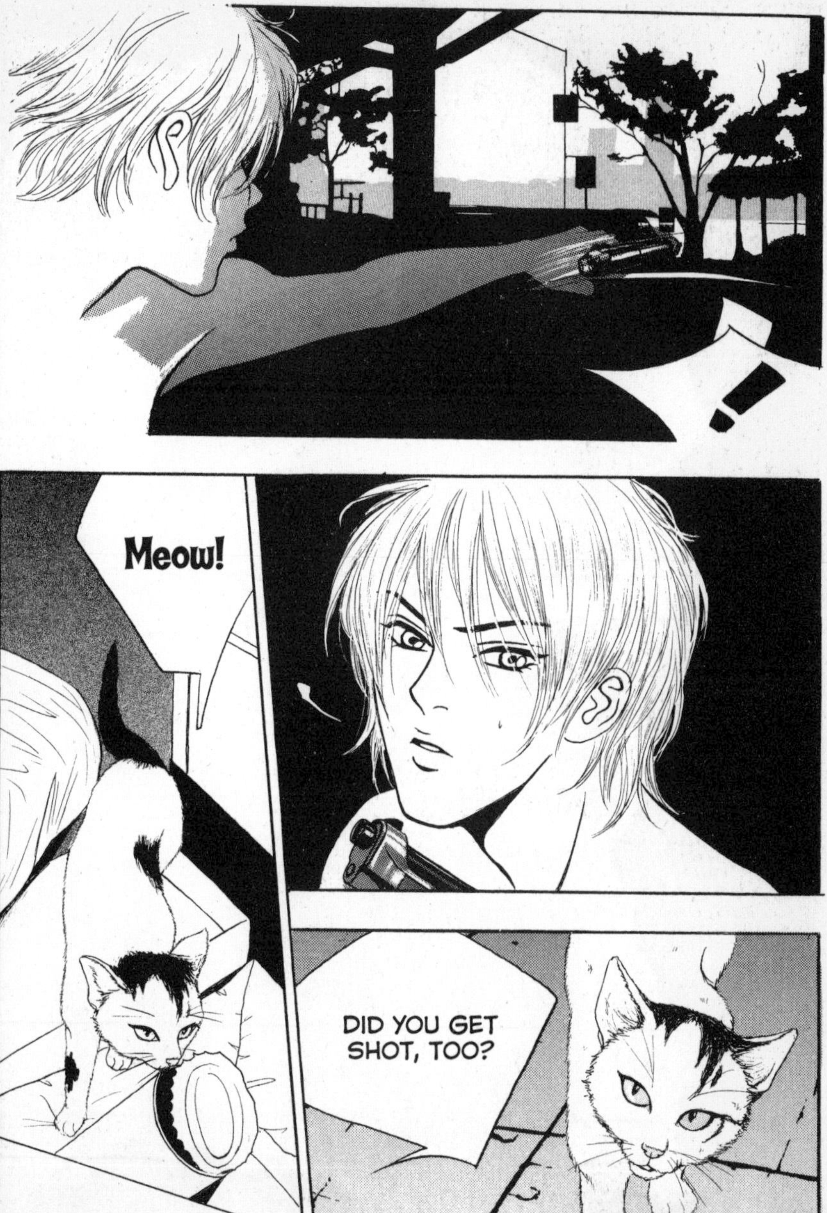
Meow!
DID YOU GET SHOT, TOO?

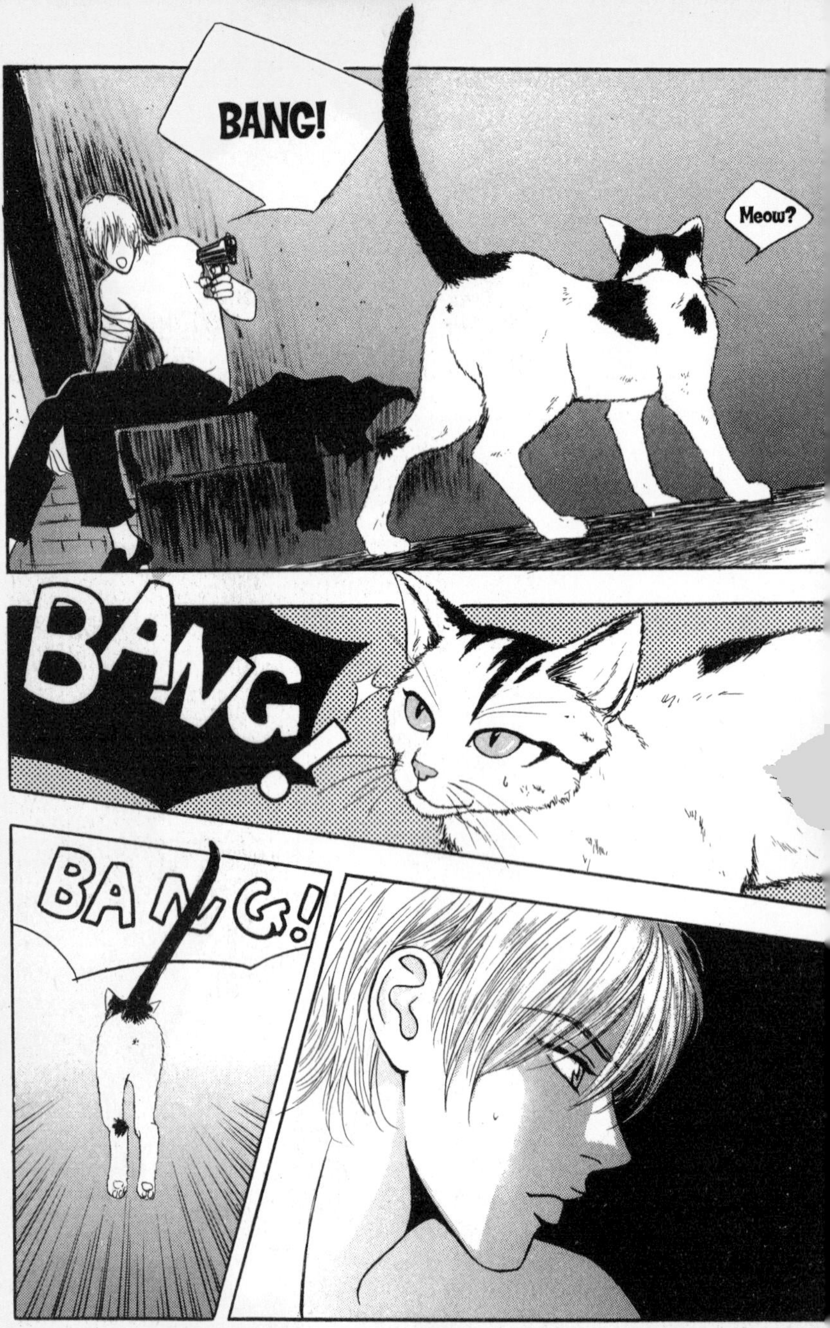
BANG!
Meow?
BANG!
BANG!

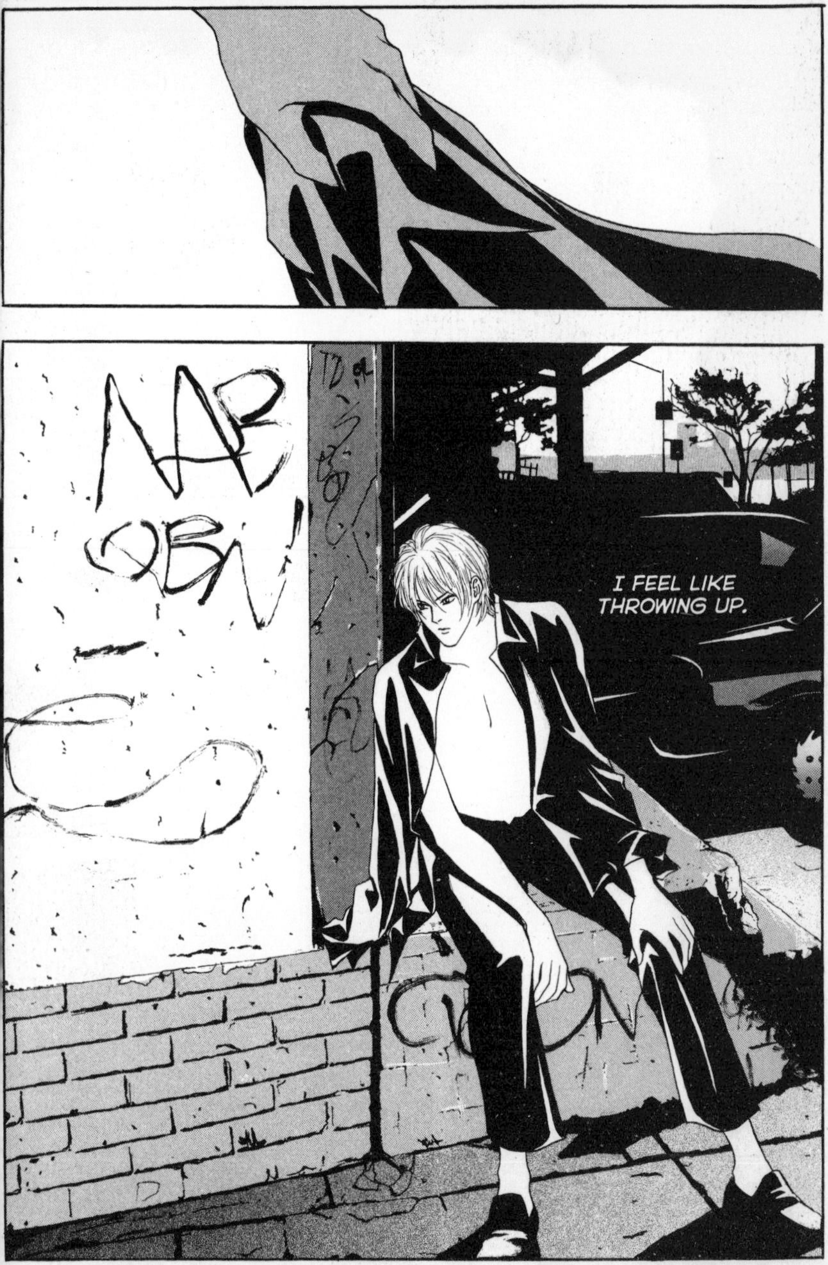
I FEEL LIKE THROWING UP.

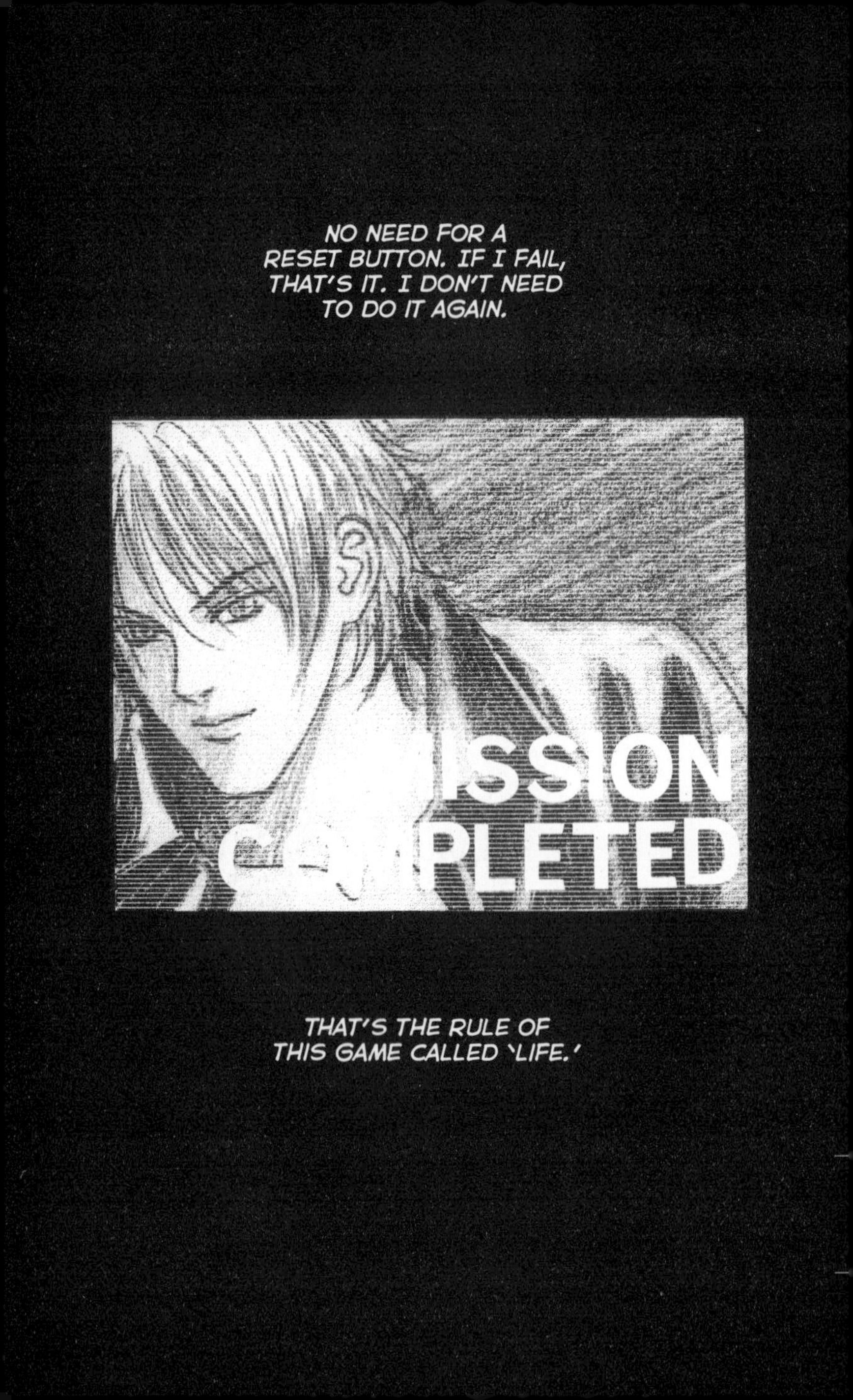
NO NEED FOR A RESET BUTTON. IF I FAIL, THAT'S IT. I DON'T NEED TO DO IT AGAIN.
SSION
PLETED
THAT'S THE RULE OF THIS GAME CALLED 'LIFE.'

SOUL TO SEOUL™

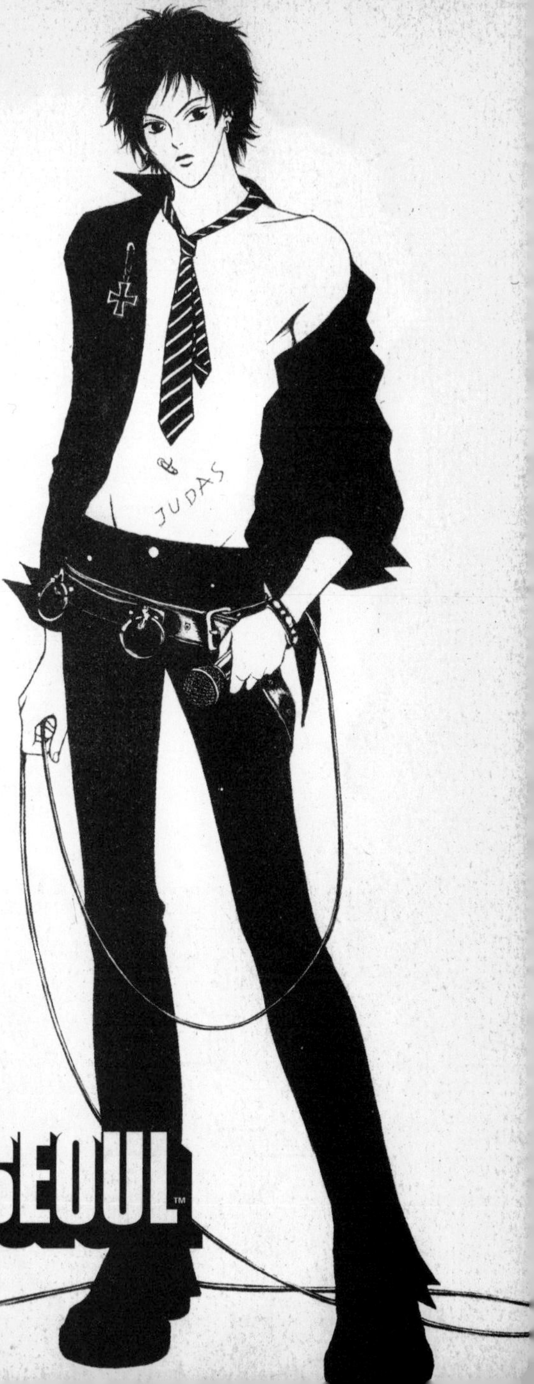
JUDAS

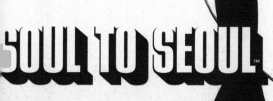

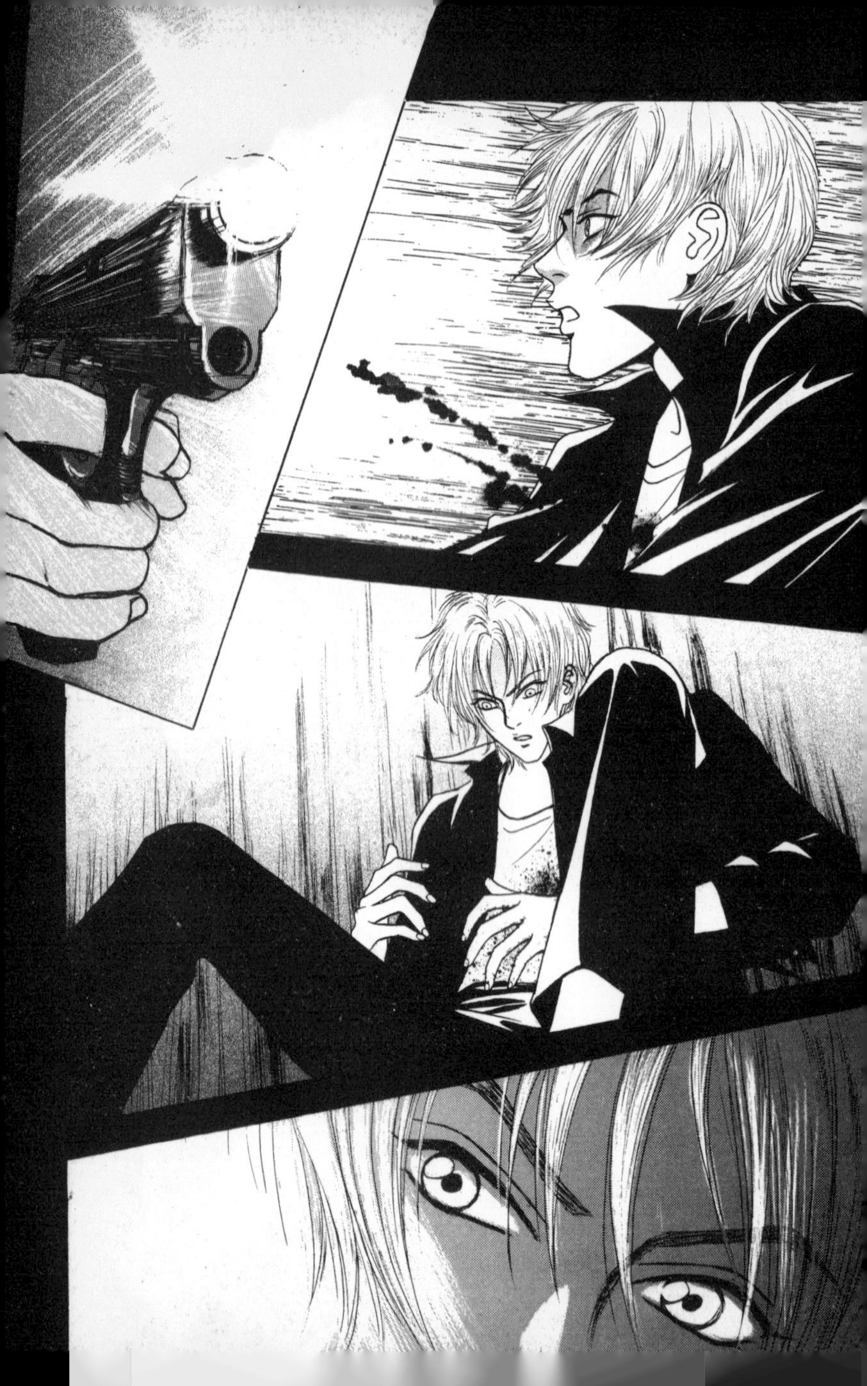

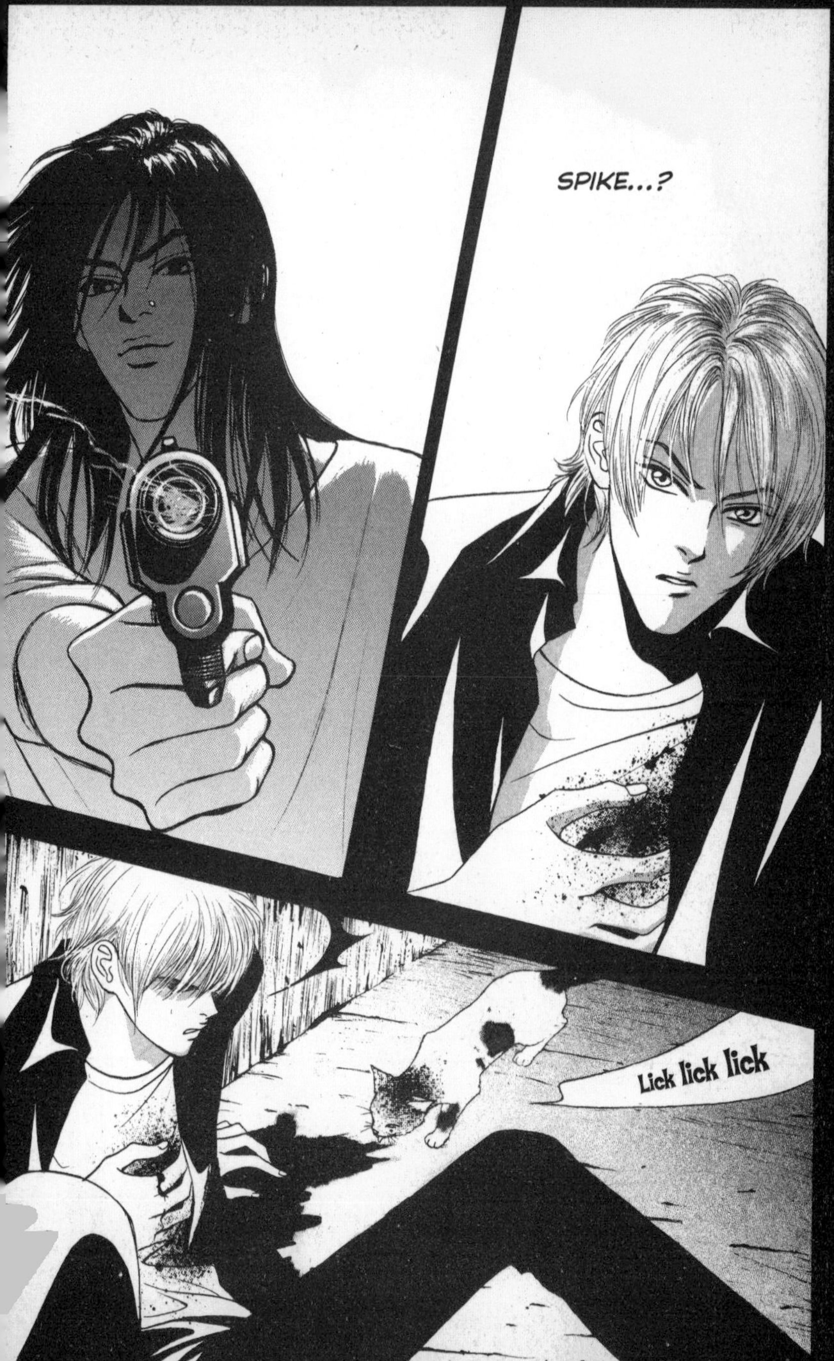
SPIKE...?
Lick lick lick

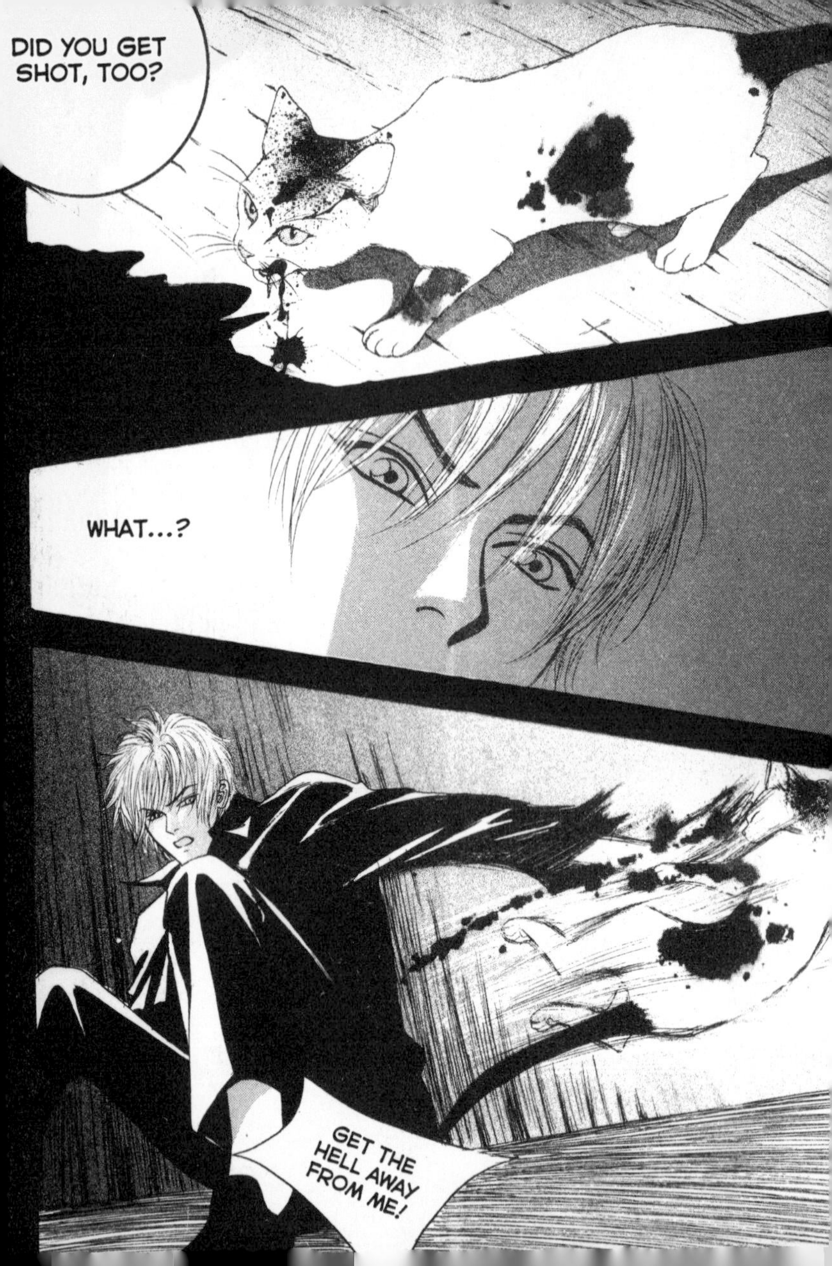
DID YOU GET SHOT, TOO?
WHAT...?
GET THE HELL AWAY FROM ME!

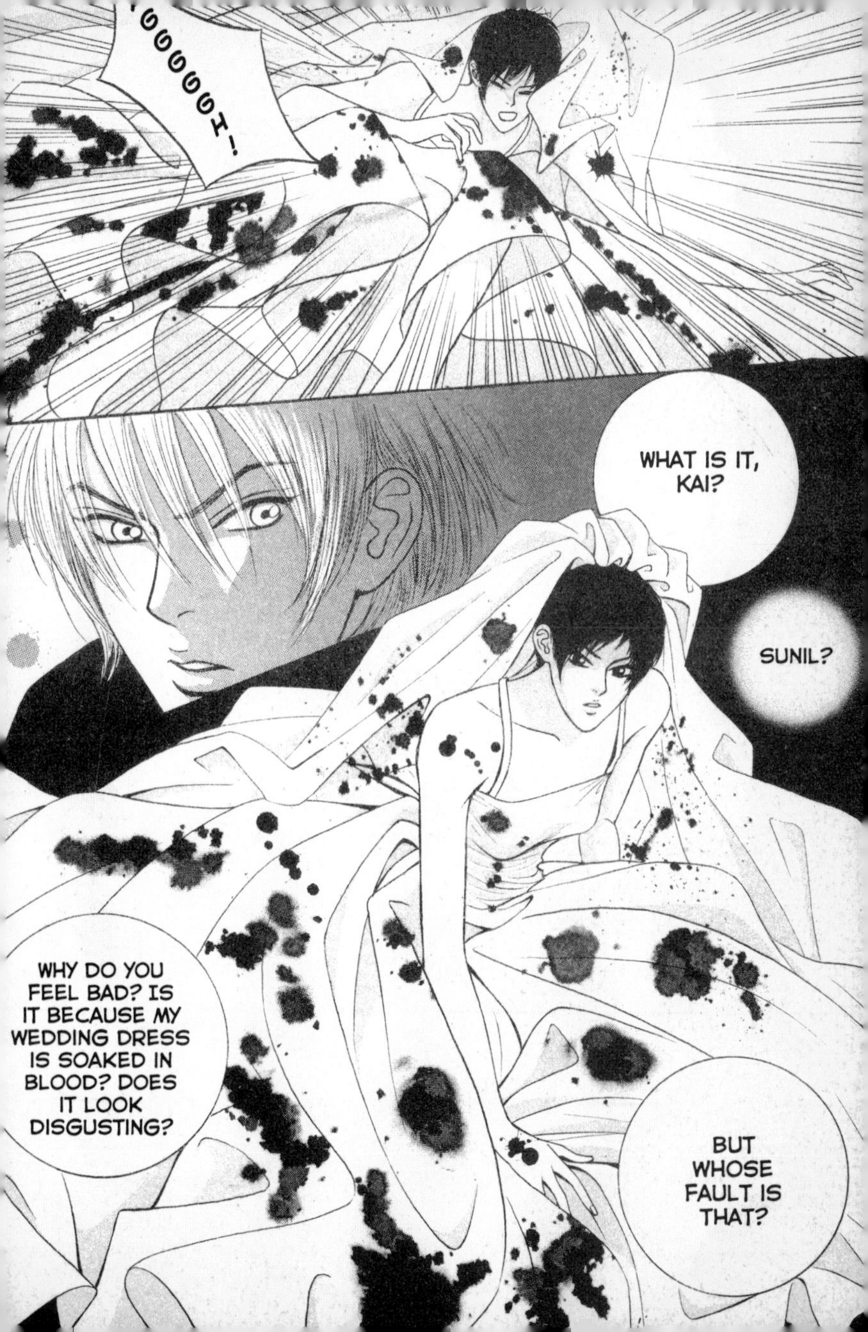
GGGGGGH!
WHAT IS IT, KAI?
SUNIL?
WHY DO YOU FEEL BAD? IS IT BECAUSE MY WEDDING DRESS IS SOAKED IN BLOOD? DOES IT LOOK DISGUSTING?
BUT WHOSE FAULT IS THAT?

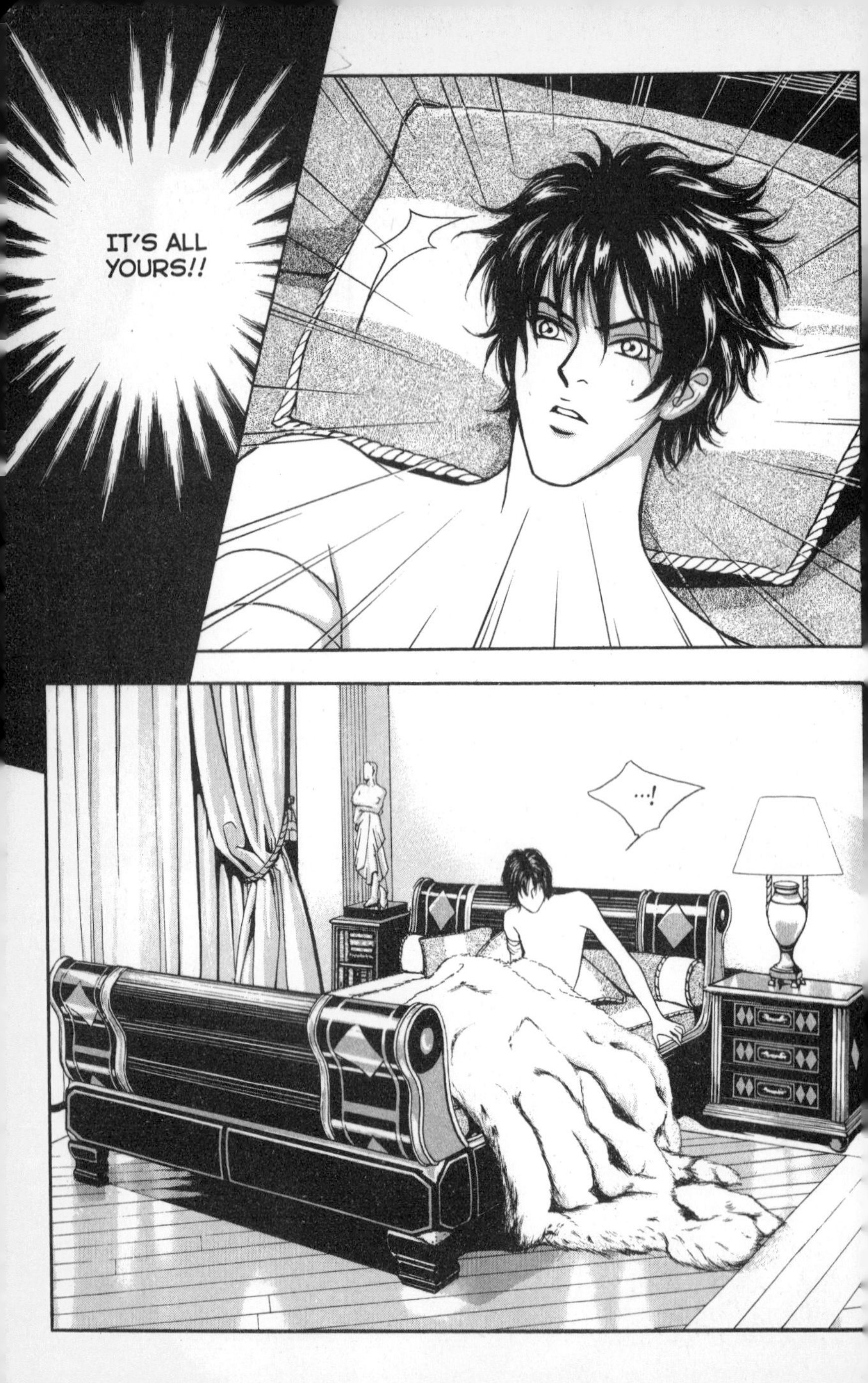
IT'S ALL YOURS!!
...!

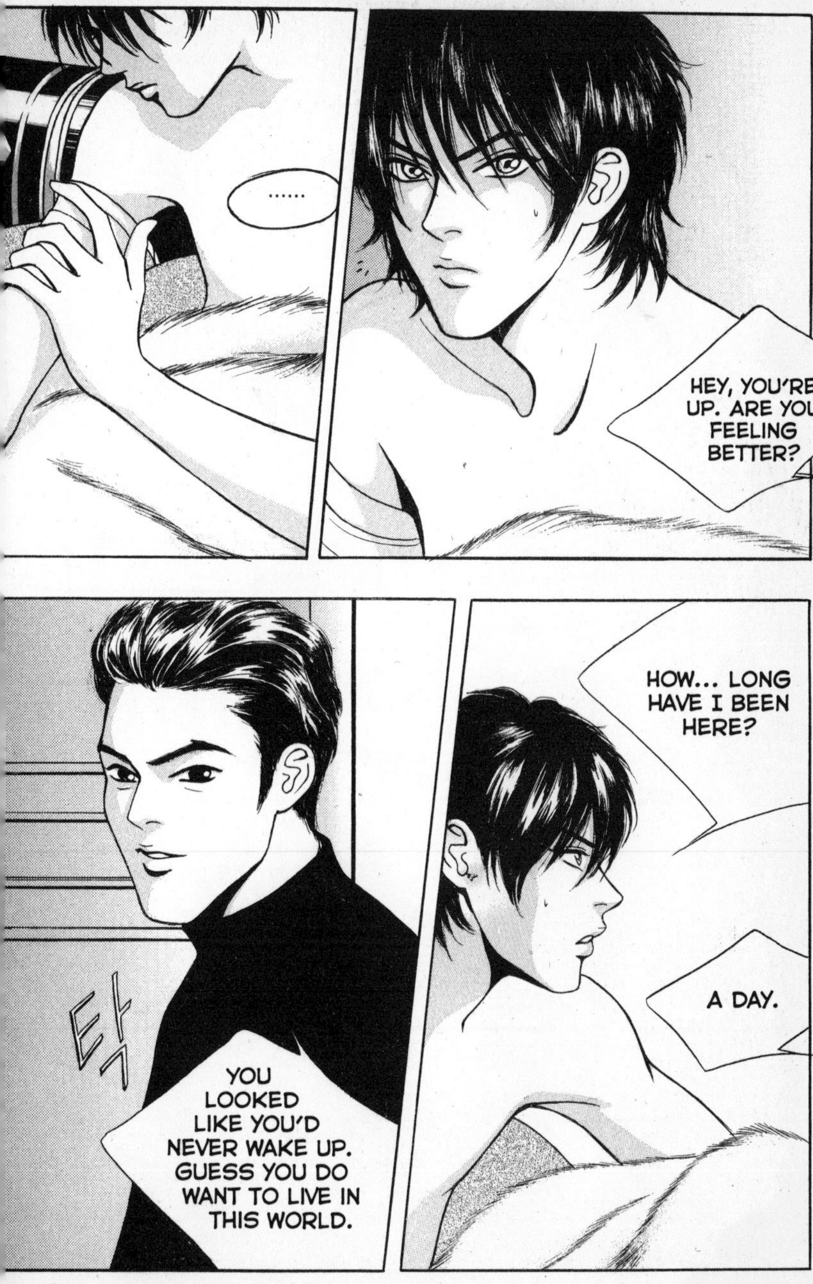
......
HEY, YOU'RE UP. ARE YOU FEELING BETTER?
탁
YOU LOOKED LIKE YOU'D NEVER WAKE UP. GUESS YOU DO WANT TO LIVE IN THIS WORLD.
HOW... LONG HAVE I BEEN HERE?
A DAY.

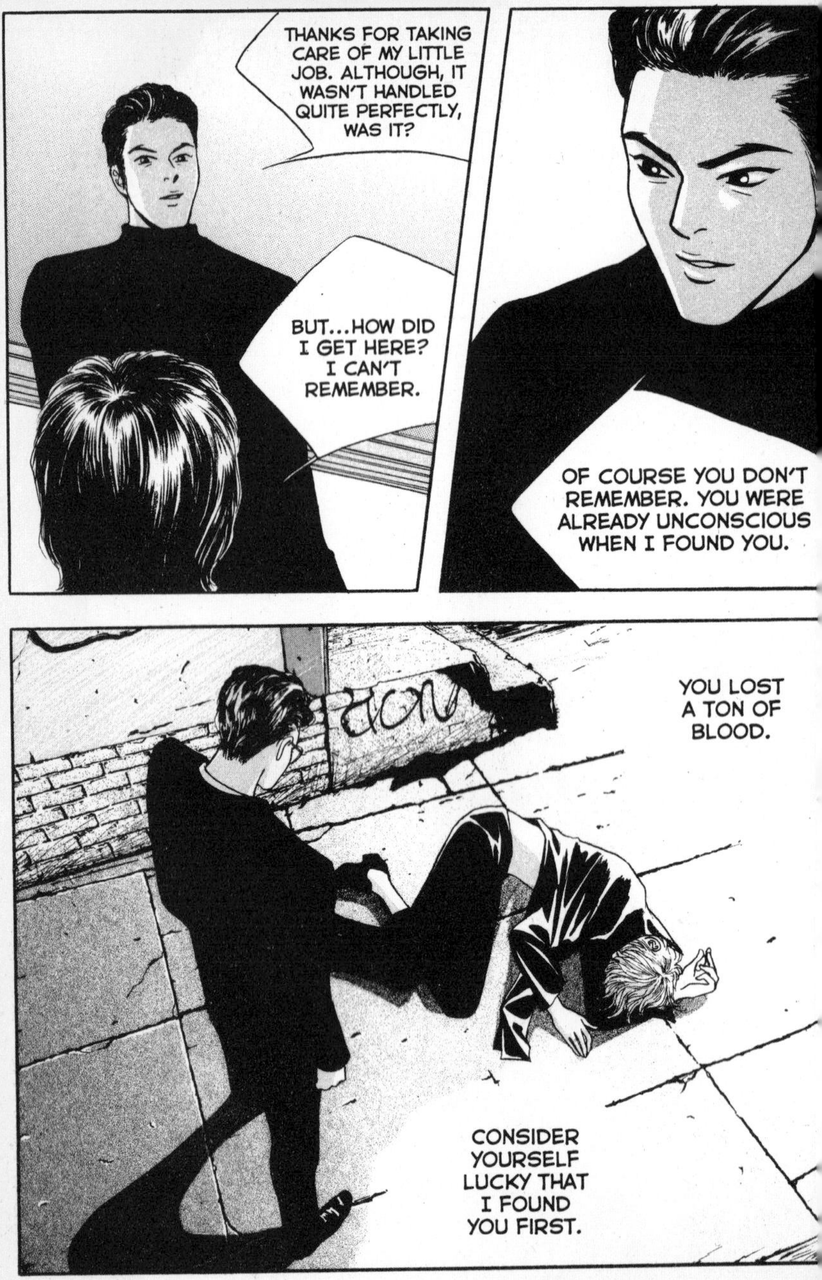
THANKS FOR TAKING CARE OF MY LITTLE JOB. ALTHOUGH, IT WASN'T HANDLED QUITE PERFECTLY, WAS IT?
BUT...HOW DID I GET HERE? I CAN'T REMEMBER.
OF COURSE YOU DON'T REMEMBER. YOU WERE ALREADY UNCONSCIOUS WHEN I FOUND YOU.
YOU LOST A TON OF BLOOD.
CONSIDER YOURSELF LUCKY THAT I FOUND YOU FIRST.

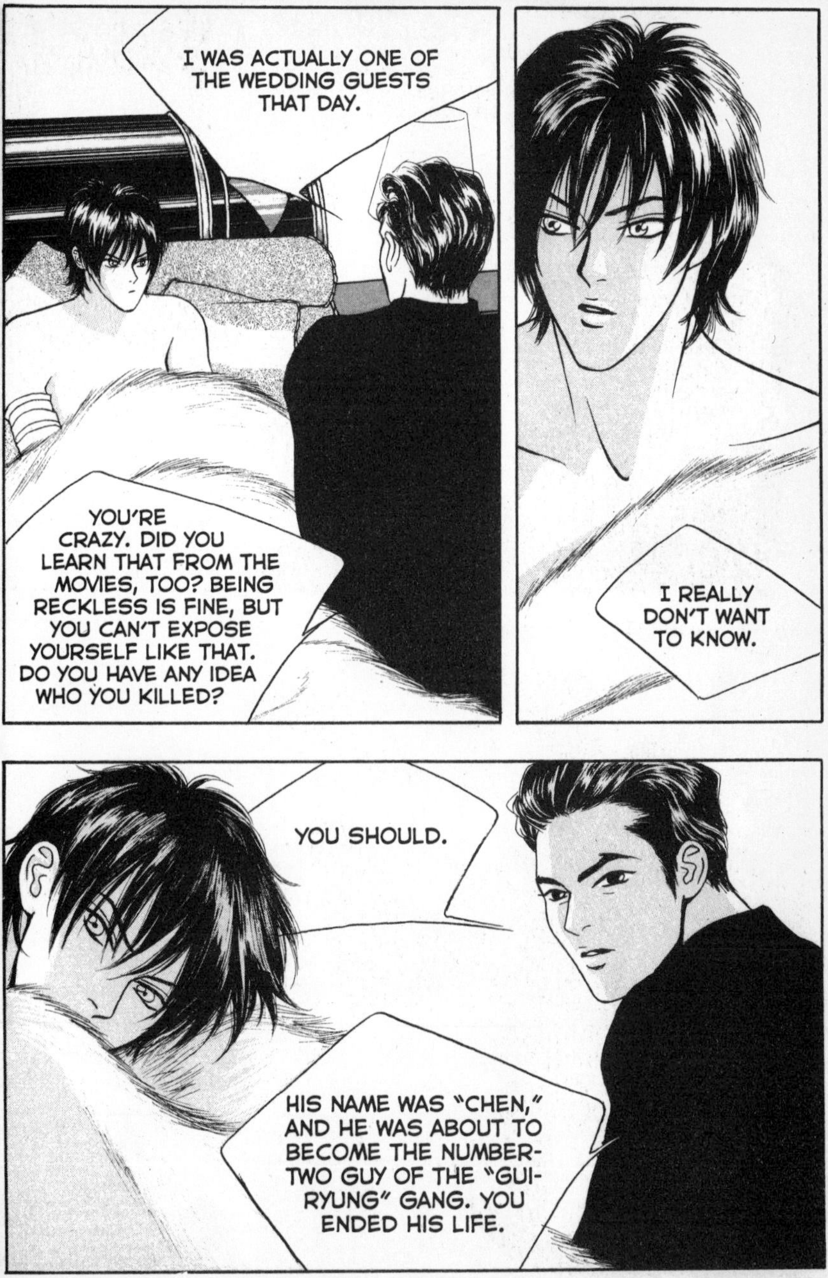
I WAS ACTUALLY ONE OF THE WEDDING GUESTS THAT DAY.
YOU'RE CRAZY. DID YOU LEARN THAT FROM THE MOVIES, TOO? BEING RECKLESS IS FINE, BUT YOU CAN'T EXPOSE YOURSELF LIKE THAT. DO YOU HAVE ANY IDEA WHO YOU KILLED?
I REALLY DON'T WANT TO KNOW.
YOU SHOULD.
HIS NAME WAS "CHEN," AND HE WAS ABOUT TO BECOME THE NUMBER-TWO GUY OF THE "GUI-RYUNG" GANG. YOU ENDED HIS LIFE.

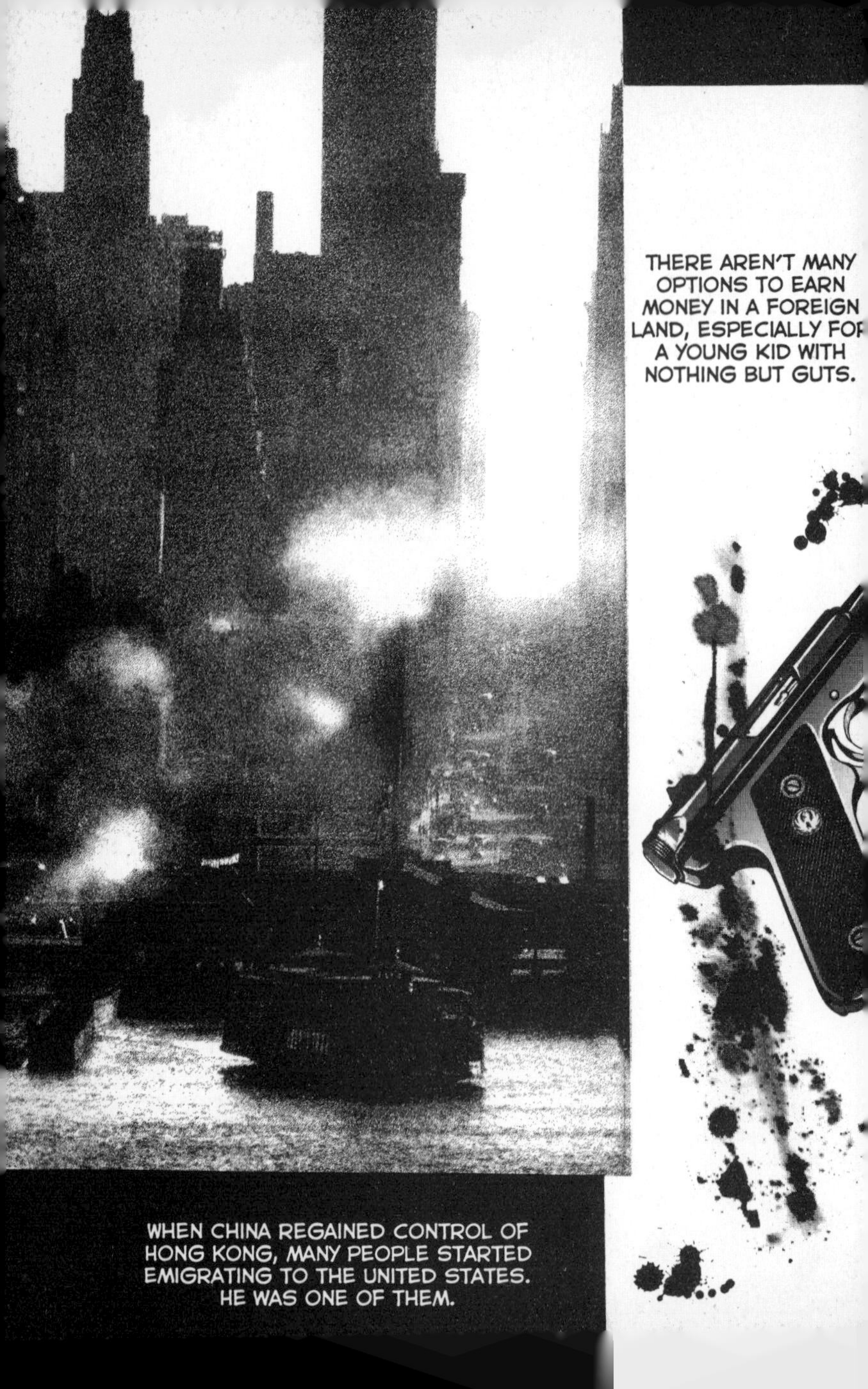
WHEN CHINA REGAINED CONTROL OF HONG KONG, MANY PEOPLE STARTED EMIGRATING TO THE UNITED STATES. HE WAS ONE OF THEM.
THERE AREN'T MANY OPTIONS TO EARN MONEY IN A FOREIGN LAND, ESPECIALLY FOR A YOUNG KID WITH NOTHING BUT GUTS.

WHEN THE NUMBER OF CHINESE IMMIGRANTS GREW AND CHINATOWN BECAME TOO CROWDED, EVERYONE WAS CALLED TO EXPAND THE TERRITORY... FROM SCHOOL TEACHERS TO STREET THUGS. FLUSHING, WHICH WAS ONCE THE KOREATOWN OF NEW YORK, BECAME A SECOND CHINATOWN.

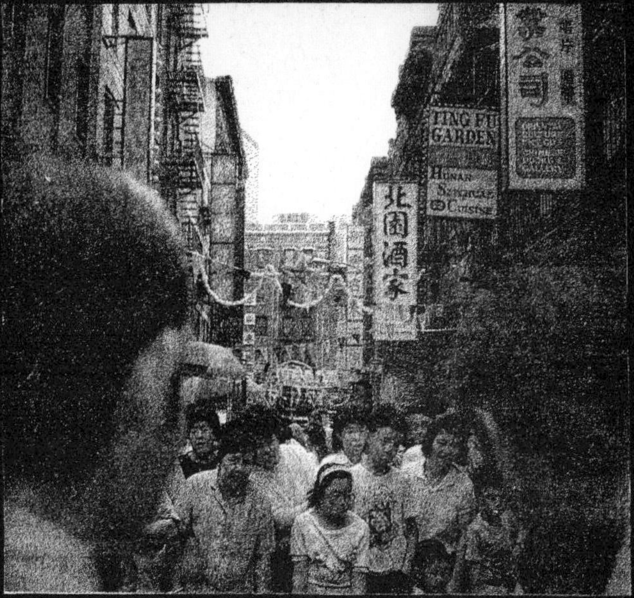
TING FU
GARDEN
北園酒家

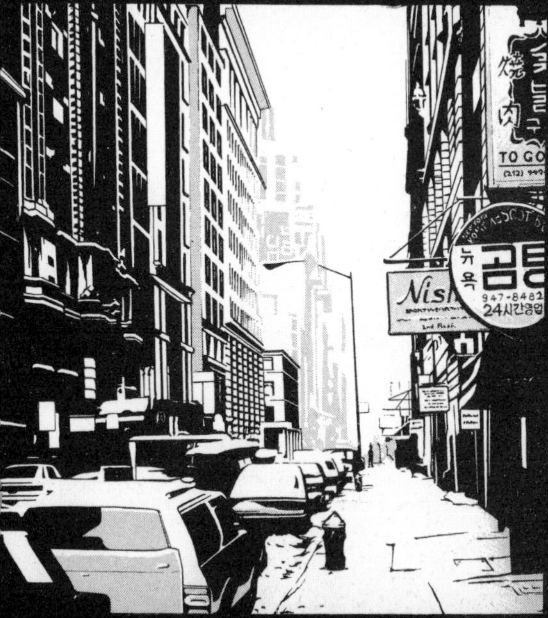
TO GO
뉴욕
947-8482
24시간영업
Nish

DURING THIS "NEW CHINATOWN" MOVEMENT, STREET THUGS LIKE CHEN WERE ALL AROUND. THEY USUALLY TARGETED KOREAN TEENAGERS AND VENDORS. WHEN THINGS GOT TOO BAD, KOREANS STARTED LEAVING FLUSHING, AND THE CHINESE TOOK OVER.

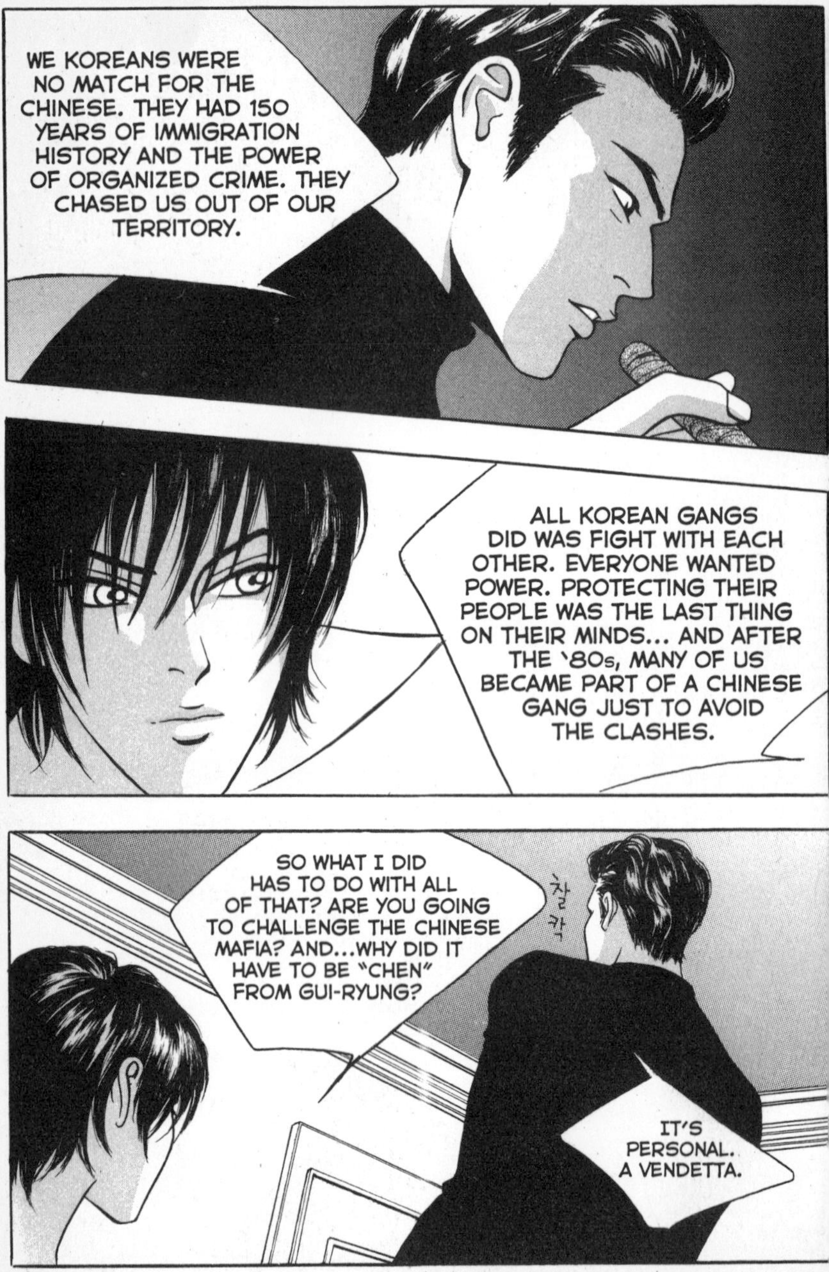
WE KOREANS WERE NO MATCH FOR THE CHINESE. THEY HAD 150 YEARS OF IMMIGRATION HISTORY AND THE POWER OF ORGANIZED CRIME. THEY CHASED US OUT OF OUR TERRITORY.
ALL KOREAN GANGS DID WAS FIGHT WITH EACH OTHER. EVERYONE WANTED POWER. PROTECTING THEIR PEOPLE WAS THE LAST THING ON THEIR MINDS... AND AFTER THE '80s, MANY OF US BECAME PART OF A CHINESE GANG JUST TO AVOID THE CLASHES.
SO WHAT I DID HAS TO DO WITH ALL OF THAT? ARE YOU GOING TO CHALLENGE THE CHINESE MAFIA? AND...WHY DID IT HAVE TO BE "CHEN" FROM GUI-RYUNG?
찰칵
IT'S PERSONAL. A VENDETTA.

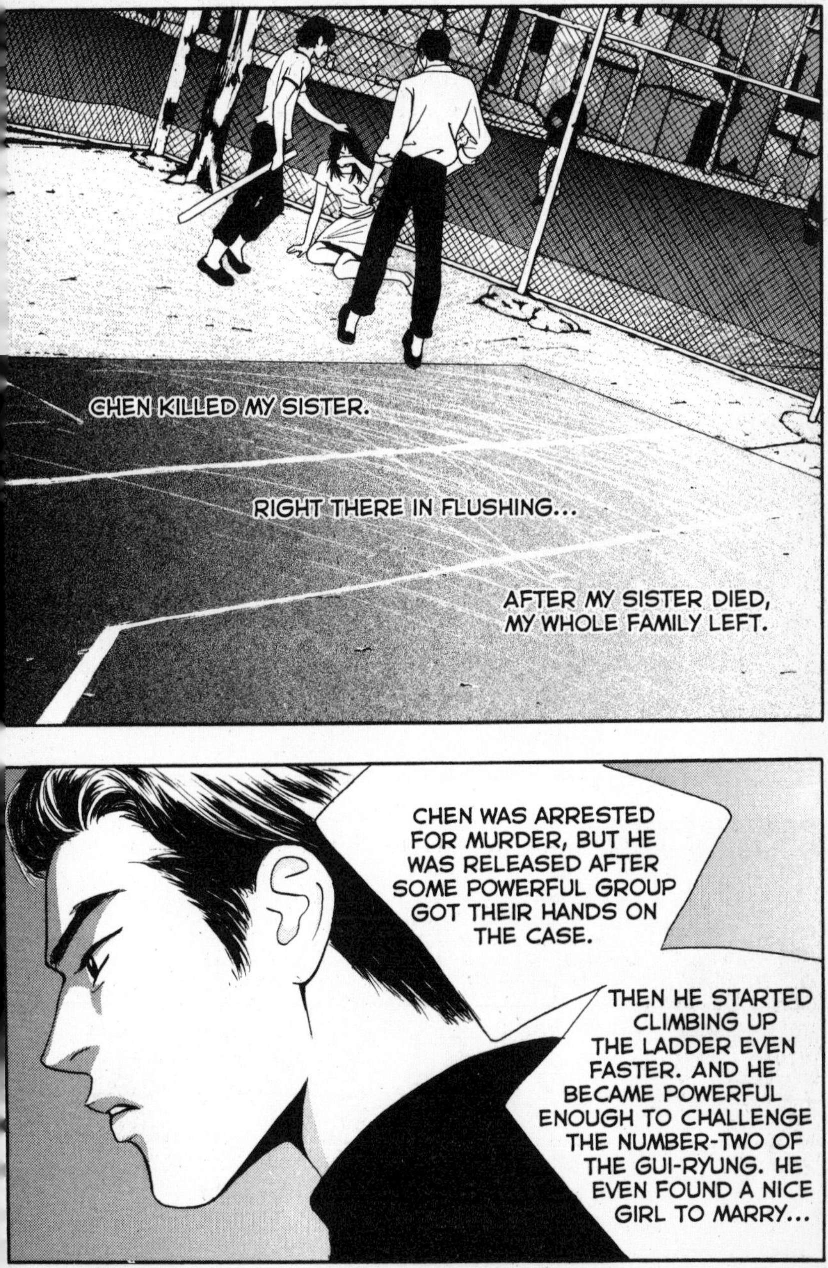
CHEN KILLED MY SISTER.
RIGHT THERE IN FLUSHING...
AFTER MY SISTER DIED, MY WHOLE FAMILY LEFT.
CHEN WAS ARRESTED FOR MURDER, BUT HE WAS RELEASED AFTER SOME POWERFUL GROUP GOT THEIR HANDS ON THE CASE.
THEN HE STARTED CLIMBING UP THE LADDER EVEN FASTER. AND HE BECAME POWERFUL ENOUGH TO CHALLENGE THE NUMBER-TWO OF THE GUI-RYUNG. HE EVEN FOUND A NICE GIRL TO MARRY...

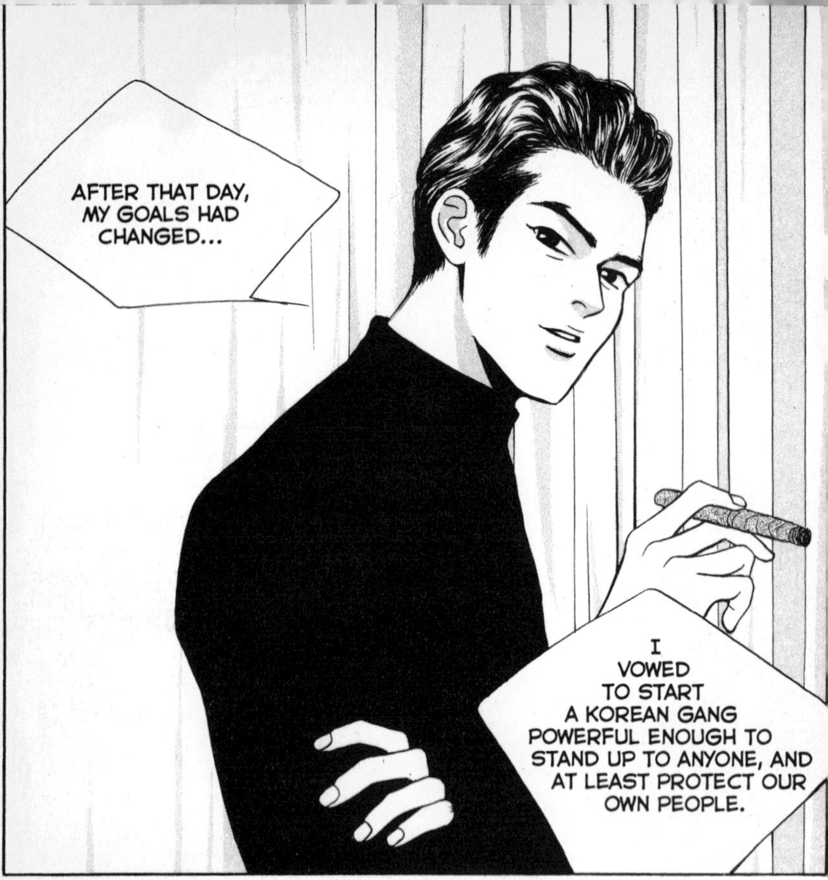
AFTER THAT DAY, MY GOALS HAD CHANGED...
I VOWED TO START A KOREAN GANG POWERFUL ENOUGH TO STAND UP TO ANYONE, AND AT LEAST PROTECT OUR OWN PEOPLE.

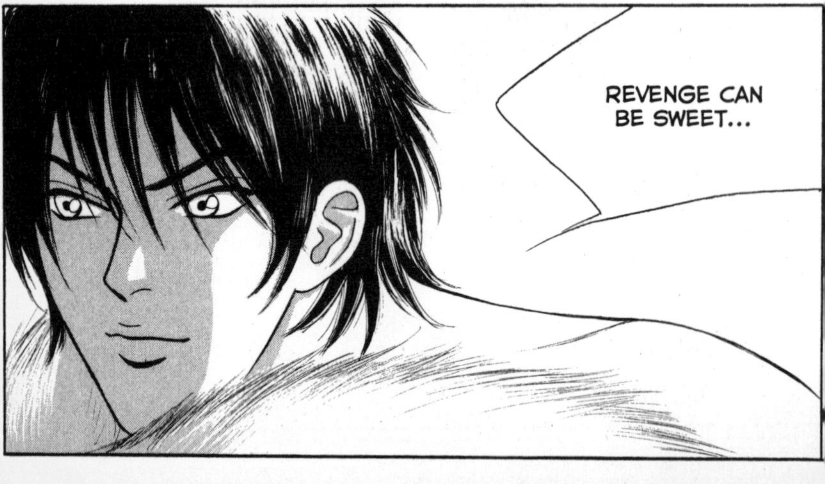
REVENGE CAN BE SWEET...

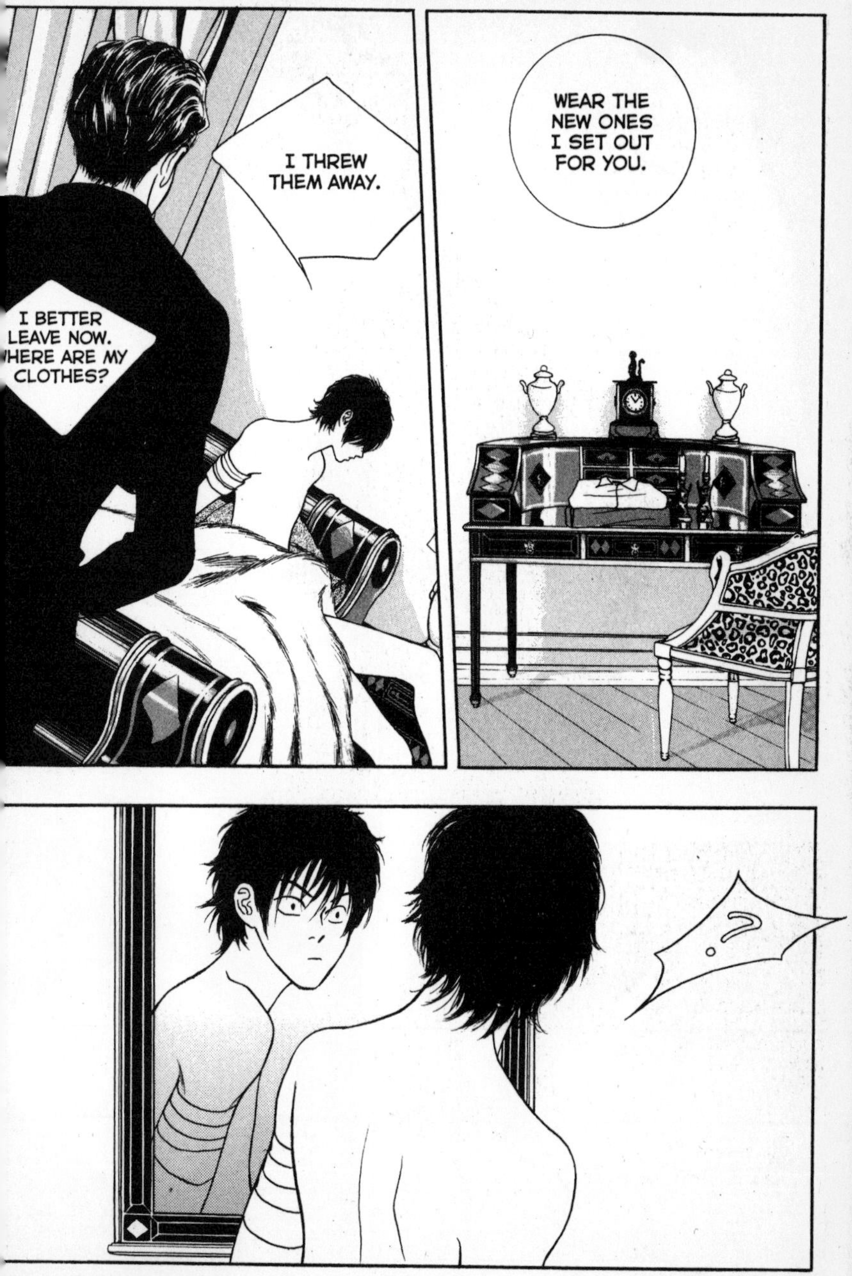
I BETTER LEAVE NOW. WHERE ARE MY CLOTHES?
I THREW THEM AWAY.
WEAR THE NEW ONES I SET OUT FOR YOU.
?

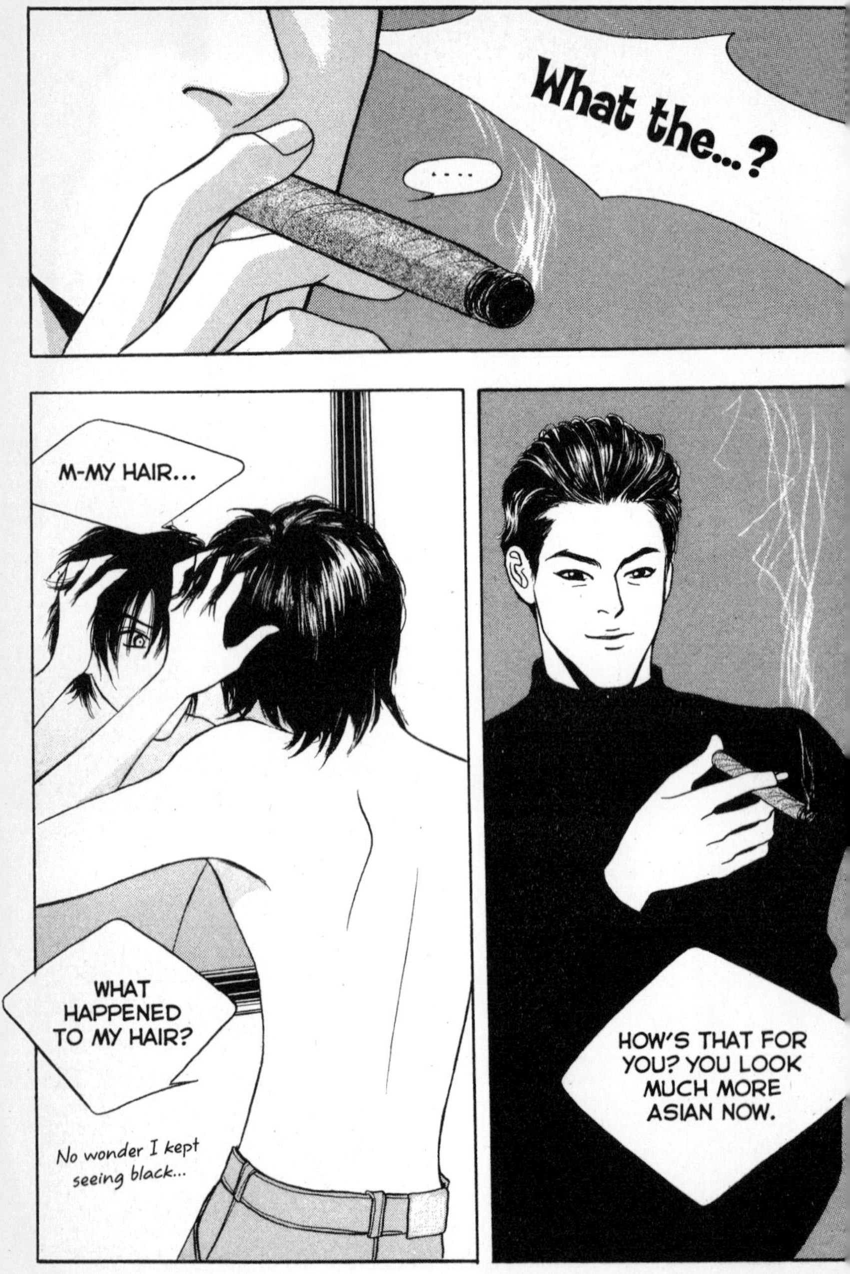

....
What the...?
M-MY HAIR...
WHAT HAPPENED TO MY HAIR?
No wonder I kept seeing black...
HOW'S THAT FOR YOU? YOU LOOK MUCH MORE ASIAN NOW.

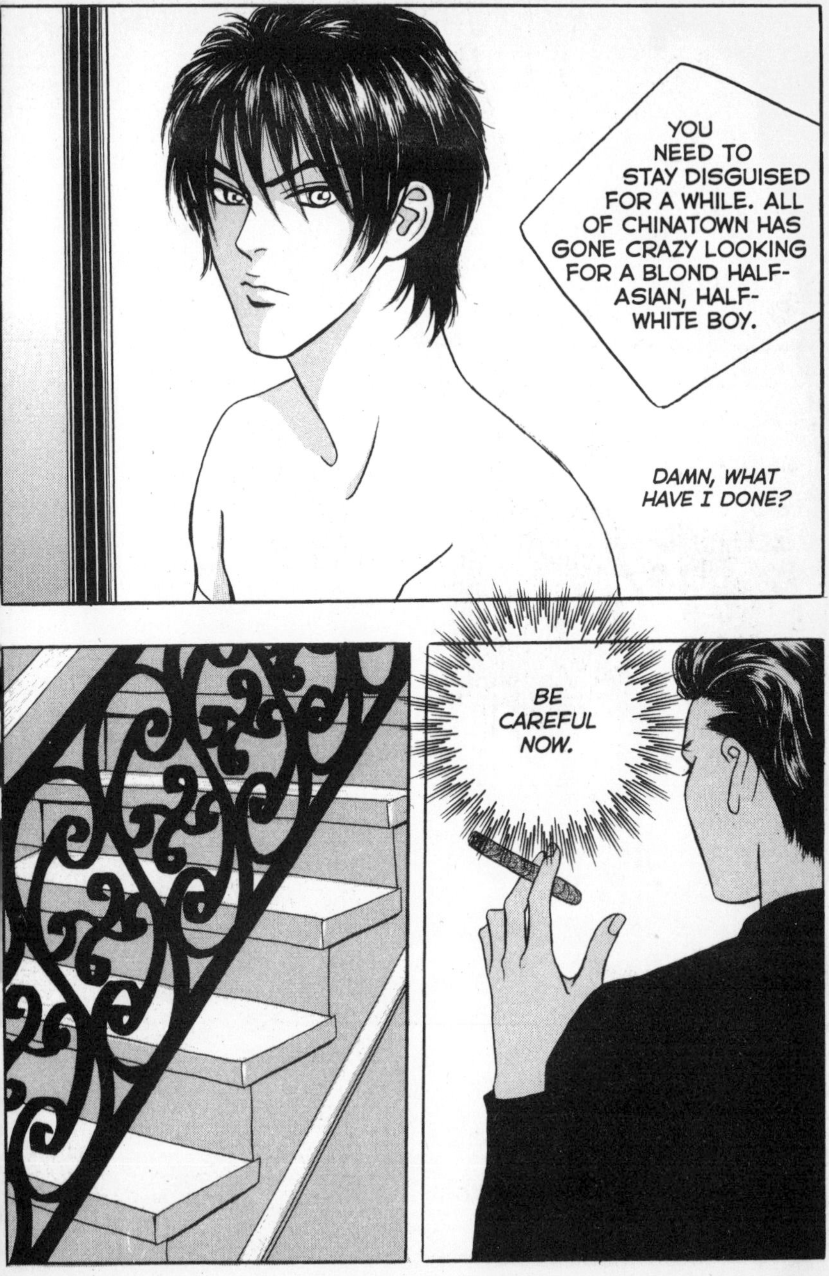
YOU NEED TO STAY DISGUISED FOR A WHILE. ALL OF CHINATOWN HAS GONE CRAZY LOOKING FOR A BLOND HALF-ASIAN, HALF-WHITE BOY.
DAMN, WHAT HAVE I DONE?
BE CAREFUL NOW.

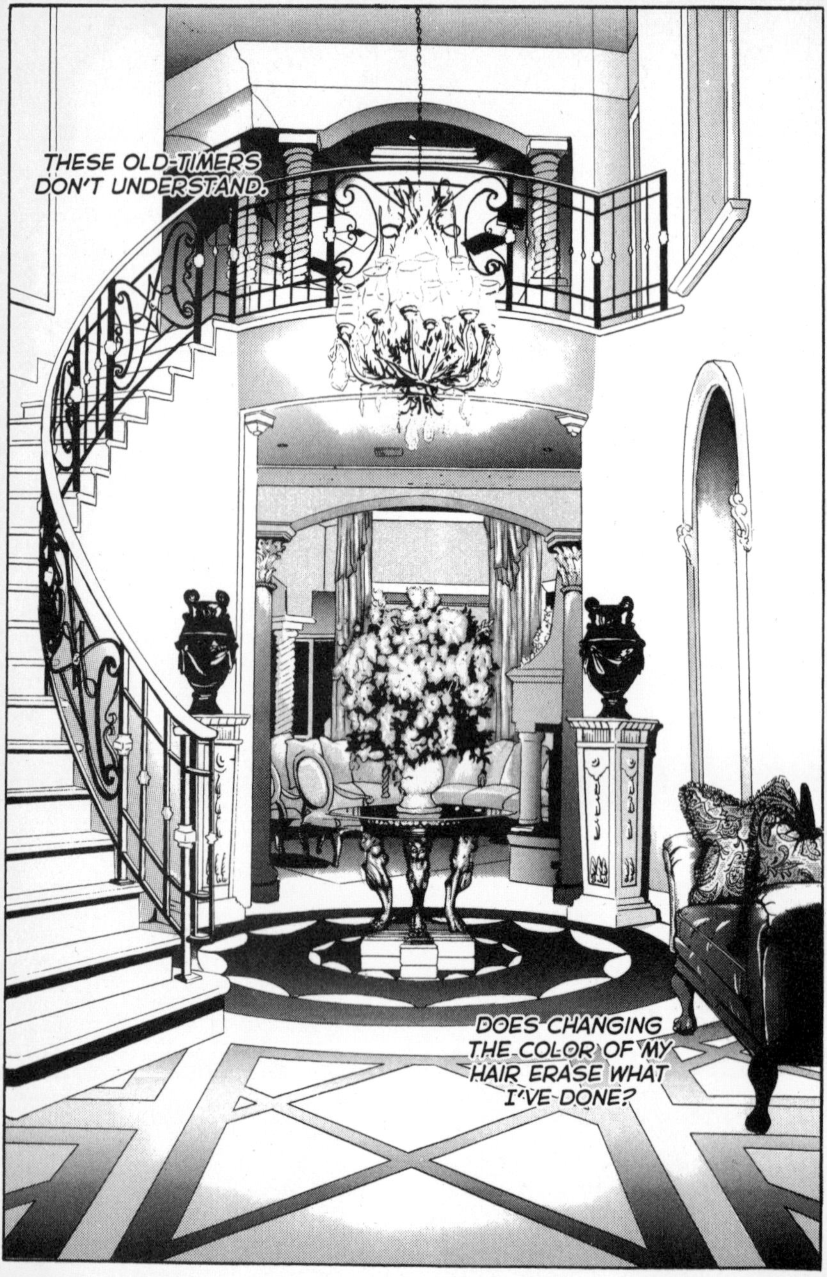
THESE OLD-TIMERS DON'T UNDERSTAND.
DOES CHANGING THE COLOR OF MY HAIR ERASE WHAT I'VE DONE?

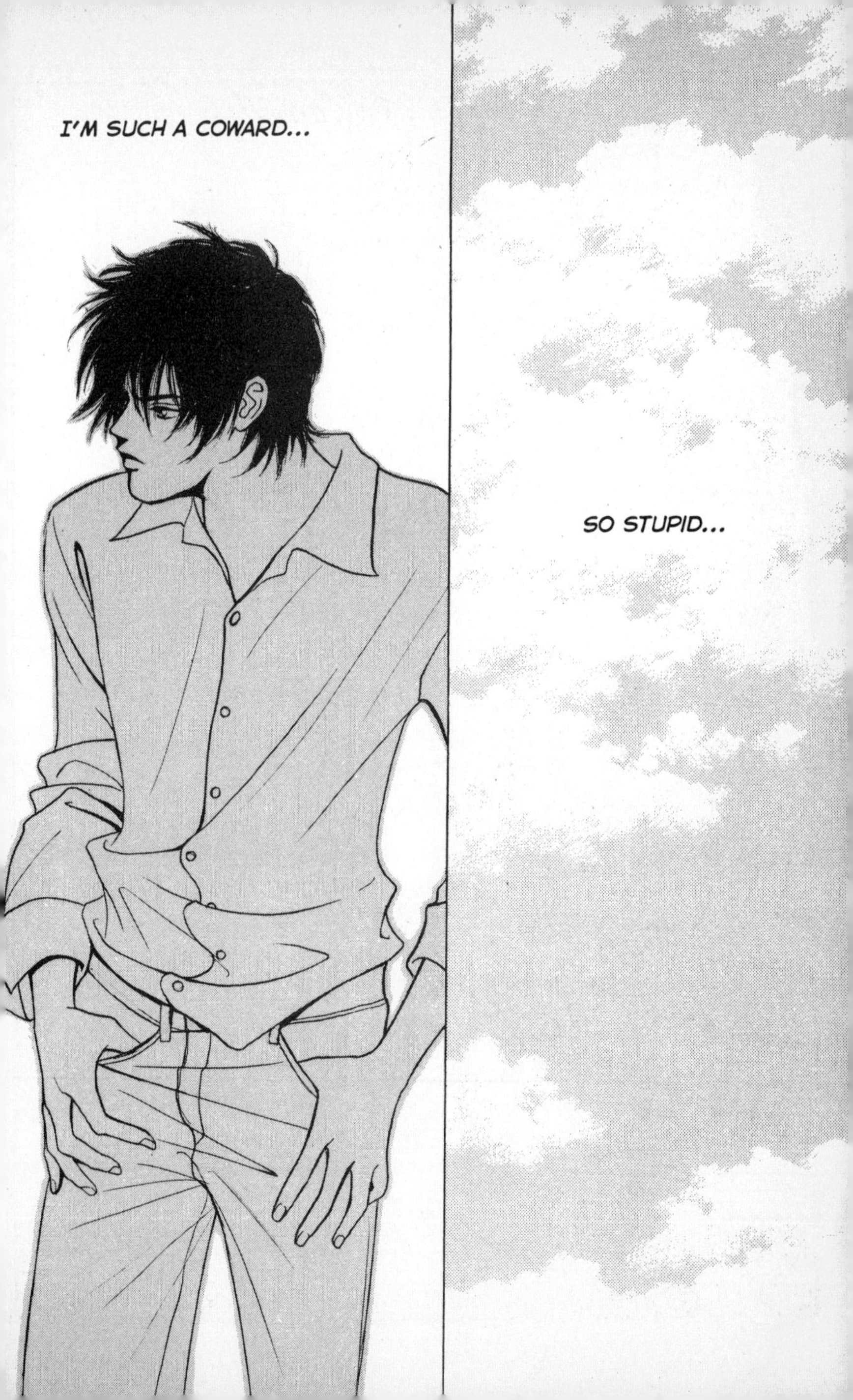
I'M SUCH A COWARD...
SO STUPID...

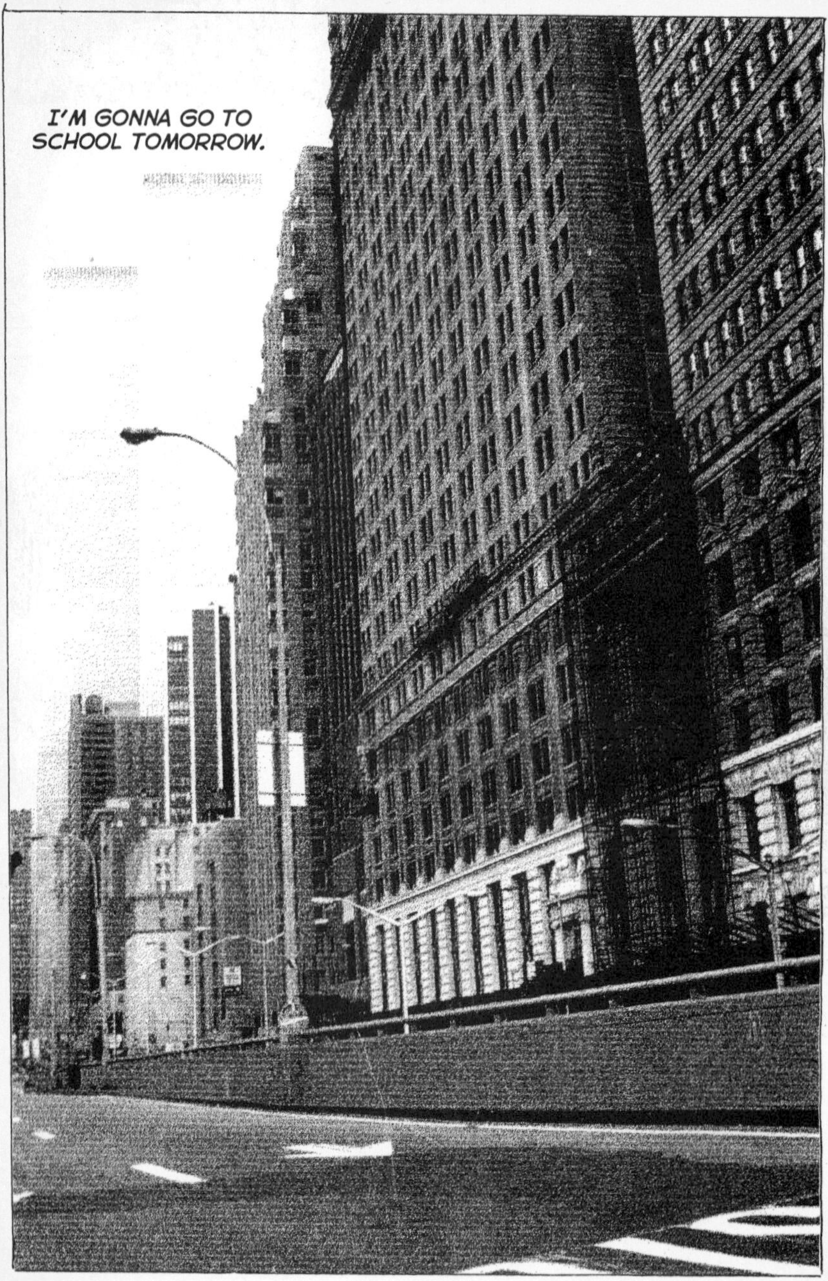
I'M GONNA GO TO
SCHOOL TOMORROW.

SOUL TO SEOUL™

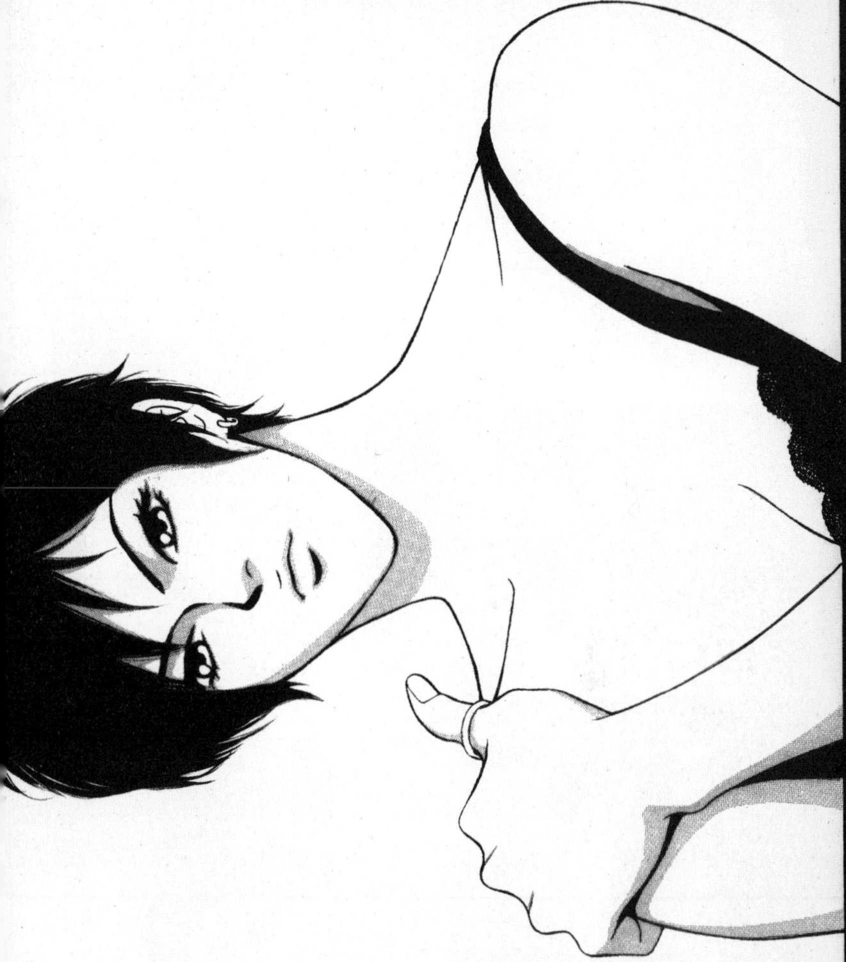

SHOT #6: JEALOUSY

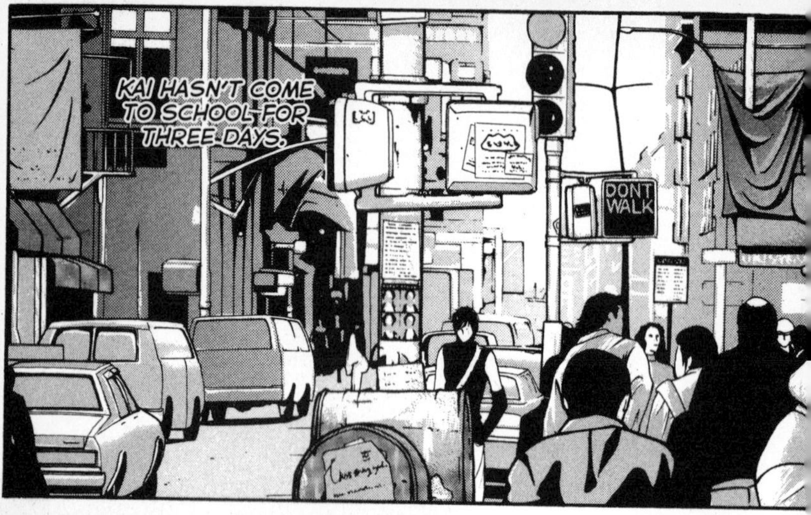
KAI HASN'T COME TO SCHOOL FOR THREE DAYS.
DONT WALK

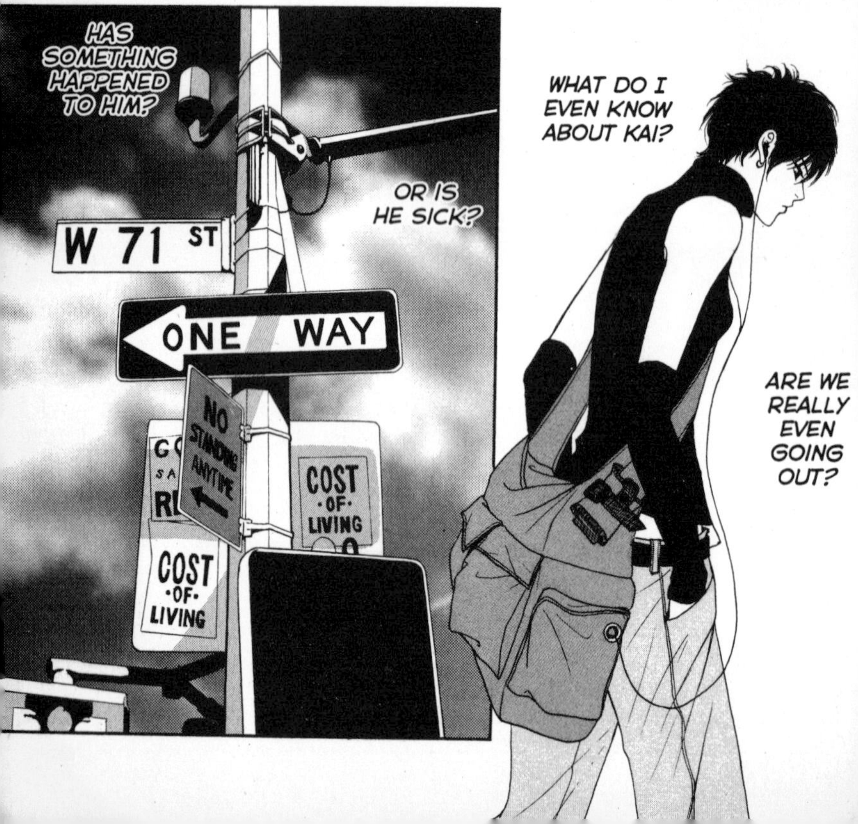
HAS SOMETHING HAPPENED TO HIM?
W 71 ST
OR IS HE SICK?
ONE WAY
NO STANDING ANYTIME
COST OF LIVING
COST OF LIVING
WHAT DO I EVEN KNOW ABOUT KAI?
ARE WE REALLY EVEN GOING OUT?

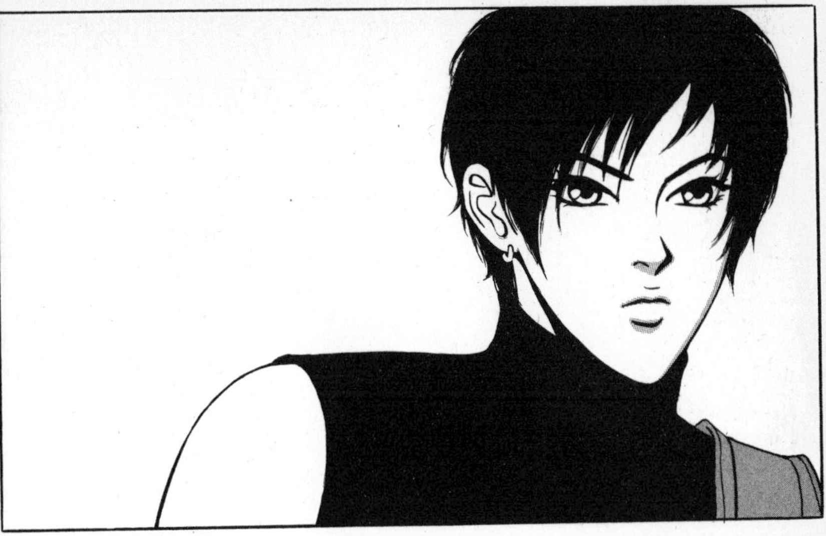

IT'S BEEN STRANGE FROM THE START. IT ALWAYS FEELS LIKE I'M BEING PULLED IN... AND I DON'T KNOW WHEN, BUT AT SOME POINT KAI HAS BECOME THE CENTER OF MY LIFE.

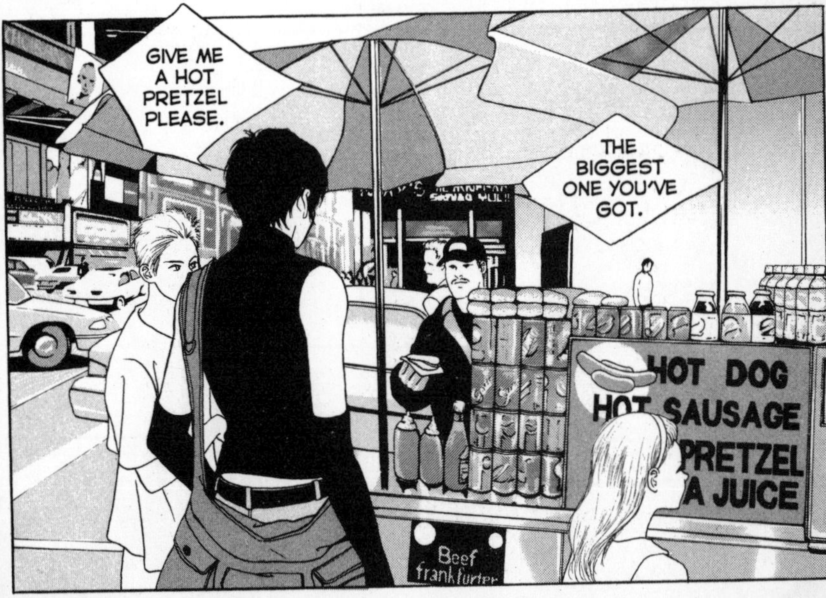
GIVE ME A HOT PRETZEL PLEASE.
THE BIGGEST ONE YOU'VE GOT.
HOT DOG
SAUSAGE
PRETZEL
A JUICE
Beef frankfurter

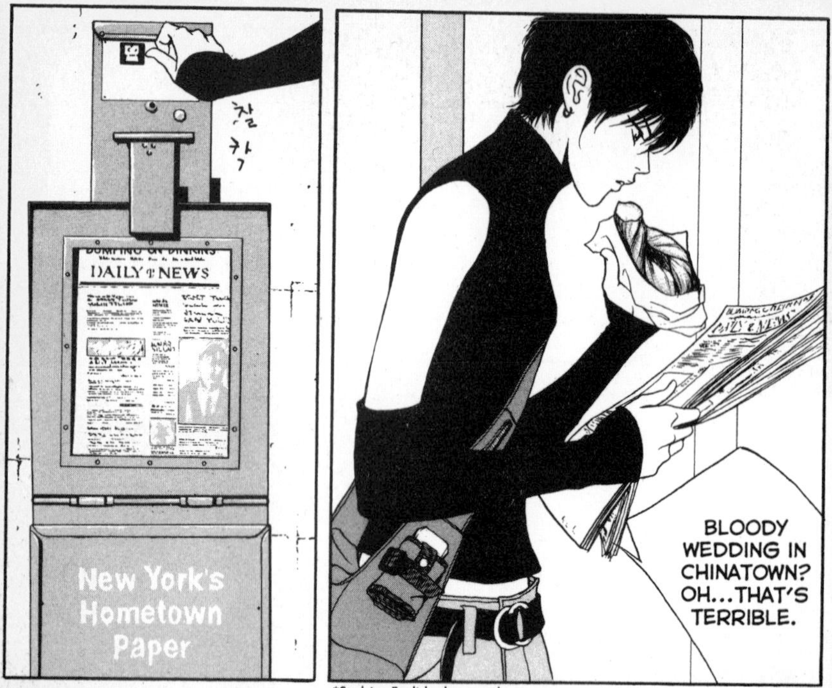
찰칵
DAILY NEWS
New York's Hometown Paper
BLOODY WEDDING IN CHINATOWN? OH...THAT'S TERRIBLE.

*Studying English whenever she can

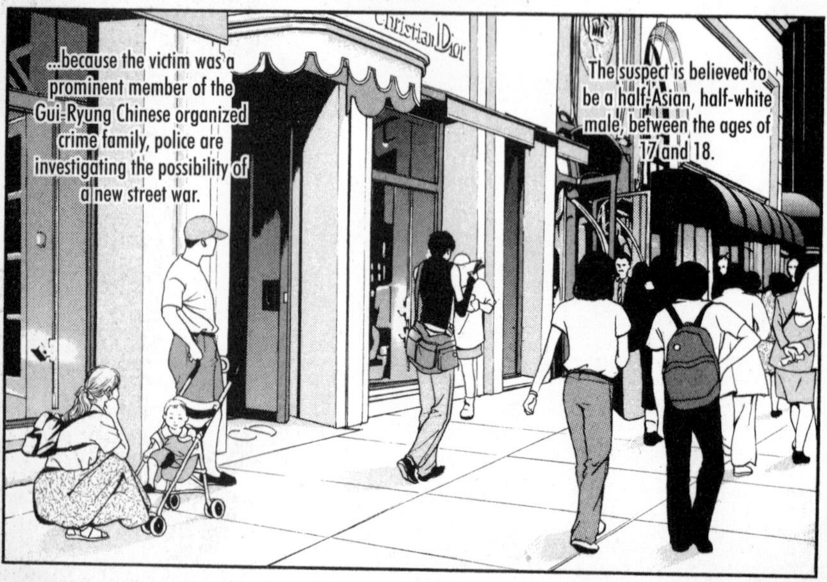
Christian Dior
...because the victim was a prominent member of the Gui-Ryung Chinese organized crime family, police are investigating the possibility of a new street war.
The suspect is believed to be a half-Asian, half-white male, between the ages of 17 and 18.

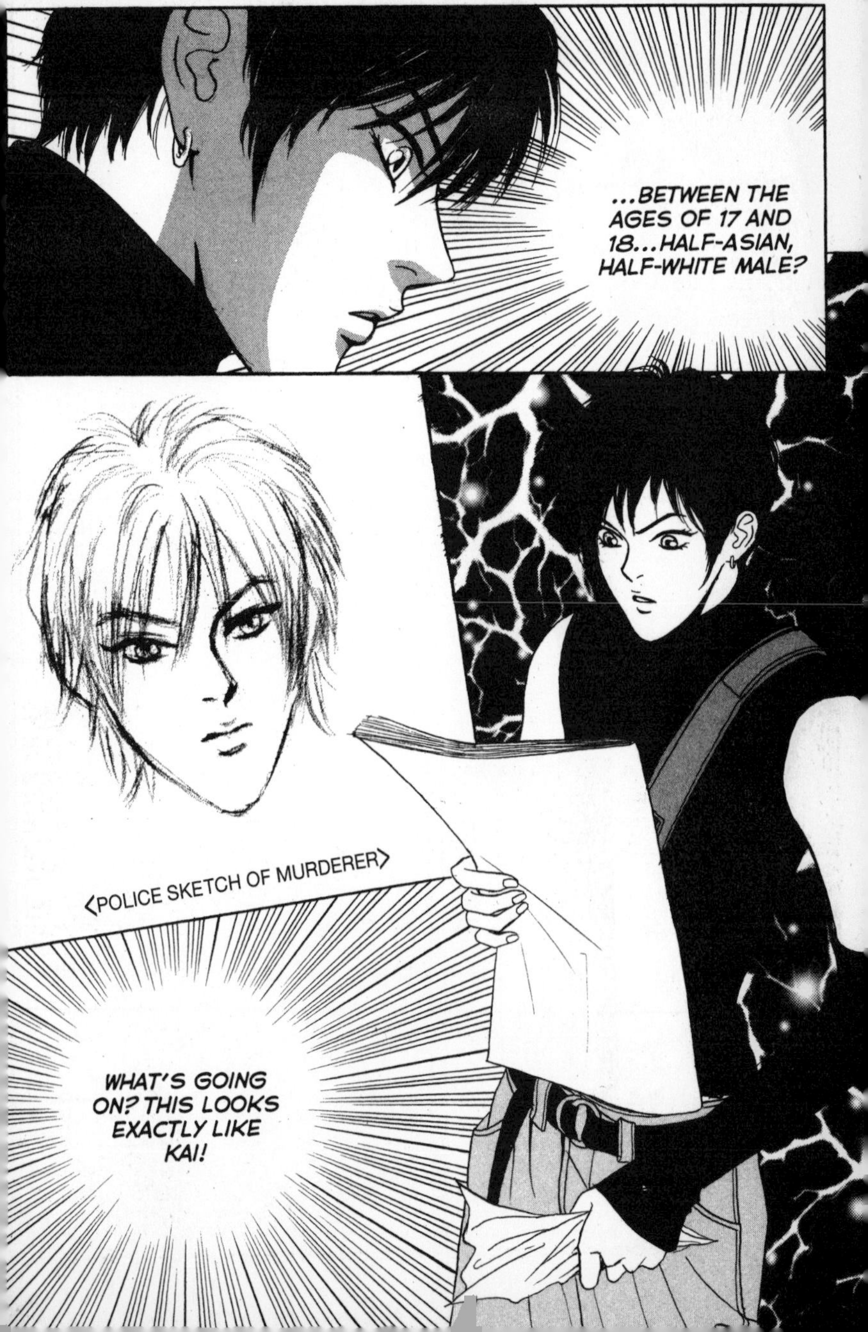
...BETWEEN THE AGES OF 17 AND 18...HALF-ASIAN, HALF-WHITE MALE?
<POLICE SKETCH OF MURDERER>
WHAT'S GOING ON? THIS LOOKS EXACTLY LIKE KAI!

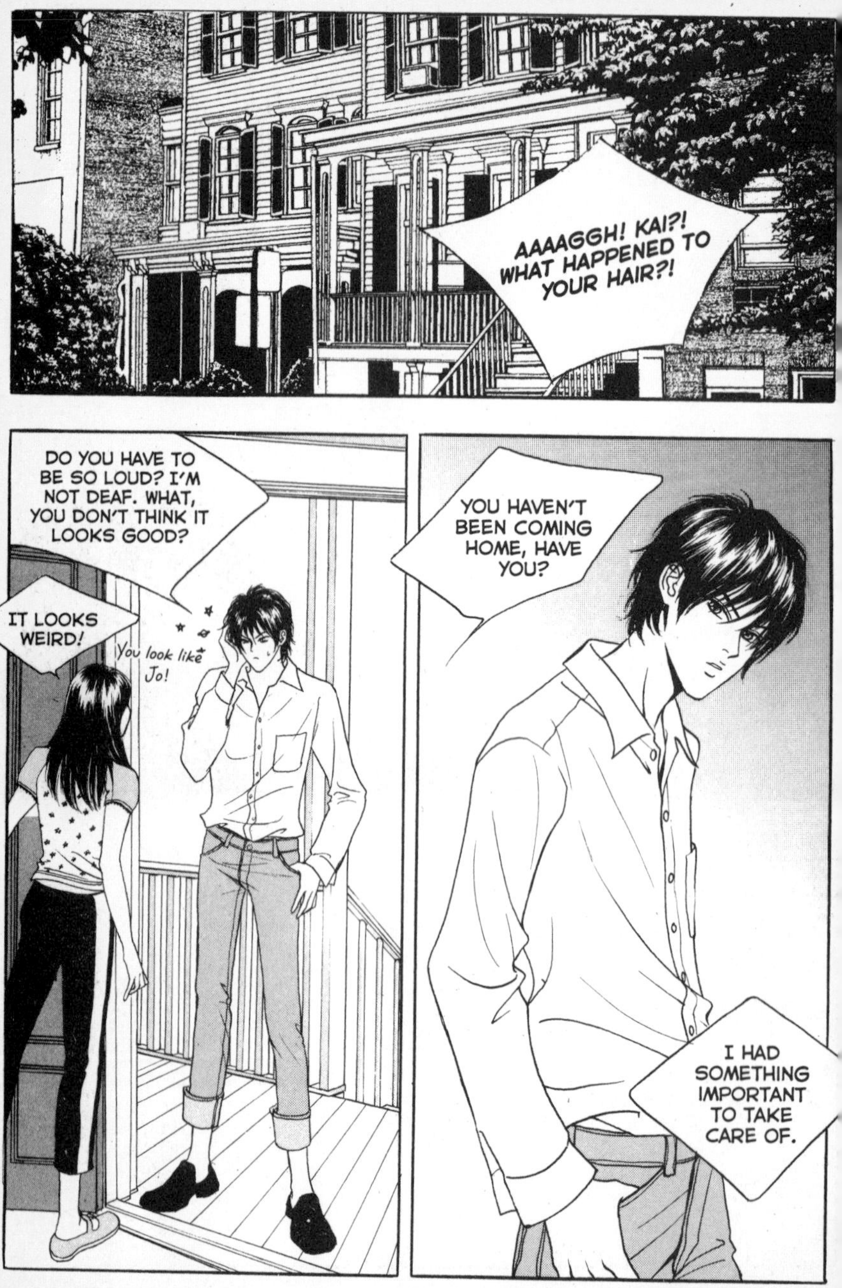
AAAAGGH! KAI?! WHAT HAPPENED TO YOUR HAIR?!
DO YOU HAVE TO BE SO LOUD? I'M NOT DEAF. WHAT, YOU DON'T THINK IT LOOKS GOOD?
IT LOOKS WEIRD!
You look like Jo!
YOU HAVEN'T BEEN COMING HOME, HAVE YOU?
I HAD SOMETHING IMPORTANT TO TAKE CARE OF.

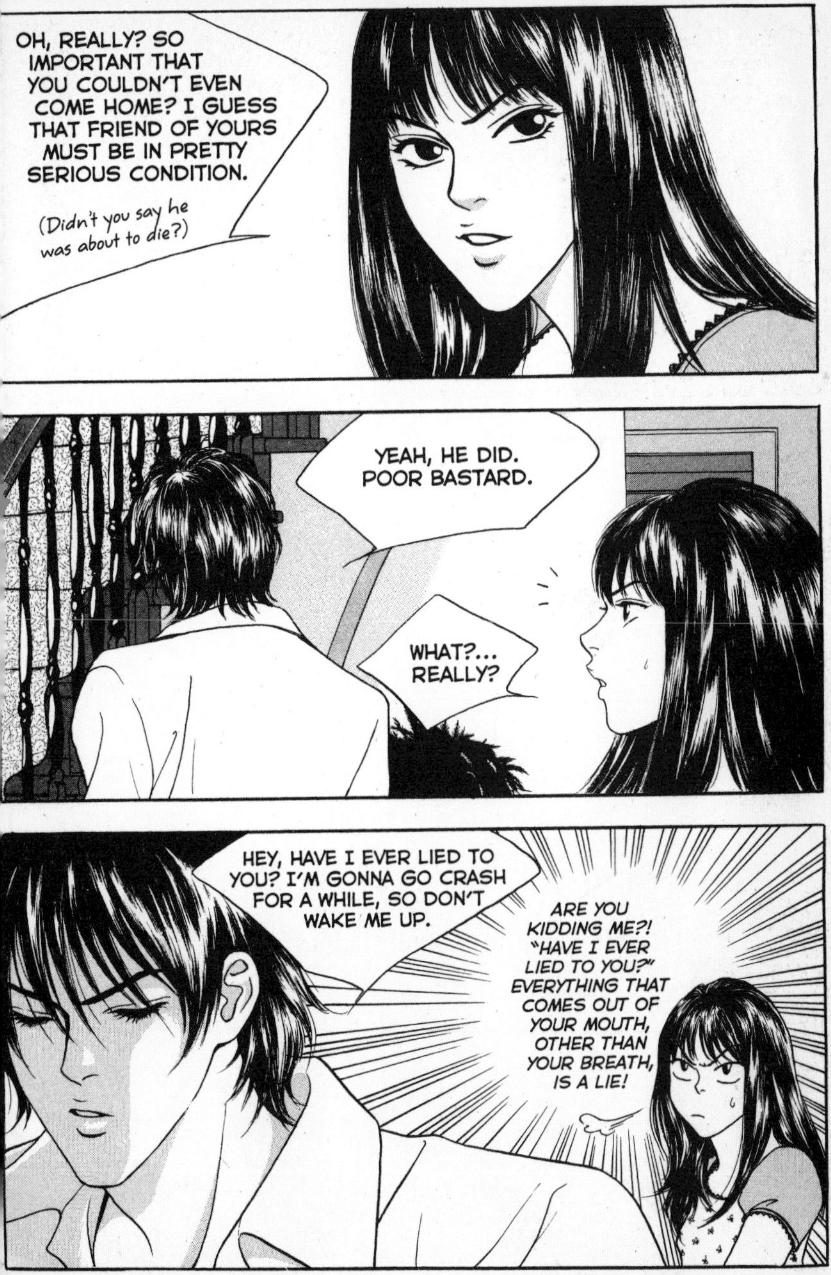
OH, REALLY? SO IMPORTANT THAT YOU COULDN'T EVEN COME HOME? I GUESS THAT FRIEND OF YOURS MUST BE IN PRETTY SERIOUS CONDITION.
(Didn't you say he was about to die?)
YEAH, HE DID. POOR BASTARD.
WHAT?... REALLY?
HEY, HAVE I EVER LIED TO YOU? I'M GONNA GO CRASH FOR A WHILE, SO DON'T WAKE ME UP.
ARE YOU KIDDING ME?! "HAVE I EVER LIED TO YOU?" EVERYTHING THAT COMES OUT OF YOUR MOUTH, OTHER THAN YOUR BREATH, IS A LIE!

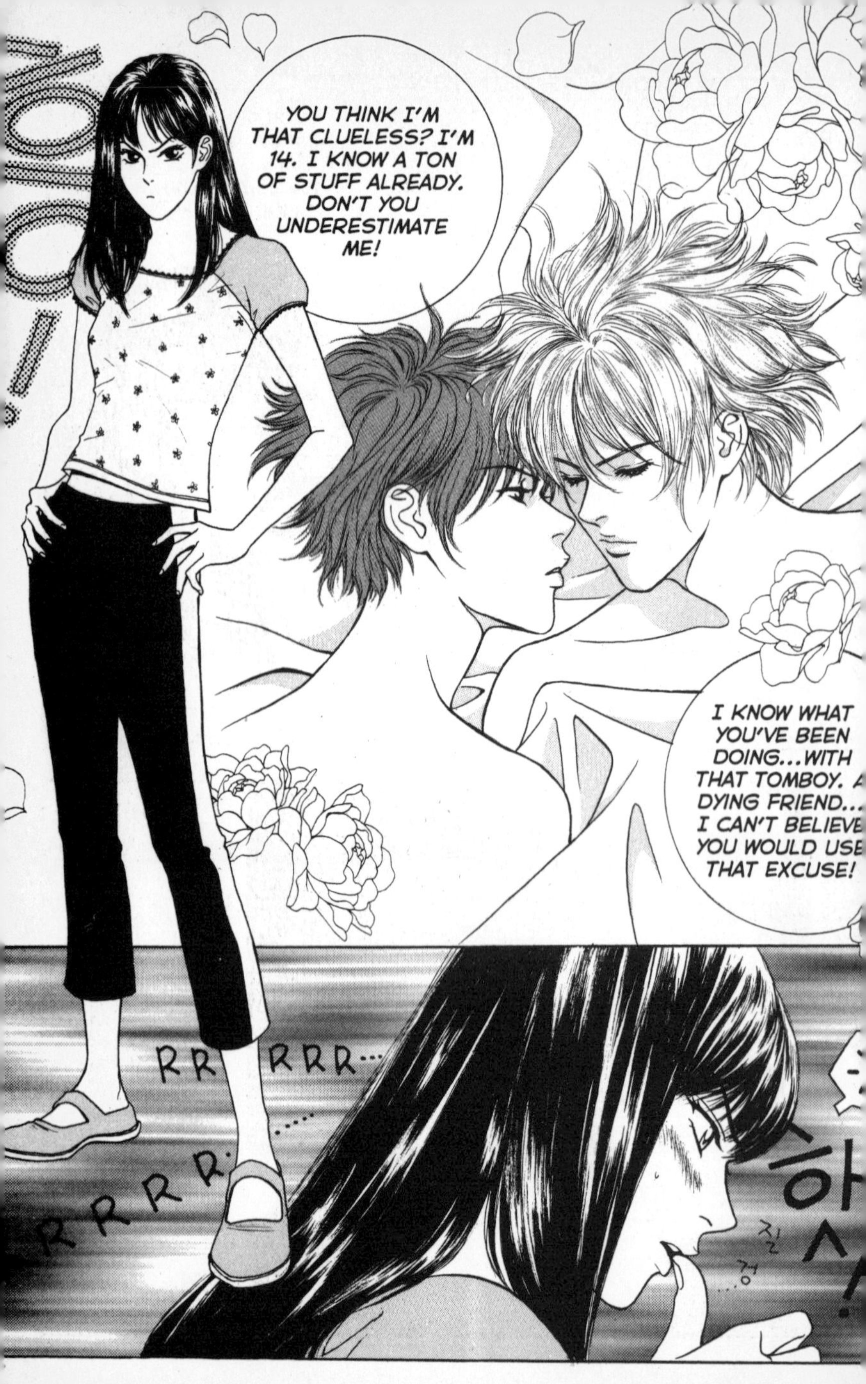
YOU THINK I'M THAT CLUELESS? I'M 14. I KNOW A TON OF STUFF ALREADY. DON'T YOU UNDERESTIMATE ME!
I KNOW WHAT YOU'VE BEEN DOING...WITH THAT TOMBOY. A DYING FRIEND... I CAN'T BELIEVE YOU WOULD USE THAT EXCUSE!
RR RRR...
RRRR...

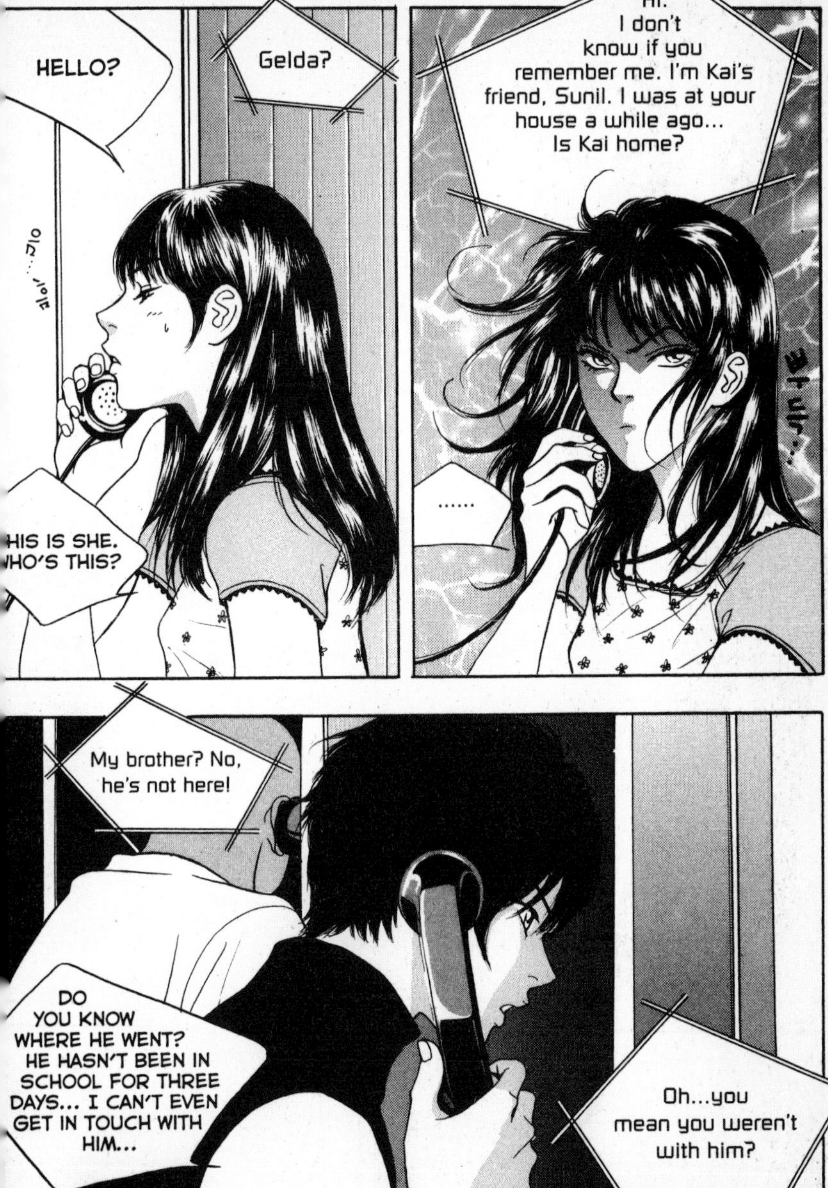

HELLO?
Gelda?
HIS IS SHE. HO'S THIS?
Hi. I don't know if you remember me. I'm Kai's friend, Sunil. I was at your house a while ago... Is Kai home?
......
My brother? No, he's not here!
DO YOU KNOW WHERE HE WENT? HE HASN'T BEEN IN SCHOOL FOR THREE DAYS... I CAN'T EVEN GET IN TOUCH WITH HIM...
Oh...you mean you weren't with him?

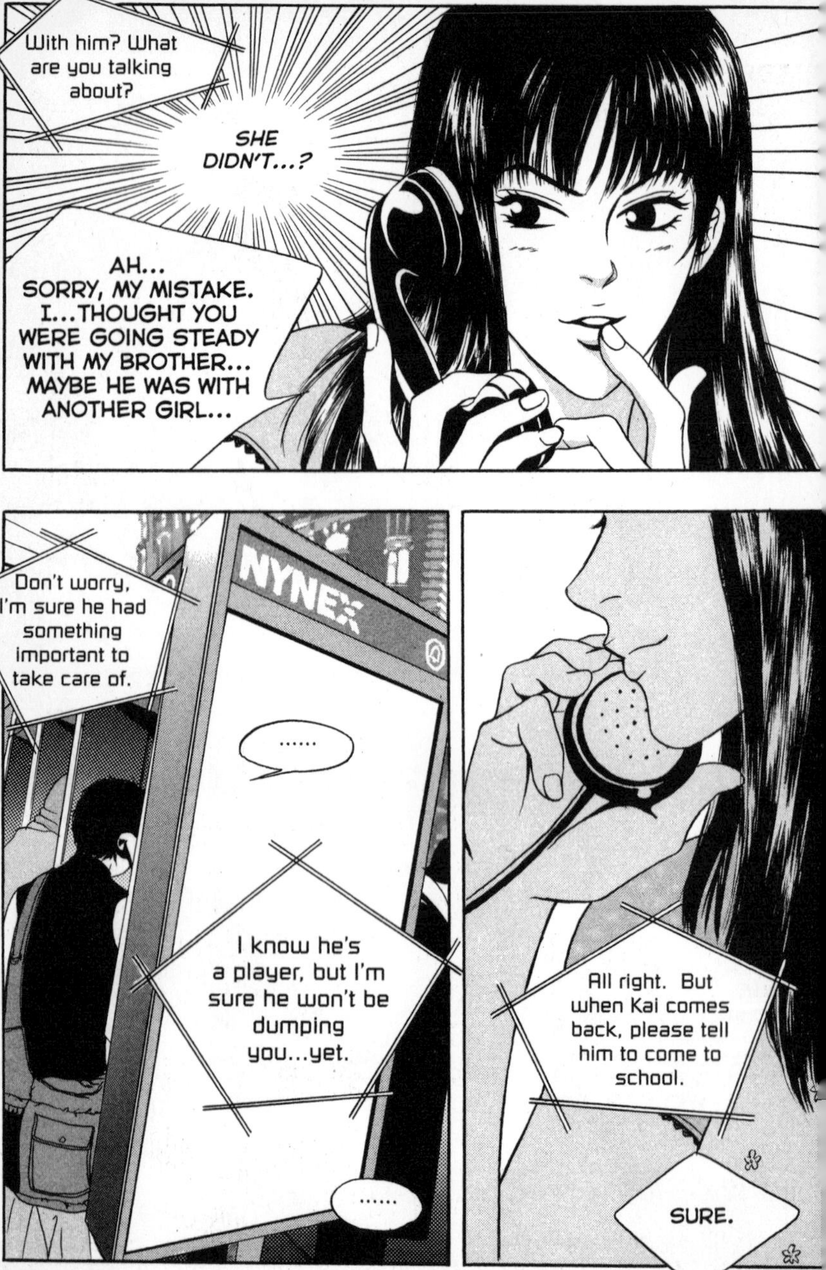
With him? What are you talking about?
SHE DIDN'T...?
AH... SORRY, MY MISTAKE. I...THOUGHT YOU WERE GOING STEADY WITH MY BROTHER... MAYBE HE WAS WITH ANOTHER GIRL...
NYNEX
Don't worry, I'm sure he had something important to take care of.
......
I know he's a player, but I'm sure he won't be dumping you...yet.
......
All right. But when Kai comes back, please tell him to come to school.
SURE.

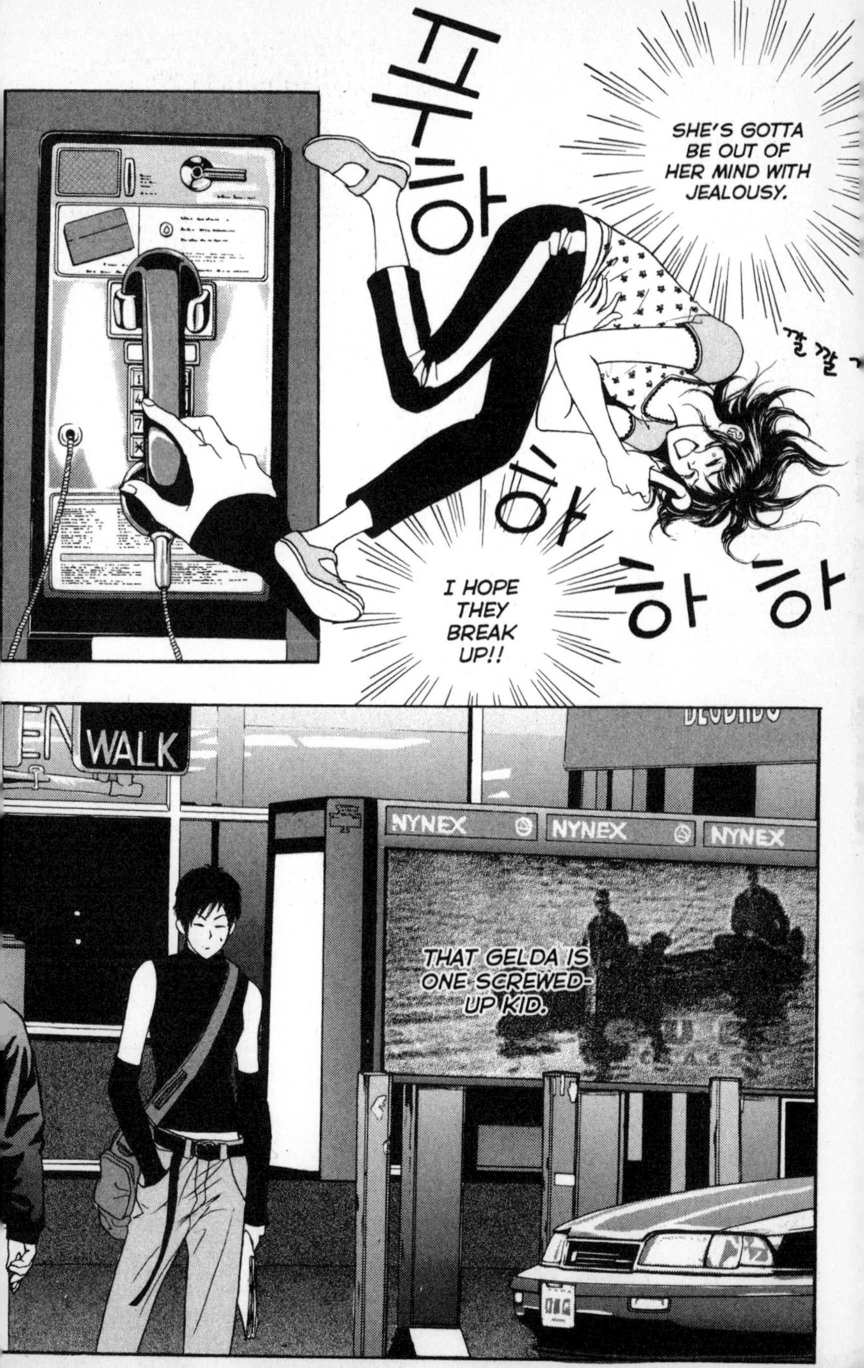
푸하
SHE'S GOTTA BE OUT OF HER MIND WITH JEALOUSY.
깔깔
하
하 하
I HOPE THEY BREAK UP!!
WALK
NYNEX
NYNEX
NYNEX
THAT GELDA IS ONE SCREWED-UP KID.

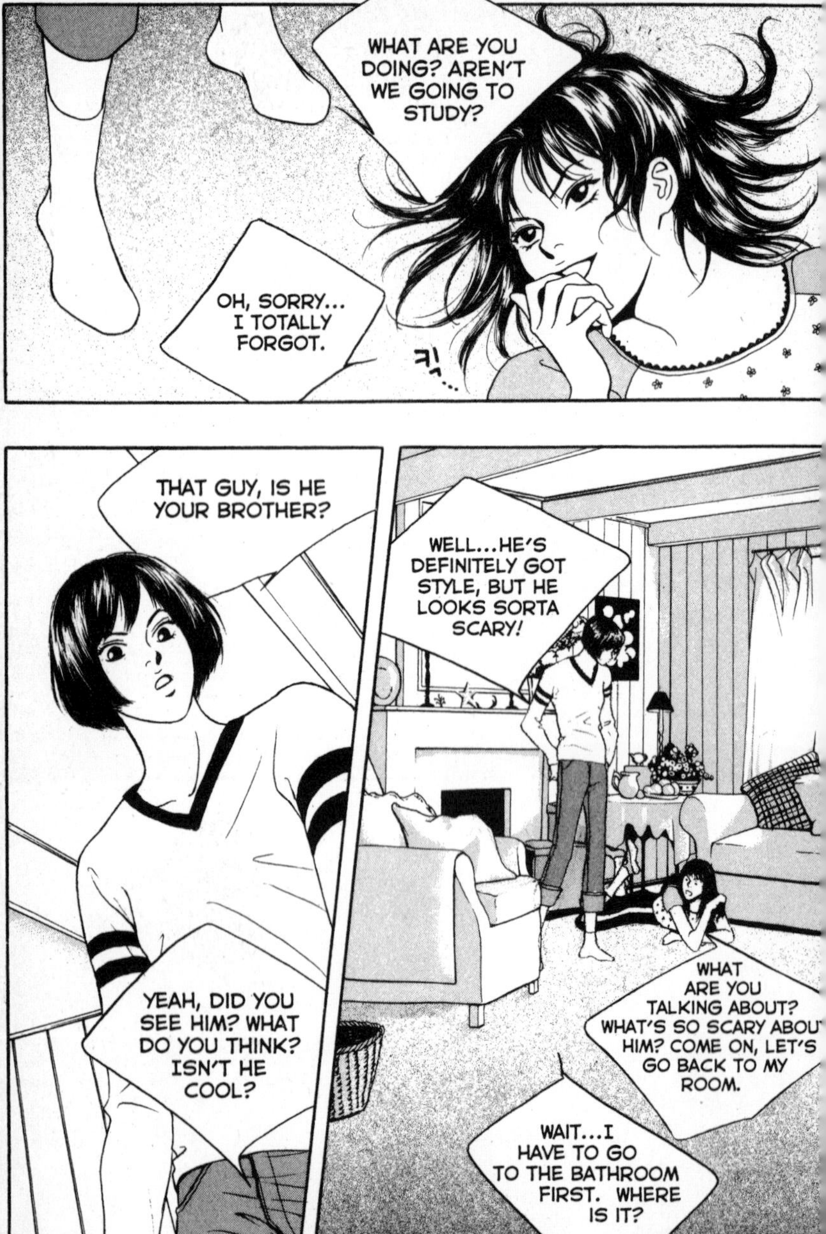
WHAT ARE YOU DOING? AREN'T WE GOING TO STUDY?
OH, SORRY... I TOTALLY FORGOT.
THAT GUY, IS HE YOUR BROTHER?
YEAH, DID YOU SEE HIM? WHAT DO YOU THINK? ISN'T HE COOL?
WELL...HE'S DEFINITELY GOT STYLE, BUT HE LOOKS SORTA SCARY!
WHAT ARE YOU TALKING ABOUT? WHAT'S SO SCARY ABOU HIM? COME ON, LET'S GO BACK TO MY ROOM.
WAIT...I HAVE TO GO TO THE BATHROOM FIRST. WHERE IS IT?

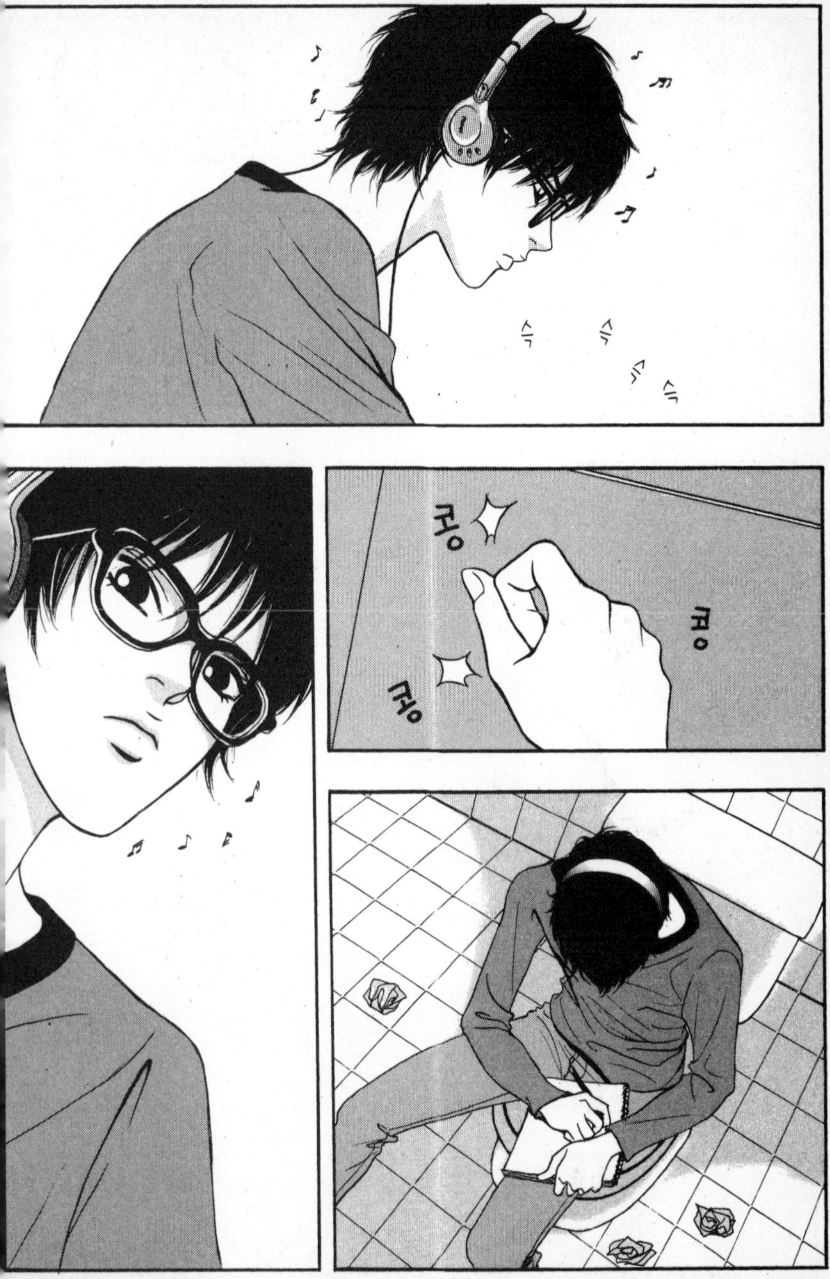

슥
슥
슥
슥
콩
콩
콩

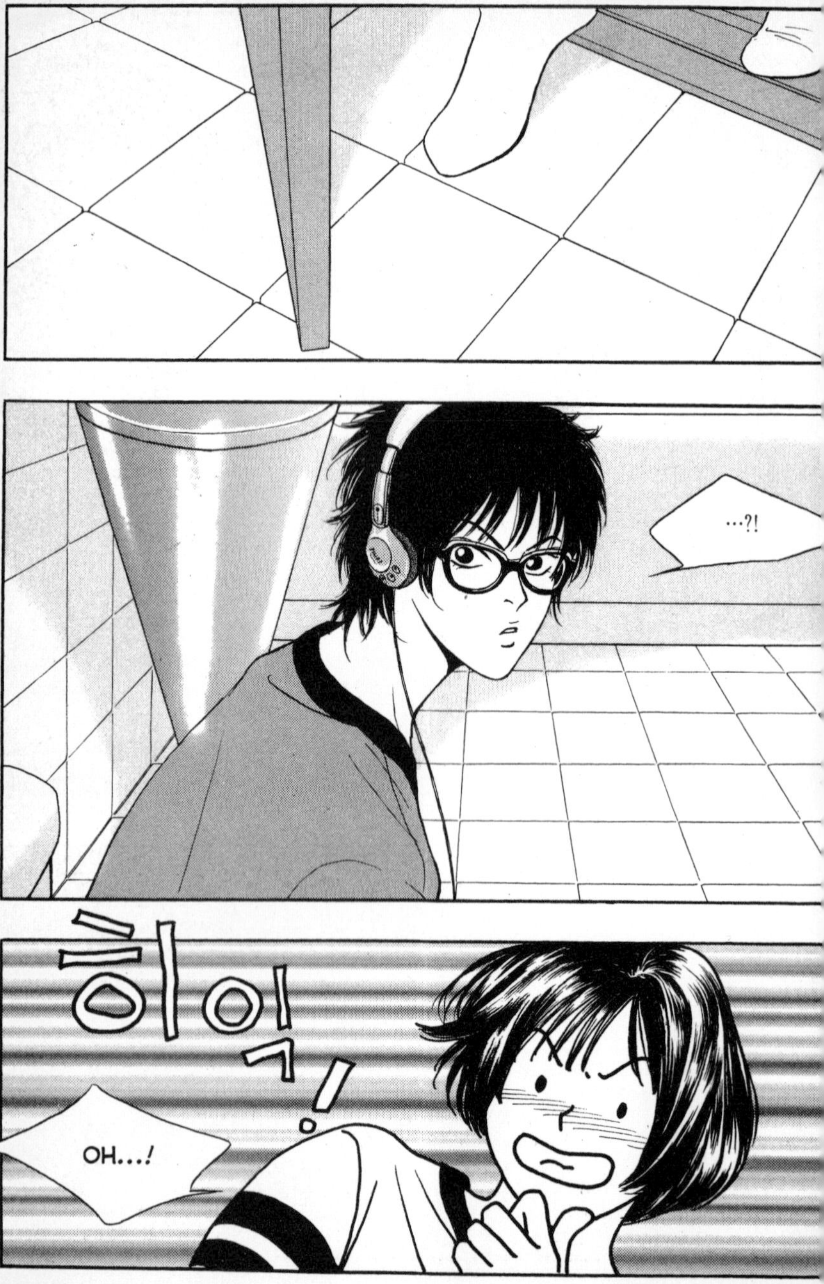
...?!
히익!
OH...!

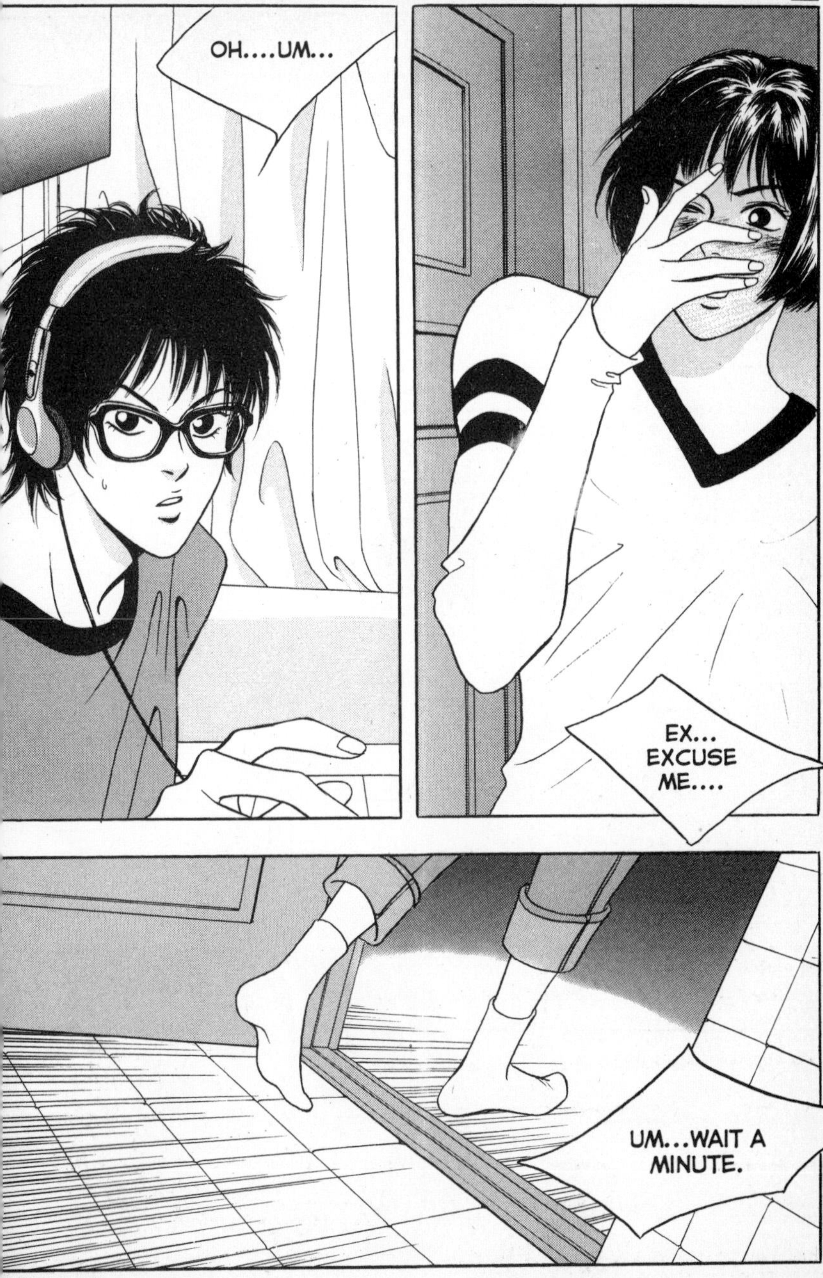
OH....UM...
EX... EXCUSE ME....
UM...WAIT A MINUTE.

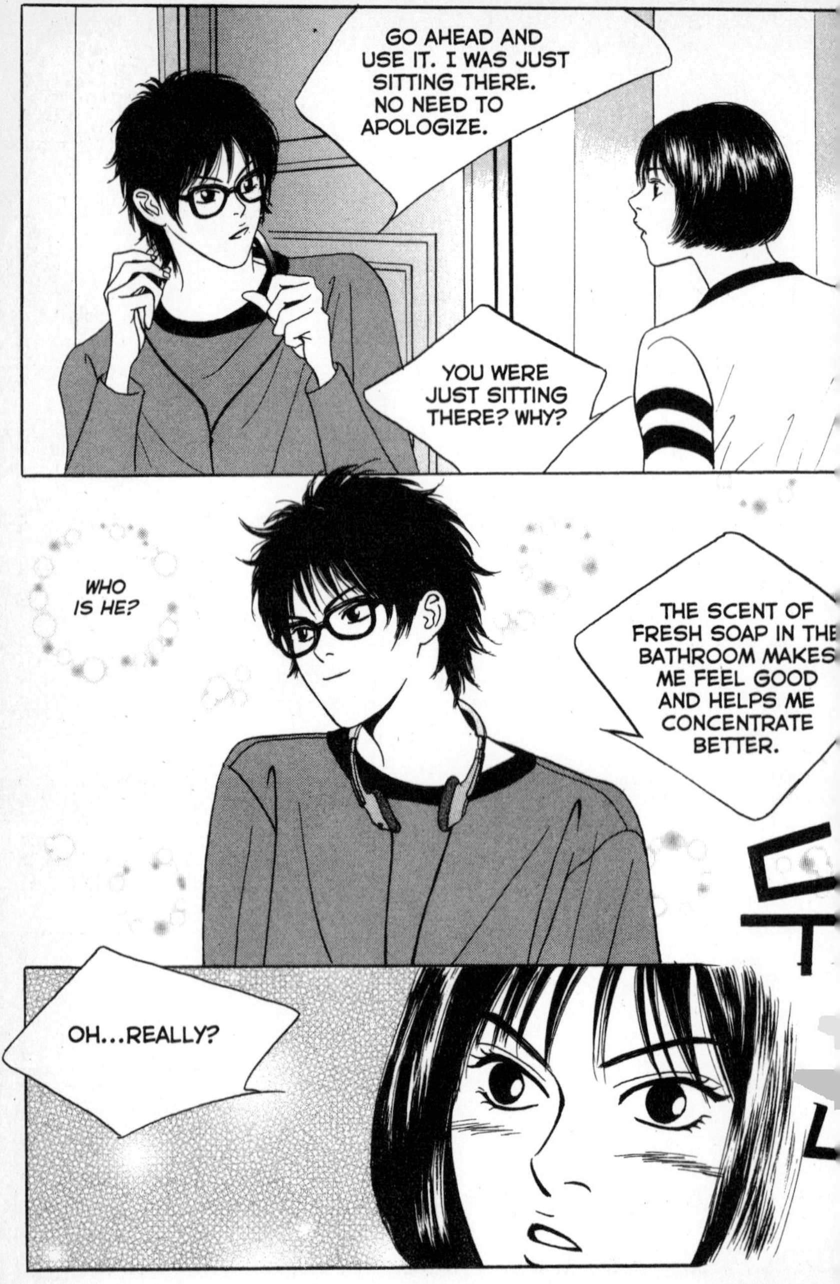
GO AHEAD AND USE IT. I WAS JUST SITTING THERE. NO NEED TO APOLOGIZE.
YOU WERE JUST SITTING THERE? WHY?
WHO IS HE?
THE SCENT OF FRESH SOAP IN THE BATHROOM MAKES ME FEEL GOOD AND HELPS ME CONCENTRATE BETTER.
OH...REALLY?

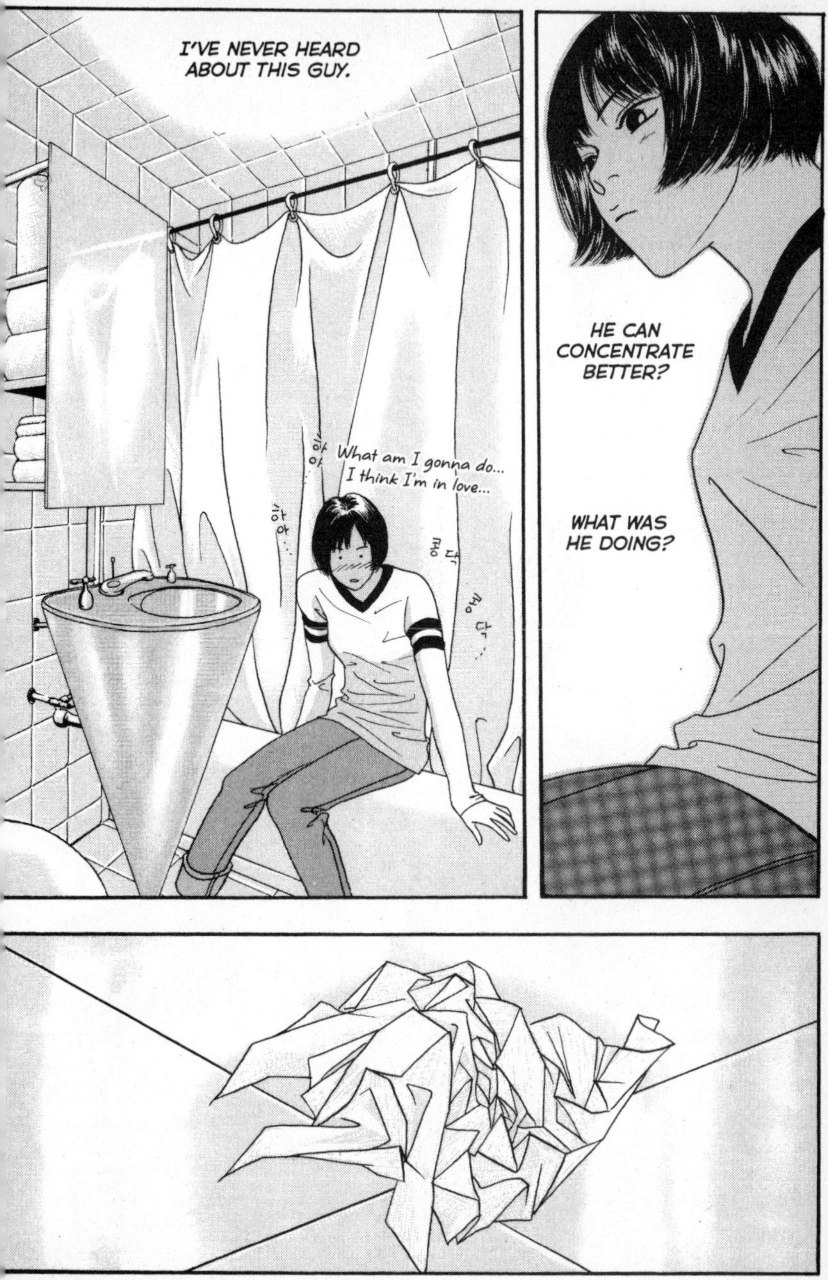
I'VE NEVER HEARD ABOUT THIS GUY.
하아...
What am I gonna do... I think I'm in love...
하아...
콩닥
콩닥...
HE CAN CONCENTRATE BETTER?
WHAT WAS HE DOING?

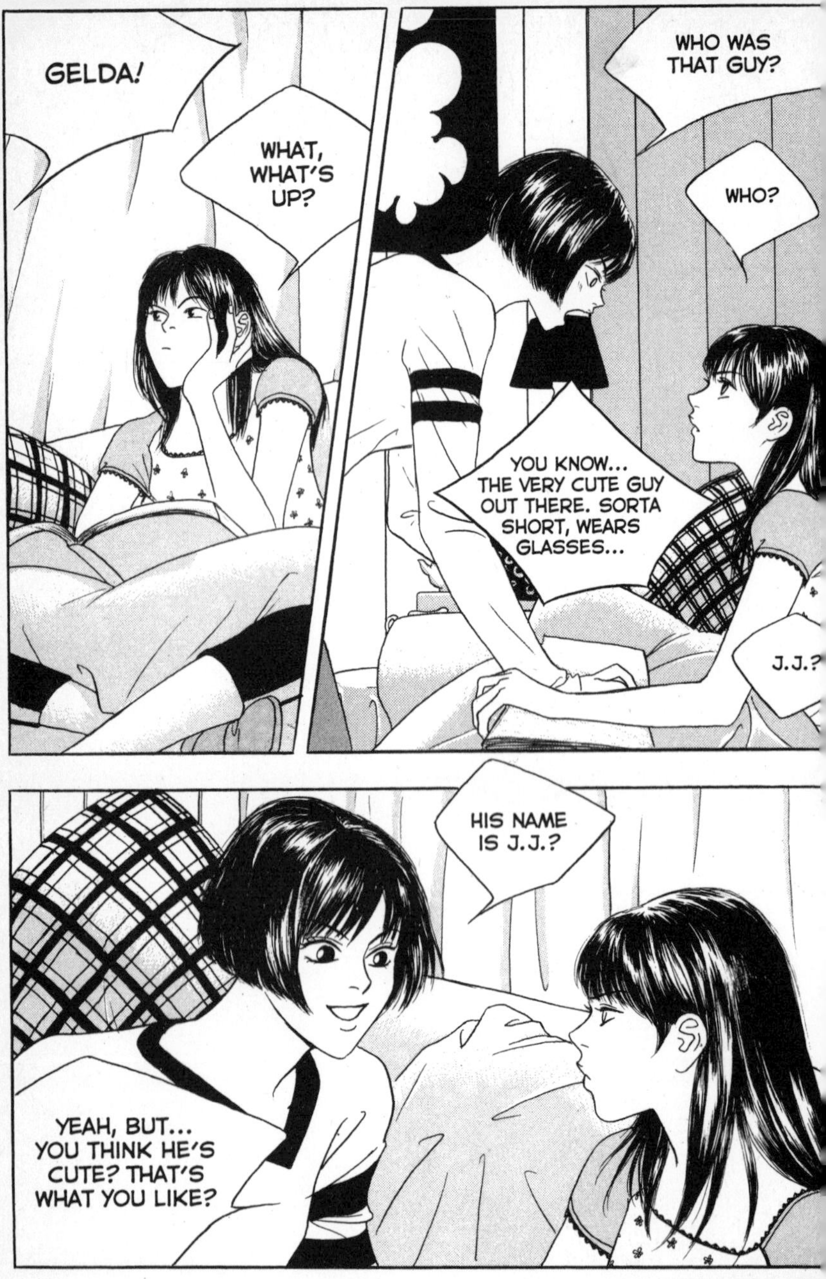
GELDA!
WHAT, WHAT'S UP?
WHO WAS THAT GUY?
WHO?
YOU KNOW... THE VERY CUTE GUY OUT THERE. SORTA SHORT, WEARS GLASSES...
J.J.?
HIS NAME IS J.J.?
YEAH, BUT... YOU THINK HE'S CUTE? THAT'S WHAT YOU LIKE?

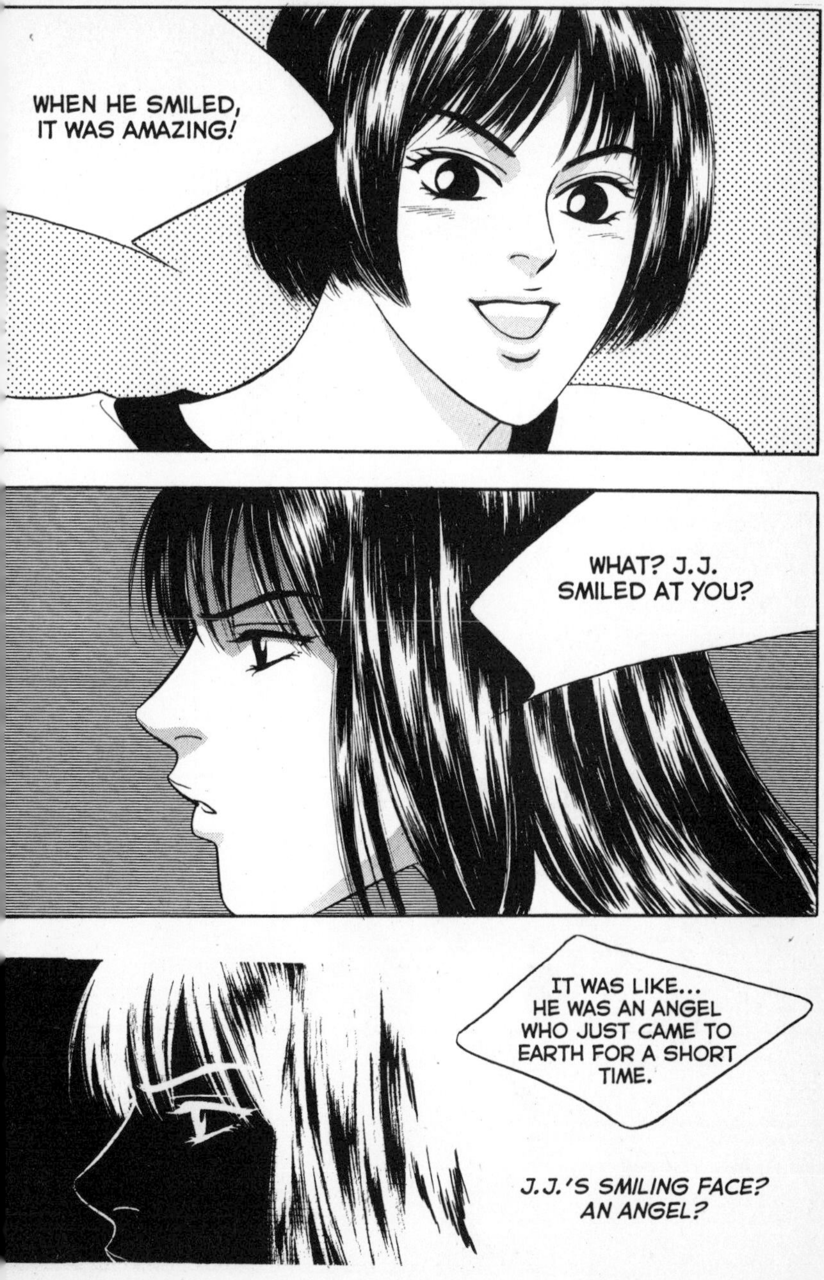
WHEN HE SMILED, IT WAS AMAZING!
WHAT? J.J. SMILED AT YOU?
IT WAS LIKE... HE WAS AN ANGEL WHO JUST CAME TO EARTH FOR A SHORT TIME.
J.J.'S SMILING FACE? AN ANGEL?

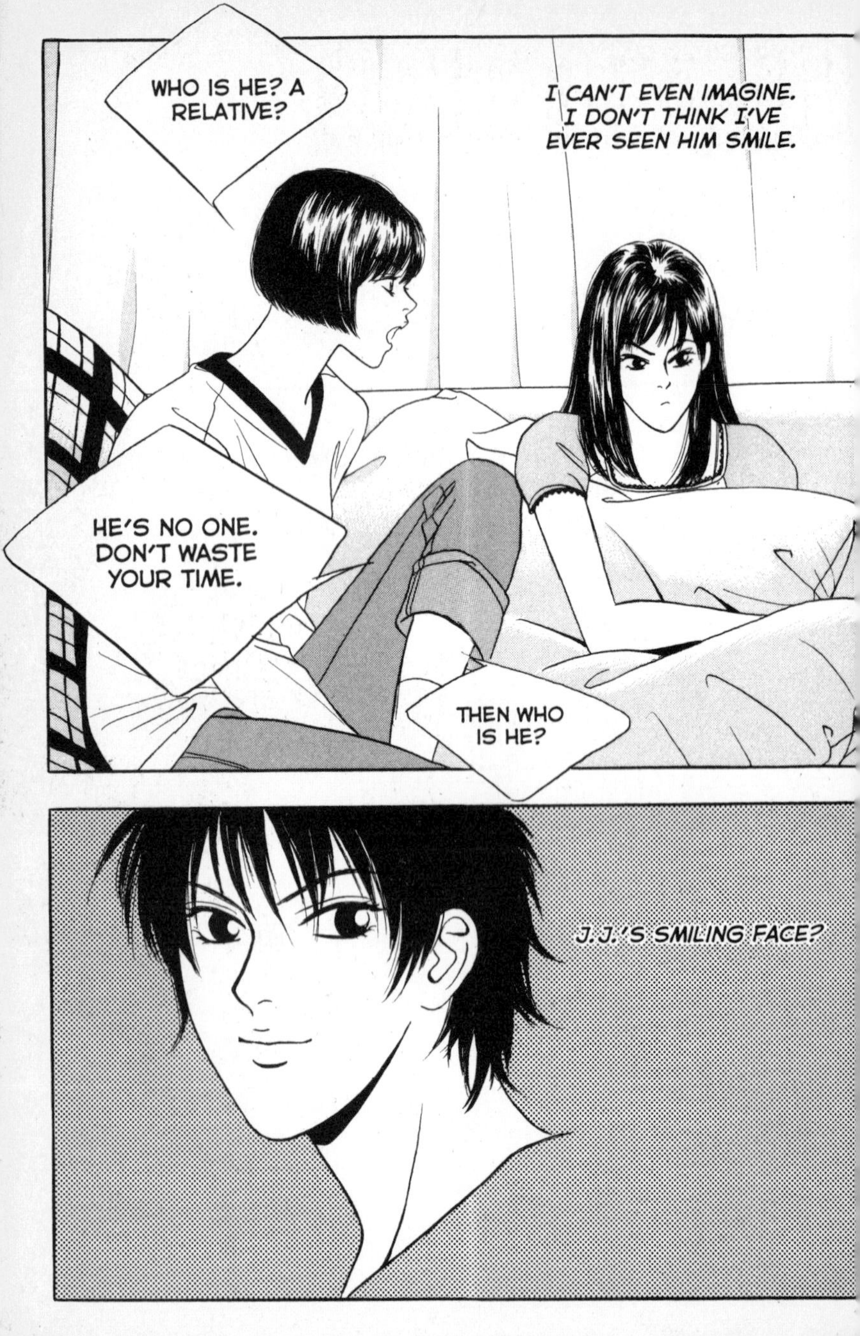
WHO IS HE? A RELATIVE?
I CAN'T EVEN IMAGINE. I DON'T THINK I'VE EVER SEEN HIM SMILE.
HE'S NO ONE. DON'T WASTE YOUR TIME.
THEN WHO IS HE?
J.J.'S SMILING FACE?

SOUL TO SEOUL™

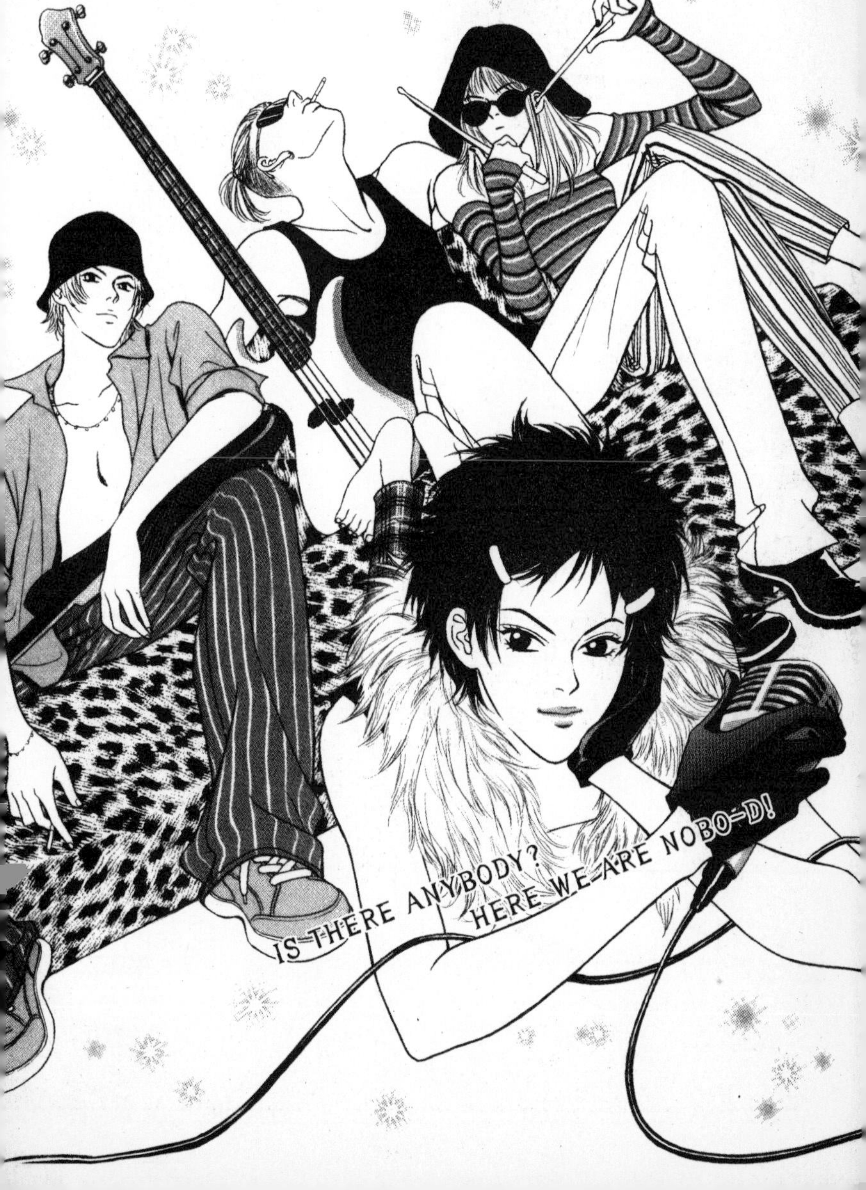

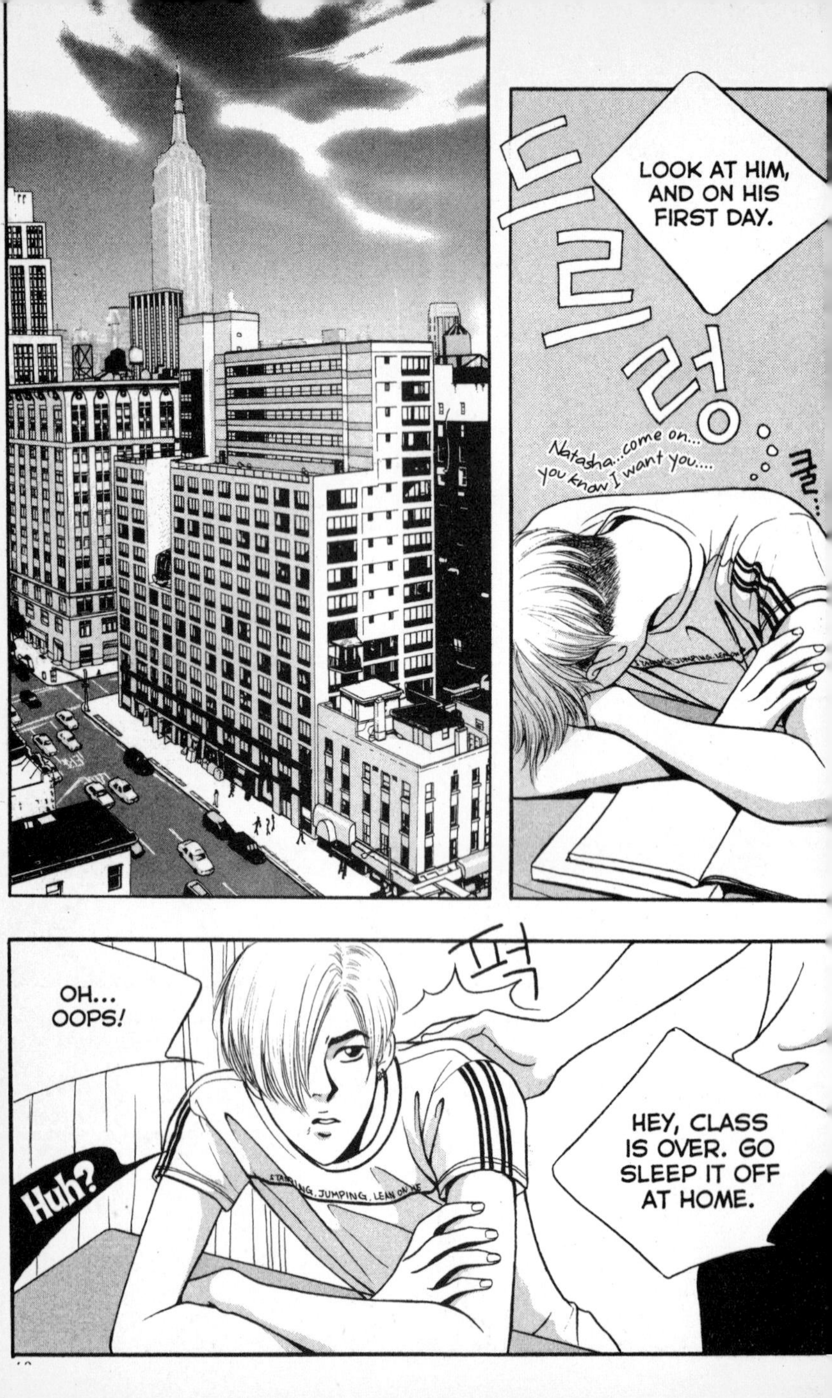
드르렁
LOOK AT HIM, AND ON HIS FIRST DAY.
Natasha...come on... you know I want you....
OH... OOPS!
Huh?
HEY, CLASS IS OVER. GO SLEEP IT OFF AT HOME.

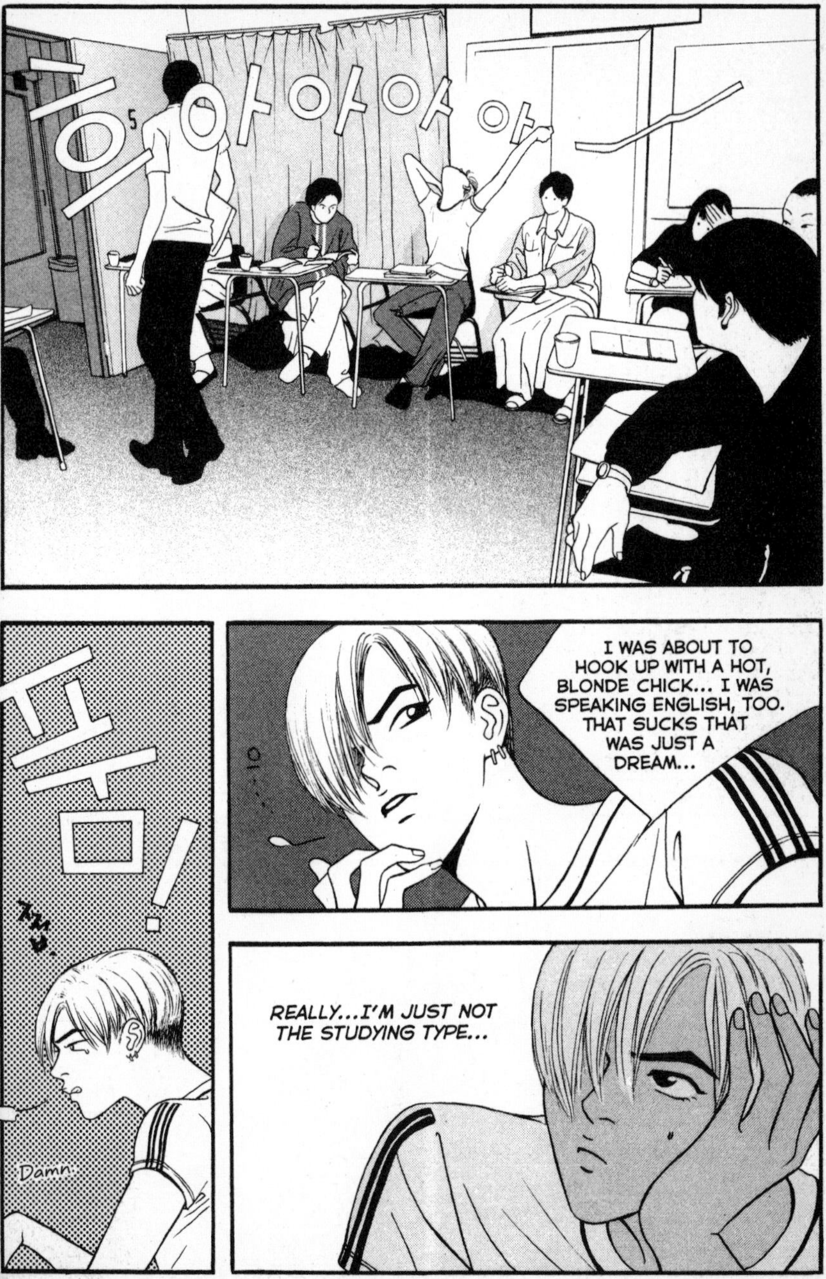
Damn.
I WAS ABOUT TO HOOK UP WITH A HOT, BLONDE CHICK... I WAS SPEAKING ENGLISH, TOO. THAT SUCKS THAT WAS JUST A DREAM...
REALLY...I'M JUST NOT THE STUDYING TYPE...

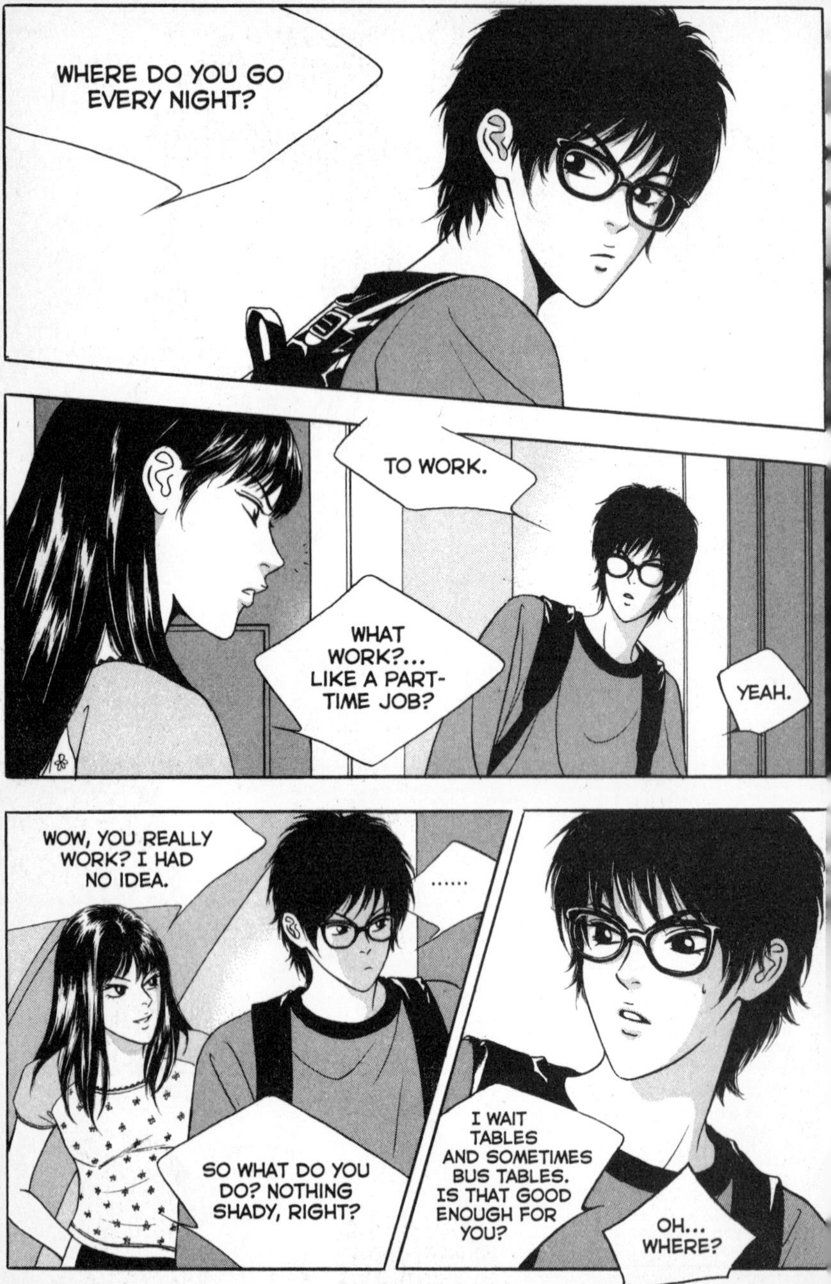
WHERE DO YOU GO EVERY NIGHT?
TO WORK.
WHAT WORK?... LIKE A PART-TIME JOB?
YEAH.
WOW, YOU REALLY WORK? I HAD NO IDEA.
......
SO WHAT DO YOU DO? NOTHING SHADY, RIGHT?
I WAIT TABLES AND SOMETIMES BUS TABLES. IS THAT GOOD ENOUGH FOR YOU?
OH... WHERE?

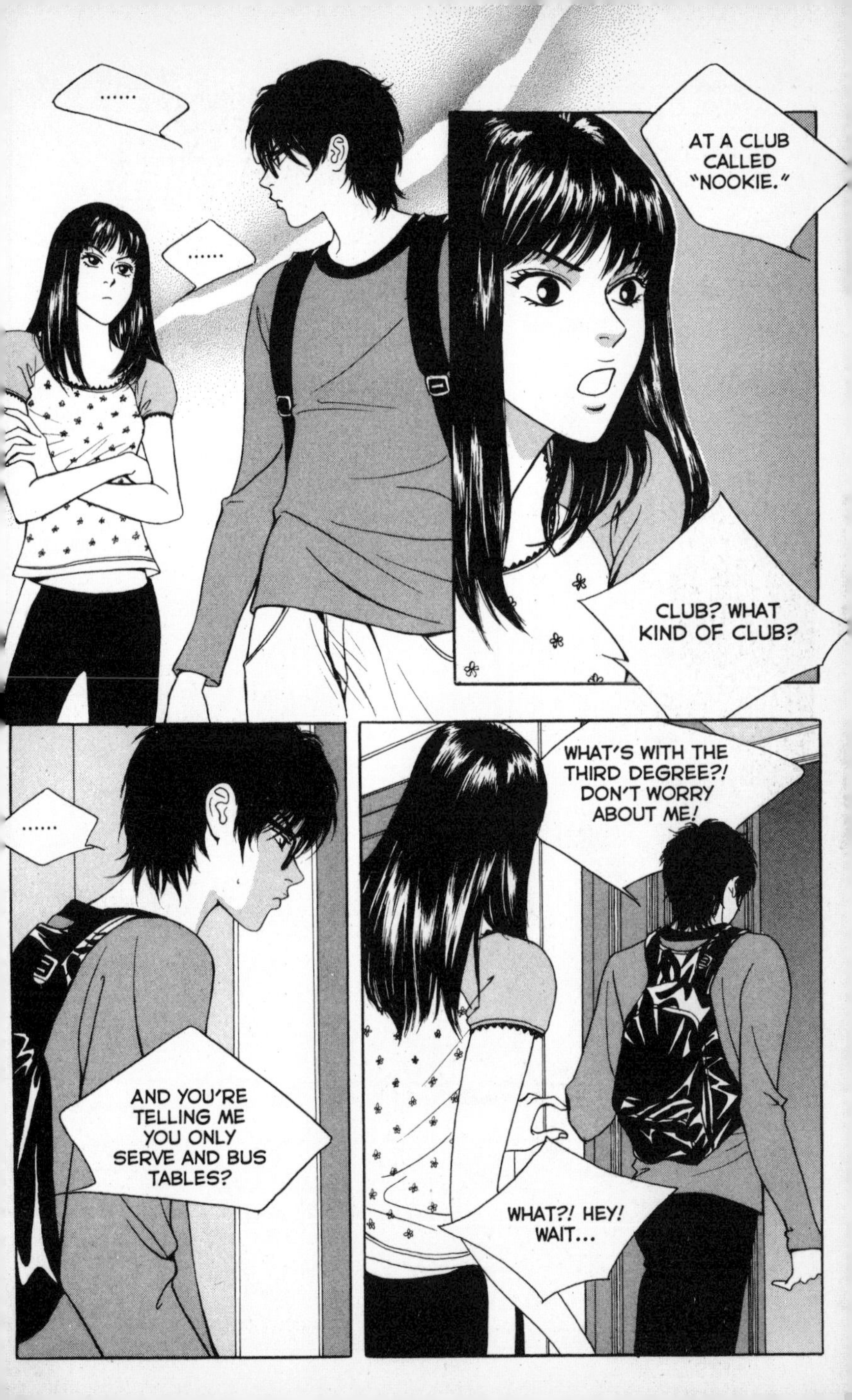
......
......
AT A CLUB CALLED "NOOKIE."
CLUB? WHAT KIND OF CLUB?
......
AND YOU'RE TELLING ME YOU ONLY SERVE AND BUS TABLES?
WHAT'S WITH THE THIRD DEGREE?! DON'T WORRY ABOUT ME!
WHAT?! HEY! WAIT...

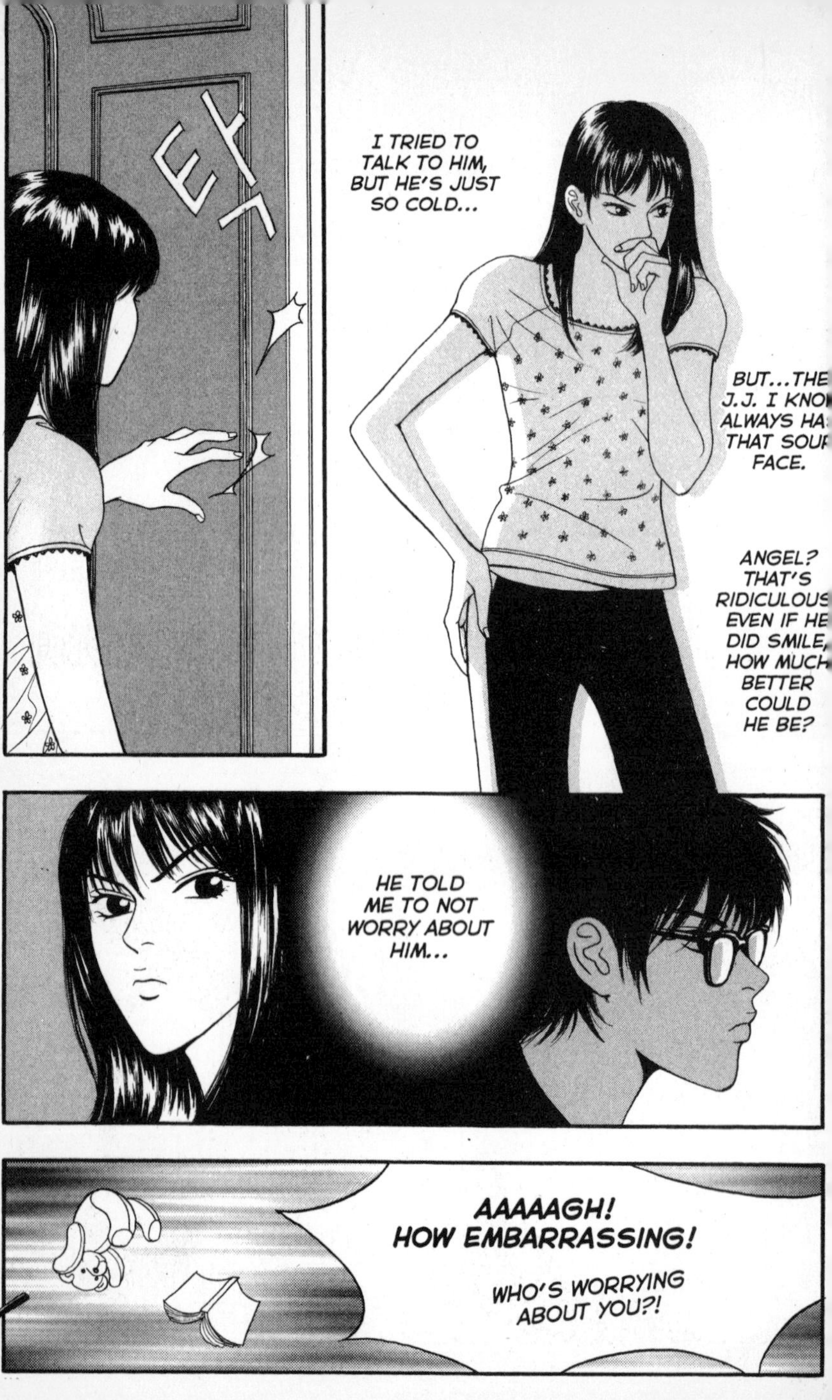
I TRIED TO TALK TO HIM, BUT HE'S JUST SO COLD...
BUT...THE J.J. I KNO ALWAYS HA THAT SOU FACE.
ANGEL? THAT'S RIDICULOUS EVEN IF HE DID SMILE, HOW MUCH BETTER COULD HE BE?
HE TOLD ME TO NOT WORRY ABOUT HIM...
AAAAAGH! HOW EMBARRASSING!
WHO'S WORRYING ABOUT YOU?!

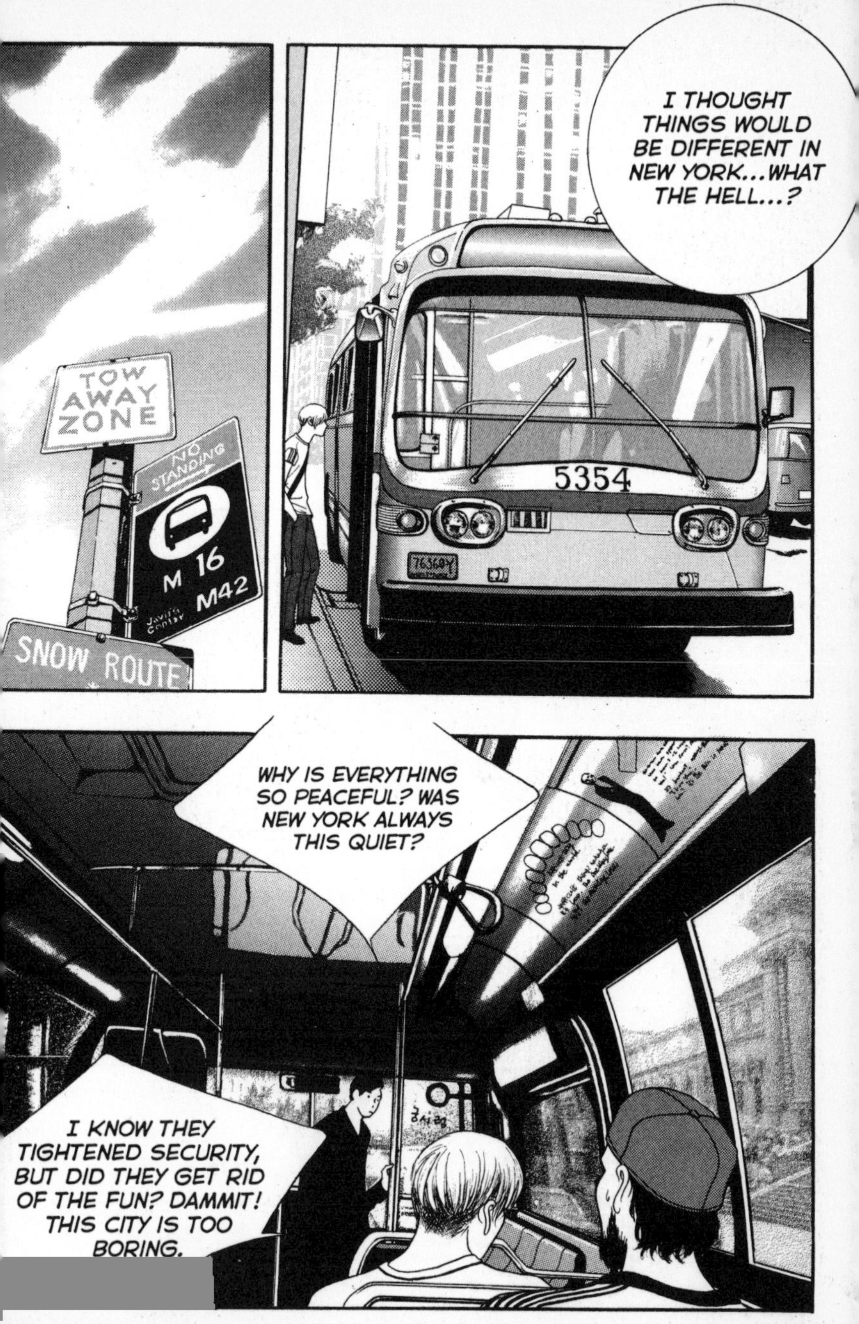
TOW AWAY ZONE
NO STANDING
M 16
M42
SNOW ROUTE
5354
I THOUGHT THINGS WOULD BE DIFFERENT IN NEW YORK...WHAT THE HELL...?
WHY IS EVERYTHING SO PEACEFUL? WAS NEW YORK ALWAYS THIS QUIET?
I KNOW THEY TIGHTENED SECURITY, BUT DID THEY GET RID OF THE FUN? DAMMIT! THIS CITY IS TOO BORING.

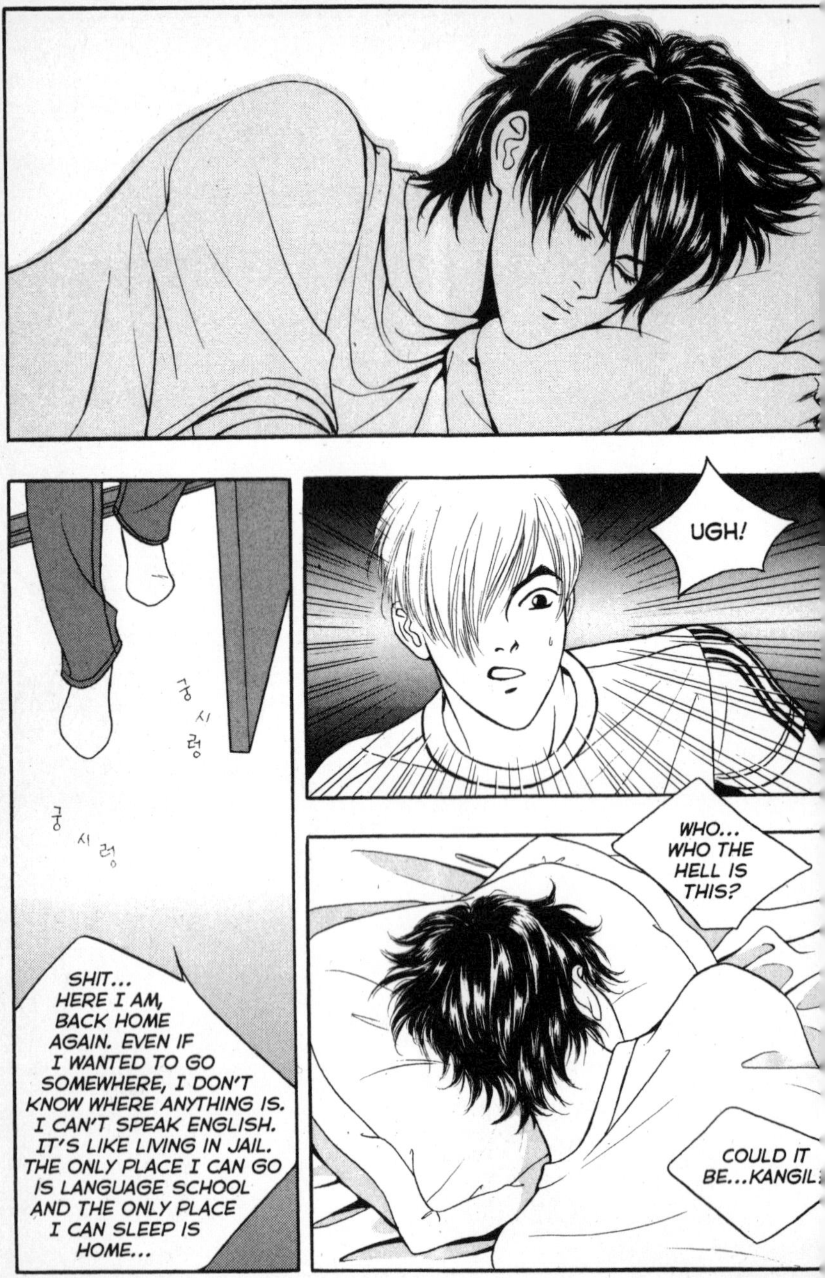
궁시렁
궁시렁
SHIT... HERE I AM, BACK HOME AGAIN. EVEN IF I WANTED TO GO SOMEWHERE, I DON'T KNOW WHERE ANYTHING IS. I CAN'T SPEAK ENGLISH. IT'S LIKE LIVING IN JAIL. THE ONLY PLACE I CAN GO IS LANGUAGE SCHOOL AND THE ONLY PLACE I CAN SLEEP IS HOME...
UGH!
WHO... WHO THE HELL IS THIS?
COULD IT BE...KANGIL

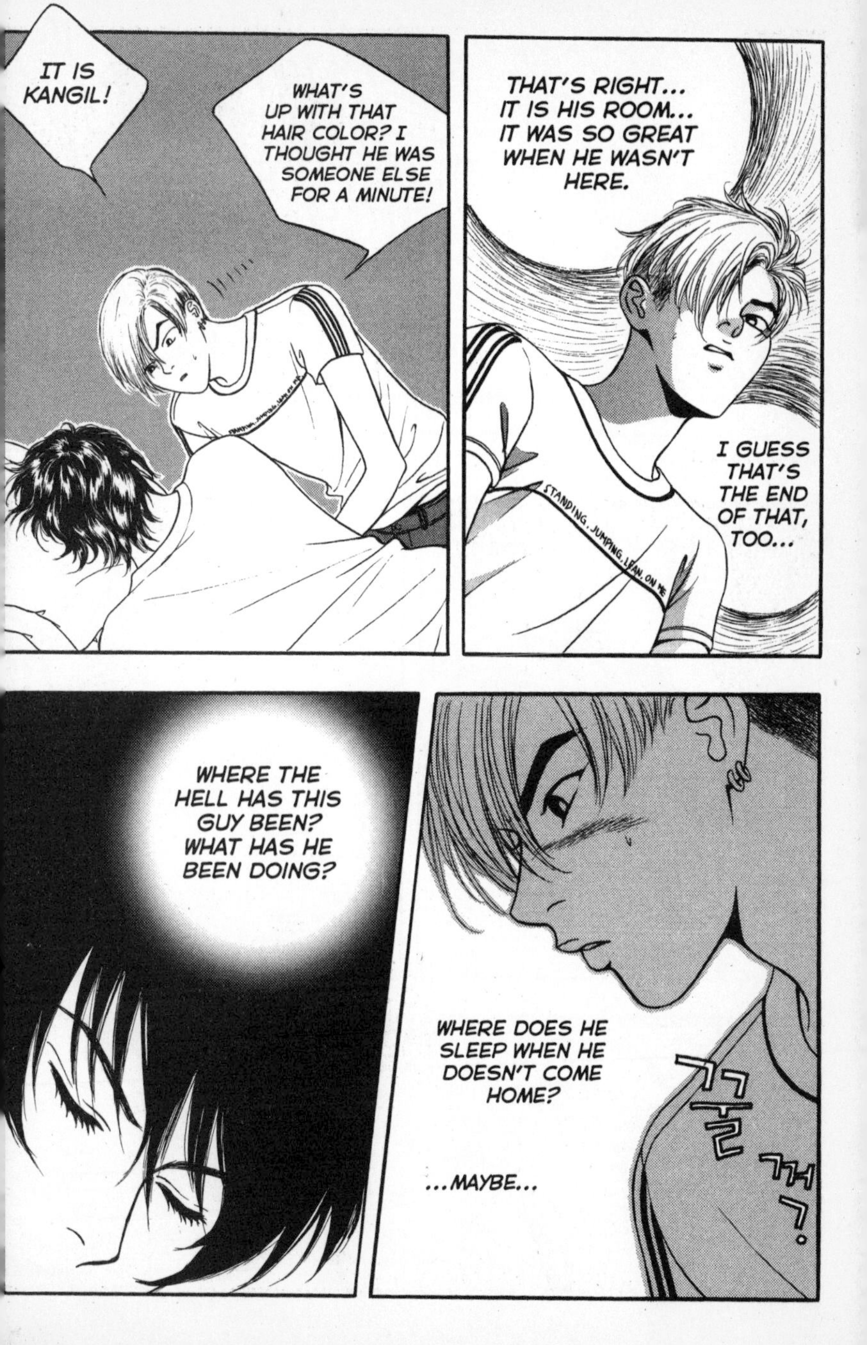
IT IS KANGIL!
WHAT'S UP WITH THAT HAIR COLOR? I THOUGHT HE WAS SOMEONE ELSE FOR A MINUTE!
THAT'S RIGHT... IT IS HIS ROOM... IT WAS SO GREAT WHEN HE WASN'T HERE.
STANDING, JUMPING, LEAN ON ME
I GUESS THAT'S THE END OF THAT, TOO...
WHERE THE HELL HAS THIS GUY BEEN? WHAT HAS HE BEEN DOING?
WHERE DOES HE SLEEP WHEN HE DOESN'T COME HOME?
...MAYBE...

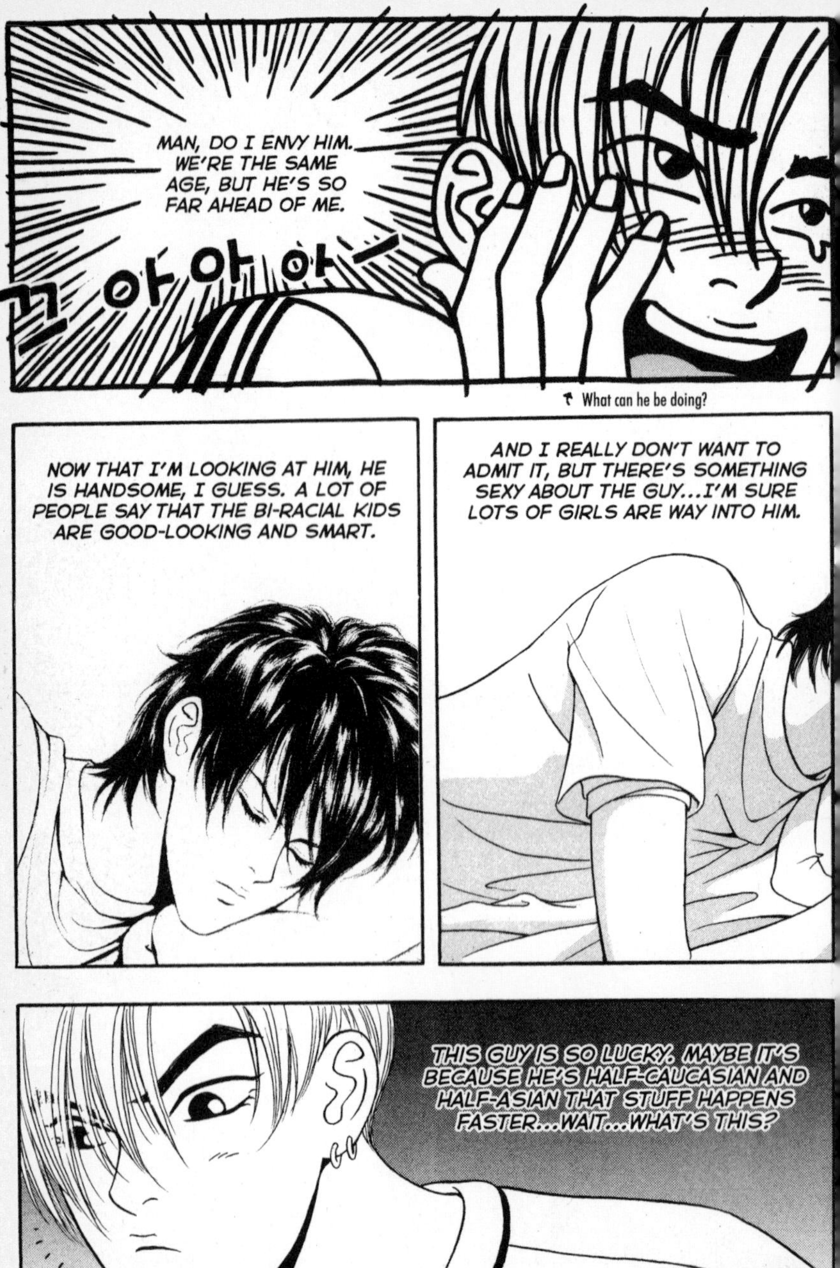
MAN, DO I ENVY HIM. WE'RE THE SAME AGE, BUT HE'S SO FAR AHEAD OF ME.
끄아아아~
What can he be doing?
NOW THAT I'M LOOKING AT HIM, HE IS HANDSOME, I GUESS. A LOT OF PEOPLE SAY THAT THE BI-RACIAL KIDS ARE GOOD-LOOKING AND SMART.
AND I REALLY DON'T WANT TO ADMIT IT, BUT THERE'S SOMETHING SEXY ABOUT THE GUY...I'M SURE LOTS OF GIRLS ARE WAY INTO HIM.
THIS GUY IS SO LUCKY. MAYBE IT'S BECAUSE HE'S HALF-CAUCASIAN AND HALF-ASIAN THAT STUFF HAPPENS FASTER...WAIT...WHAT'S THIS?

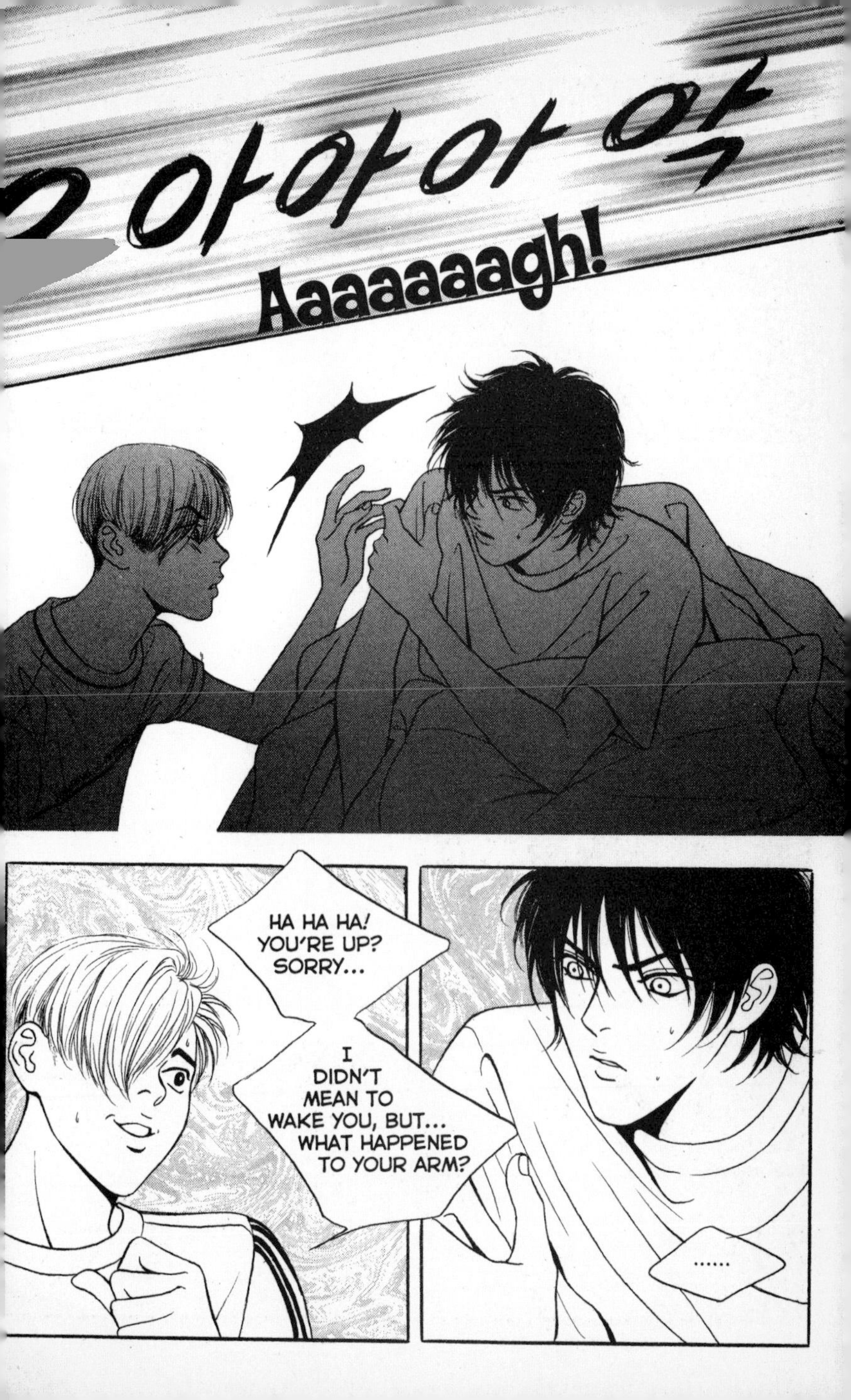
아아아악
Aaaaaaagh!
HA HA HA! YOU'RE UP? SORRY...
I DIDN'T MEAN TO WAKE YOU, BUT... WHAT HAPPENED TO YOUR ARM?
......

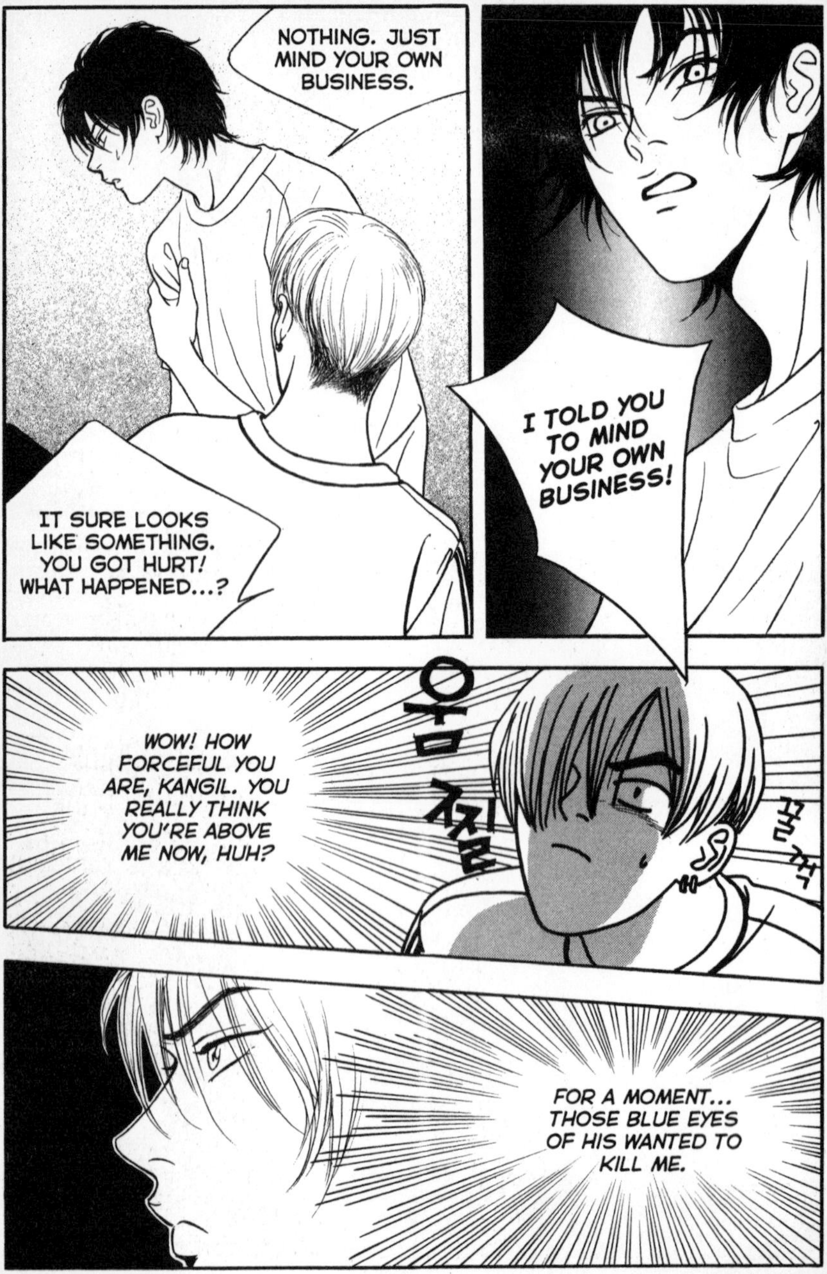
NOTHING. JUST MIND YOUR OWN BUSINESS.
IT SURE LOOKS LIKE SOMETHING. YOU GOT HURT! WHAT HAPPENED...?
I TOLD YOU TO MIND YOUR OWN BUSINESS!
움찔
WOW! HOW FORCEFUL YOU ARE, KANGIL. YOU REALLY THINK YOU'RE ABOVE ME NOW, HUH?
FOR A MOMENT... THOSE BLUE EYES OF HIS WANTED TO KILL ME.

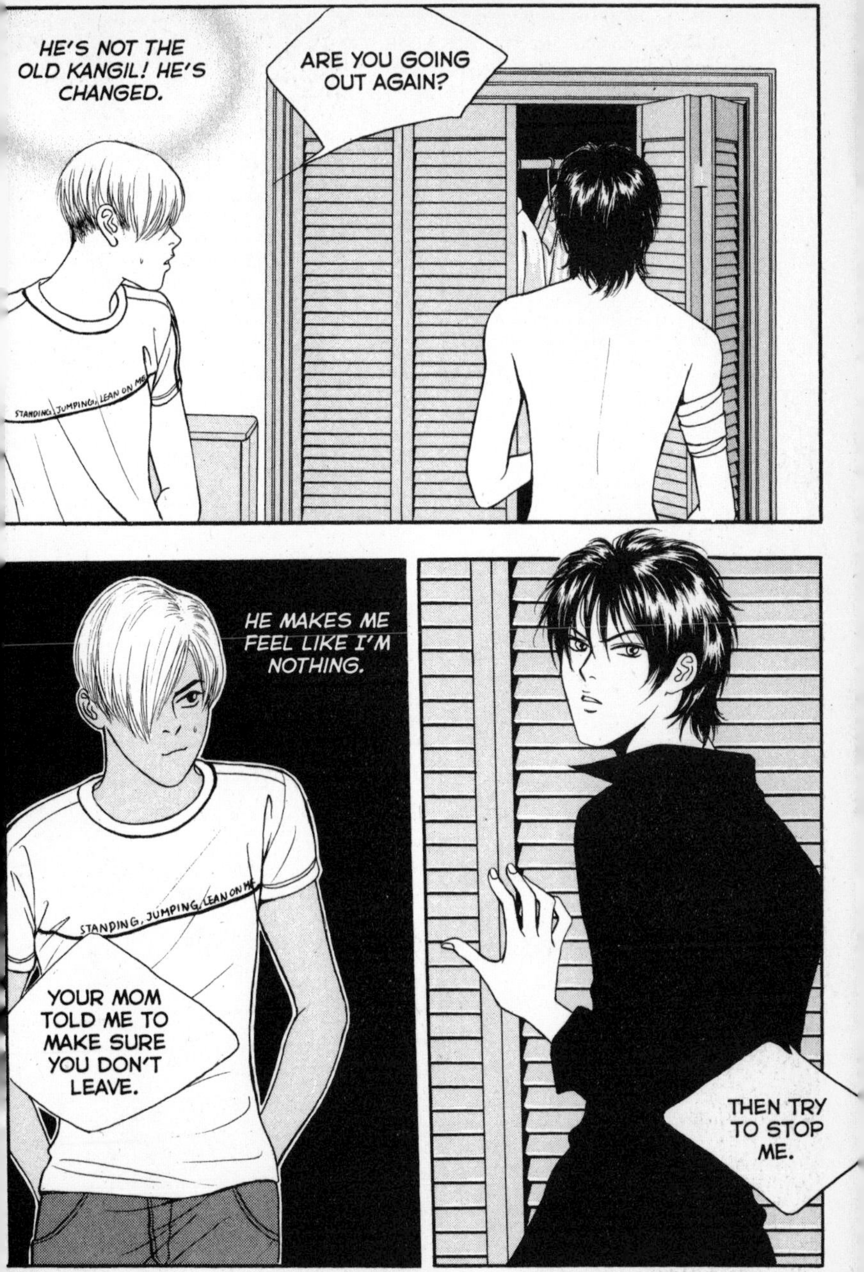

HE'S NOT THE OLD KANGIL! HE'S CHANGED.
ARE YOU GOING OUT AGAIN?
STANDING, JUMPING, LEAN ON ME
HE MAKES ME FEEL LIKE I'M NOTHING.
STANDING, JUMPING, LEAN ON ME
YOUR MOM TOLD ME TO MAKE SURE YOU DON'T LEAVE.
THEN TRY TO STOP ME.

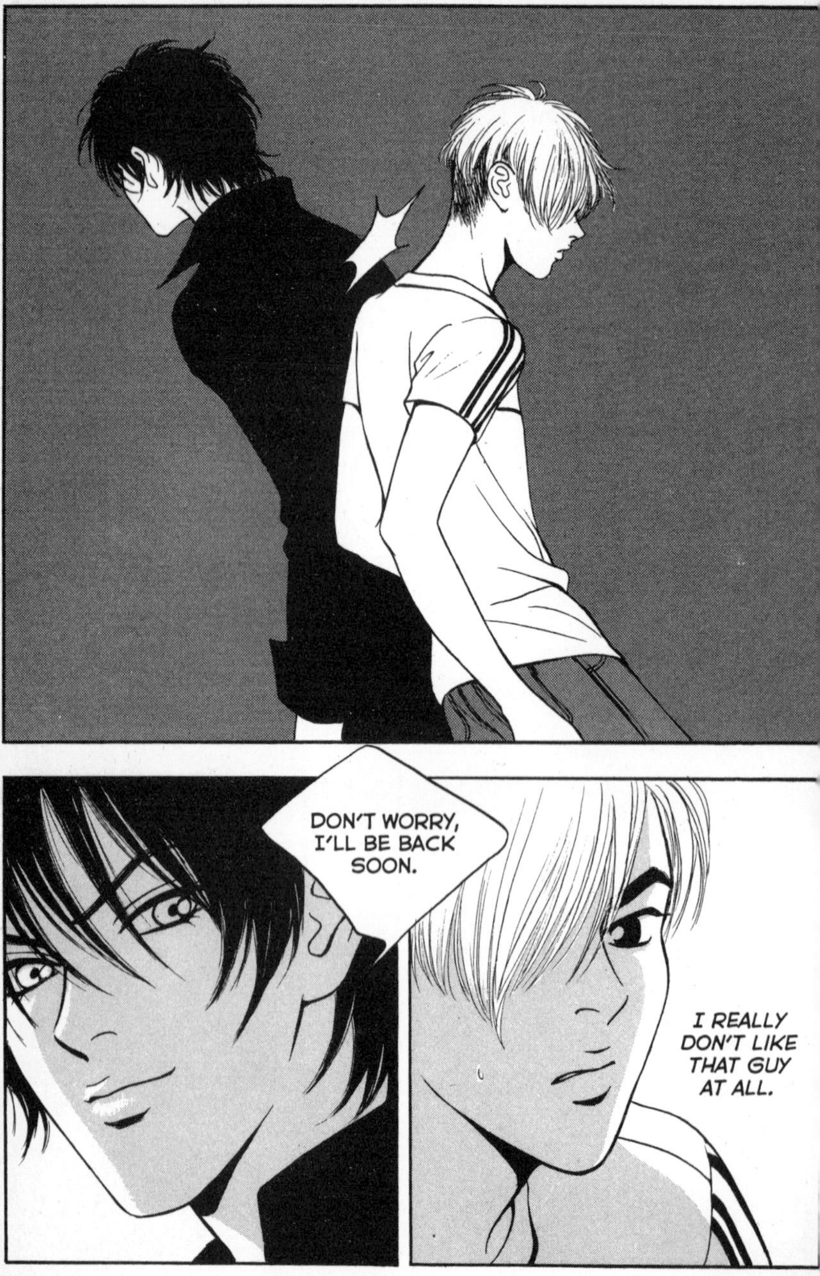
DON'T WORRY, I'LL BE BACK SOON.
I REALLY DON'T LIKE THAT GUY AT ALL.

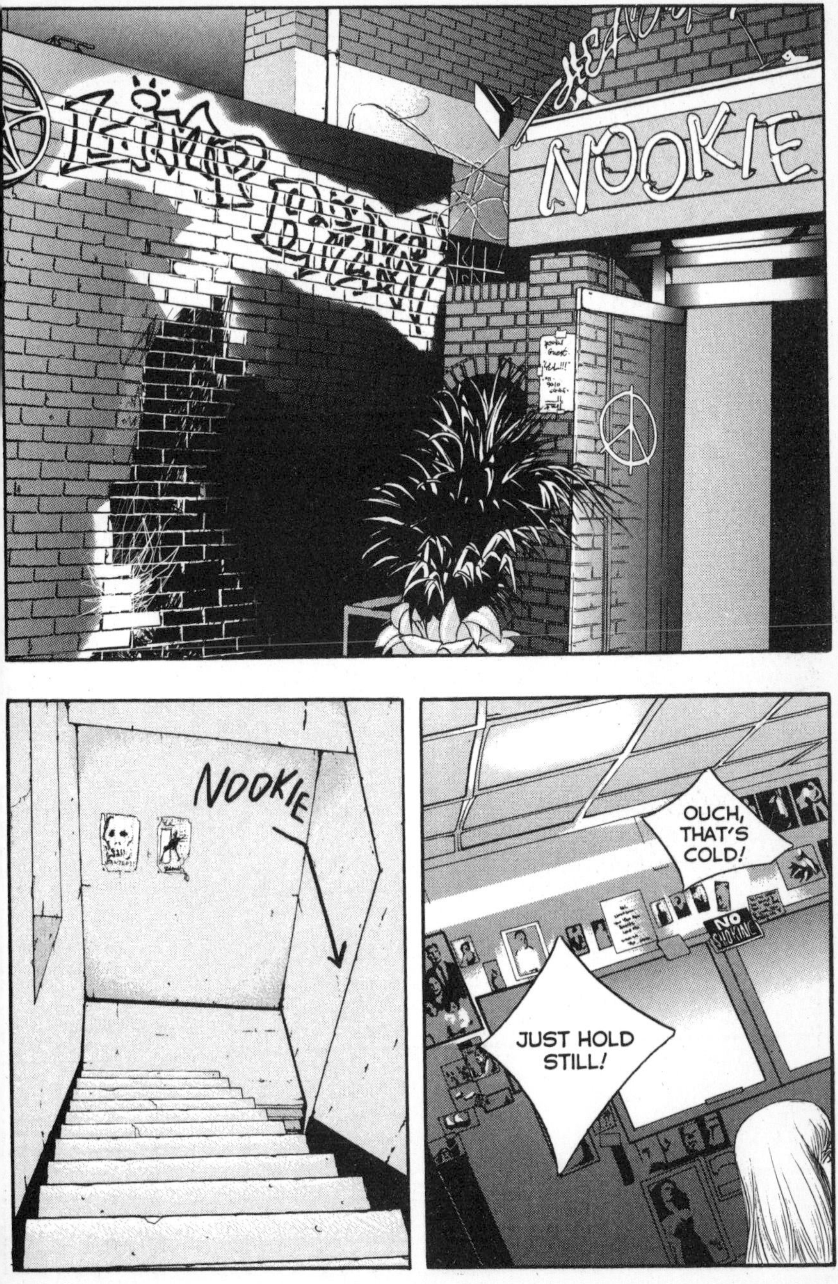
NOOKIE
NOOKIE
OUCH, THAT'S COLD!
NO SMOKING
JUST HOLD STILL!

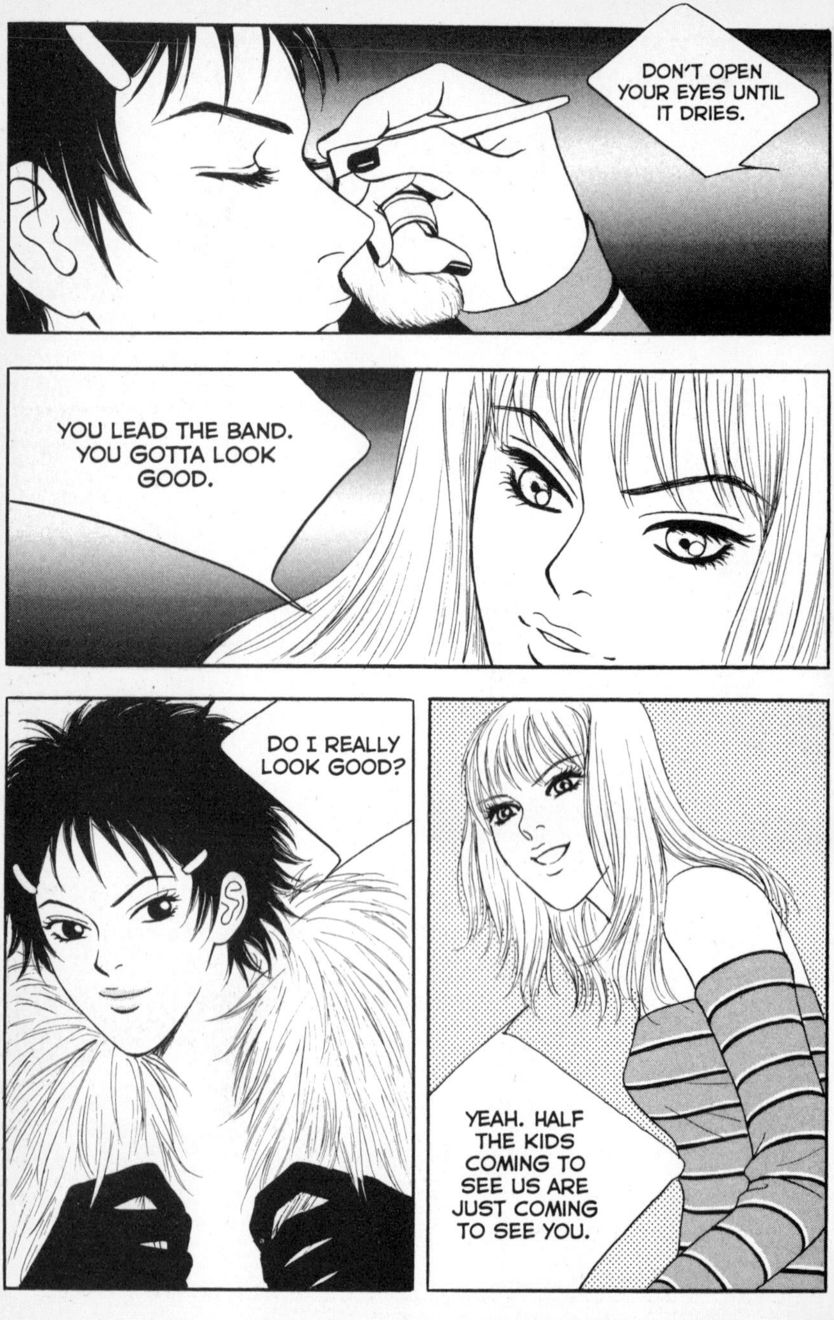
DON'T OPEN YOUR EYES UNTIL IT DRIES.
YOU LEAD THE BAND. YOU GOTTA LOOK GOOD.
DO I REALLY LOOK GOOD?
YEAH. HALF THE KIDS COMING TO SEE US ARE JUST COMING TO SEE YOU.

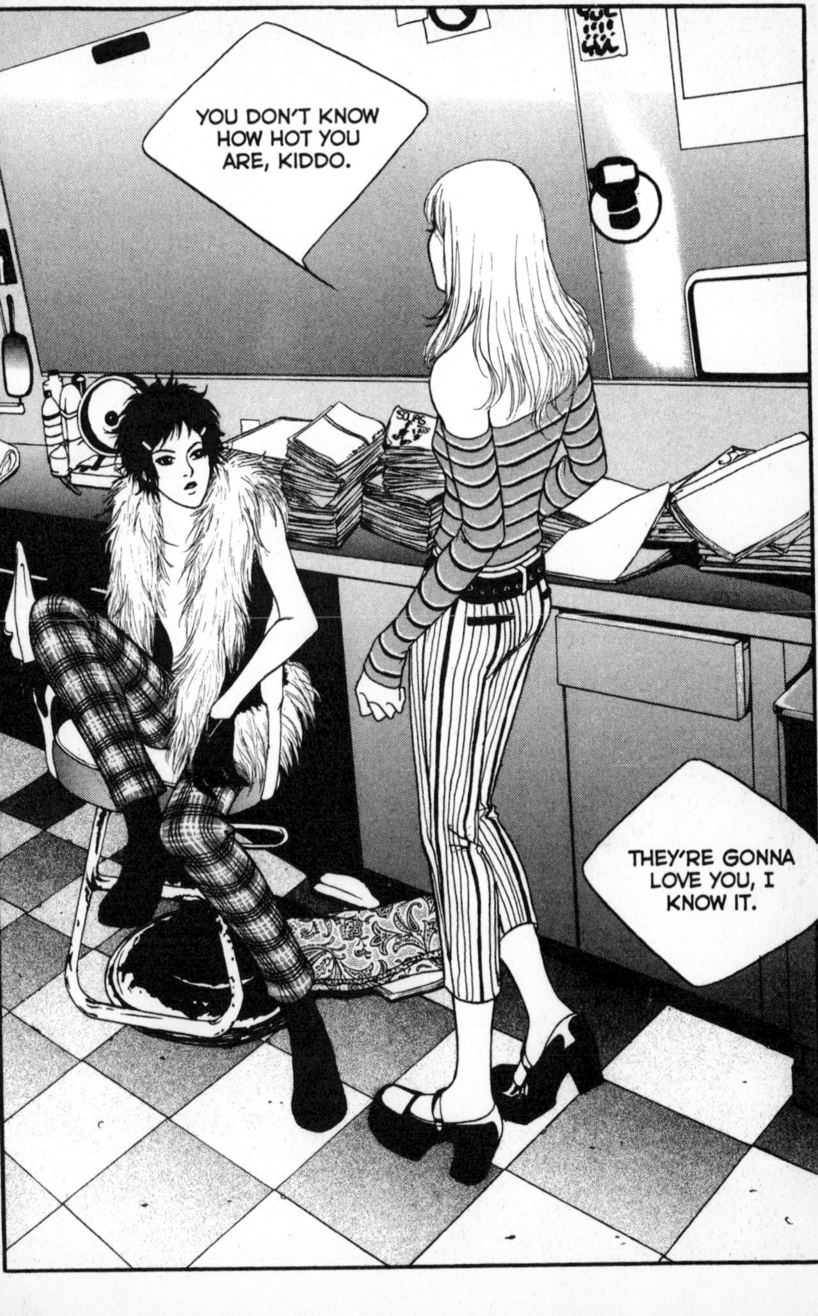
YOU DON'T KNOW HOW HOT YOU ARE, KIDDO.
THEY'RE GONNA LOVE YOU, I KNOW IT.

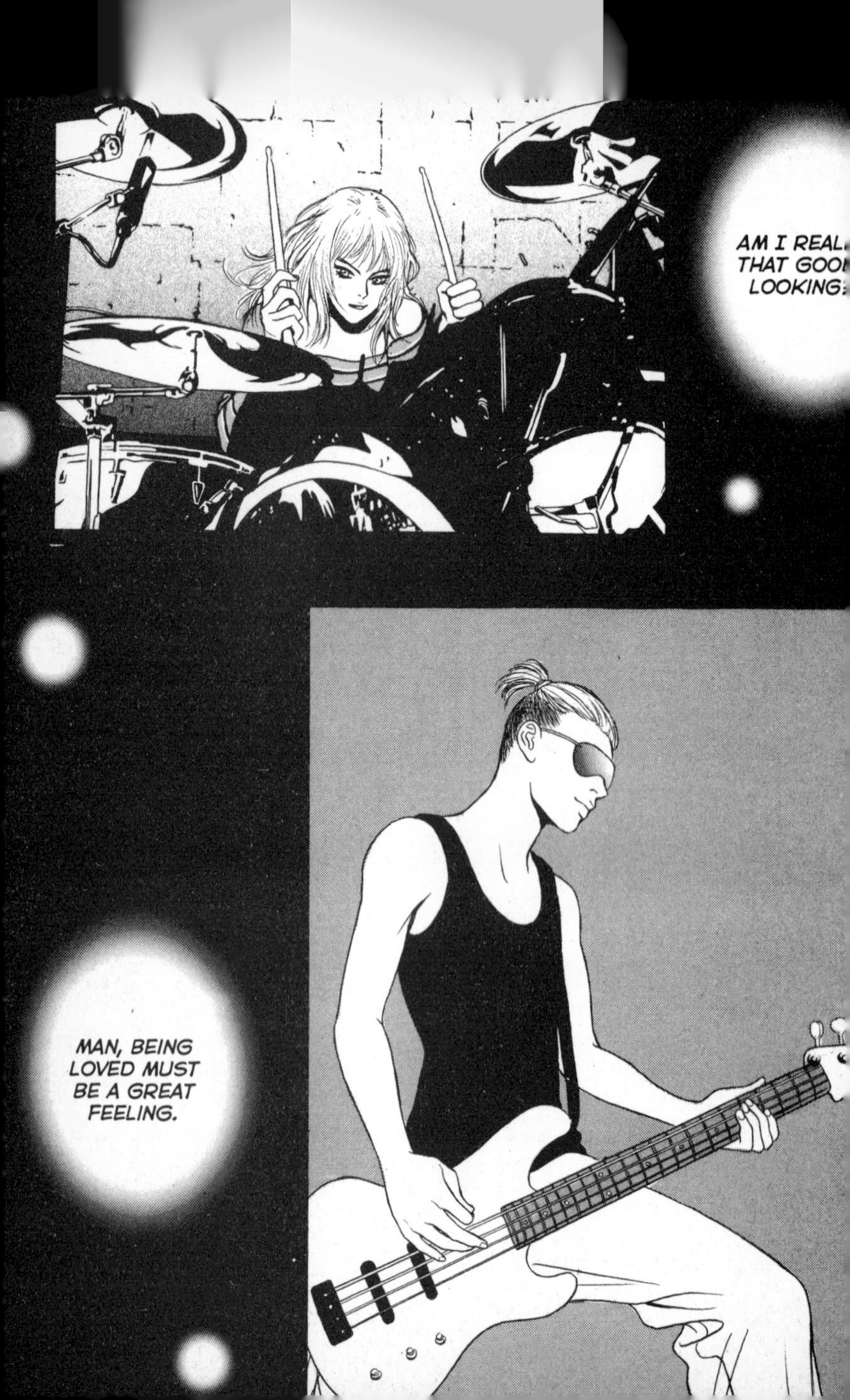
AM I REAL
THAT GOO
LOOKING?
MAN, BEING LOVED MUST BE A GREAT FEELING.

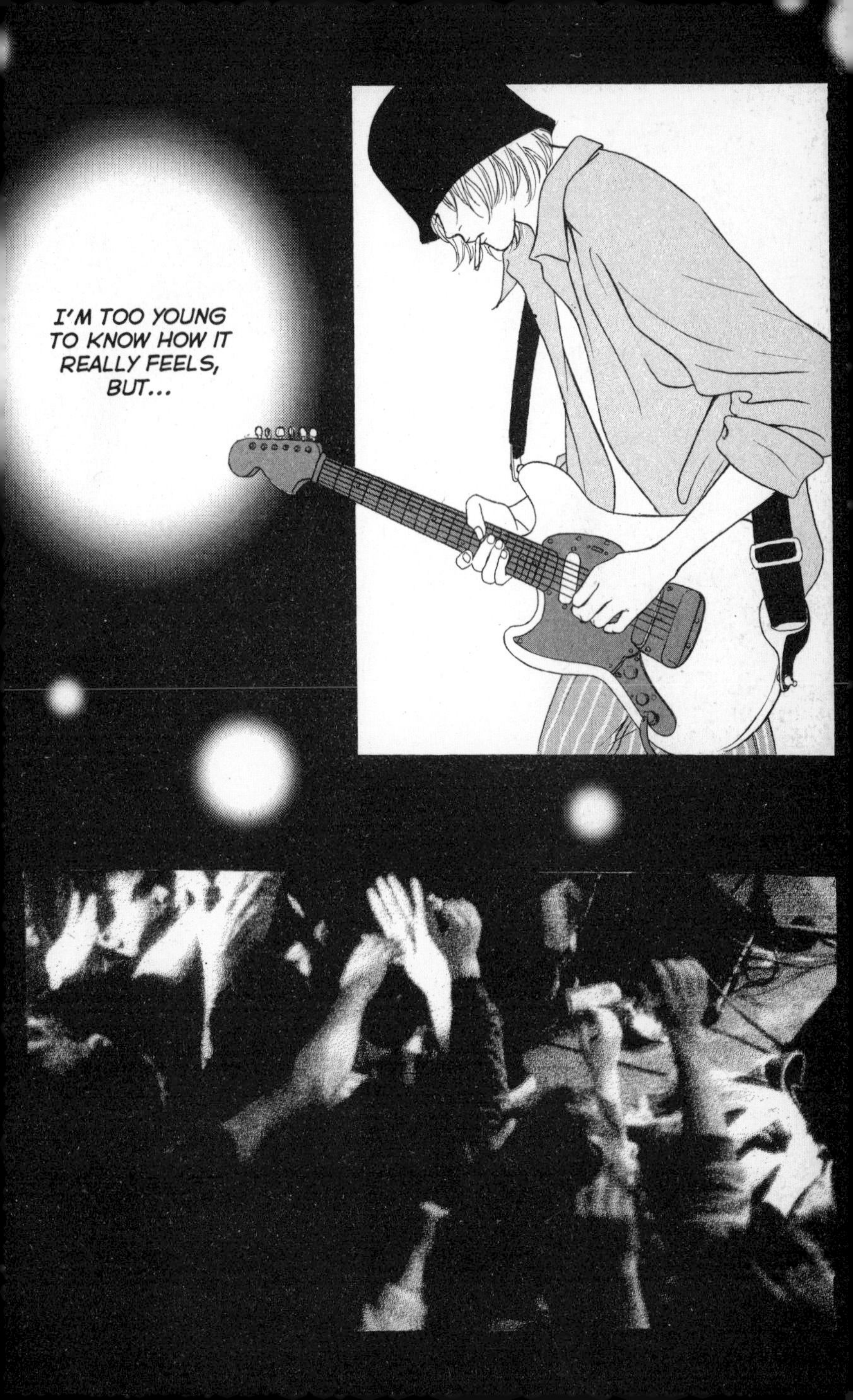
I'M TOO YOUNG TO KNOW HOW IT REALLY FEELS, BUT...

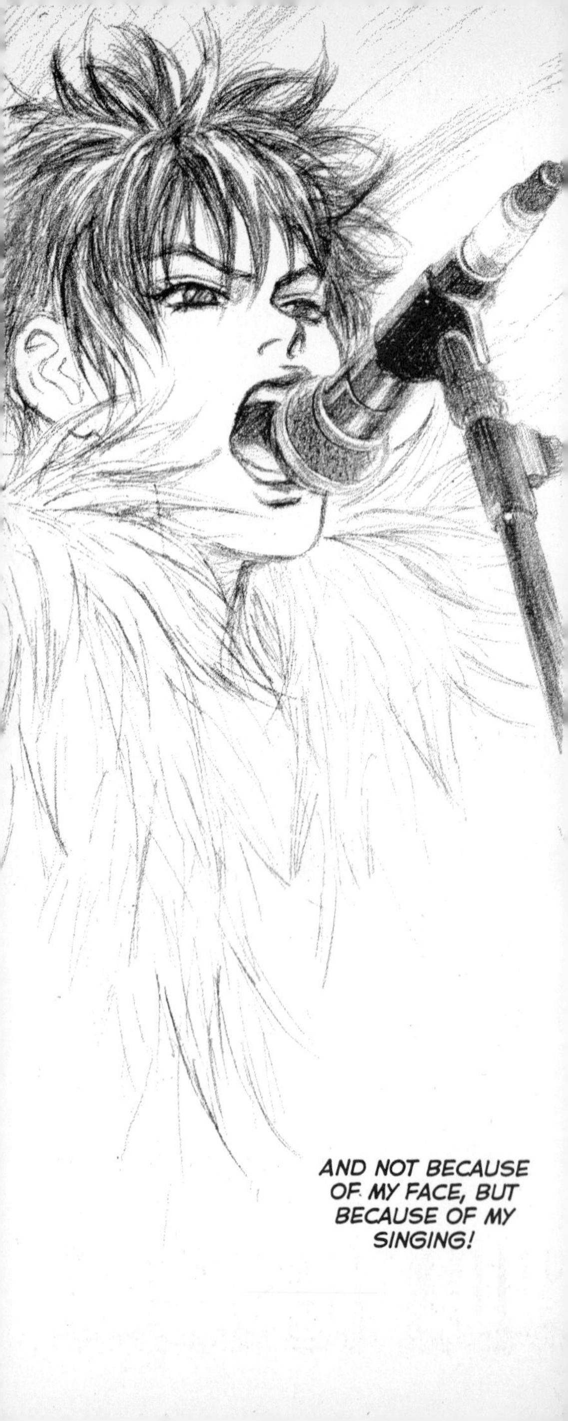
AND NOT BECAUSE OF MY FACE, BUT BECAUSE OF MY SINGING!

SOUL TO SEOUL™

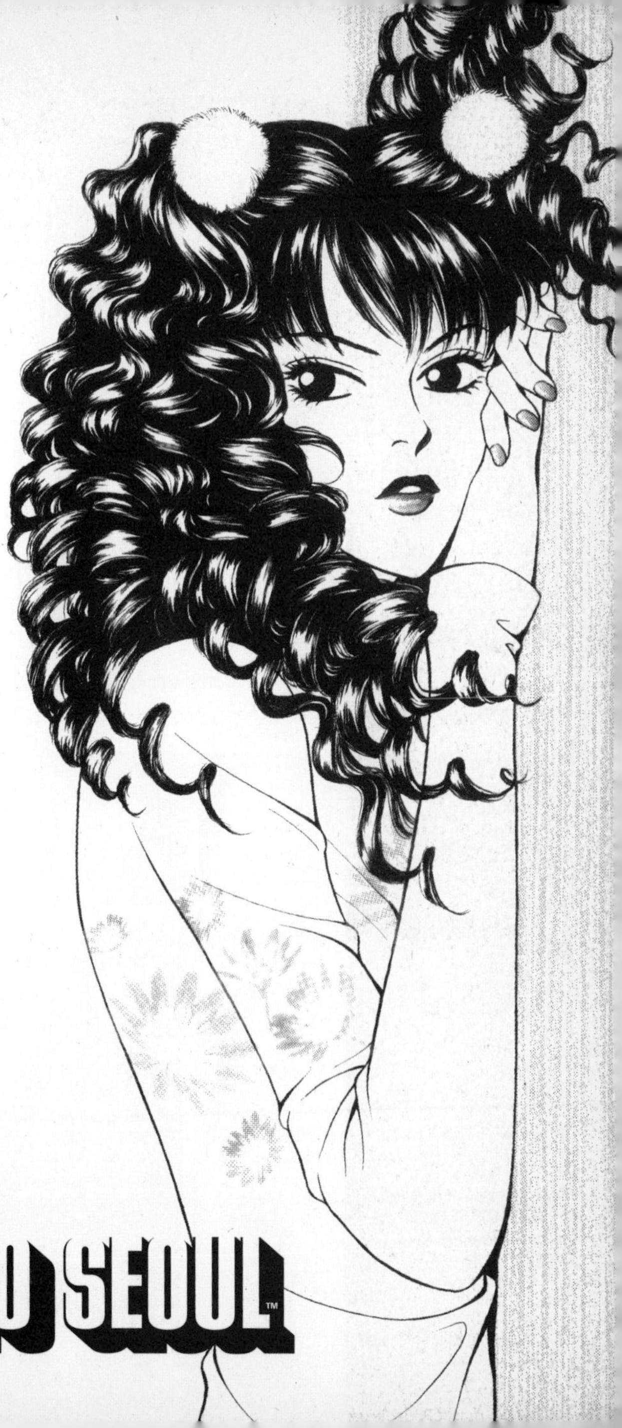

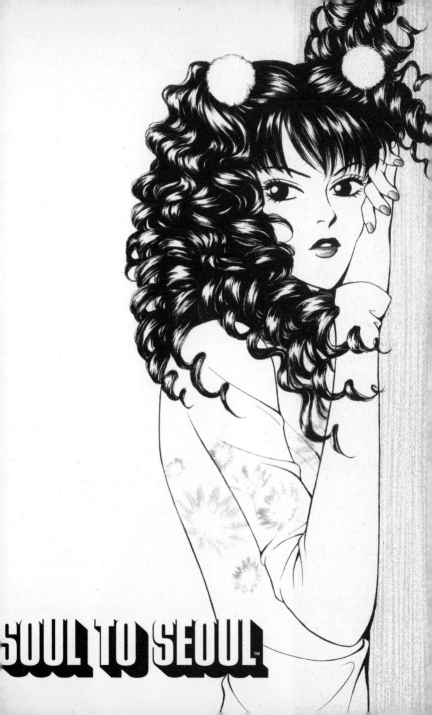

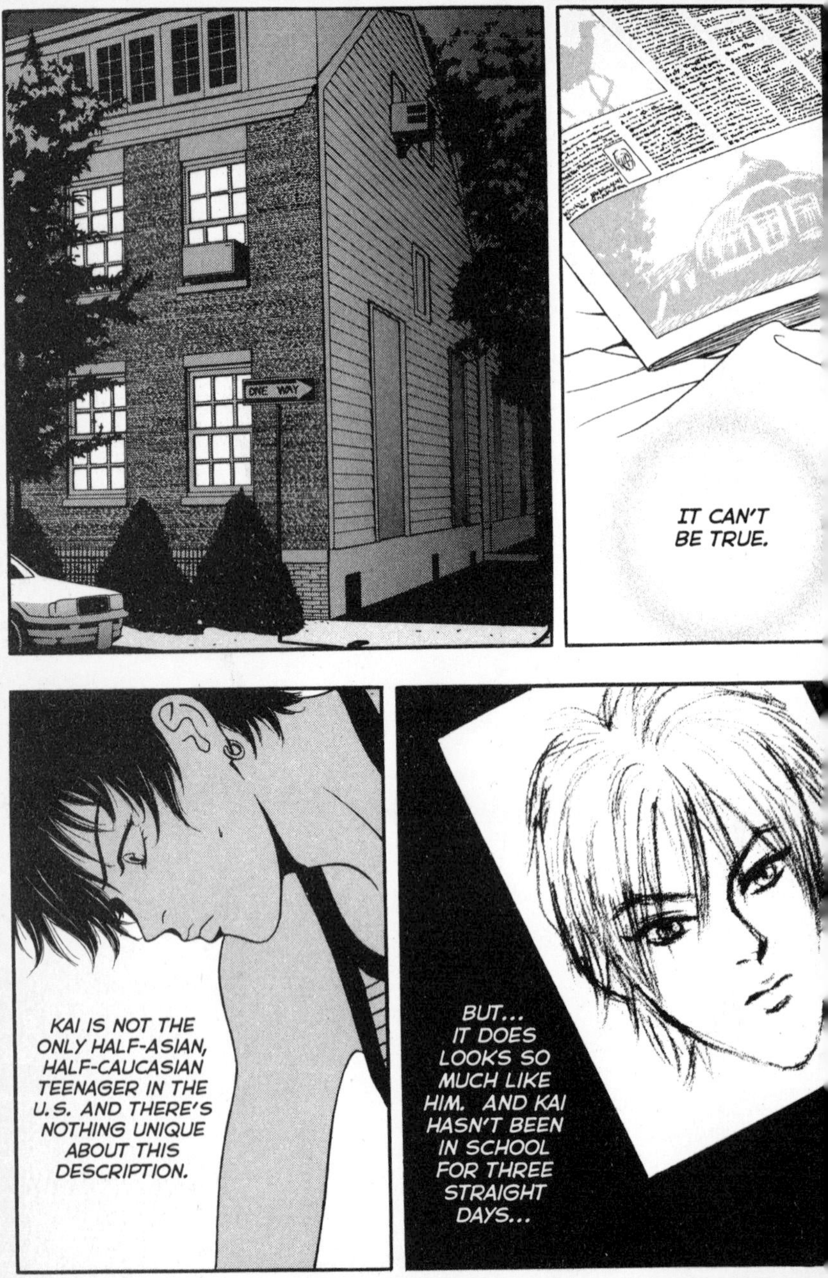
ONE WAY
IT CAN'T BE TRUE.
KAI IS NOT THE ONLY HALF-ASIAN, HALF-CAUCASIAN TEENAGER IN THE U.S. AND THERE'S NOTHING UNIQUE ABOUT THIS DESCRIPTION.
BUT... IT DOES LOOKS SO MUCH LIKE HIM. AND KAI HASN'T BEEN IN SCHOOL FOR THREE STRAIGHT DAYS...

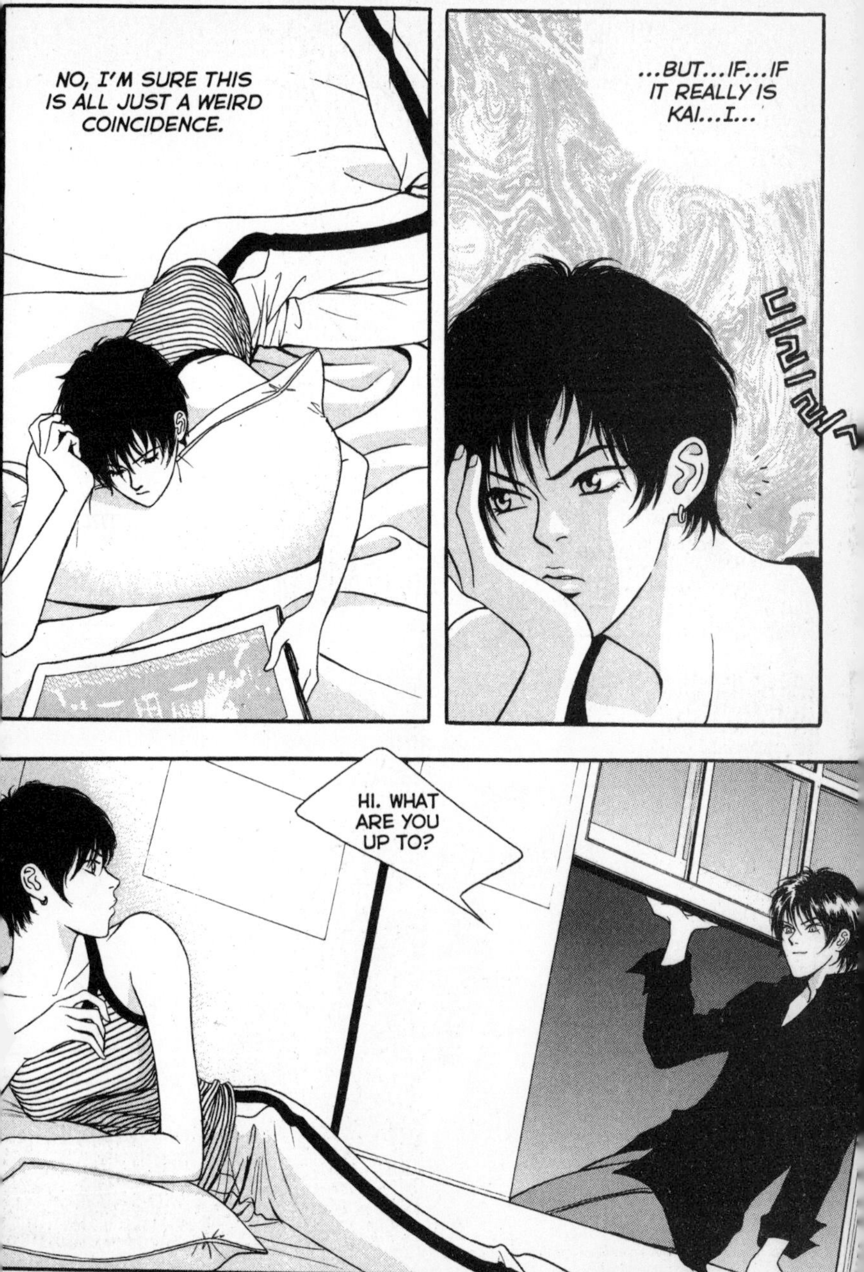
NO, I'M SURE THIS IS ALL JUST A WEIRD COINCIDENCE.
...BUT...IF...IF IT REALLY IS KAI...I...
HI. WHAT ARE YOU UP TO?

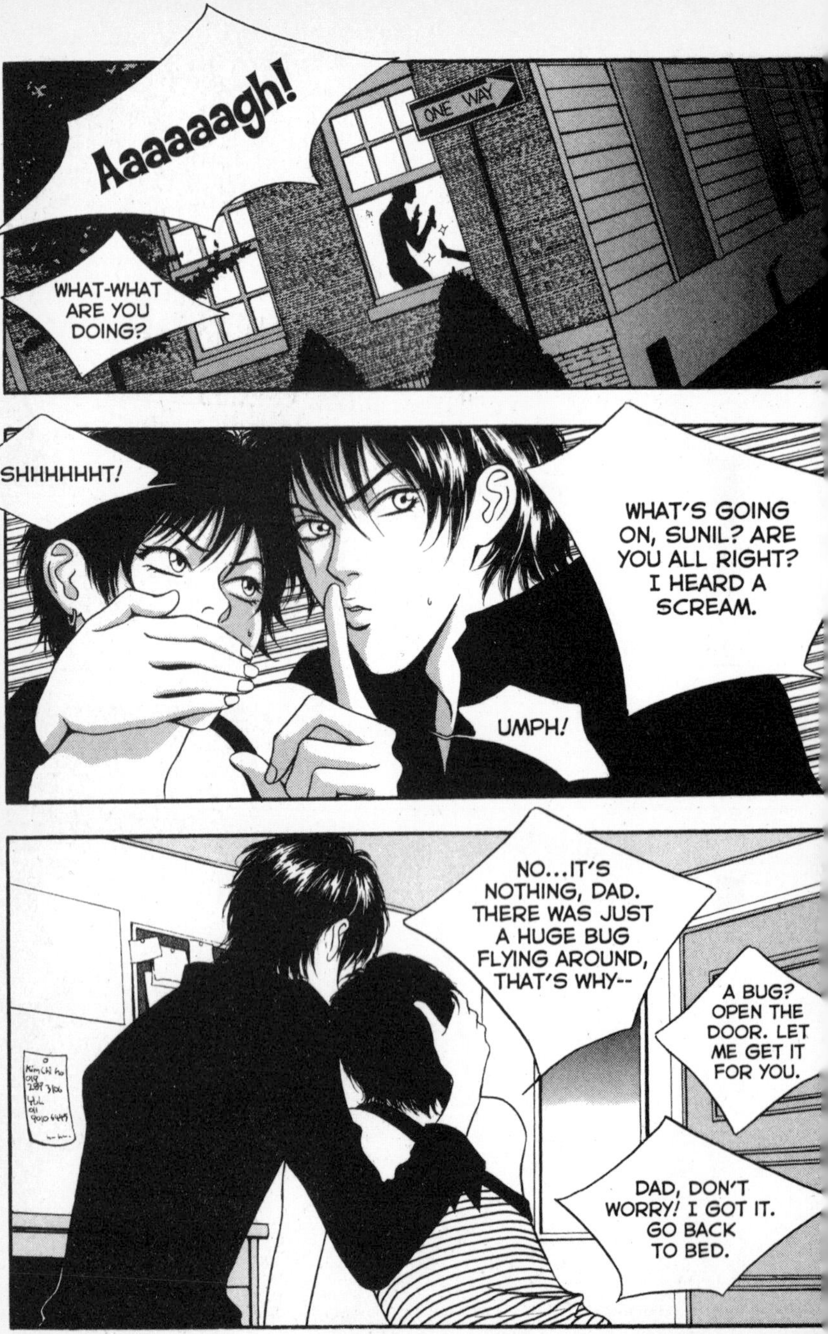
Aaaaaagh!
ONE WAY
WHAT-WHAT ARE YOU DOING?
SHHHHHHT!
WHAT'S GOING ON, SUNIL? ARE YOU ALL RIGHT? I HEARD A SCREAM.
UMPH!
NO...IT'S NOTHING, DAD. THERE WAS JUST A HUGE BUG FLYING AROUND, THAT'S WHY--
A BUG? OPEN THE DOOR. LET ME GET IT FOR YOU.
DAD, DON'T WORRY! I GOT IT. GO BACK TO BED.

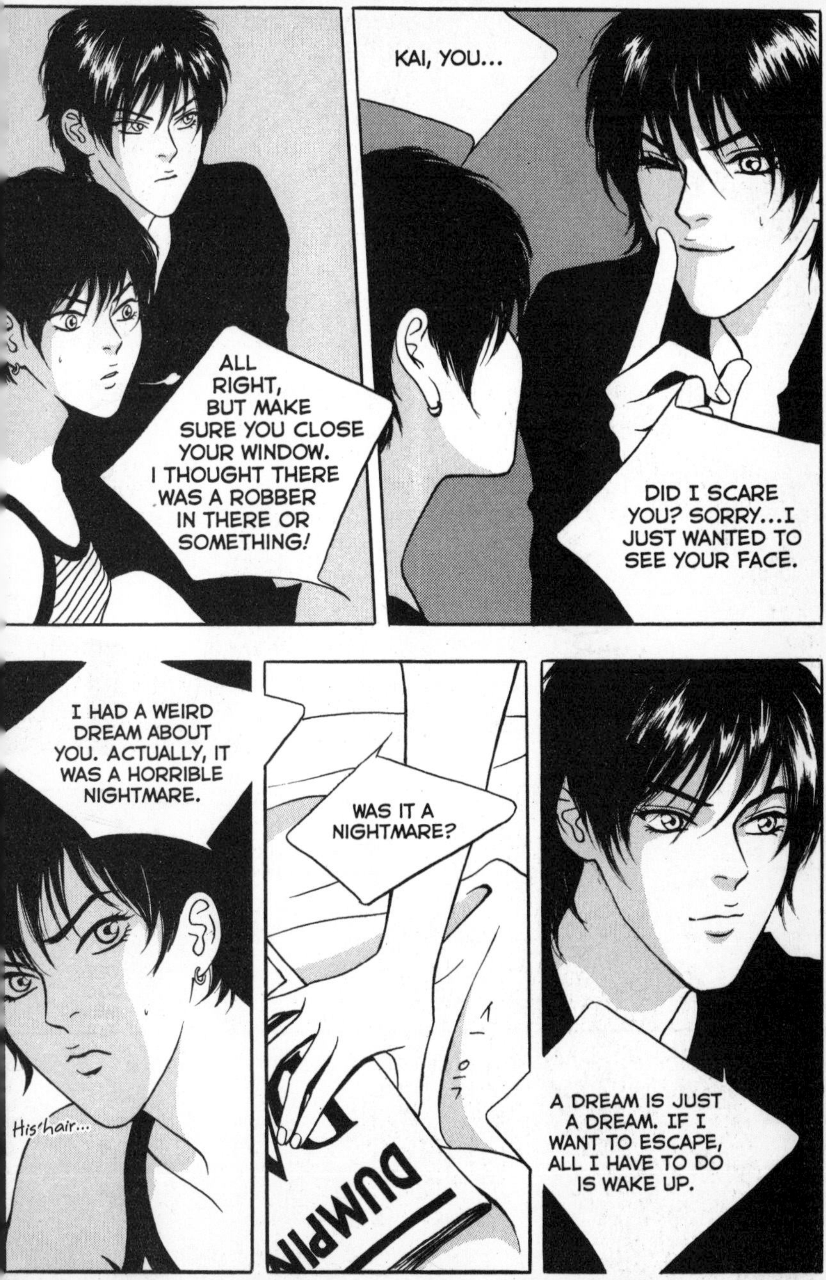
ALL RIGHT, BUT MAKE SURE YOU CLOSE YOUR WINDOW. I THOUGHT THERE WAS A ROBBER IN THERE OR SOMETHING!
KAI, YOU...
DID I SCARE YOU? SORRY...I JUST WANTED TO SEE YOUR FACE.
I HAD A WEIRD DREAM ABOUT YOU. ACTUALLY, IT WAS A HORRIBLE NIGHTMARE.
His hair...
WAS IT A NIGHTMARE?
A DREAM IS JUST A DREAM. IF I WANT TO ESCAPE, ALL I HAVE TO DO IS WAKE UP.

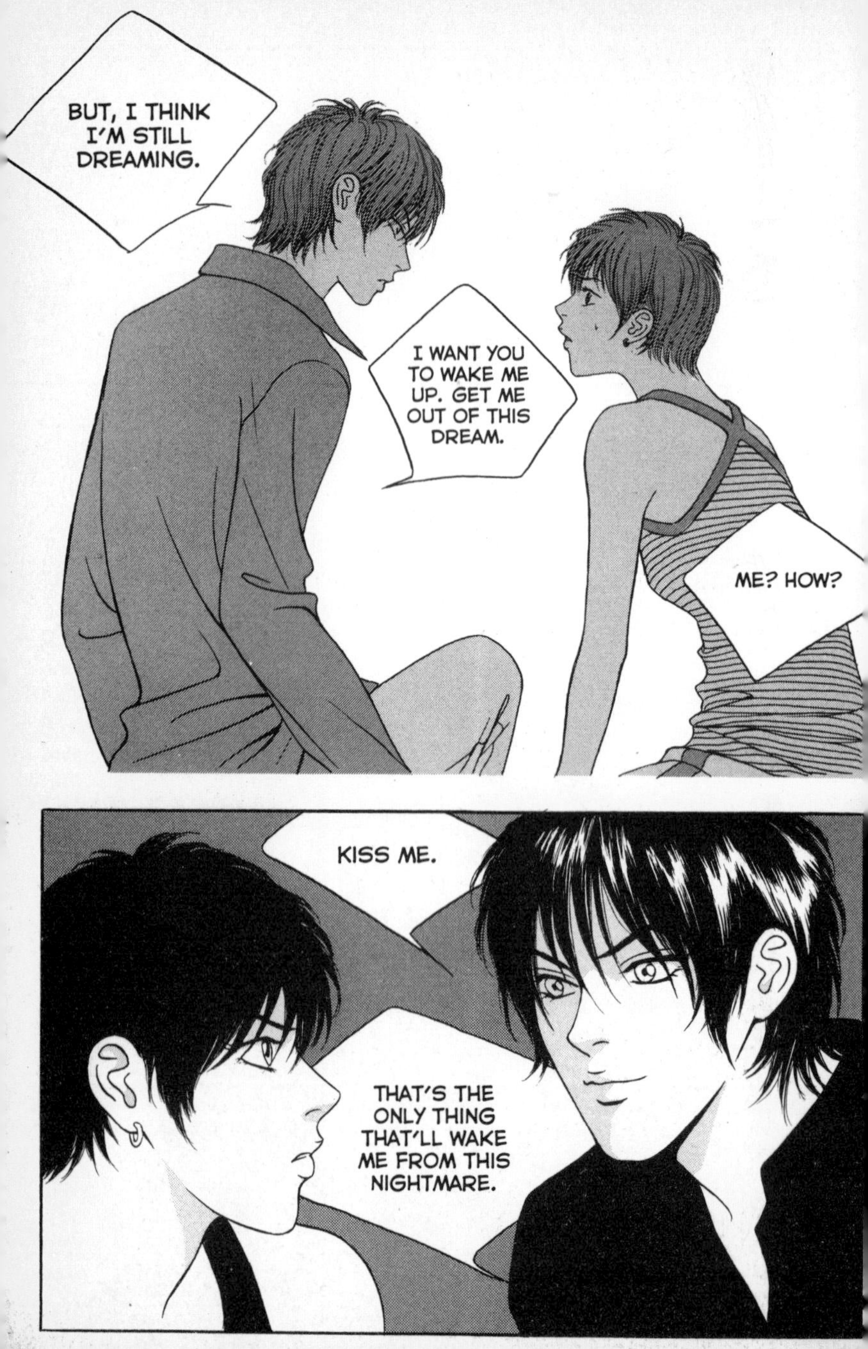
BUT, I THINK I'M STILL DREAMING.
I WANT YOU TO WAKE ME UP. GET ME OUT OF THIS DREAM.
ME? HOW?
KISS ME.
THAT'S THE ONLY THING THAT'LL WAKE ME FROM THIS NIGHTMARE.

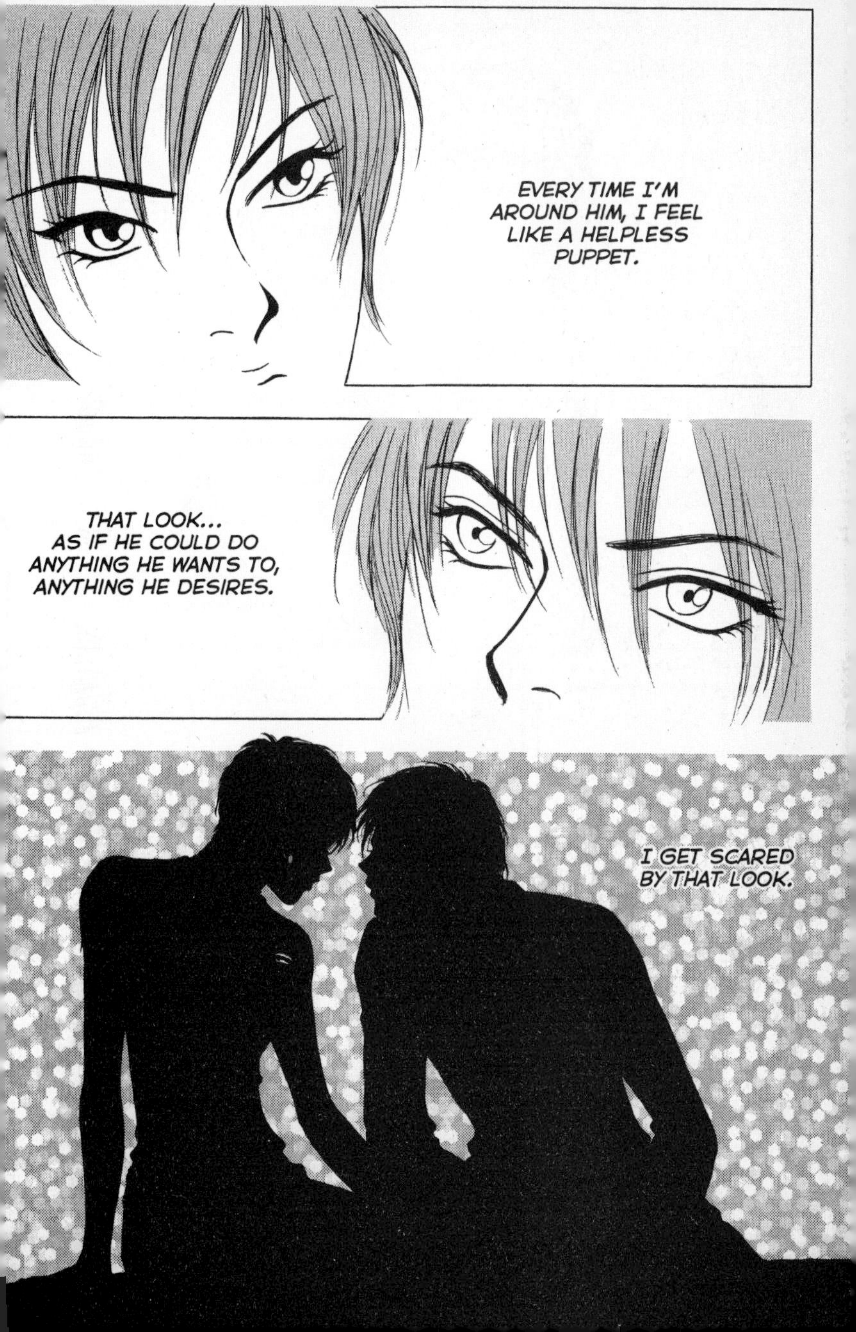
EVERY TIME I'M AROUND HIM, I FEEL LIKE A HELPLESS PUPPET.
THAT LOOK... AS IF HE COULD DO ANYTHING HE WANTS TO, ANYTHING HE DESIRES.
I GET SCARED BY THAT LOOK.

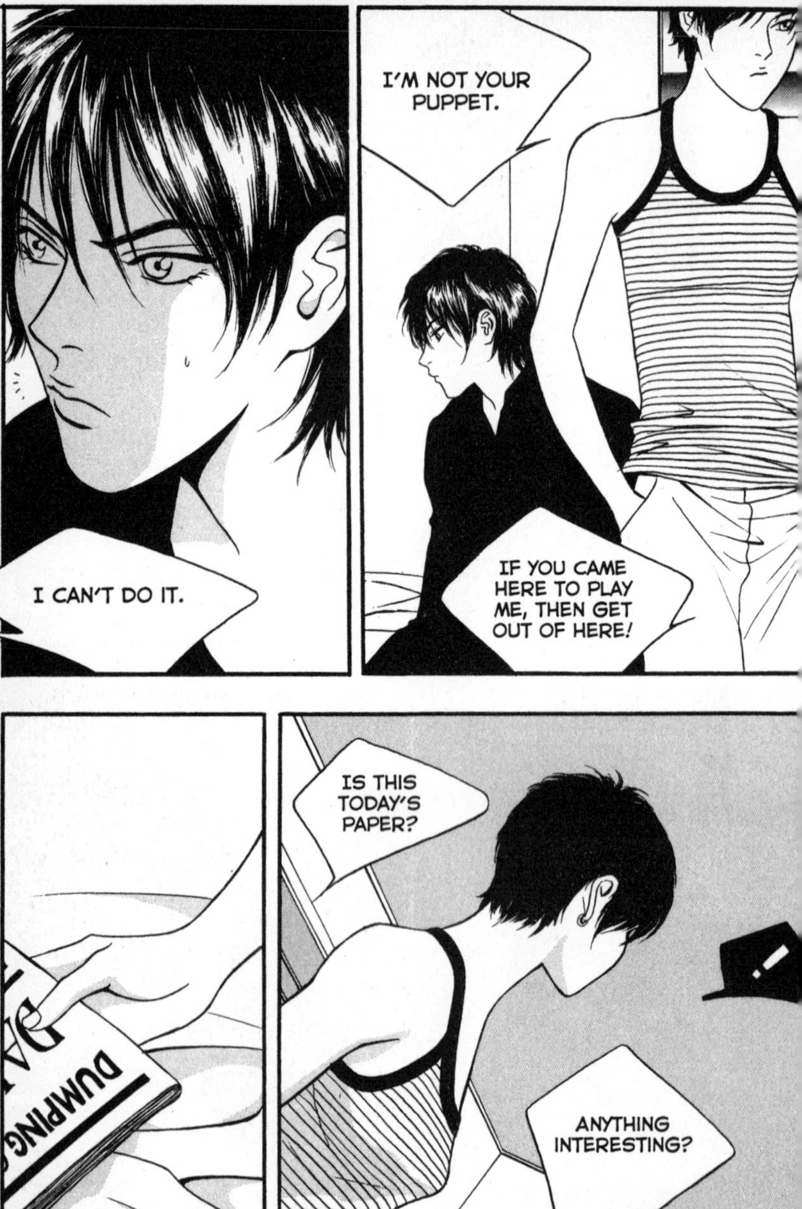
I CAN'T DO IT.
I'M NOT YOUR PUPPET.
IF YOU CAME HERE TO PLAY ME, THEN GET OUT OF HERE!
DUMPING
IS THIS TODAY'S PAPER?
ANYTHING INTERESTING?

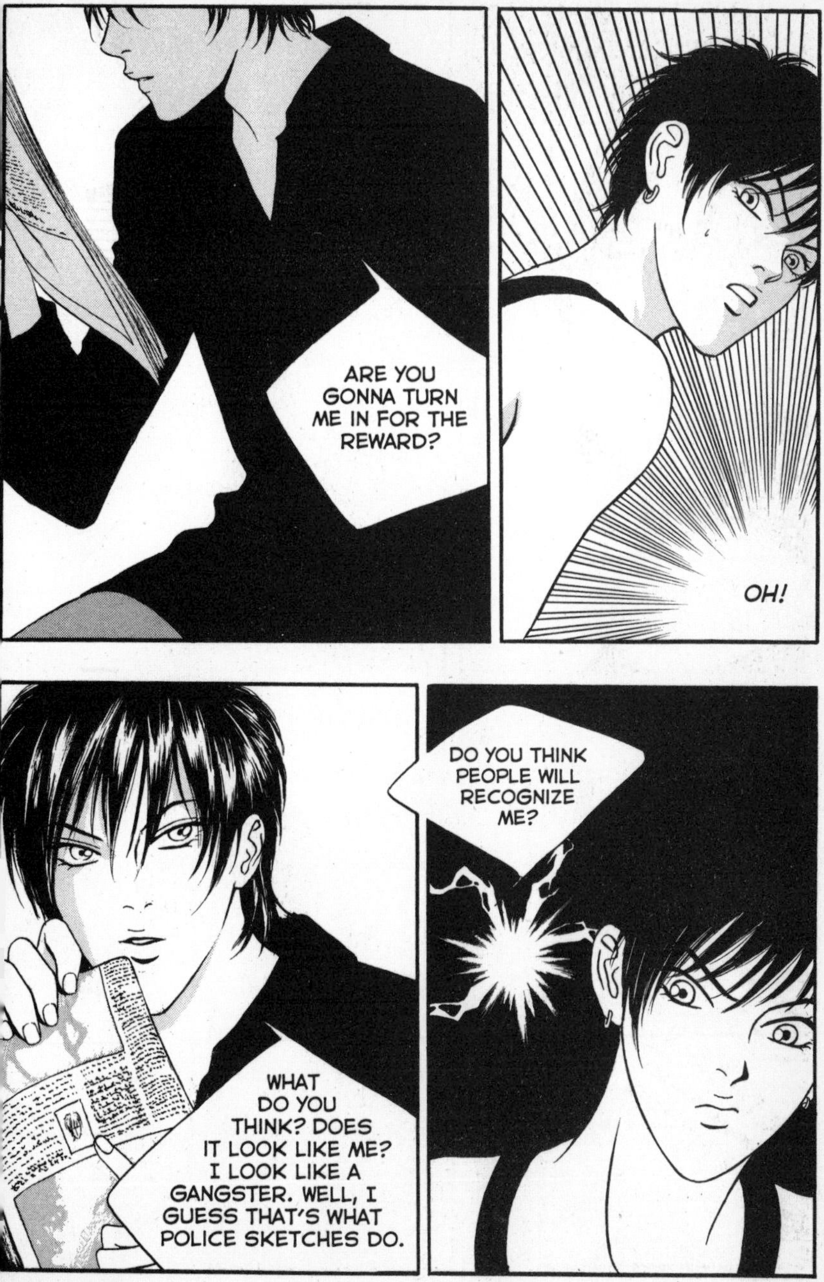
ARE YOU GONNA TURN ME IN FOR THE REWARD?
OH!
WHAT DO YOU THINK? DOES IT LOOK LIKE ME? I LOOK LIKE A GANGSTER. WELL, I GUESS THAT'S WHAT POLICE SKETCHES DO.
DO YOU THINK PEOPLE WILL RECOGNIZE ME?

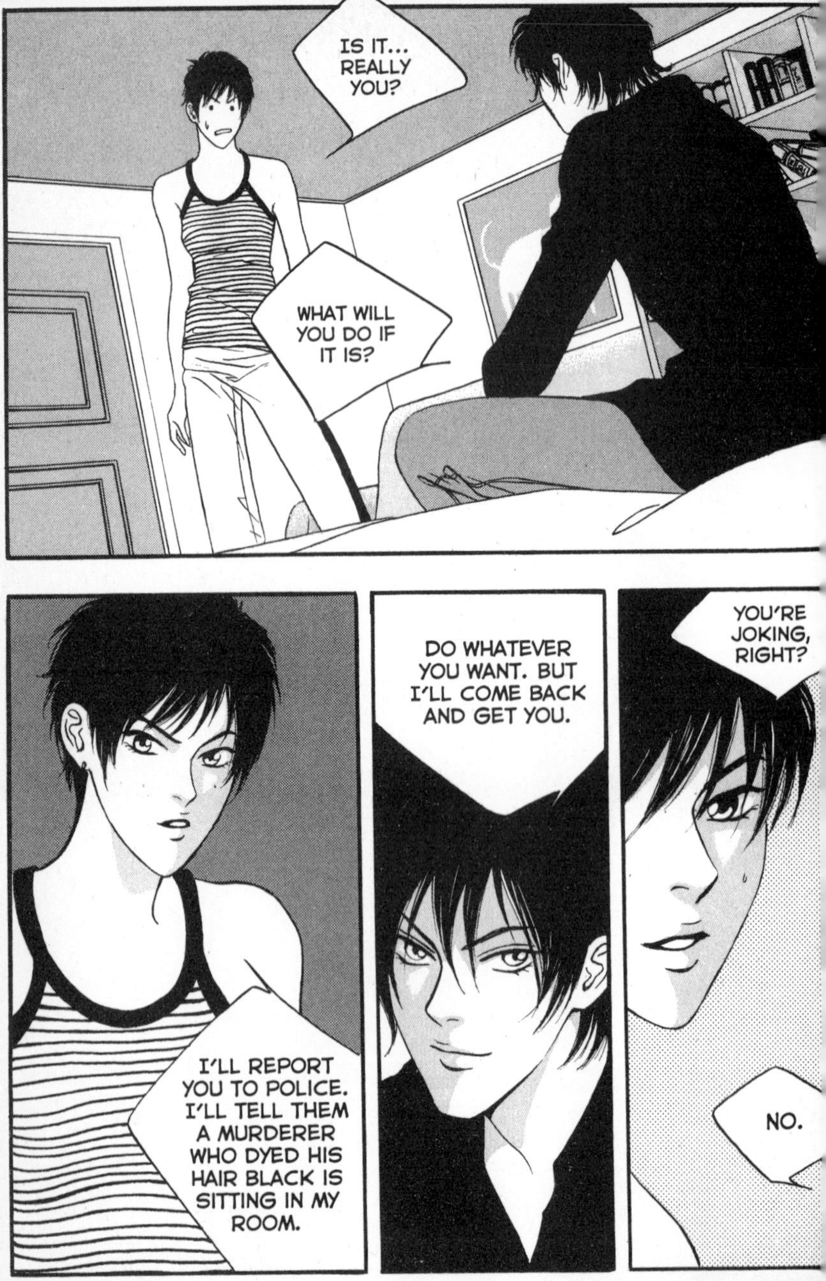
IS IT... REALLY YOU?
WHAT WILL YOU DO IF IT IS?
I'LL REPORT YOU TO POLICE. I'LL TELL THEM A MURDERER WHO DYED HIS HAIR BLACK IS SITTING IN MY ROOM.
DO WHATEVER YOU WANT. BUT I'LL COME BACK AND GET YOU.
YOU'RE JOKING, RIGHT?
NO.

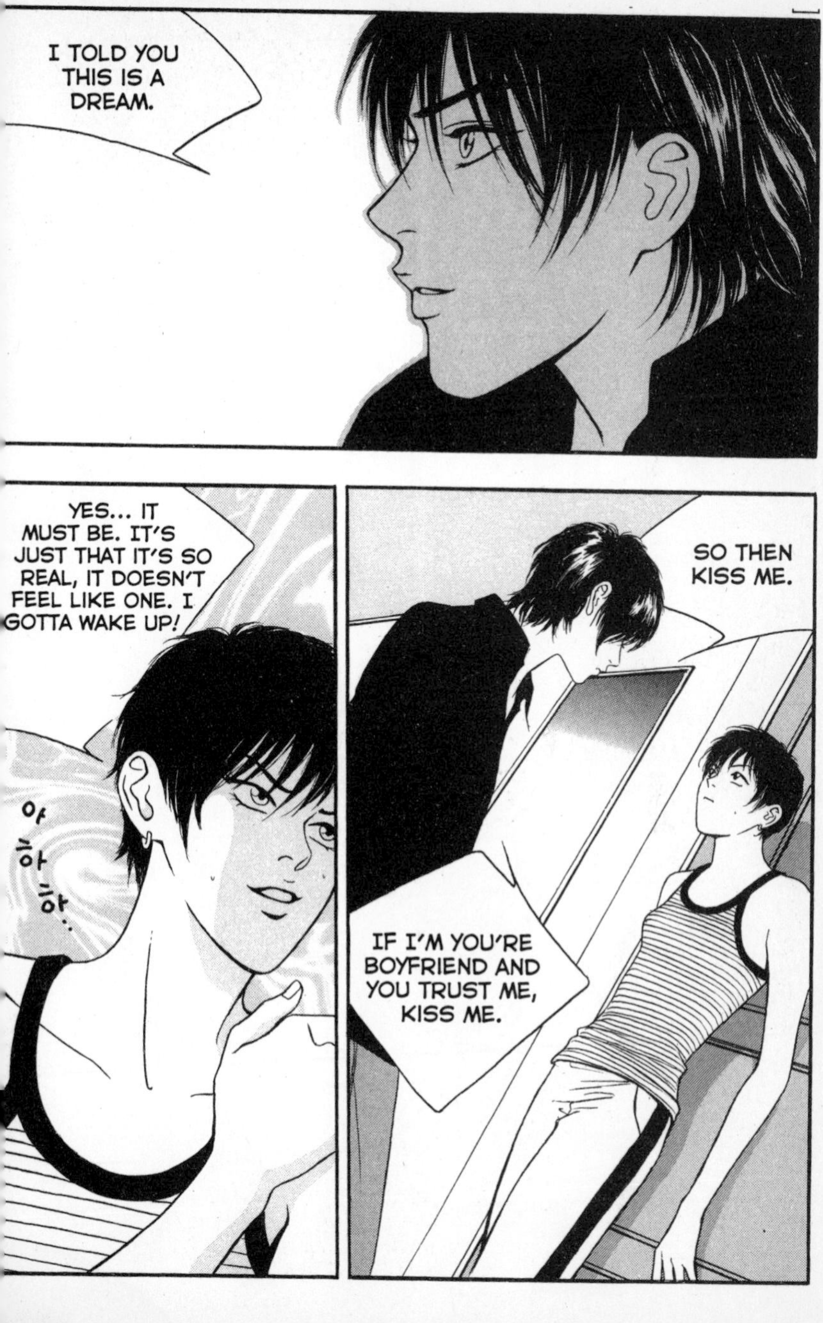
I TOLD YOU THIS IS A DREAM.
YES... IT MUST BE. IT'S JUST THAT IT'S SO REAL, IT DOESN'T FEEL LIKE ONE. I GOTTA WAKE UP!
아하하...
SO THEN KISS ME.
IF I'M YOU'RE BOYFRIEND AND YOU TRUST ME, KISS ME.

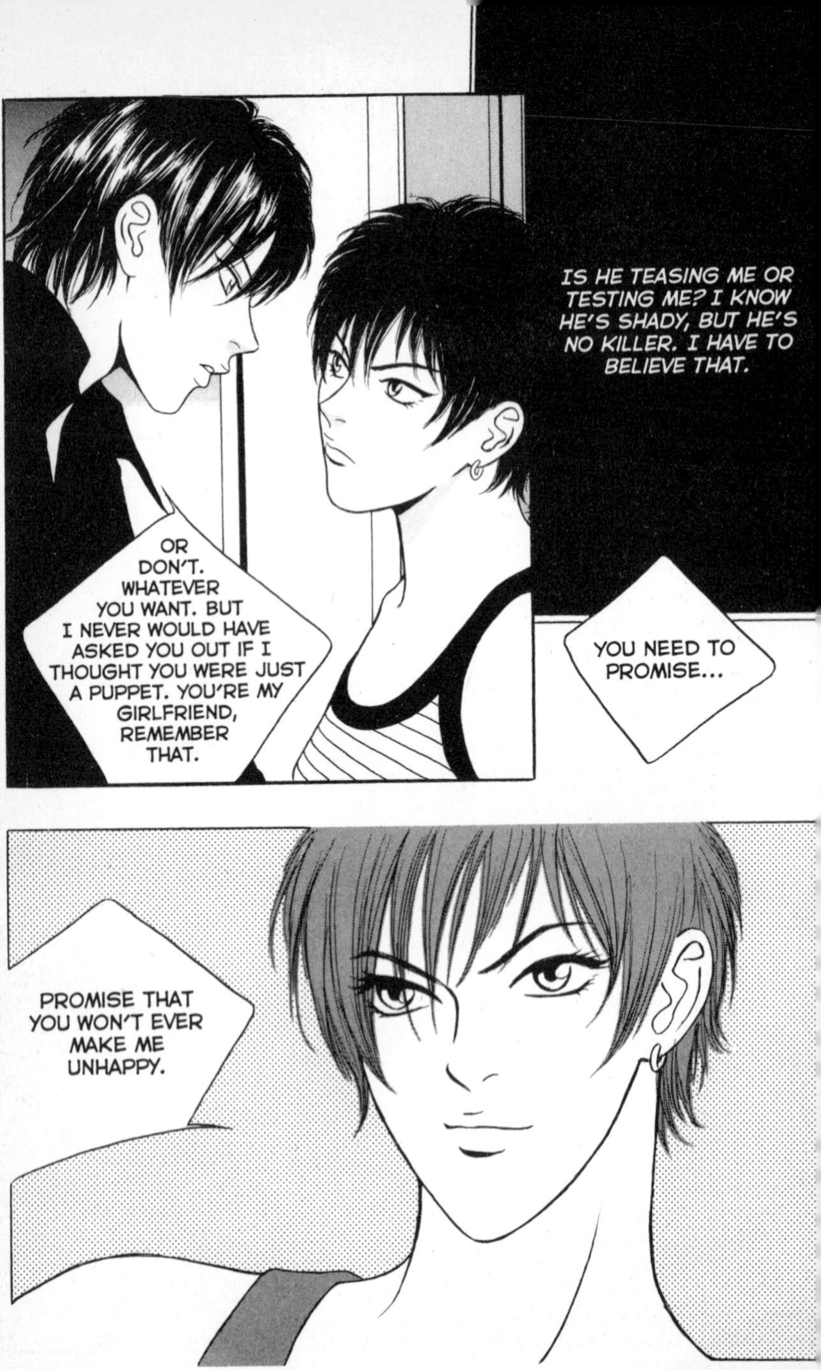
OR DON'T. WHATEVER YOU WANT. BUT I NEVER WOULD HAVE ASKED YOU OUT IF I THOUGHT YOU WERE JUST A PUPPET. YOU'RE MY GIRLFRIEND, REMEMBER THAT.
IS HE TEASING ME OR TESTING ME? I KNOW HE'S SHADY, BUT HE'S NO KILLER. I HAVE TO BELIEVE THAT.
YOU NEED TO PROMISE...
PROMISE THAT YOU WON'T EVER MAKE ME UNHAPPY.

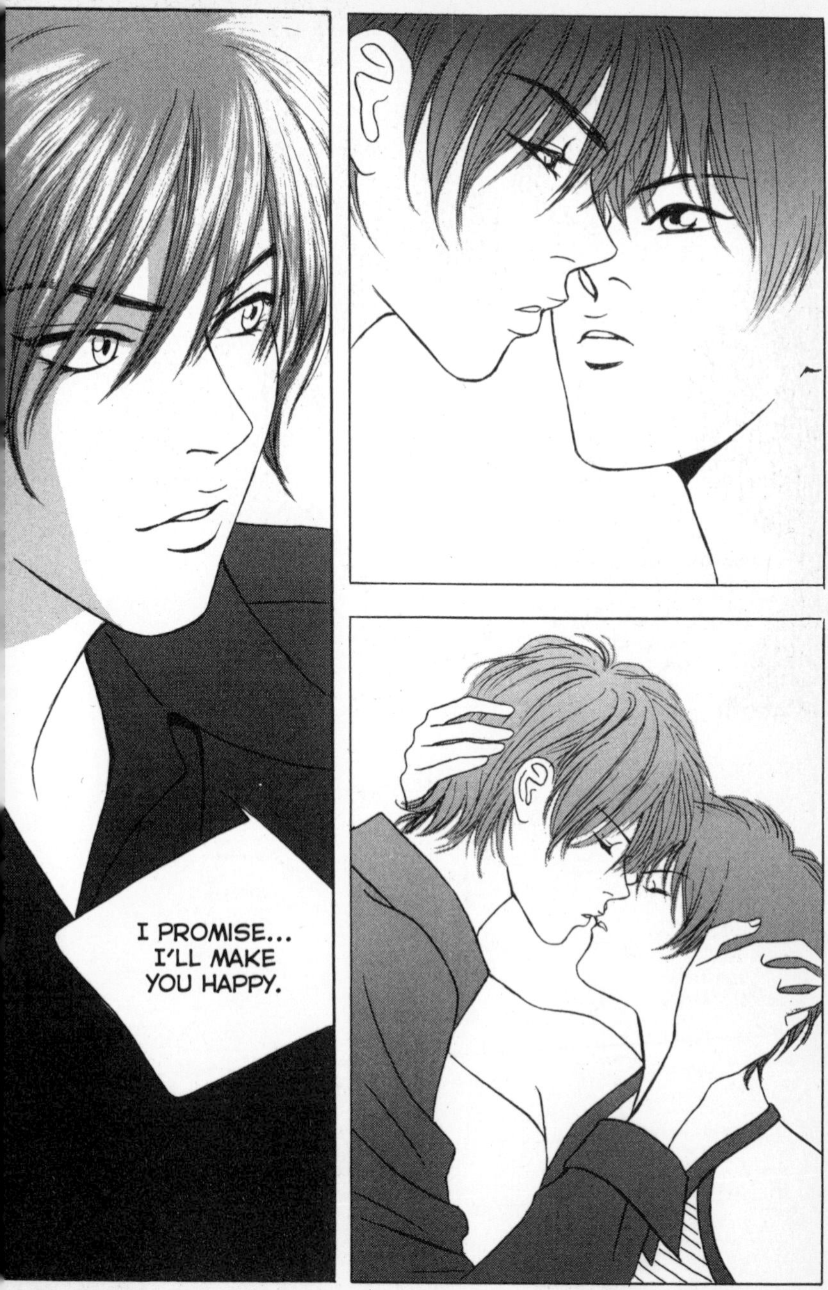
I PROMISE... I'LL MAKE YOU HAPPY.

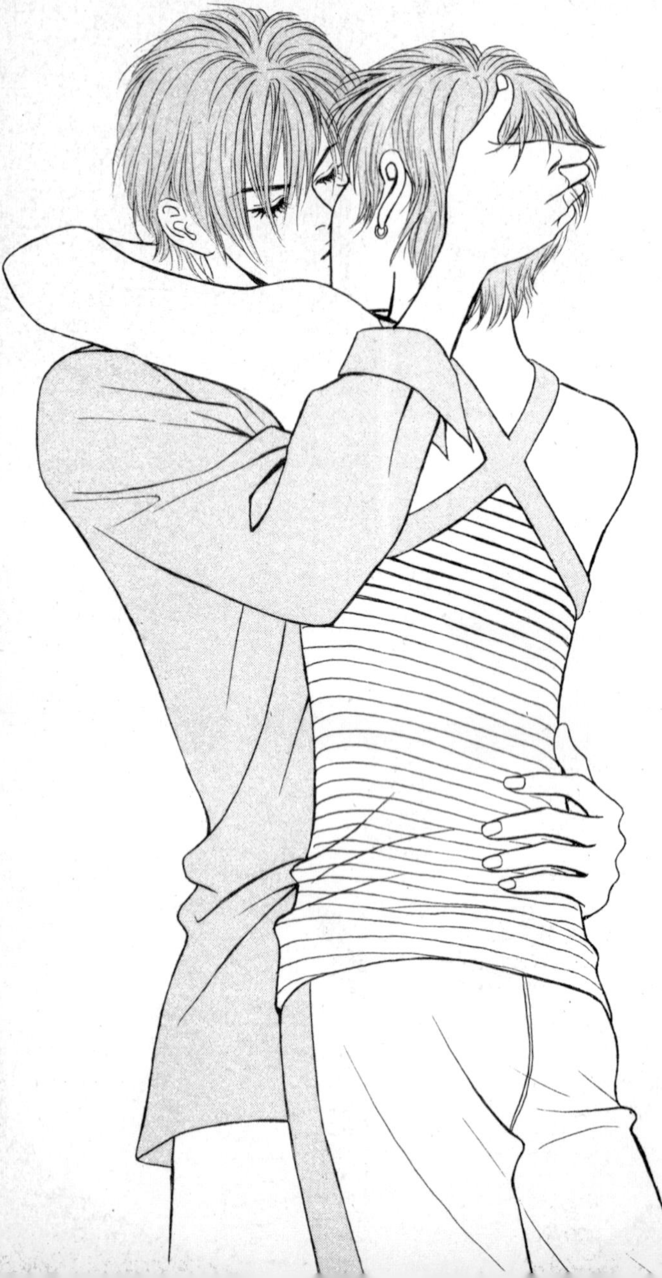

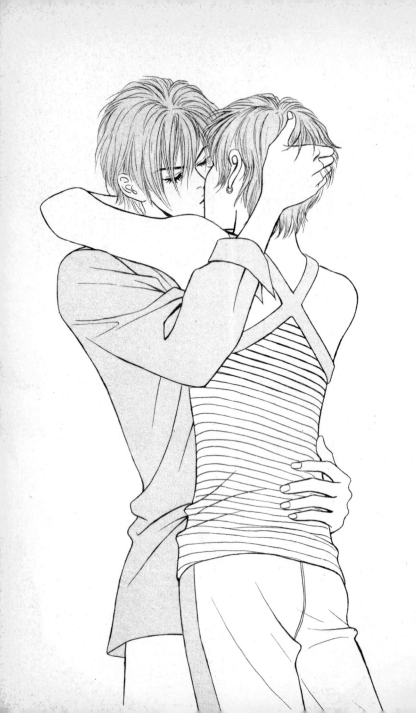

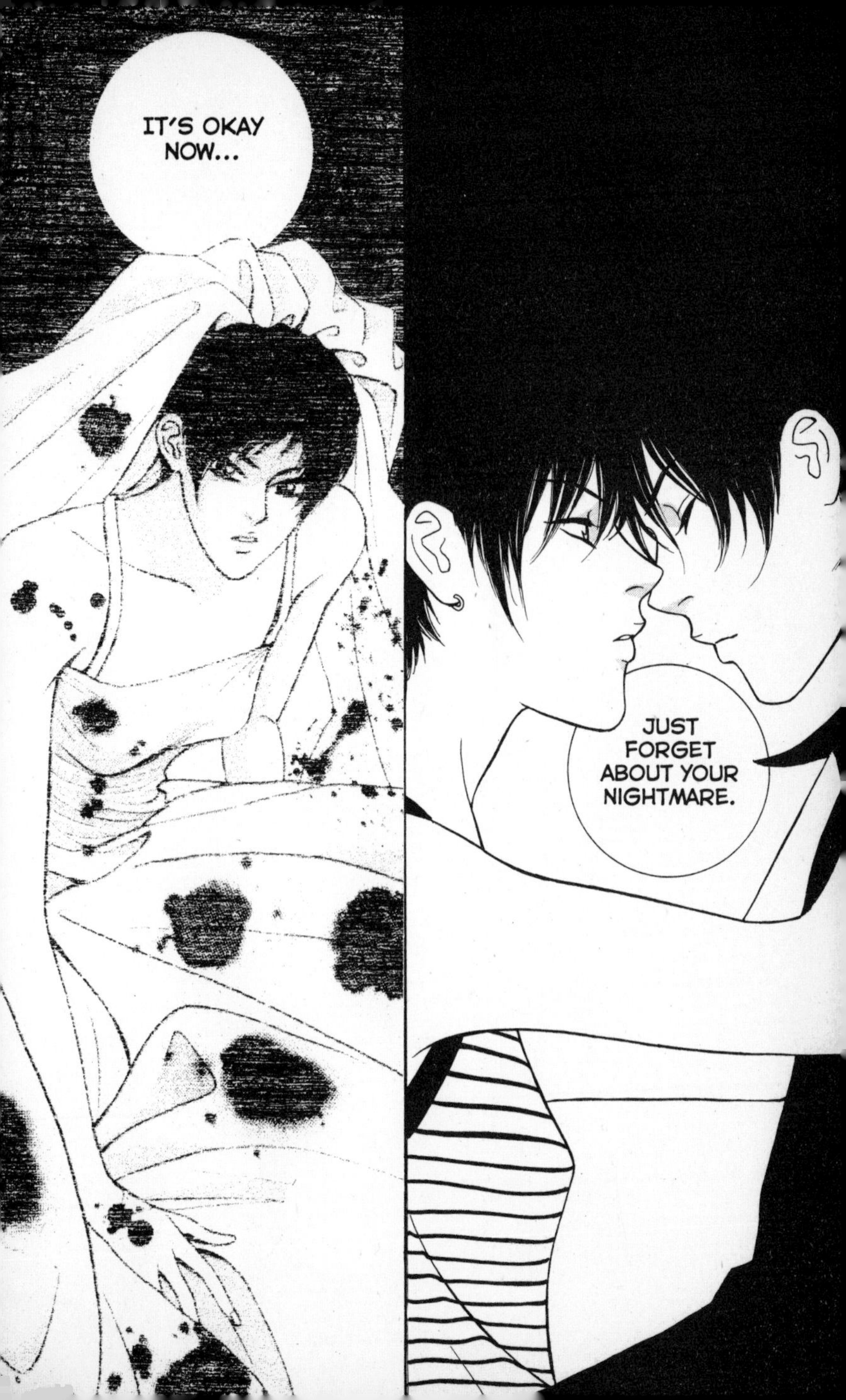
IT'S OKAY NOW...
JUST FORGET ABOUT YOUR NIGHTMARE.

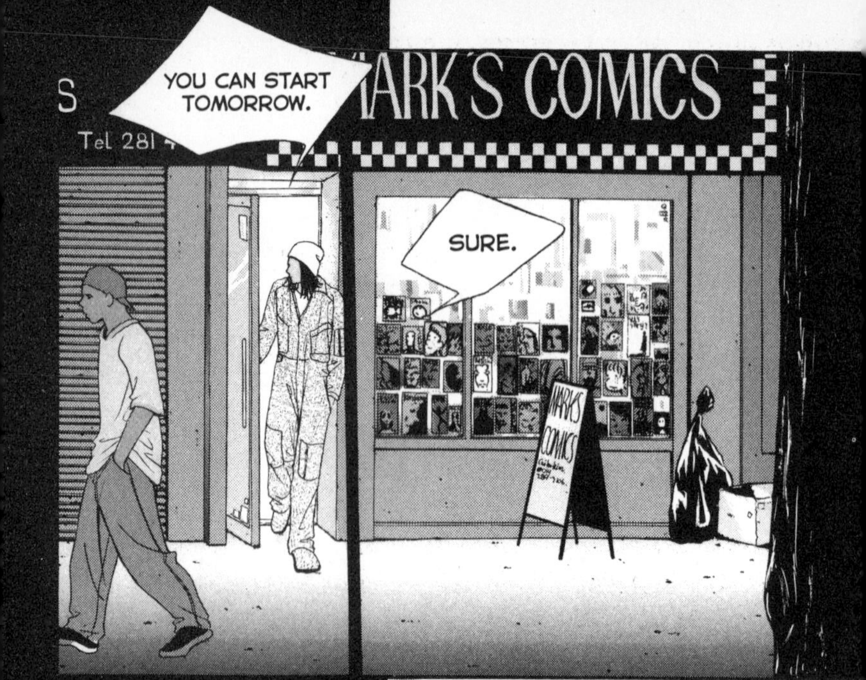
YOU CAN START TOMORROW.
SURE.
MARK'S COMICS

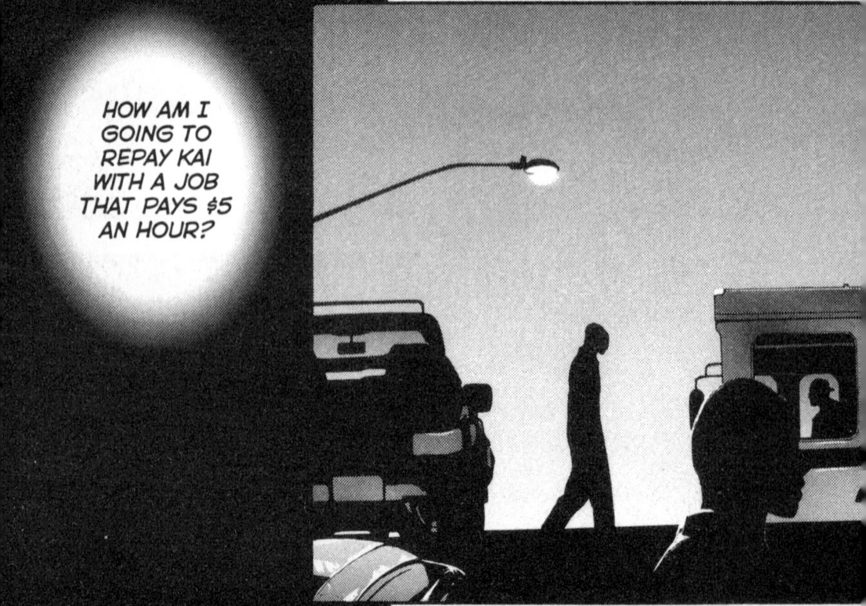
HOW AM I GOING TO REPAY KAI WITH A JOB THAT PAYS $5 AN HOUR?

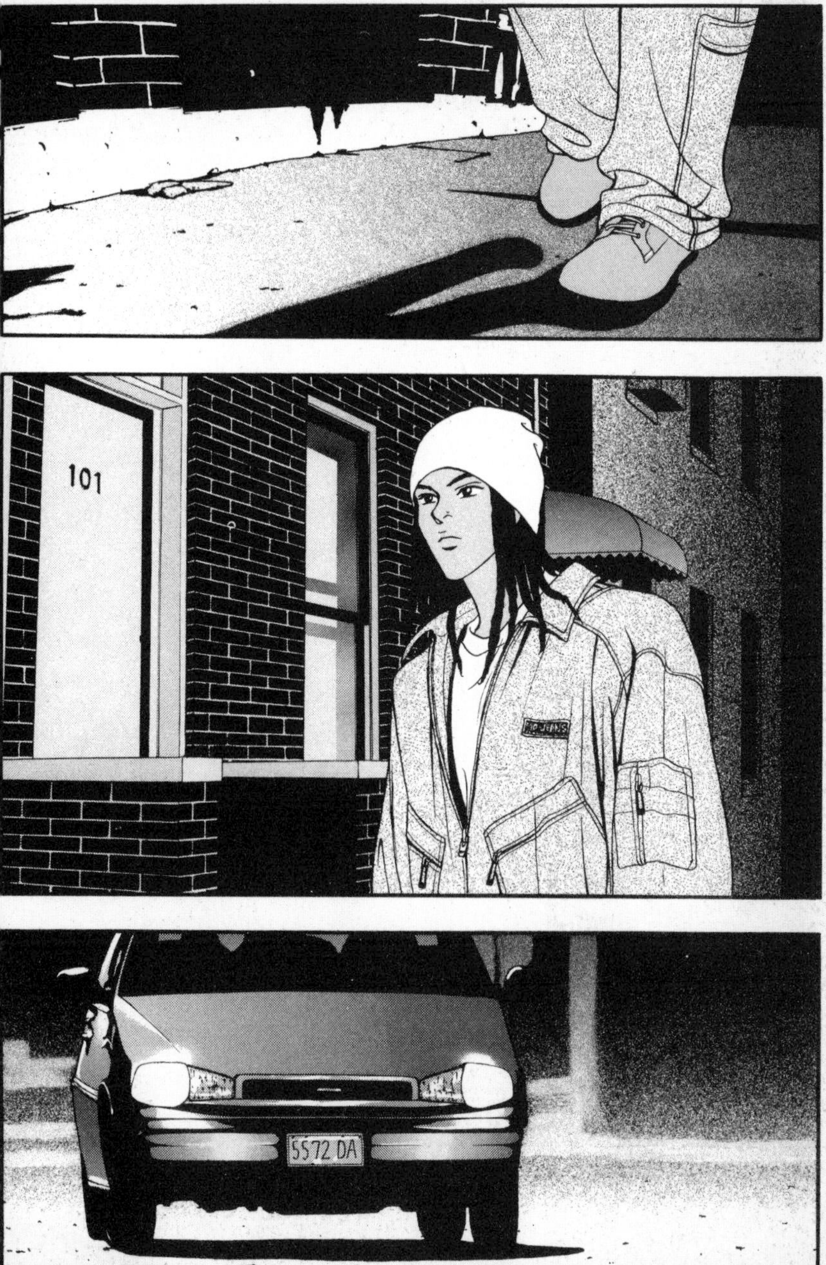
101
5572 DA

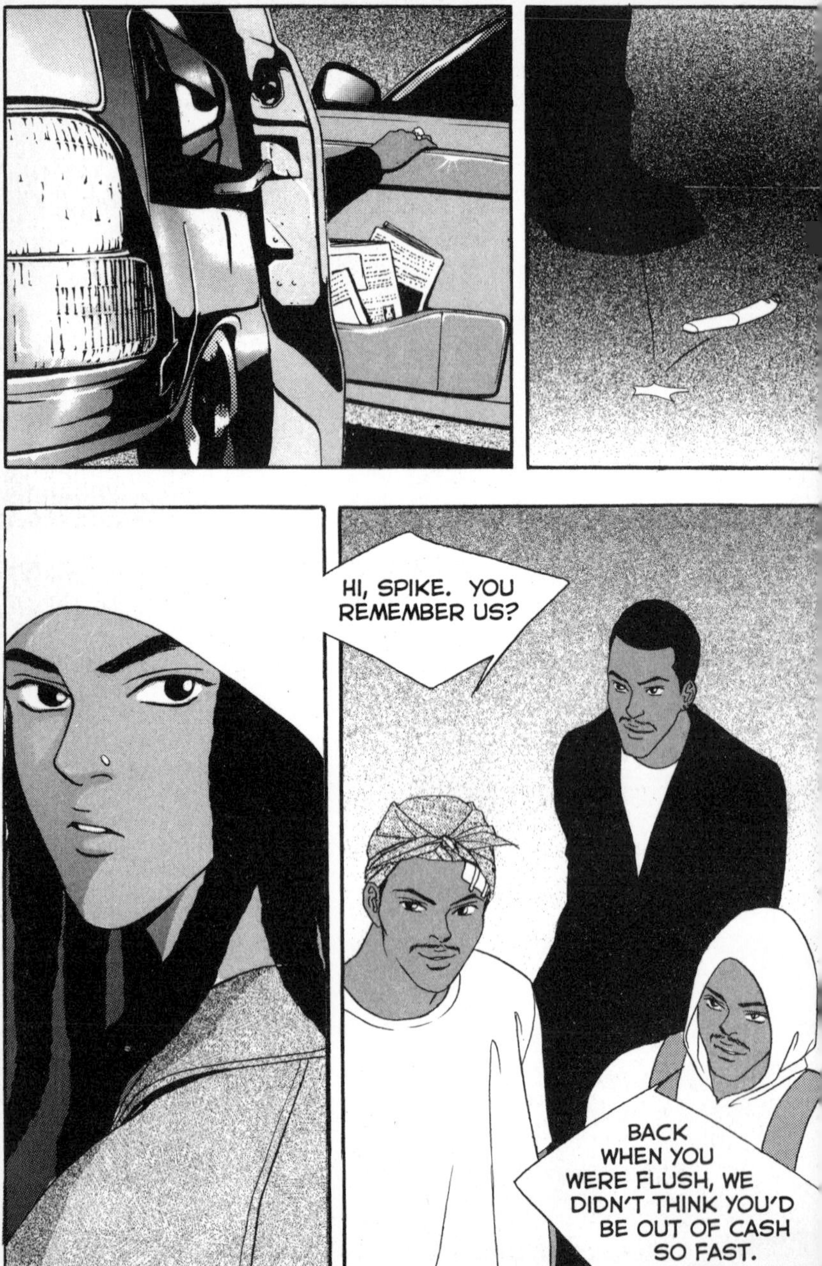
HI, SPIKE. YOU REMEMBER US?
BACK WHEN YOU WERE FLUSH, WE DIDN'T THINK YOU'D BE OUT OF CASH SO FAST.

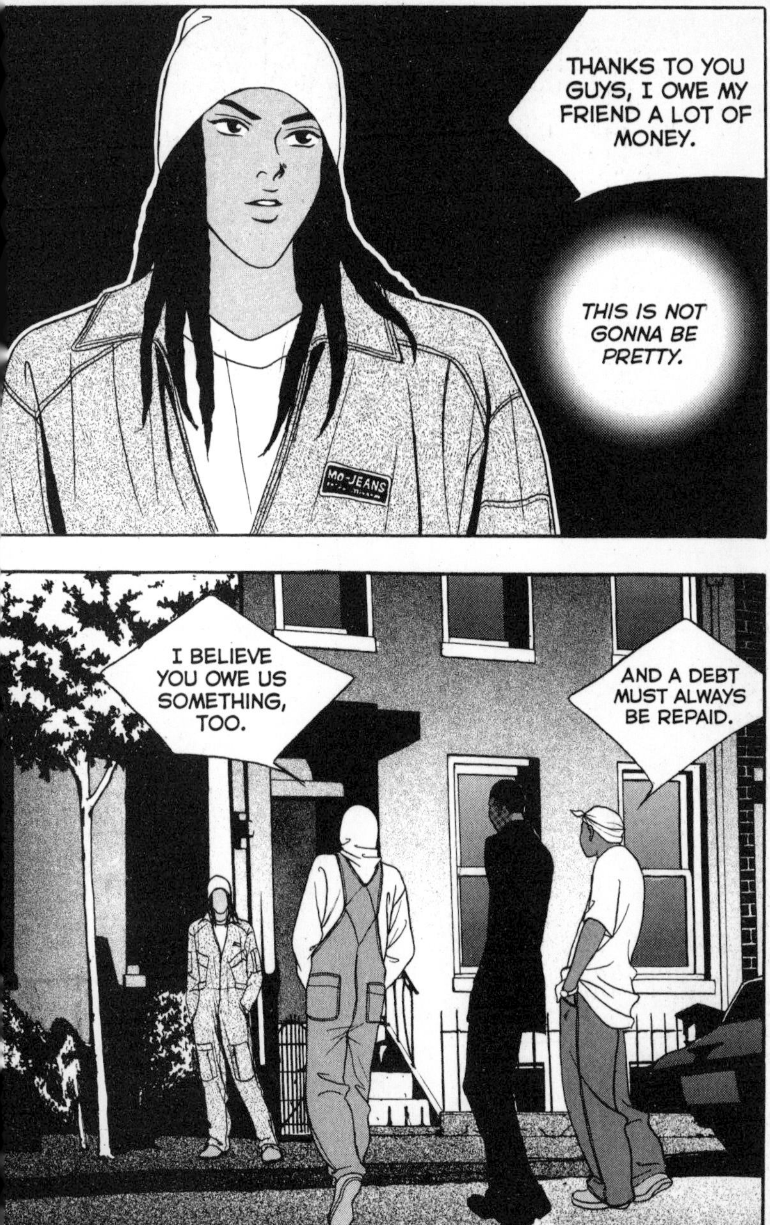
THANKS TO YOU GUYS, I OWE MY FRIEND A LOT OF MONEY.
THIS IS NOT GONNA BE PRETTY.
MO-JEANS
I BELIEVE YOU OWE US SOMETHING, TOO.
AND A DEBT MUST ALWAYS BE REPAID.

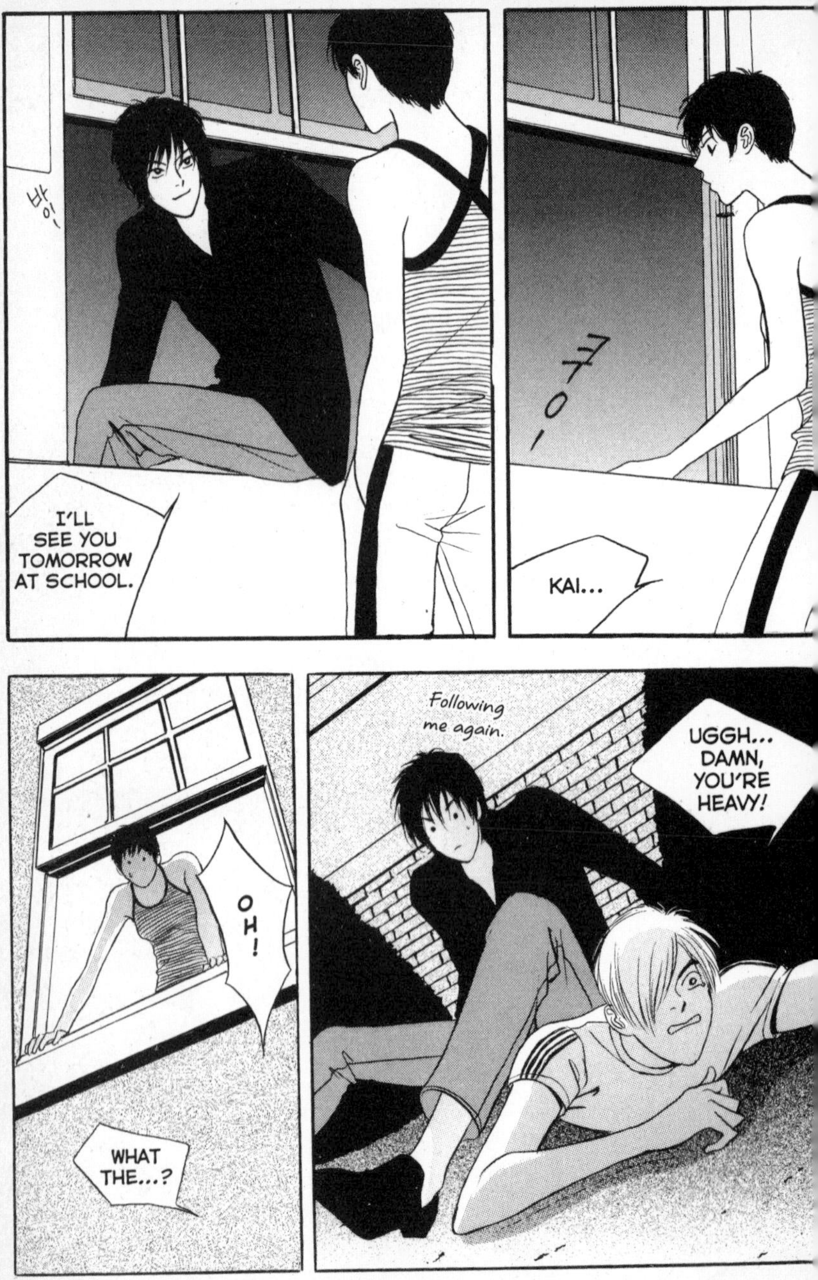
바이
I'LL SEE YOU TOMORROW AT SCHOOL.
KAI...
OH!
WHAT THE...?
Following me again.
UGGH... DAMN, YOU'RE HEAVY!

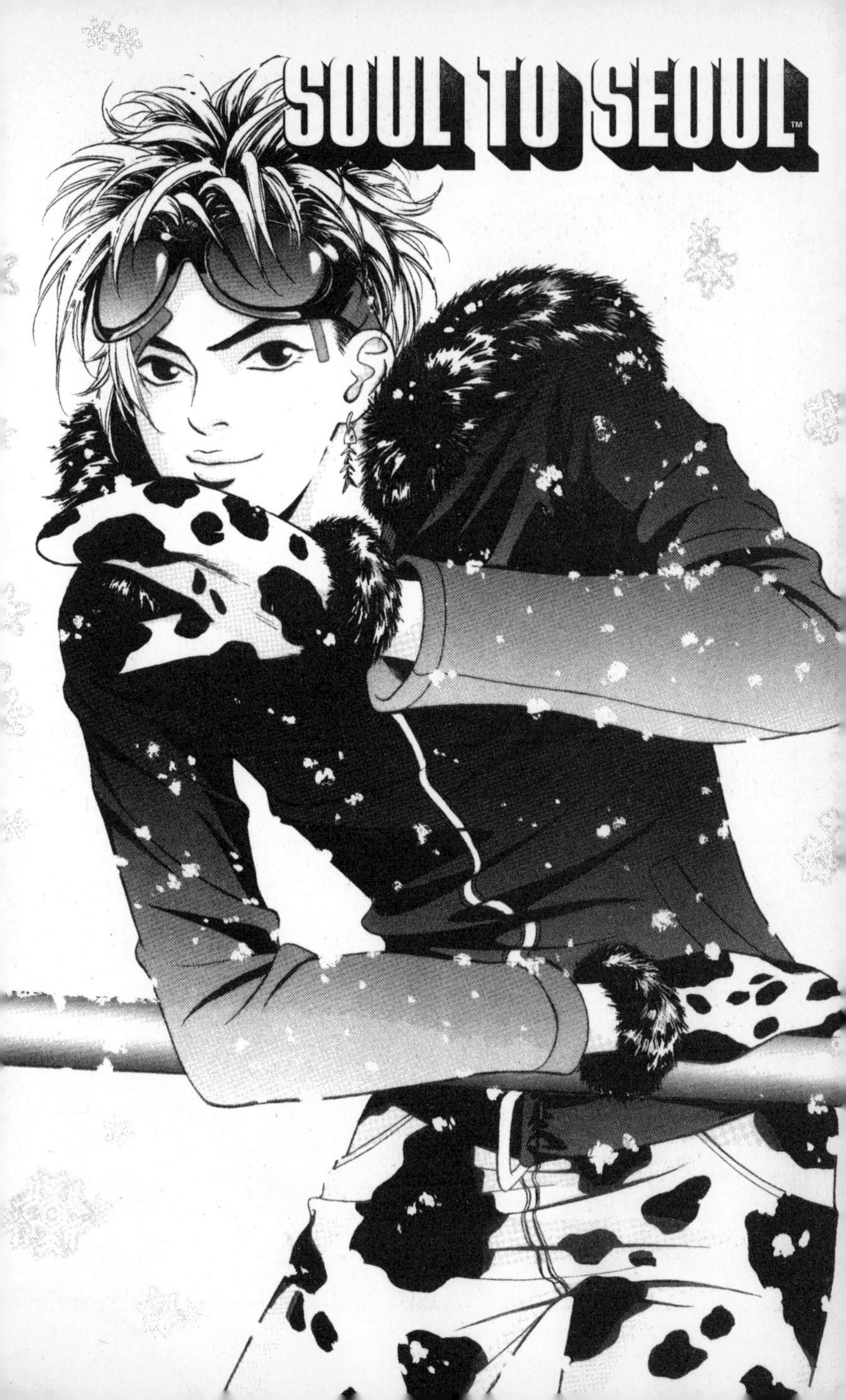
SOUL TO SEOUL™

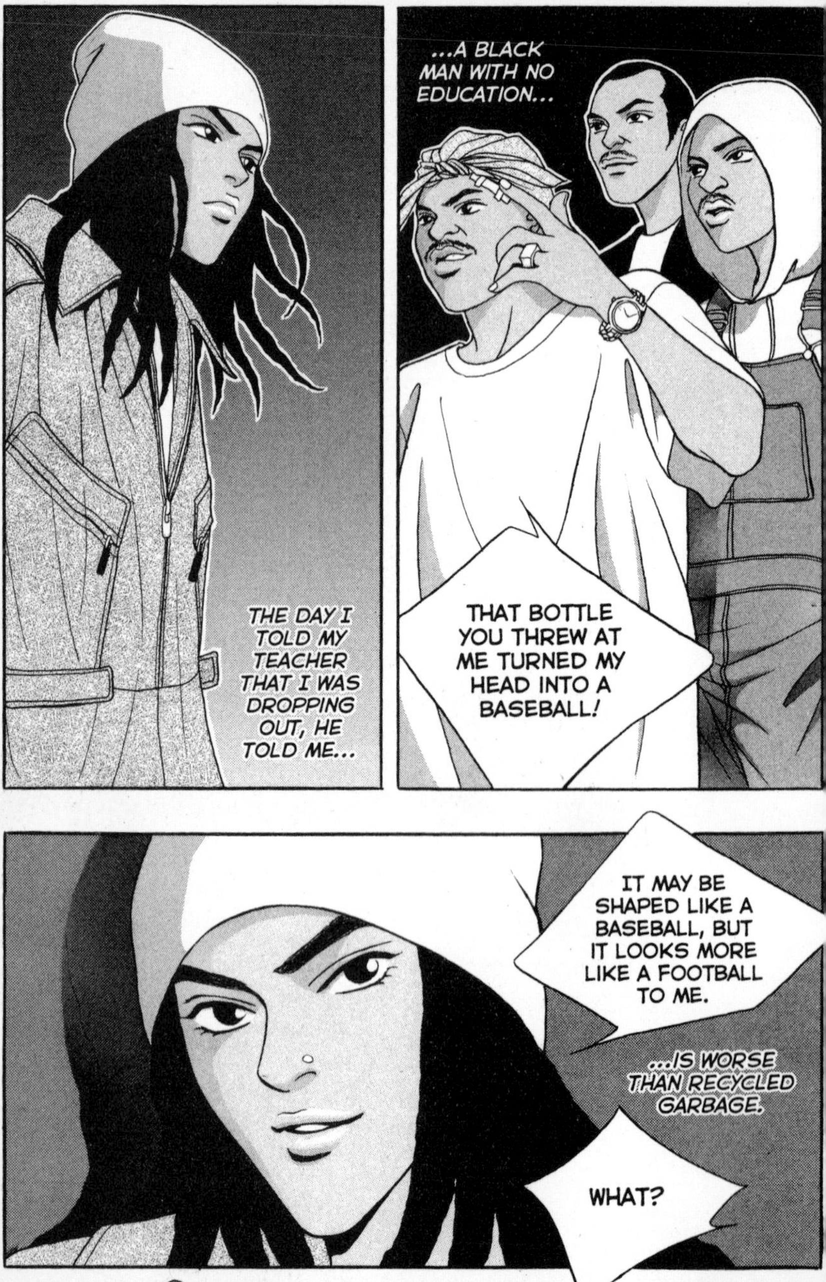
THE DAY I TOLD MY TEACHER THAT I WAS DROPPING OUT, HE TOLD ME...
...A BLACK MAN WITH NO EDUCATION...
THAT BOTTLE YOU THREW AT ME TURNED MY HEAD INTO A BASEBALL!
IT MAY BE SHAPED LIKE A BASEBALL, BUT IT LOOKS MORE LIKE A FOOTBALL TO ME.
...IS WORSE THAN RECYCLED GARBAGE.
WHAT?

Baseball = = = = Football

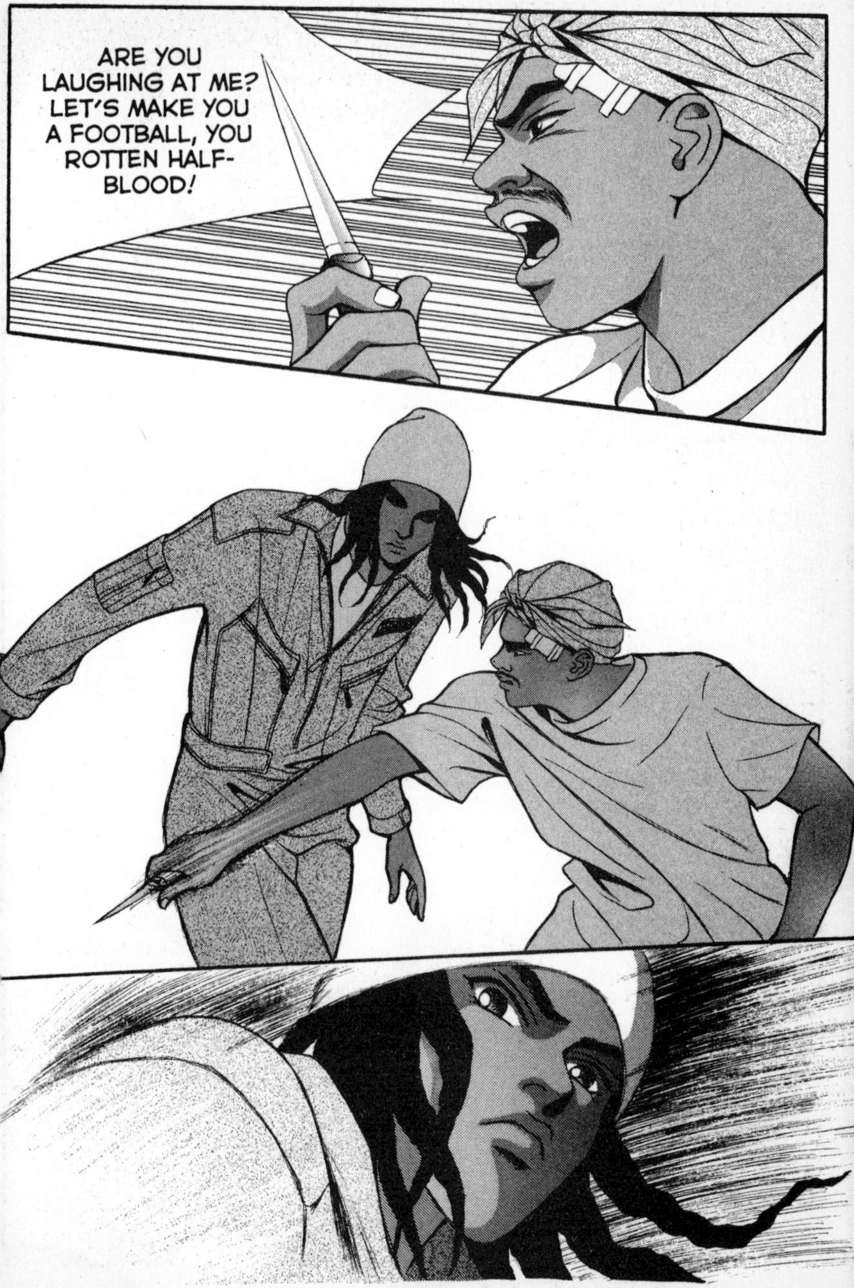
ARE YOU LAUGHING AT ME? LET'S MAKE YOU A FOOTBALL, YOU ROTTEN HALF-BLOOD!

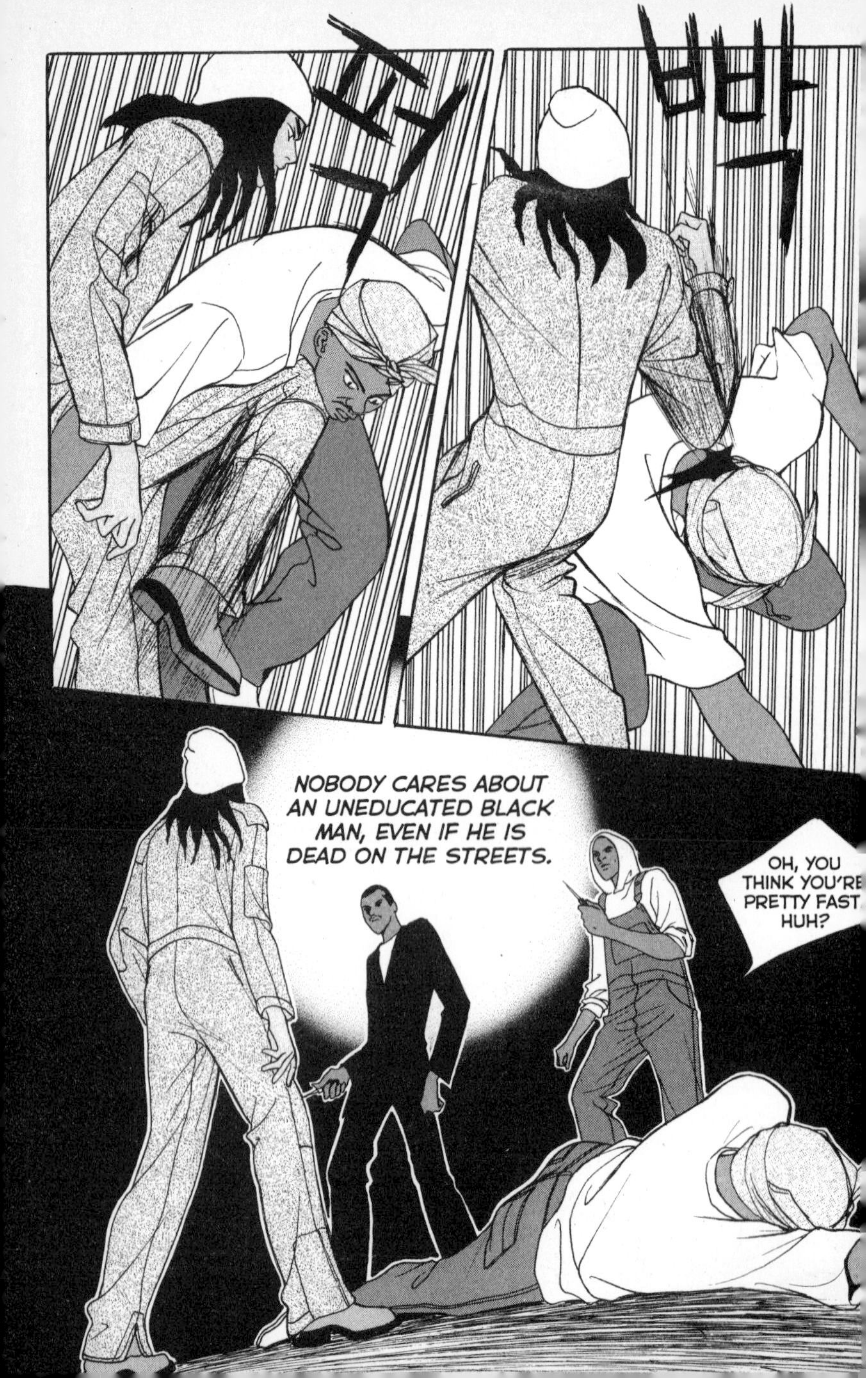
퍽
빠각
NOBODY CARES ABOUT AN UNEDUCATED BLACK MAN, EVEN IF HE IS DEAD ON THE STREETS.
OH, YOU THINK YOU'RE PRETTY FAST, HUH?

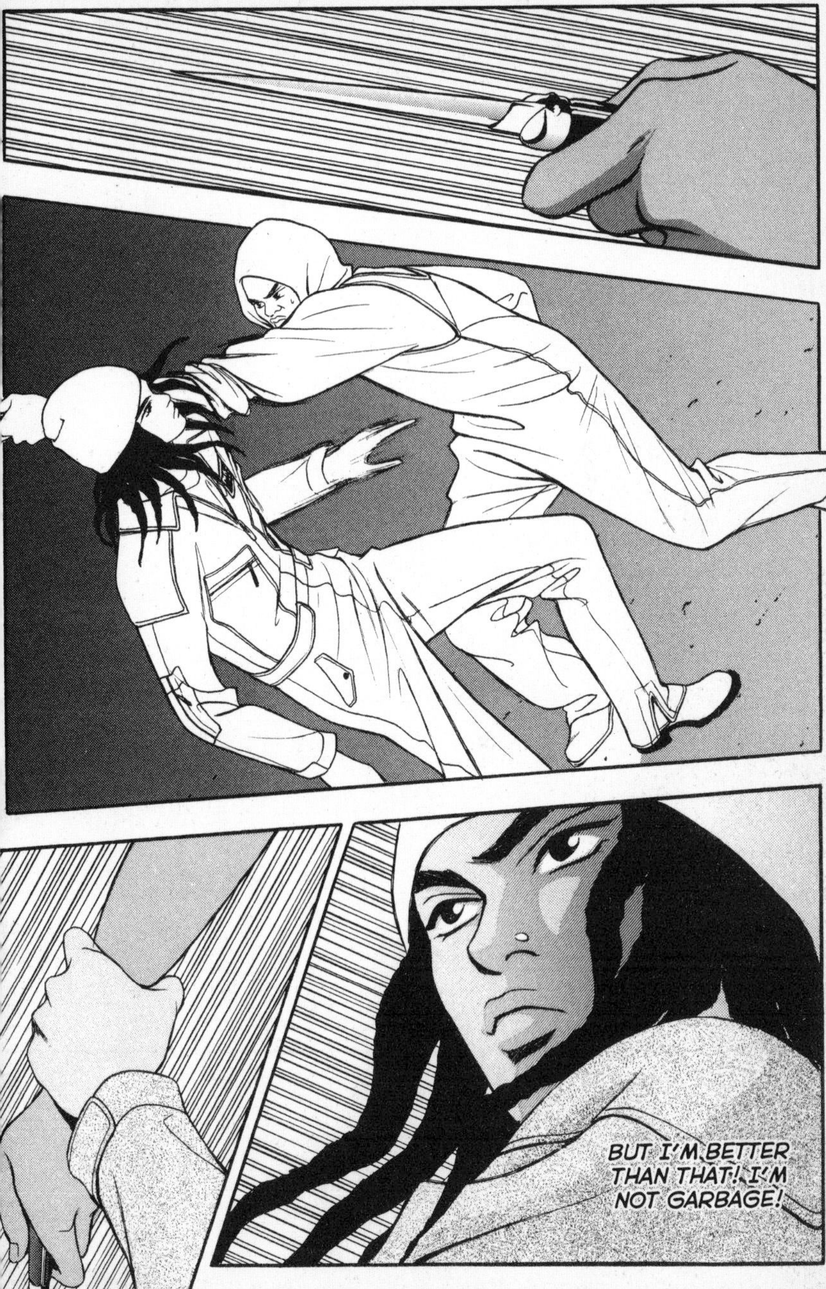
BUT I'M BETTER THAN THAT! I'M NOT GARBAGE!

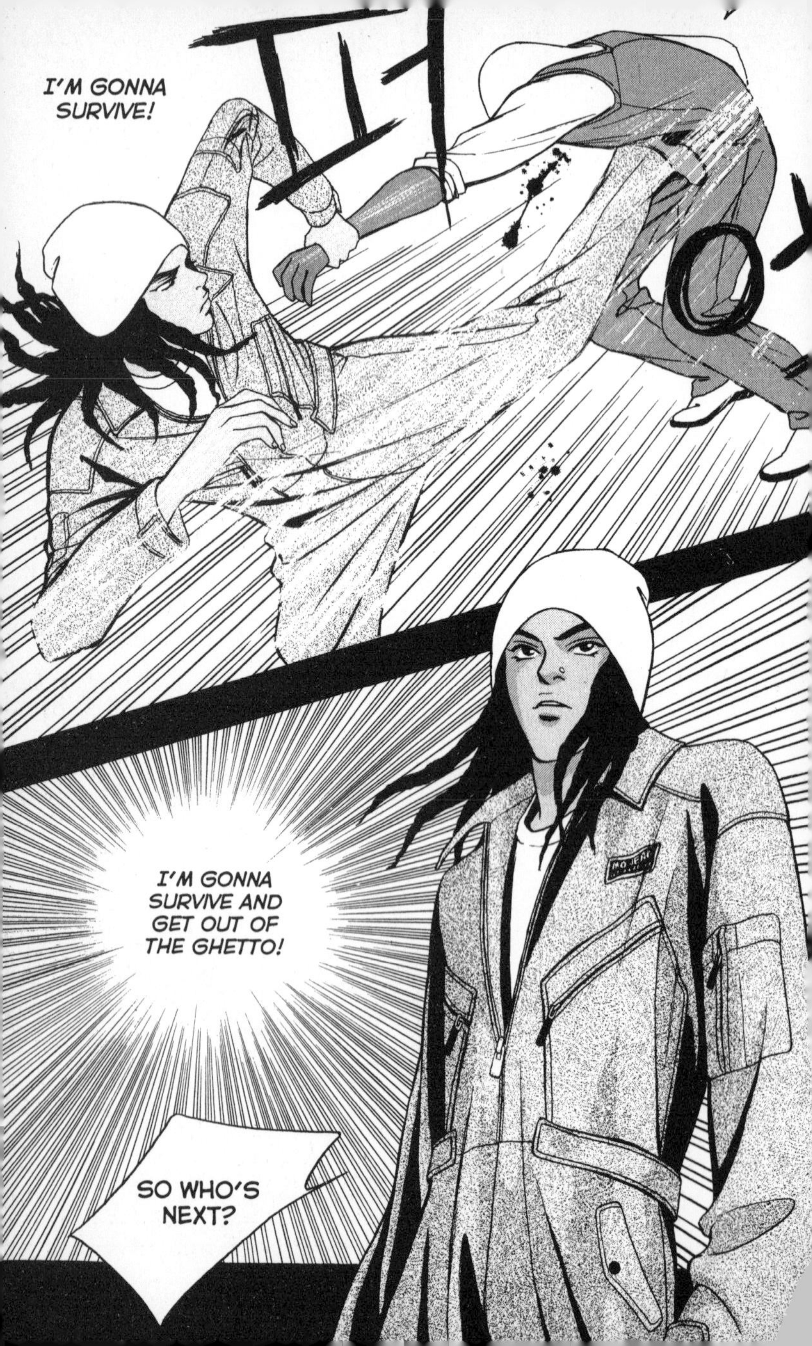
I'M GONNA SURVIVE!
I'M GONNA SURVIVE AND GET OUT OF THE GHETTO!
SO WHO'S NEXT?

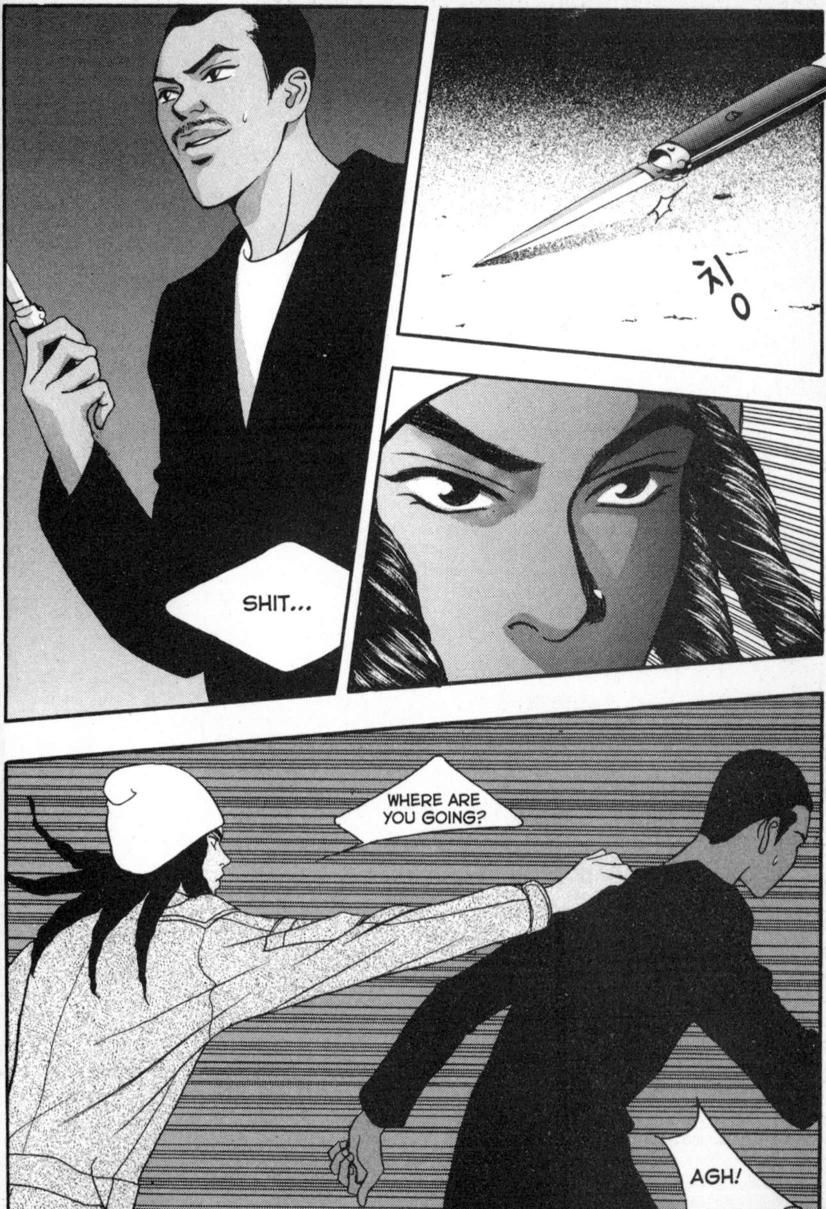
SHIT...
징
WHERE ARE YOU GOING?
AGH!

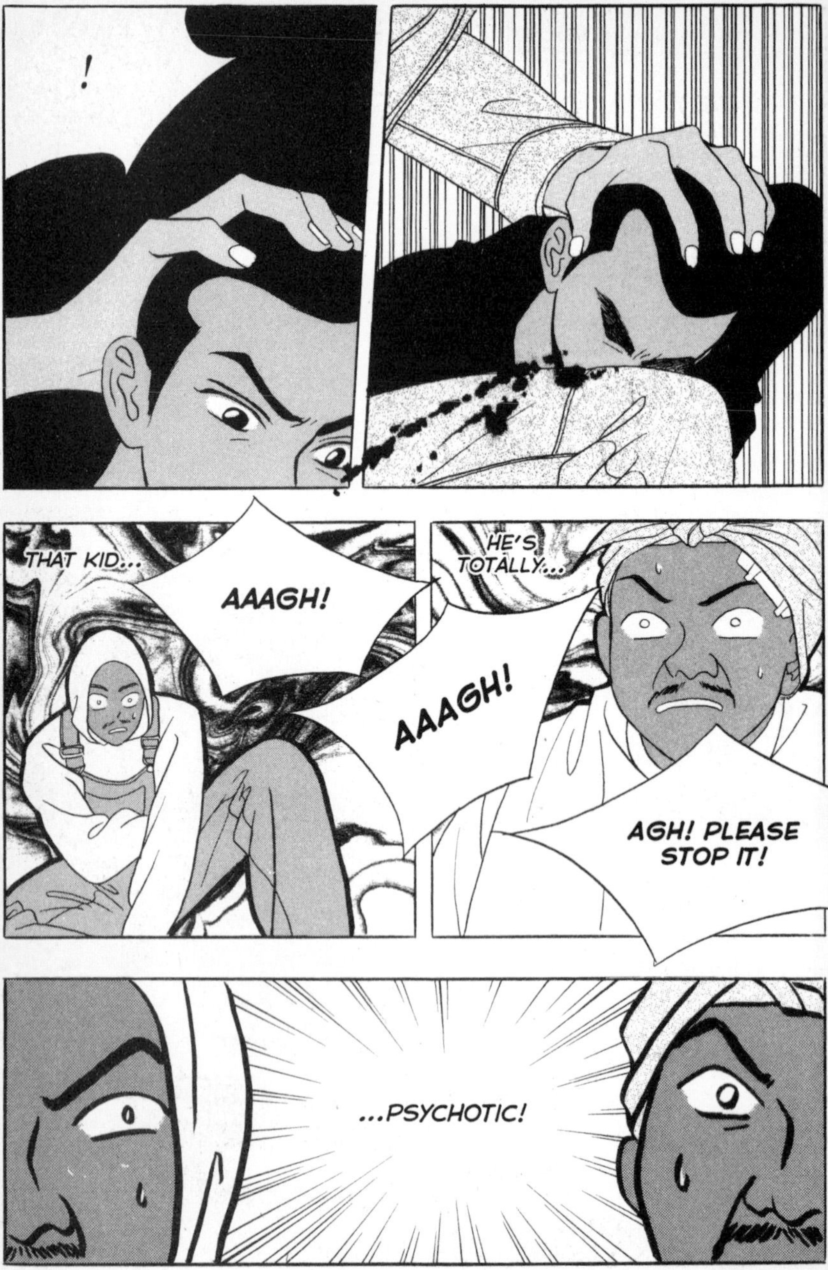
!
THAT KID...
AAAGH!
HE'S TOTALLY...
AAAGH!
AGH! PLEASE STOP IT!
...PSYCHOTIC!

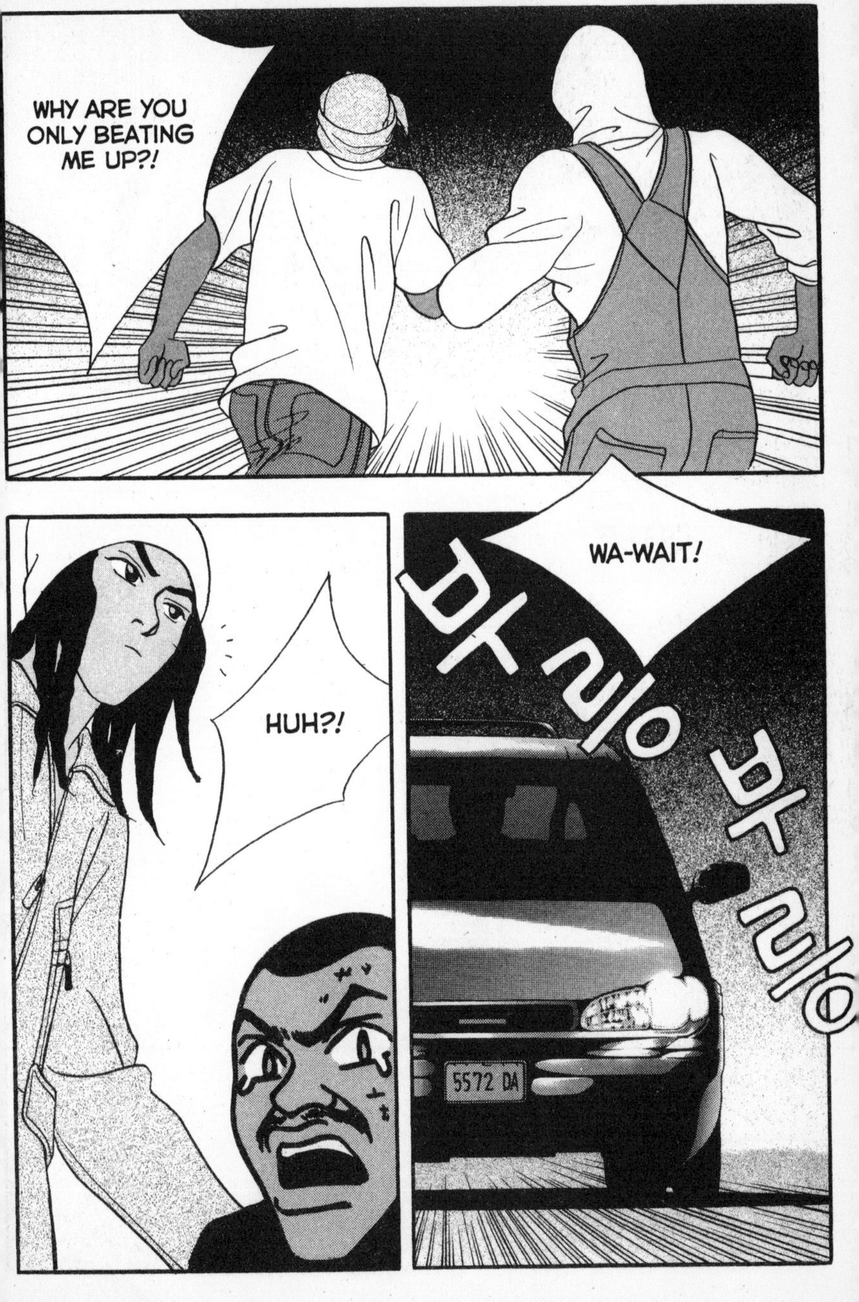
WHY ARE YOU ONLY BEATING ME UP?!
HUH?!
WA-WAIT!
5572 DA

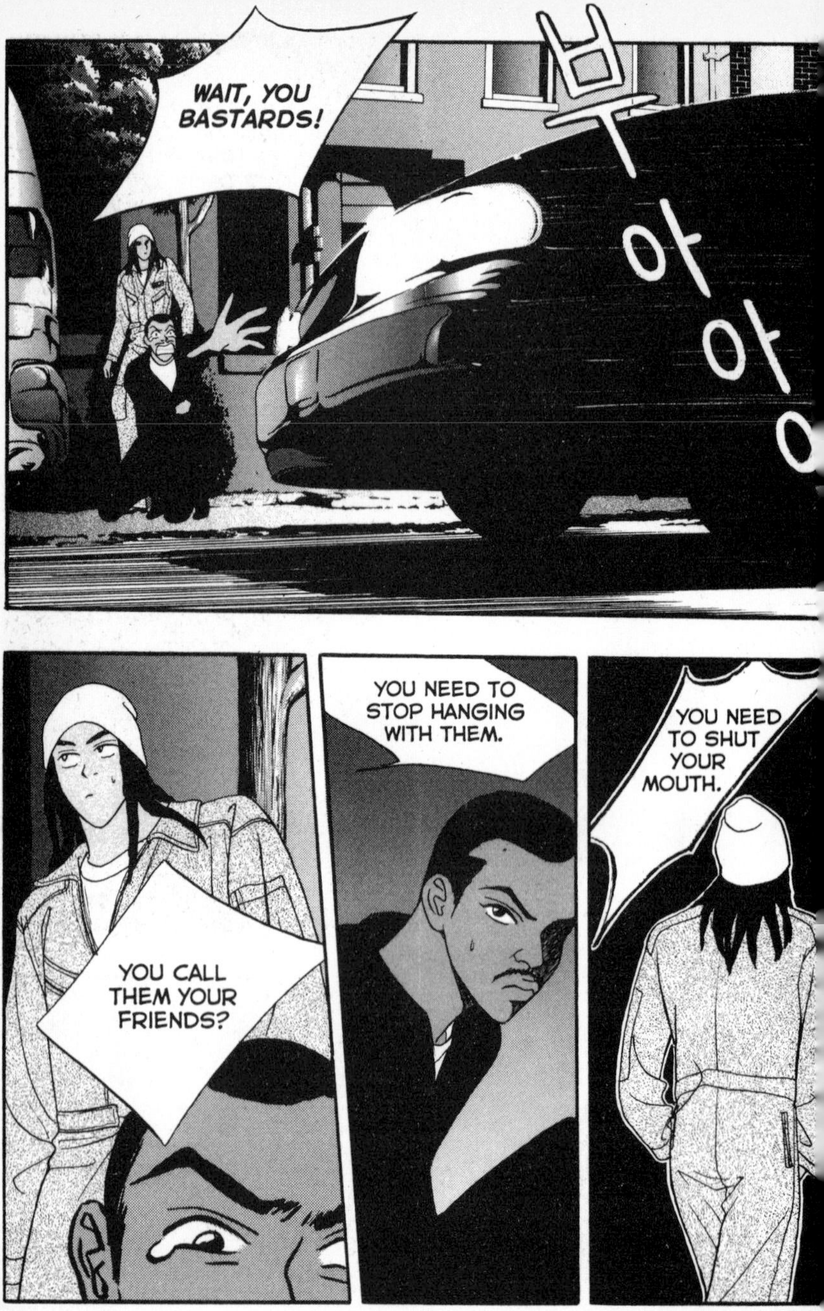
WAIT, YOU BASTARDS!
부아아
YOU CALL THEM YOUR FRIENDS?
YOU NEED TO STOP HANGING WITH THEM.
YOU NEED TO SHUT YOUR MOUTH.

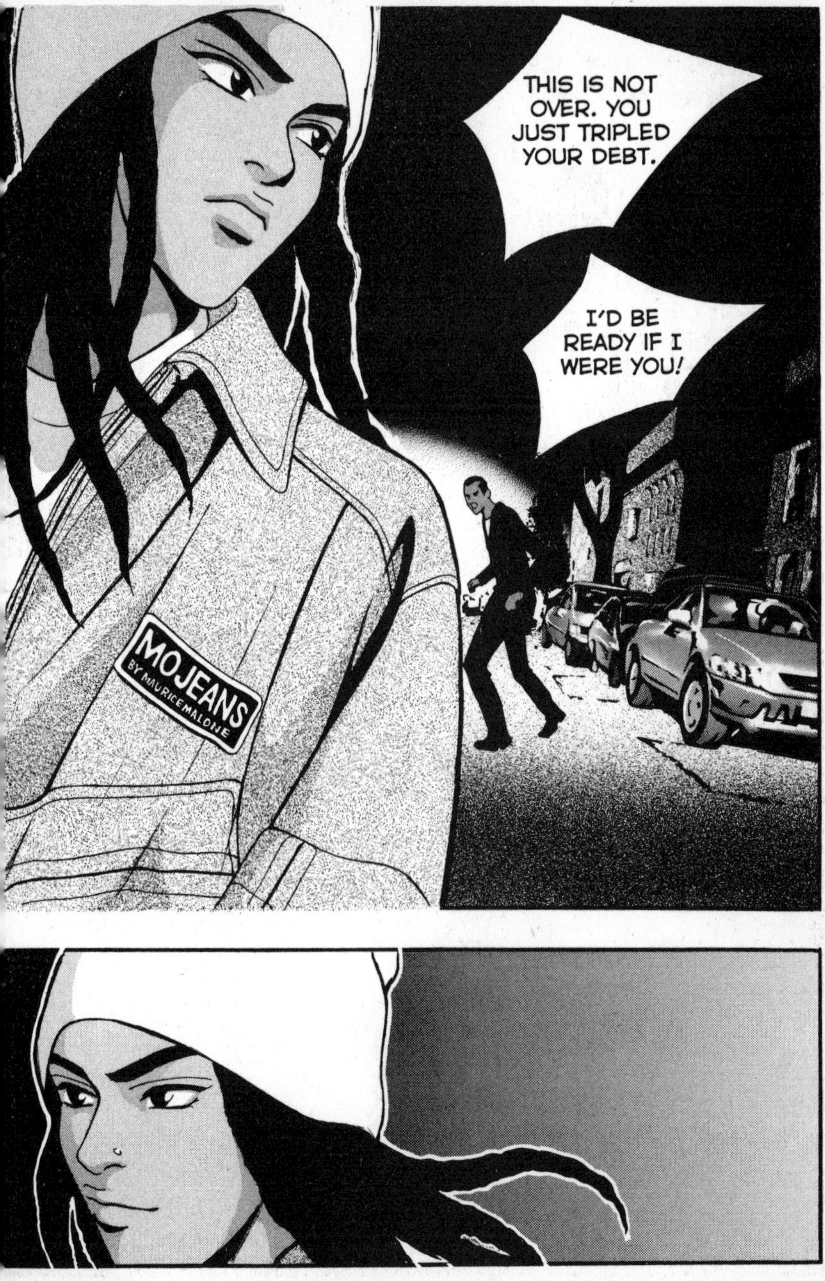
THIS IS NOT OVER. YOU JUST TRIPLED YOUR DEBT.
I'D BE READY IF I WERE YOU!
MOJEANS
BY MAURICEMALONE

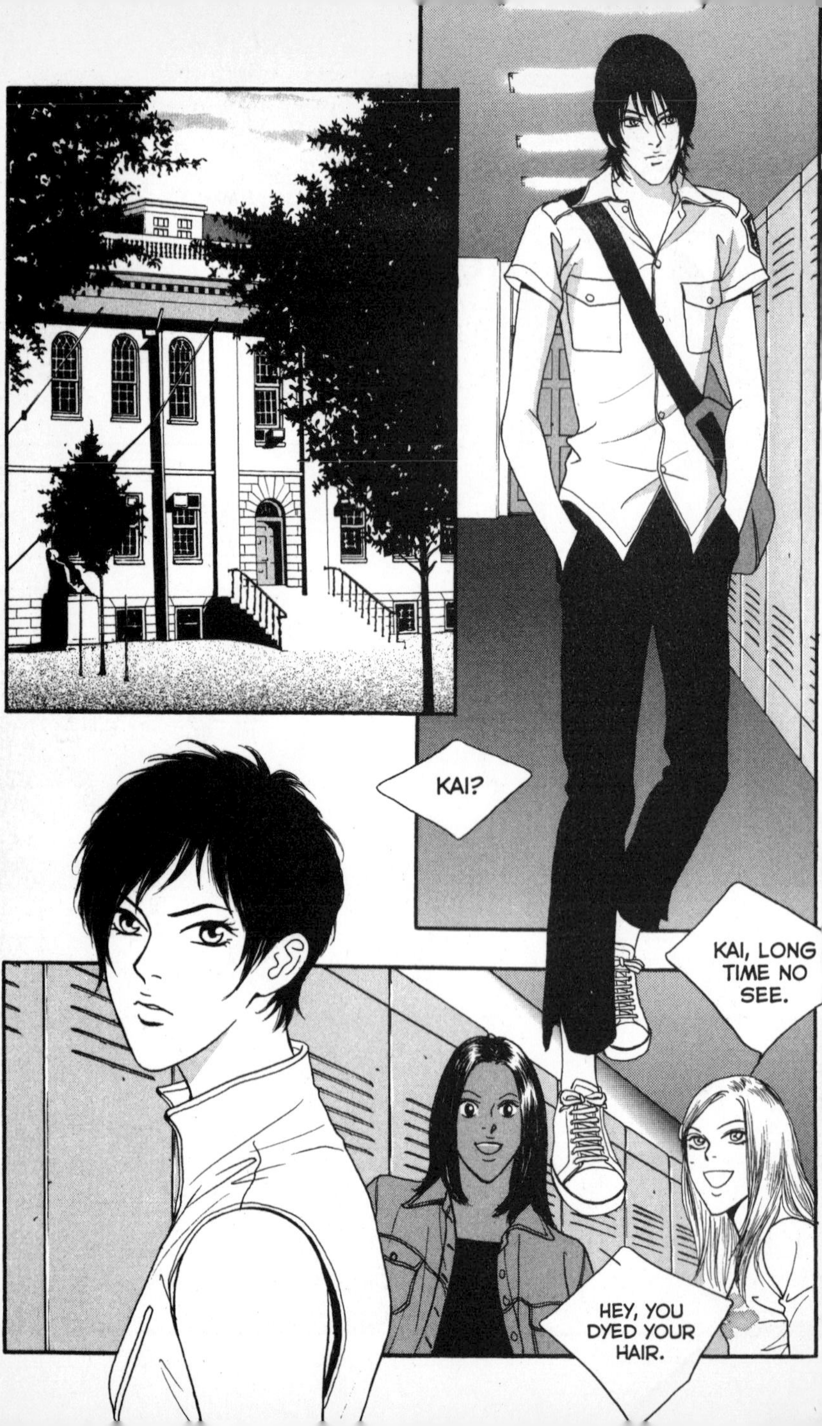
KAI?
KAI, LONG TIME NO SEE.
HEY, YOU DYED YOUR HAIR.

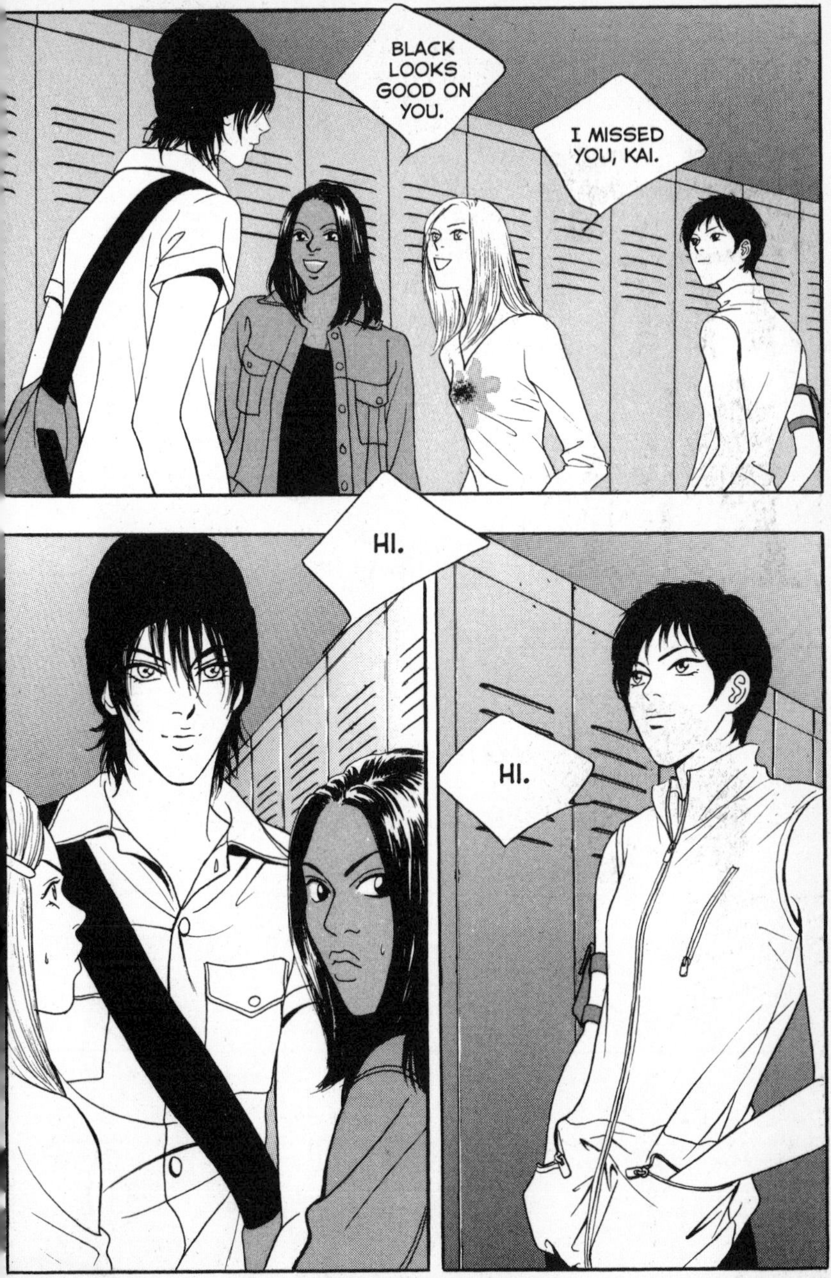
BLACK LOOKS GOOD ON YOU.
I MISSED YOU, KAI.
HI.
HI.

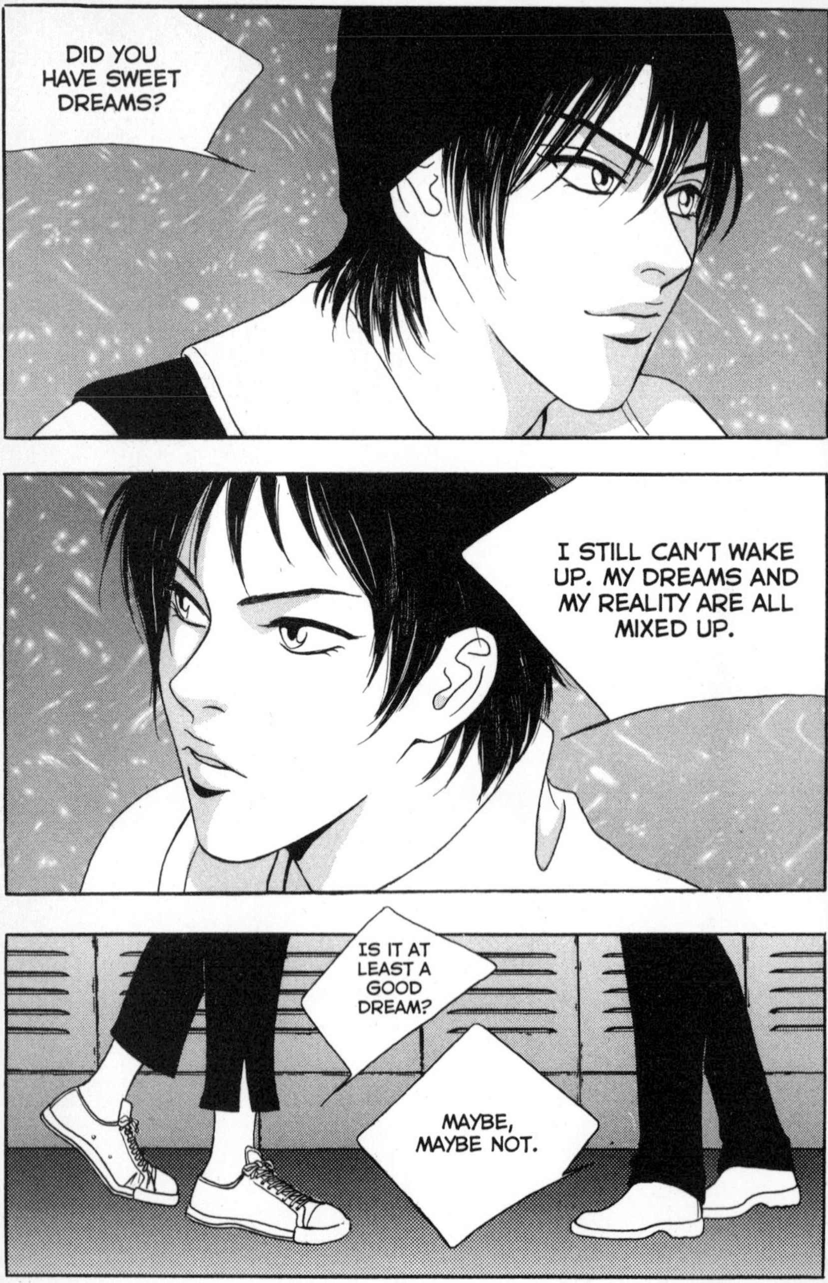
DID YOU HAVE SWEET DREAMS?
I STILL CAN'T WAKE UP. MY DREAMS AND MY REALITY ARE ALL MIXED UP.
IS IT AT LEAST A GOOD DREAM?
MAYBE, MAYBE NOT.

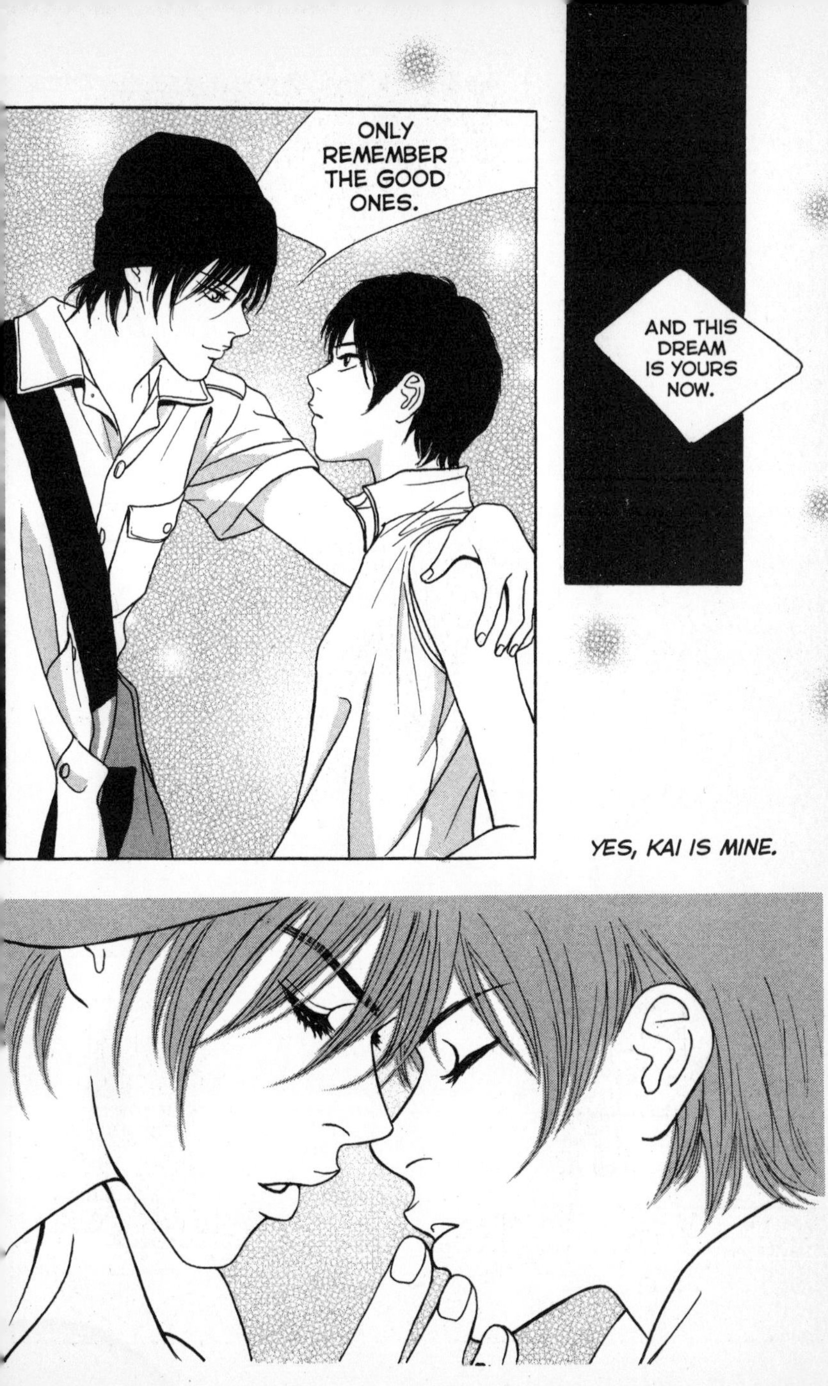
ONLY REMEMBER THE GOOD ONES.
AND THIS DREAM IS YOURS NOW.
YES, KAI IS MINE.

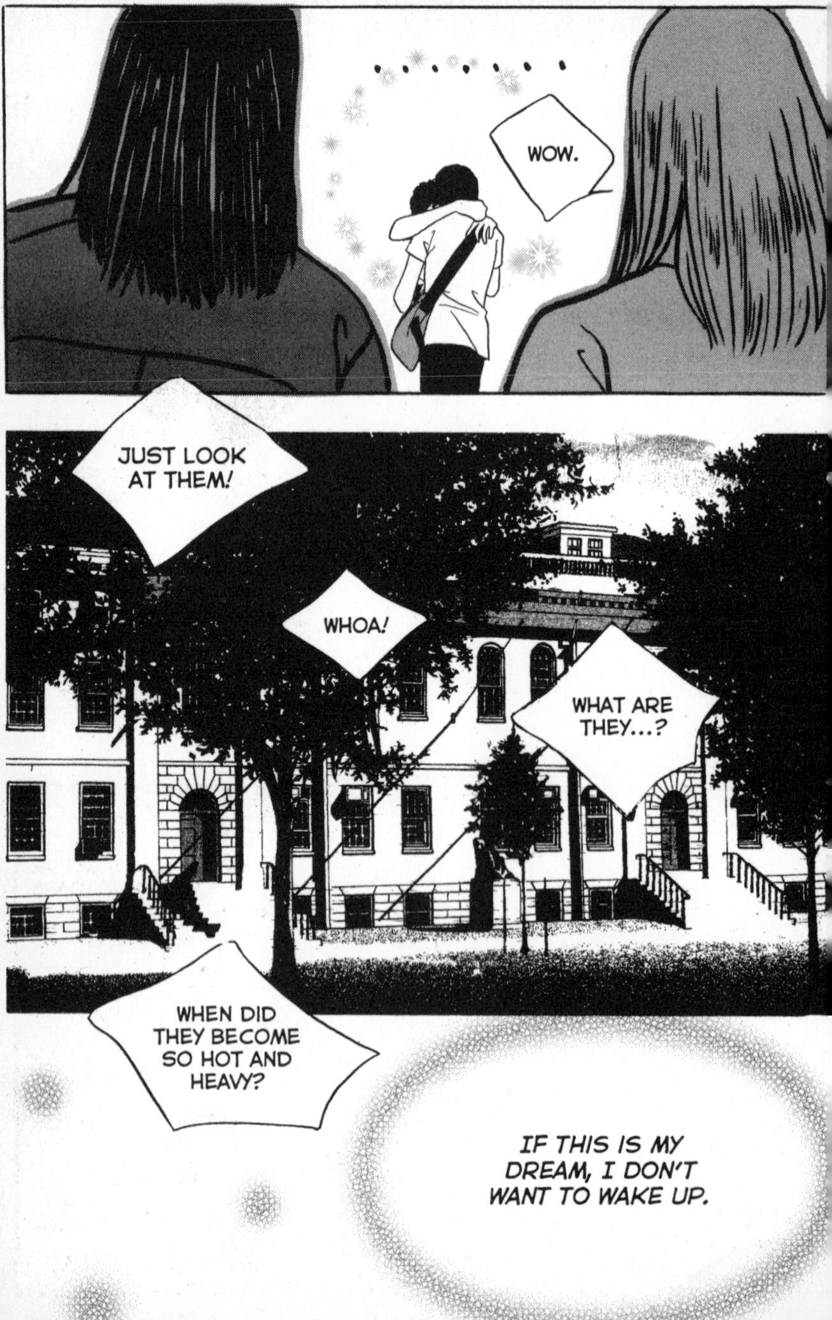
WOW.
JUST LOOK AT THEM!
WHOA!
WHAT ARE THEY...?
WHEN DID THEY BECOME SO HOT AND HEAVY?
IF THIS IS MY DREAM, I DON'T WANT TO WAKE UP.

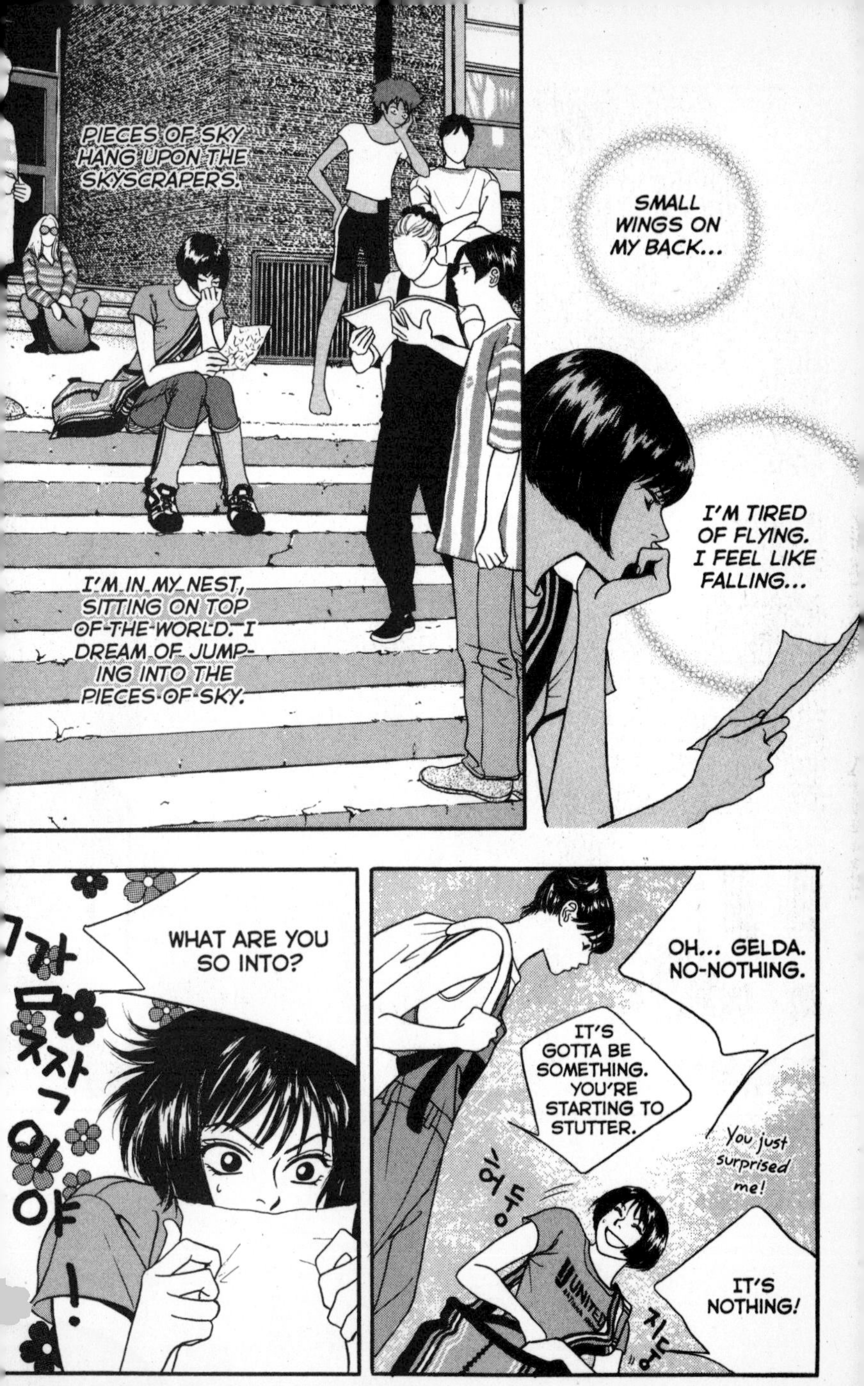
PIECES OF SKY HANG UPON THE SKYSCRAPERS.
I'M IN MY NEST, SITTING ON TOP OF THE WORLD. I DREAM OF JUMPING INTO THE PIECES OF SKY.
SMALL WINGS ON MY BACK...
I'M TIRED OF FLYING. I FEEL LIKE FALLING...
WHAT ARE YOU SO INTO?
깜짝이야—!
OH... GELDA. NO-NOTHING.
IT'S GOTTA BE SOMETHING. YOU'RE STARTING TO STUTTER.
허둥
You just surprised me!
IT'S NOTHING!
지잉
UNITED

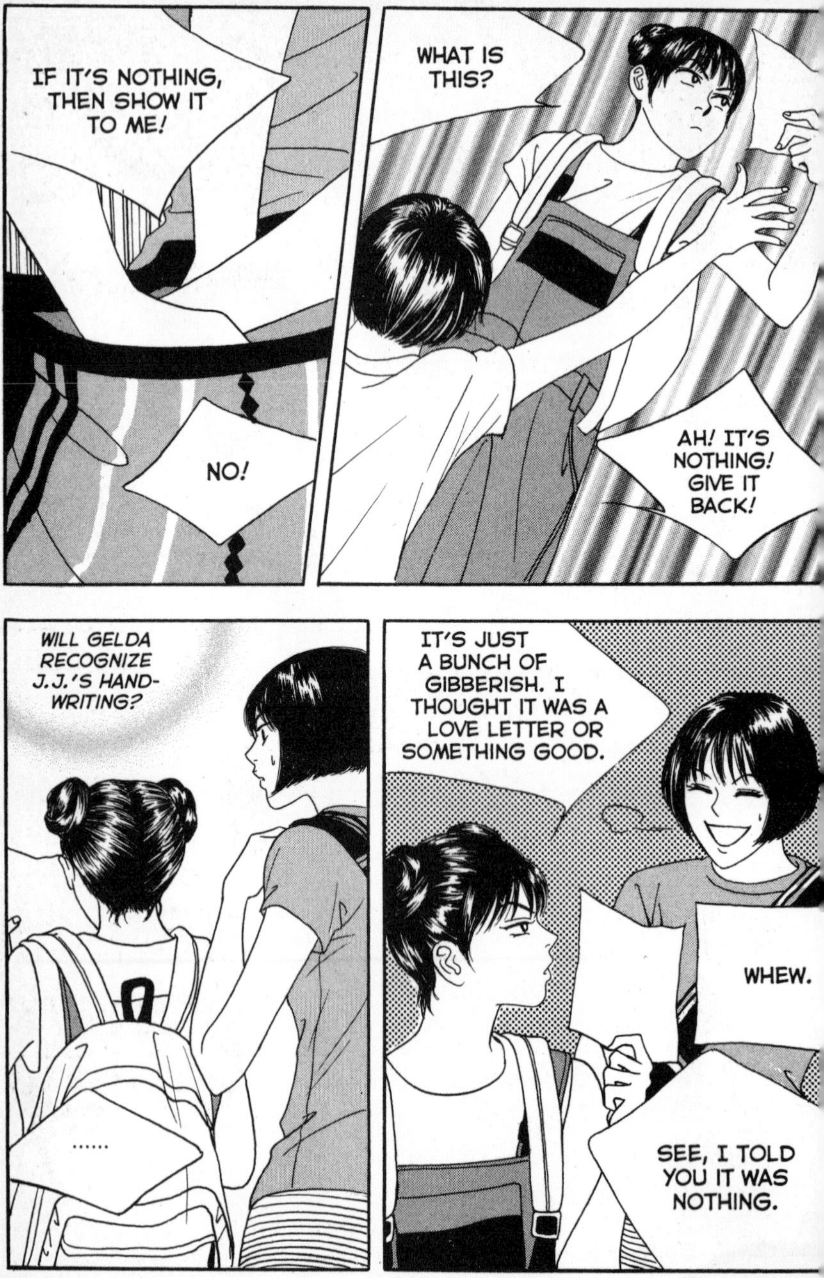
IF IT'S NOTHING, THEN SHOW IT TO ME!
NO!
WHAT IS THIS?
AH! IT'S NOTHING! GIVE IT BACK!
WILL GELDA RECOGNIZE J.J.'S HAND-WRITING?
......
IT'S JUST A BUNCH OF GIBBERISH. I THOUGHT IT WAS A LOVE LETTER OR SOMETHING GOOD.
WHEW.
SEE, I TOLD YOU IT WAS NOTHING.

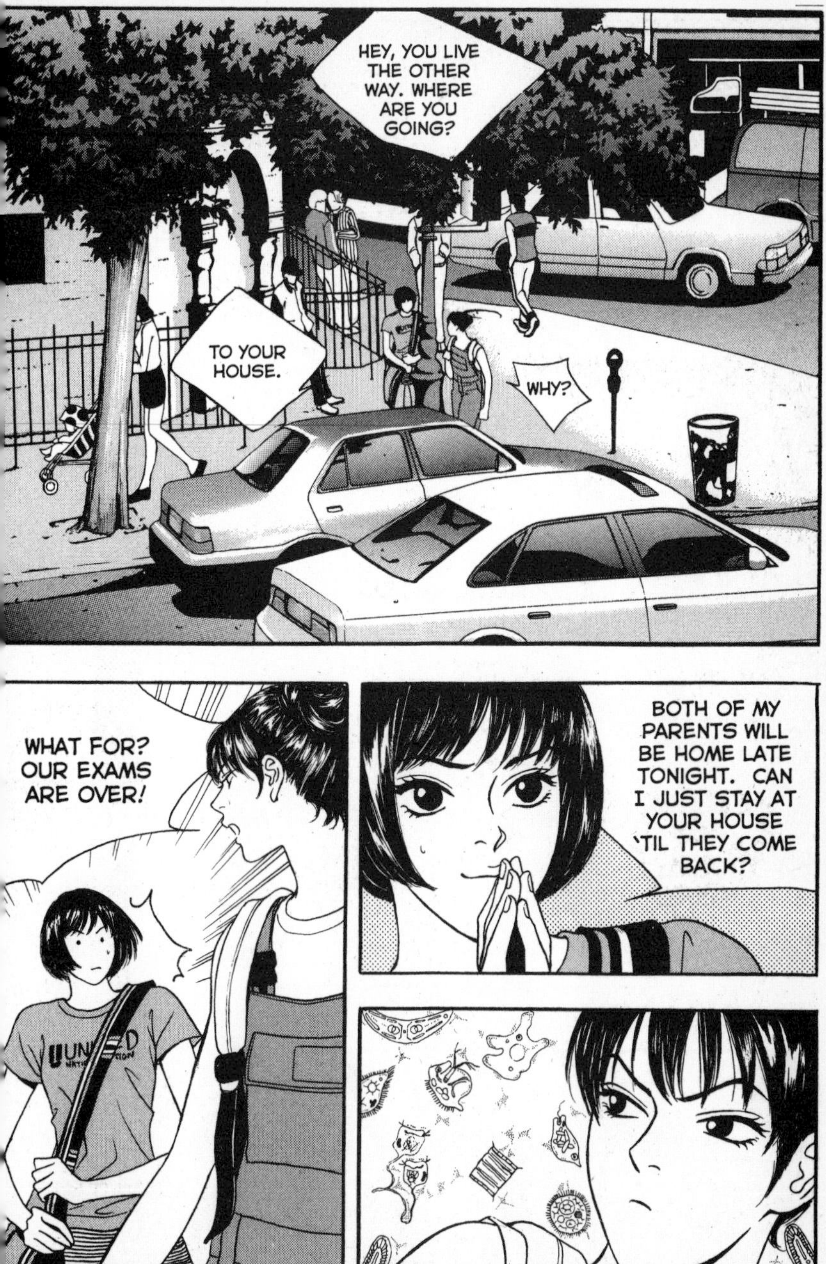
HEY, YOU LIVE THE OTHER WAY. WHERE ARE YOU GOING?
TO YOUR HOUSE.
WHY?
WHAT FOR? OUR EXAMS ARE OVER!
BOTH OF MY PARENTS WILL BE HOME LATE TONIGHT. CAN I JUST STAY AT YOUR HOUSE 'TIL THEY COME BACK?

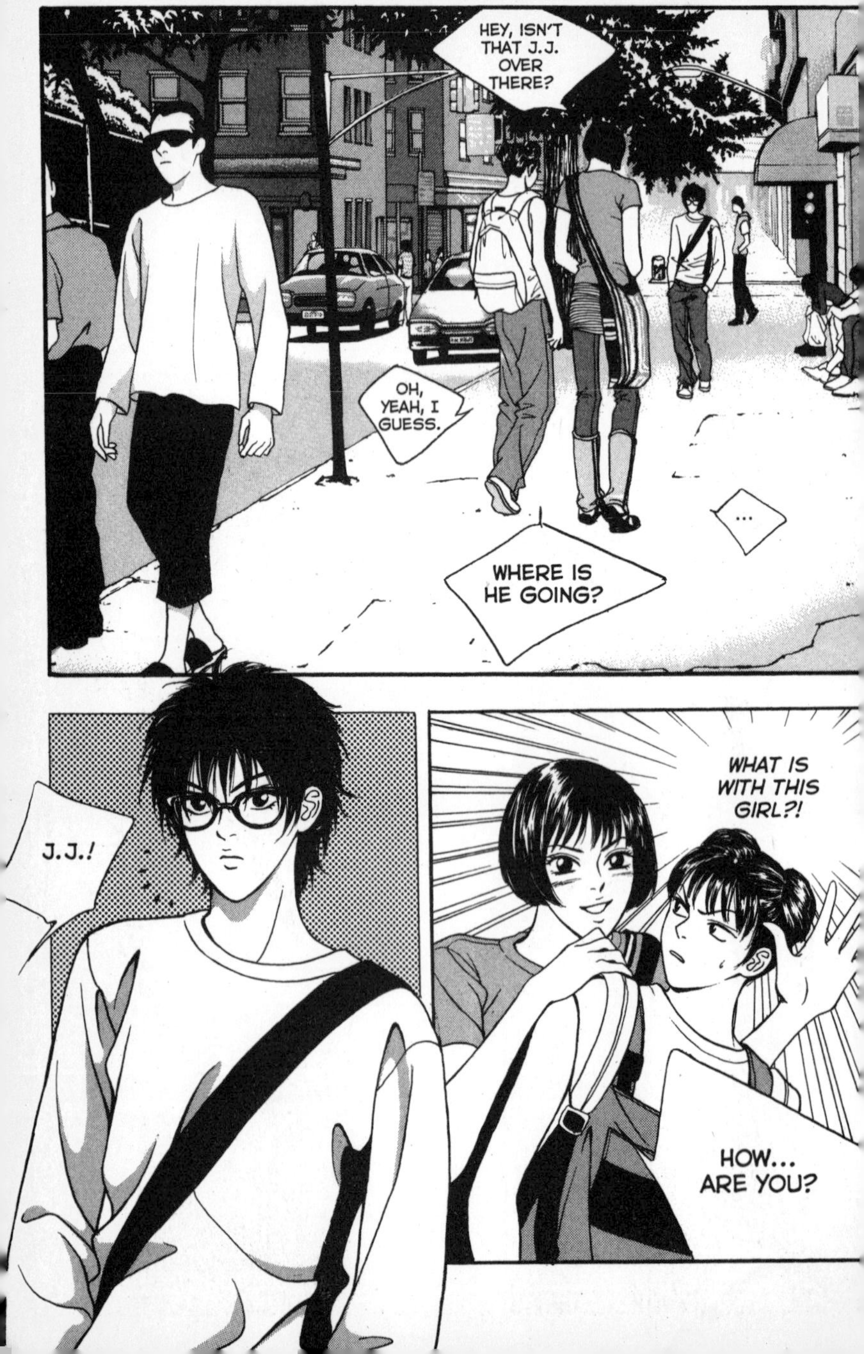
HEY, ISN'T THAT J.J. OVER THERE?
OH, YEAH, I GUESS.
...
WHERE IS HE GOING?
J.J.!
WHAT IS WITH THIS GIRL?!
HOW... ARE YOU?

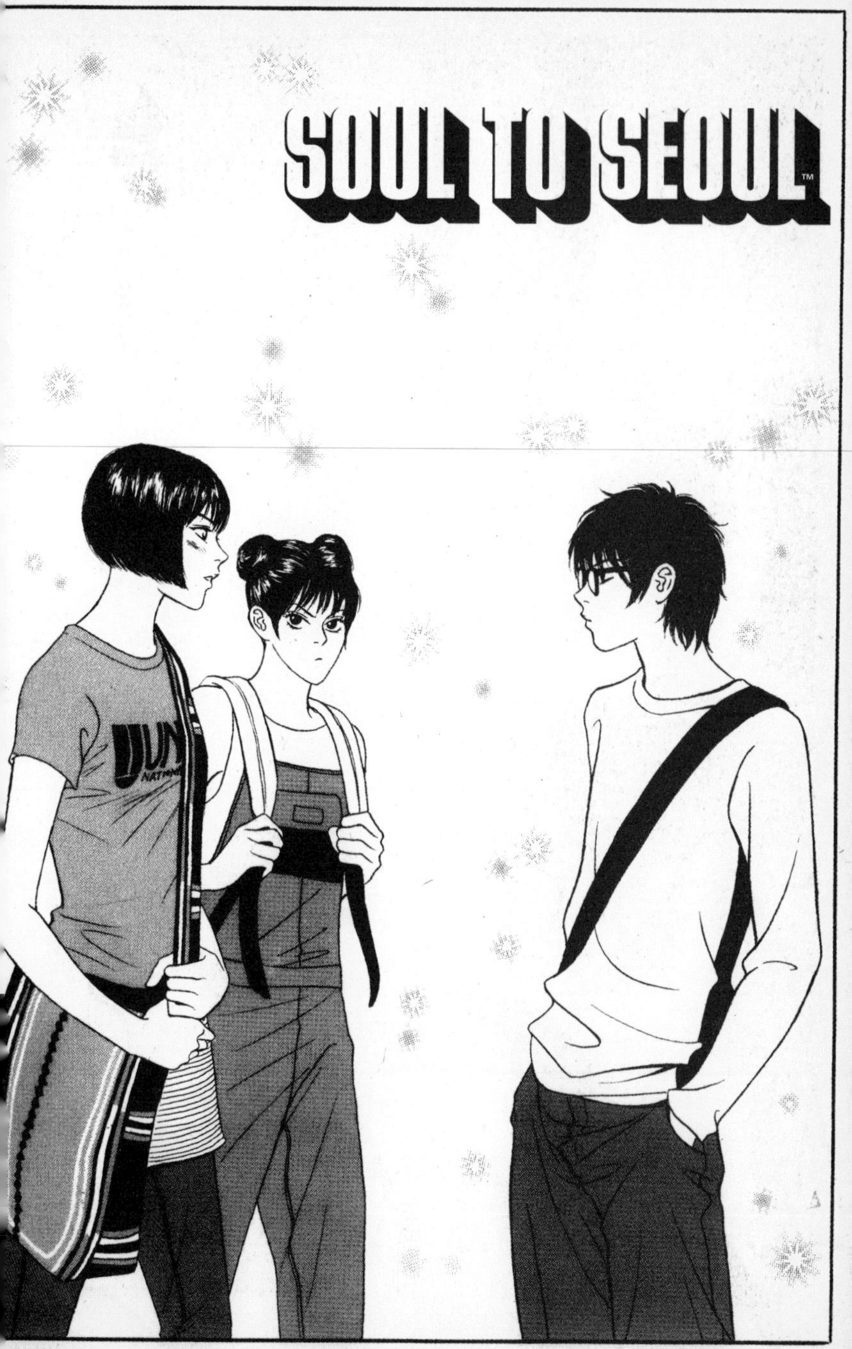
SOUL TO SEOUL™

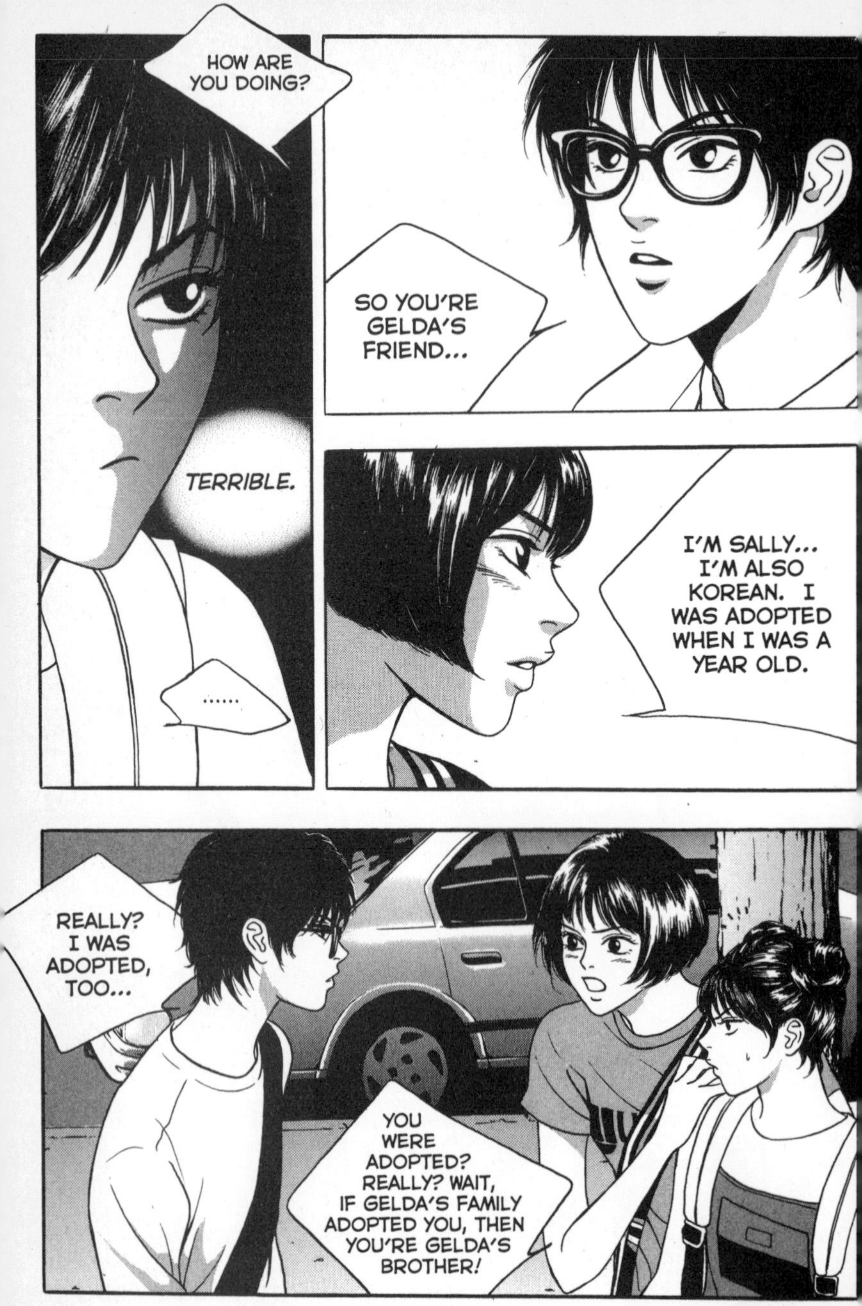
HOW ARE YOU DOING?
TERRIBLE.
......
SO YOU'RE GELDA'S FRIEND...
I'M SALLY... I'M ALSO KOREAN. I WAS ADOPTED WHEN I WAS A YEAR OLD.
REALLY? I WAS ADOPTED, TOO...
YOU WERE ADOPTED? REALLY? WAIT, IF GELDA'S FAMILY ADOPTED YOU, THEN YOU'RE GELDA'S BROTHER!

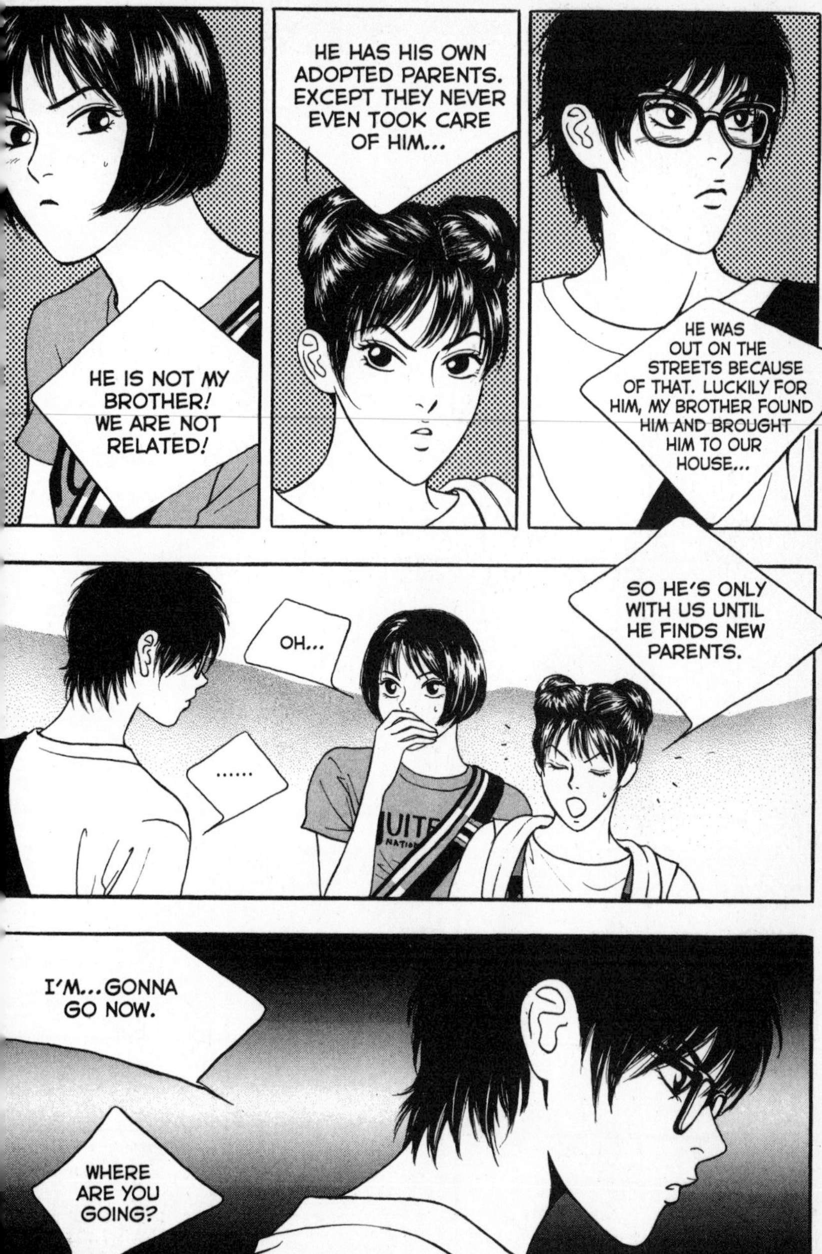

HE IS NOT MY BROTHER! WE ARE NOT RELATED!
HE HAS HIS OWN ADOPTED PARENTS. EXCEPT THEY NEVER EVEN TOOK CARE OF HIM...
HE WAS OUT ON THE STREETS BECAUSE OF THAT. LUCKILY FOR HIM, MY BROTHER FOUND HIM AND BROUGHT HIM TO OUR HOUSE...
OH...
......
SO HE'S ONLY WITH US UNTIL HE FINDS NEW PARENTS.
I'M...GONNA GO NOW.
WHERE ARE YOU GOING?

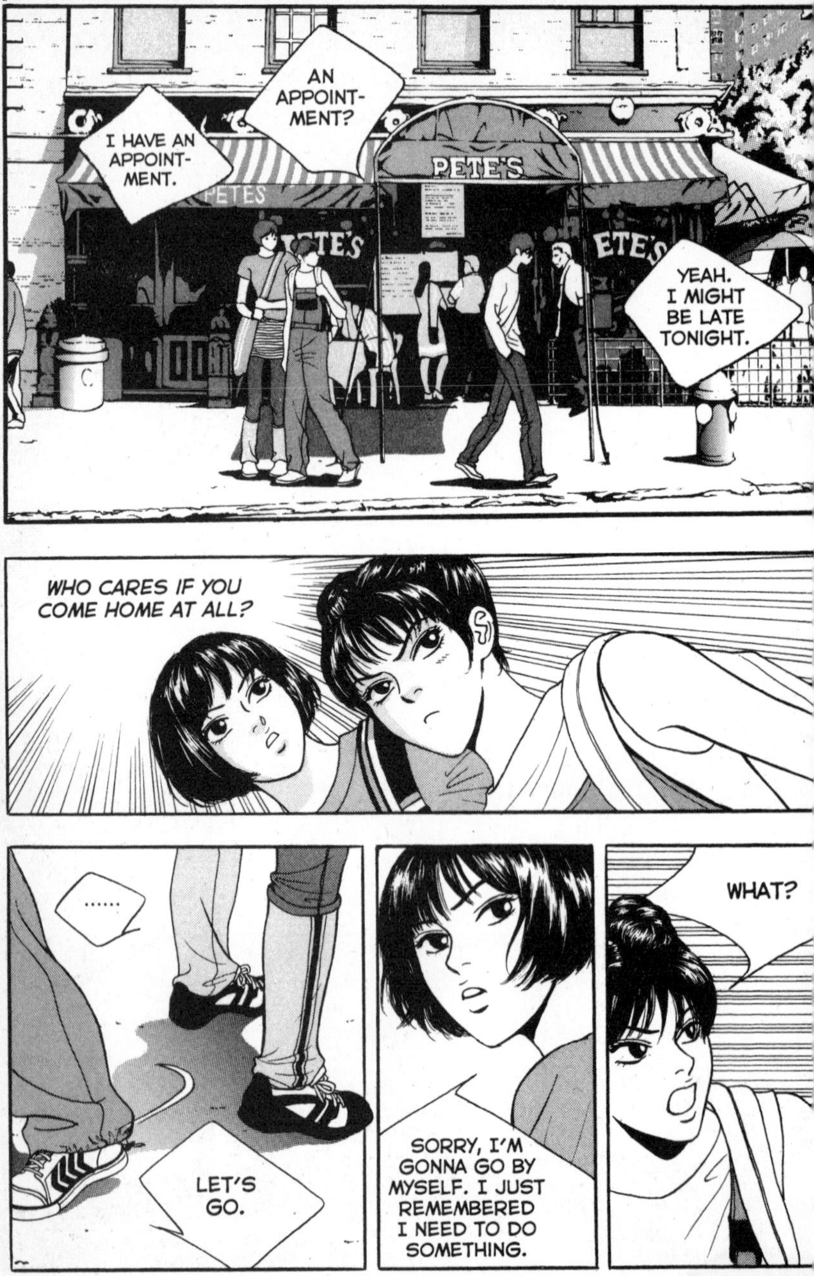
I HAVE AN APPOINT-MENT.
AN APPOINT-MENT?
PETE'S
PETES
PETE'S
ETE'S
YEAH. I MIGHT BE LATE TONIGHT.
WHO CARES IF YOU COME HOME AT ALL?
......
LET'S GO.
SORRY, I'M GONNA GO BY MYSELF. I JUST REMEMBERED I NEED TO DO SOMETHING.
WHAT?

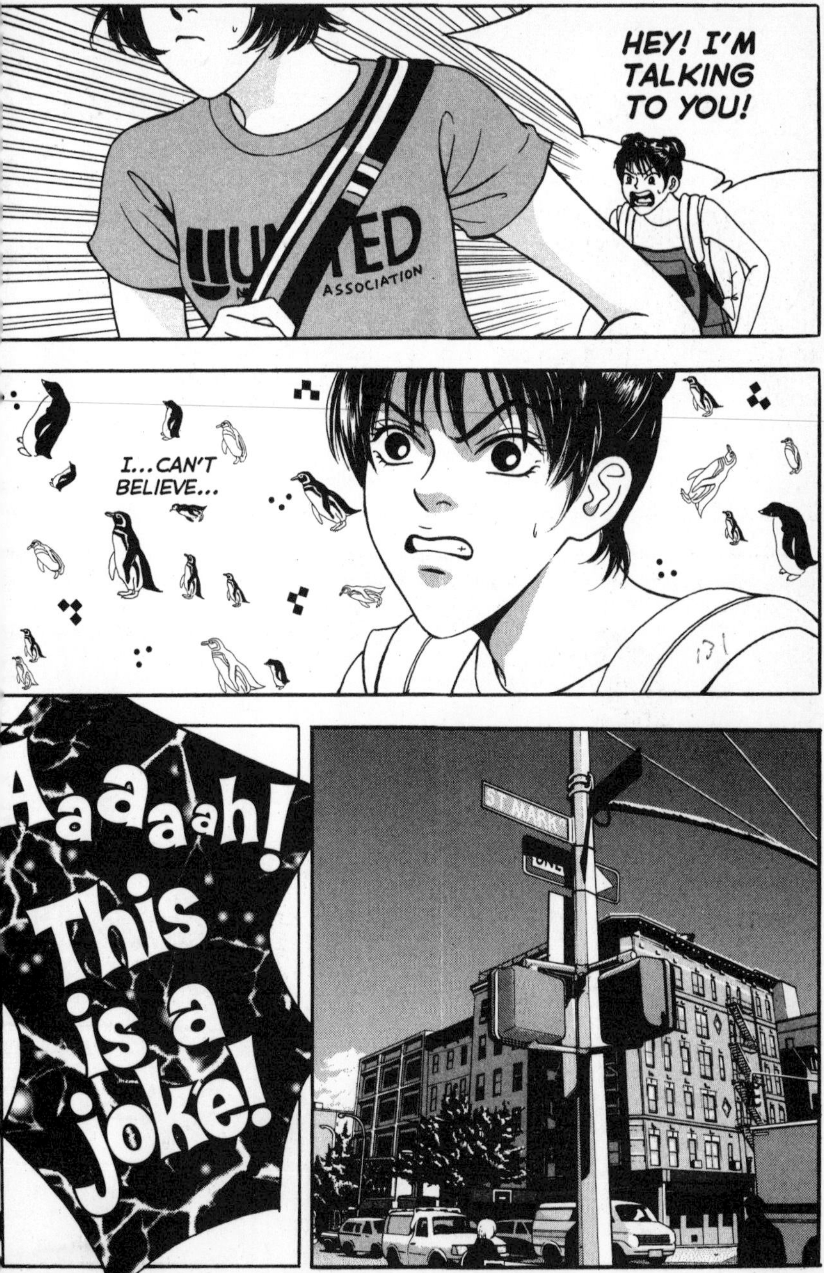
HEY! I'M TALKING TO YOU!
ASSOCIATION
I...CAN'T BELIEVE...
Aaaaah! This is a joke!

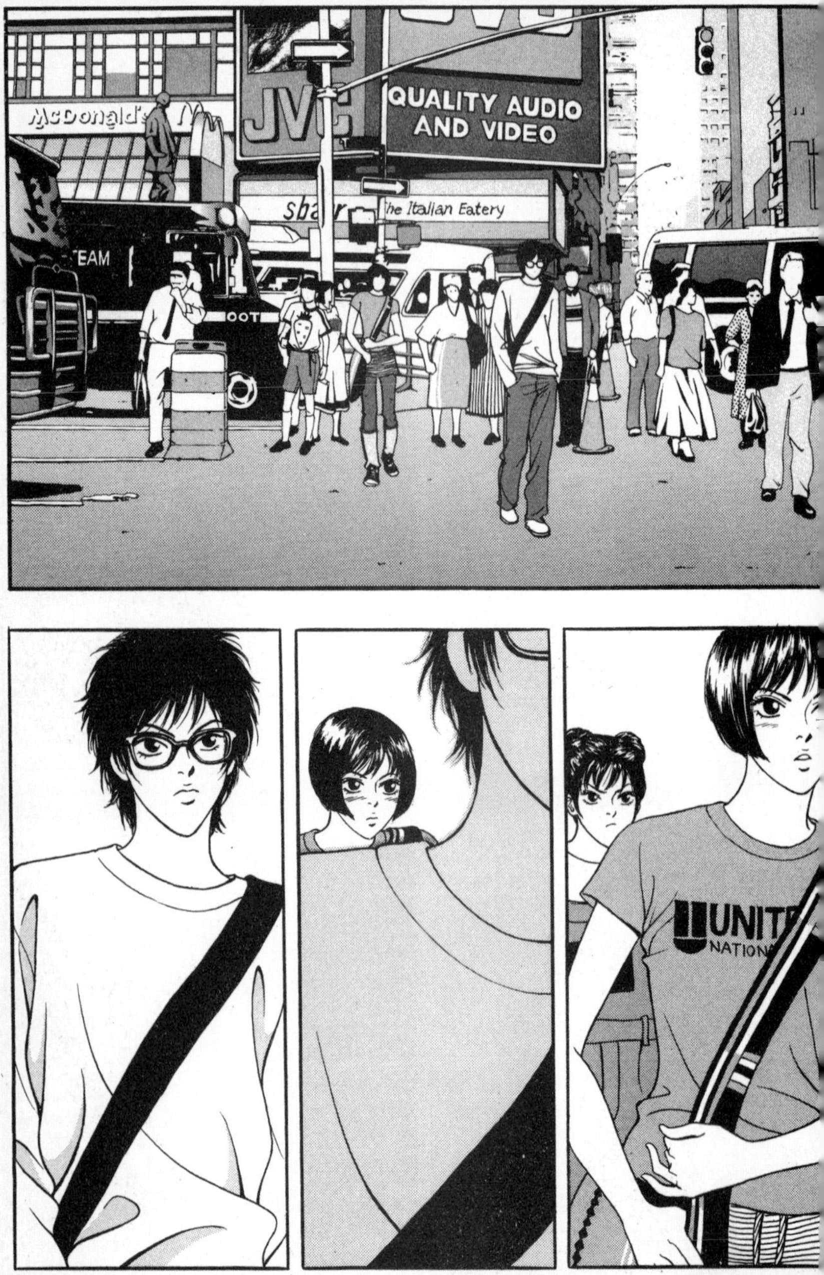
McDonald's
QUALITY AUDIO
AND VIDEO
The Italian Eatery

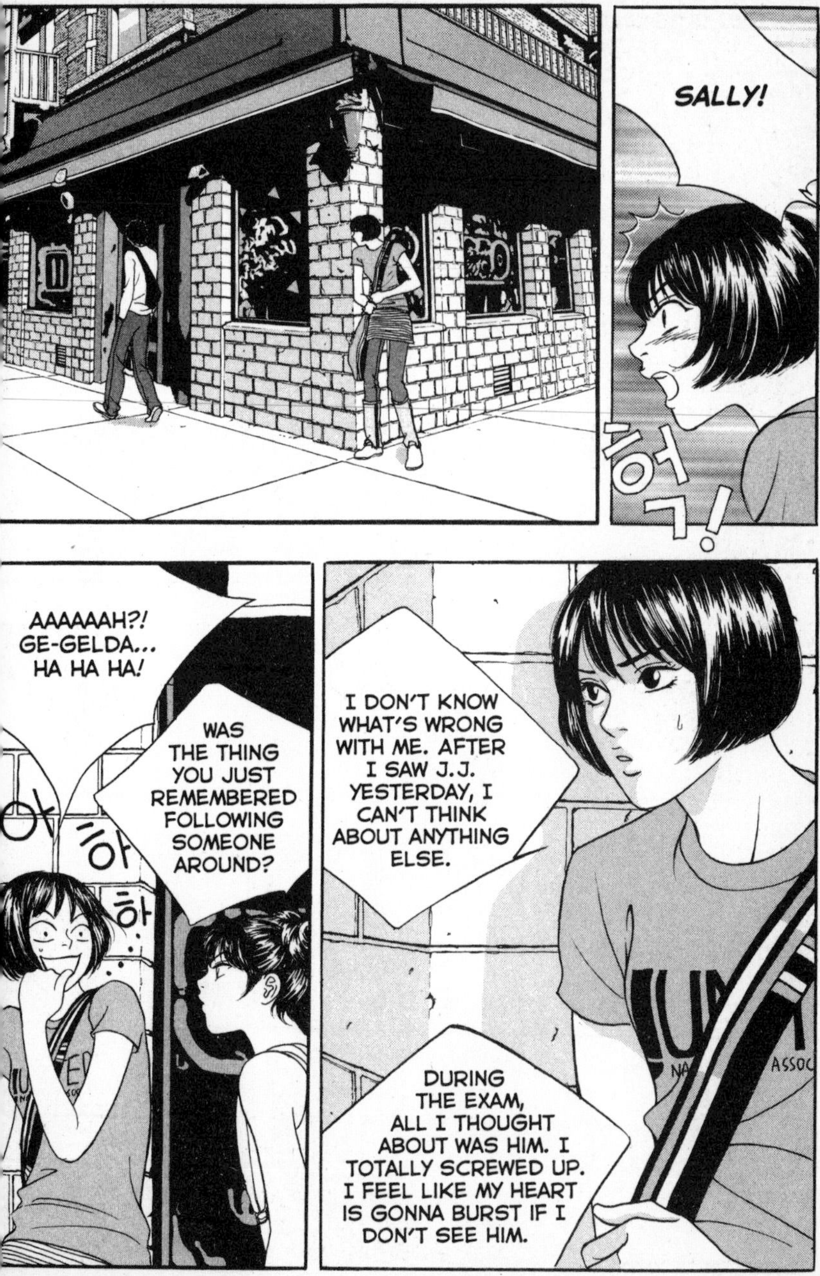
SALLY!
허억!
AAAAAAH?! GE-GELDA... HA HA HA!
아하하
WAS THE THING YOU JUST REMEMBERED FOLLOWING SOMEONE AROUND?
I DON'T KNOW WHAT'S WRONG WITH ME. AFTER I SAW J.J. YESTERDAY, I CAN'T THINK ABOUT ANYTHING ELSE.
DURING THE EXAM, ALL I THOUGHT ABOUT WAS HIM. I TOTALLY SCREWED UP. I FEEL LIKE MY HEART IS GONNA BURST IF I DON'T SEE HIM.

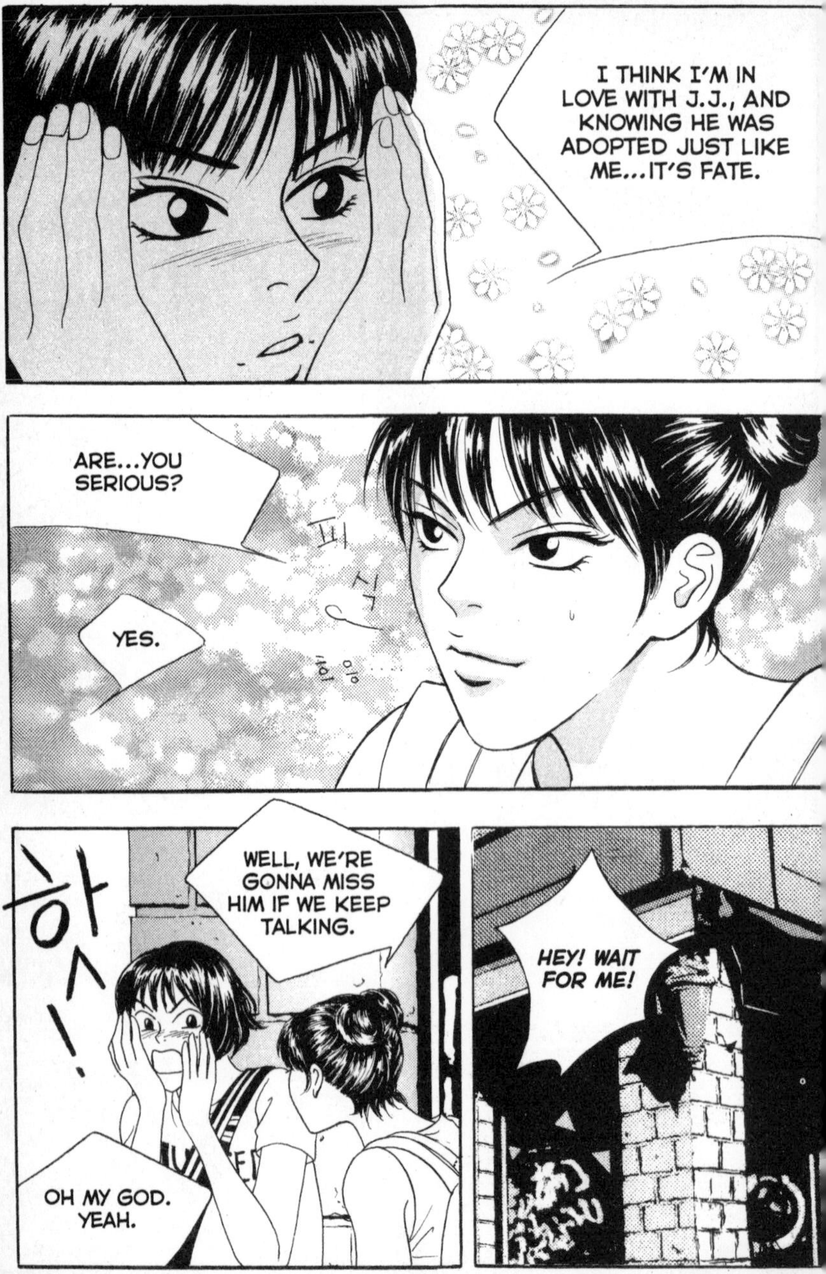
I THINK I'M IN LOVE WITH J.J., AND KNOWING HE WAS ADOPTED JUST LIKE ME...IT'S FATE.
ARE...YOU SERIOUS?
YES.
하
WELL, WE'RE GONNA MISS HIM IF WE KEEP TALKING.
OH MY GOD. YEAH.
HEY! WAIT FOR ME!

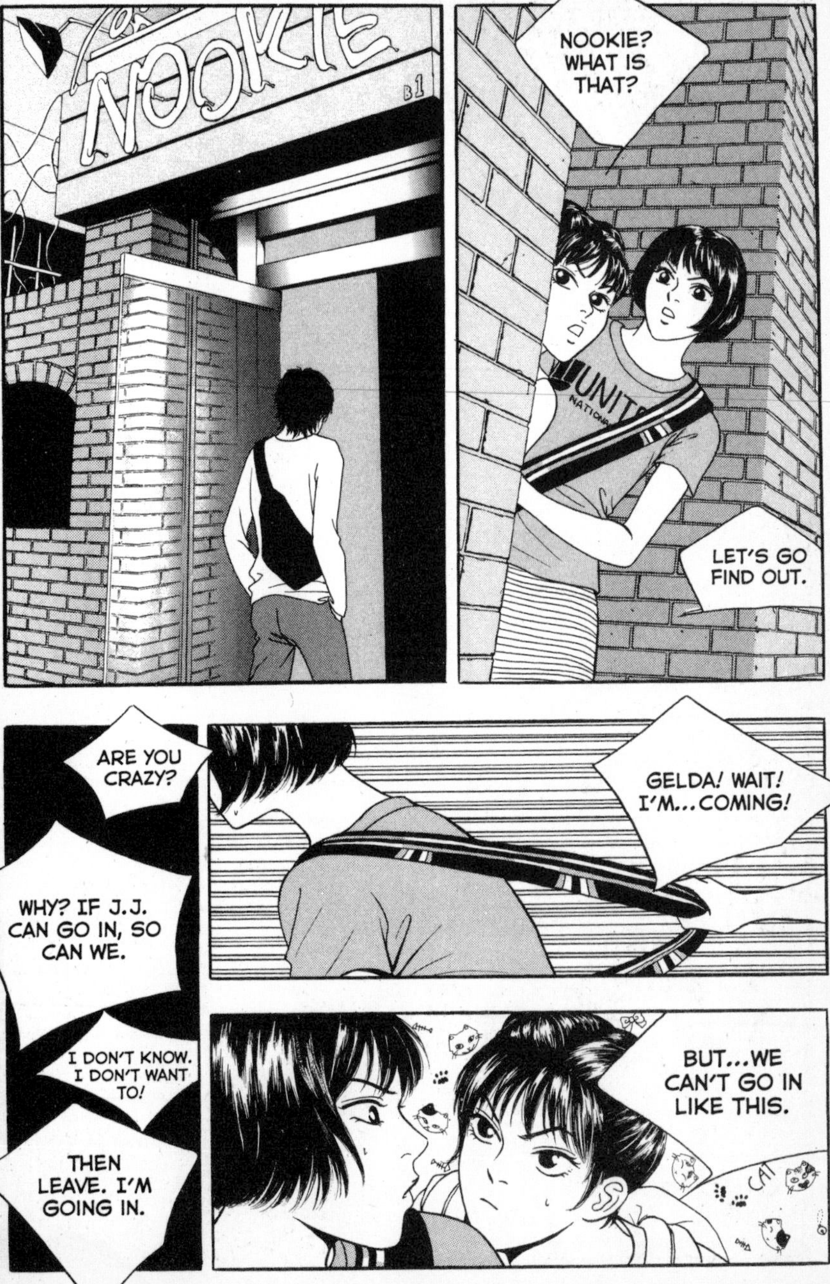
NOOKIE
B1
NOOKIE? WHAT IS THAT?
LET'S GO FIND OUT.
ARE YOU CRAZY?
WHY? IF J.J. CAN GO IN, SO CAN WE.
I DON'T KNOW. I DON'T WANT TO!
THEN LEAVE. I'M GOING IN.
GELDA! WAIT! I'M...COMING!
BUT...WE CAN'T GO IN LIKE THIS.
CAT

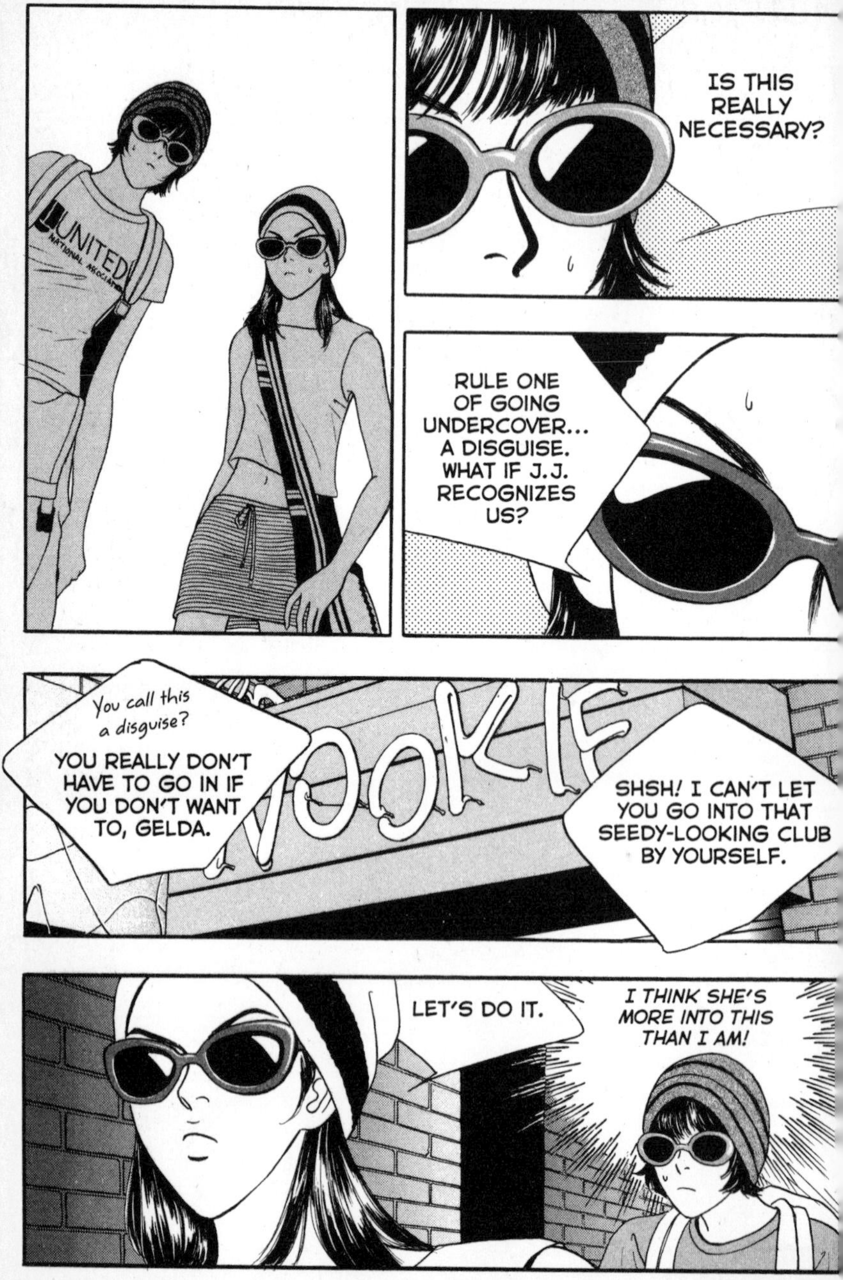
IS THIS REALLY NECESSARY?
RULE ONE OF GOING UNDERCOVER... A DISGUISE. WHAT IF J.J. RECOGNIZES US?
You call this a disguise?
YOU REALLY DON'T HAVE TO GO IN IF YOU DON'T WANT TO, GELDA.
SHSH! I CAN'T LET YOU GO INTO THAT SEEDY-LOOKING CLUB BY YOURSELF.
LET'S DO IT.
I THINK SHE'S MORE INTO THIS THAN I AM!

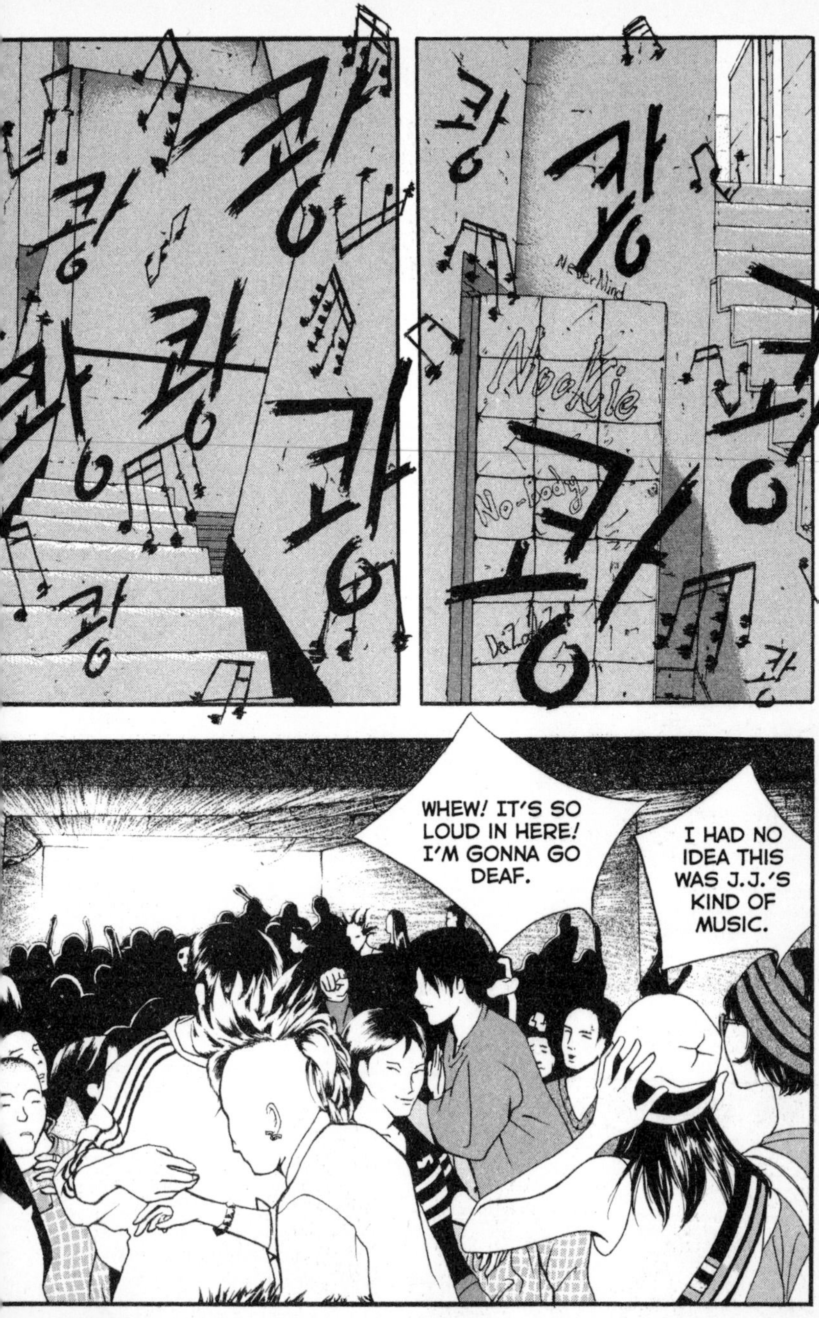
쾅
쾅
쾅
쾅
쾅
쾅
쾅
NeverMind
Nookie
No-body
쾅
쾅
쾅
WHEW! IT'S SO LOUD IN HERE! I'M GONNA GO DEAF.
I HAD NO IDEA THIS WAS J.J.'S KIND OF MUSIC.

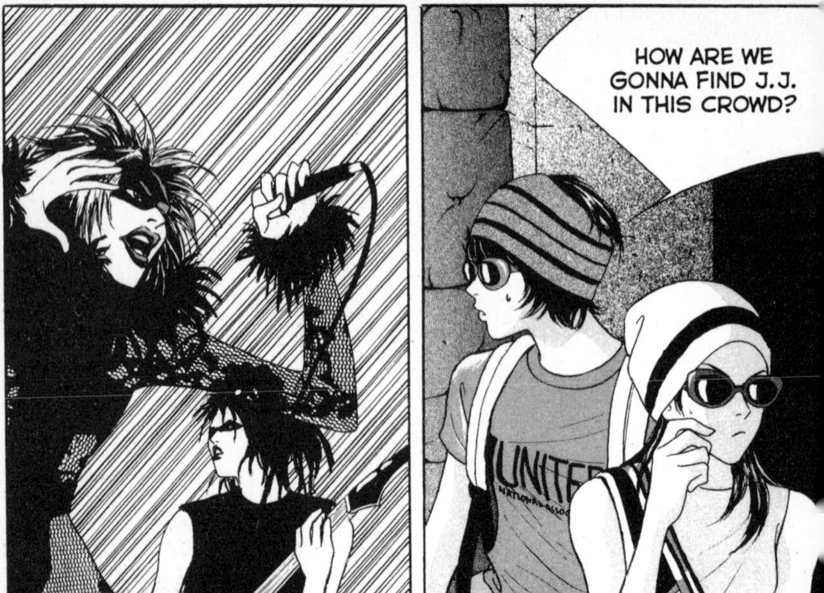
HOW ARE WE GONNA FIND J.J. IN THIS CROWD?

*A Marilyn Manson cover band... "Charlie Monroe"

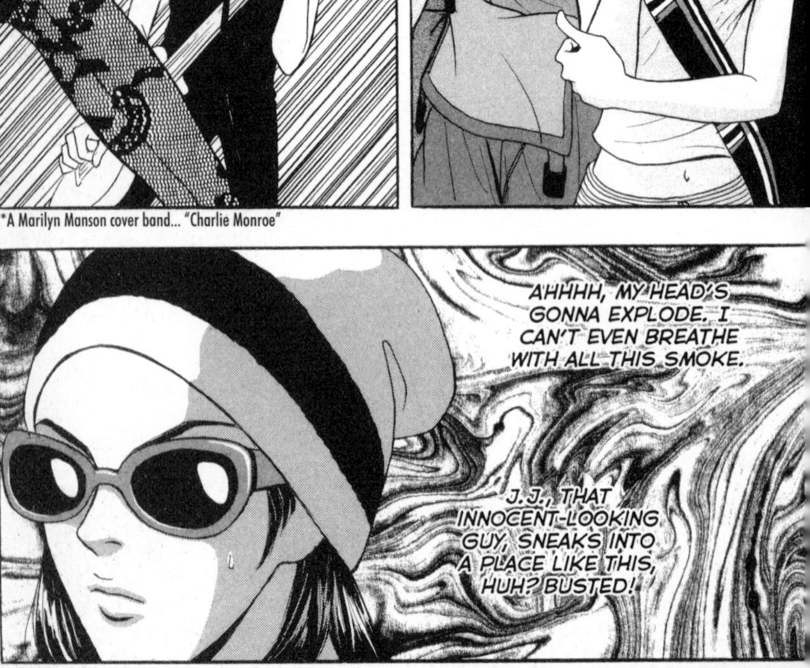
AHHHH, MY HEAD'S GONNA EXPLODE. I CAN'T EVEN BREATHE WITH ALL THIS SMOKE.
J.J., THAT INNOCENT-LOOKING GUY, SNEAKS INTO A PLACE LIKE THIS, HUH? BUSTED!

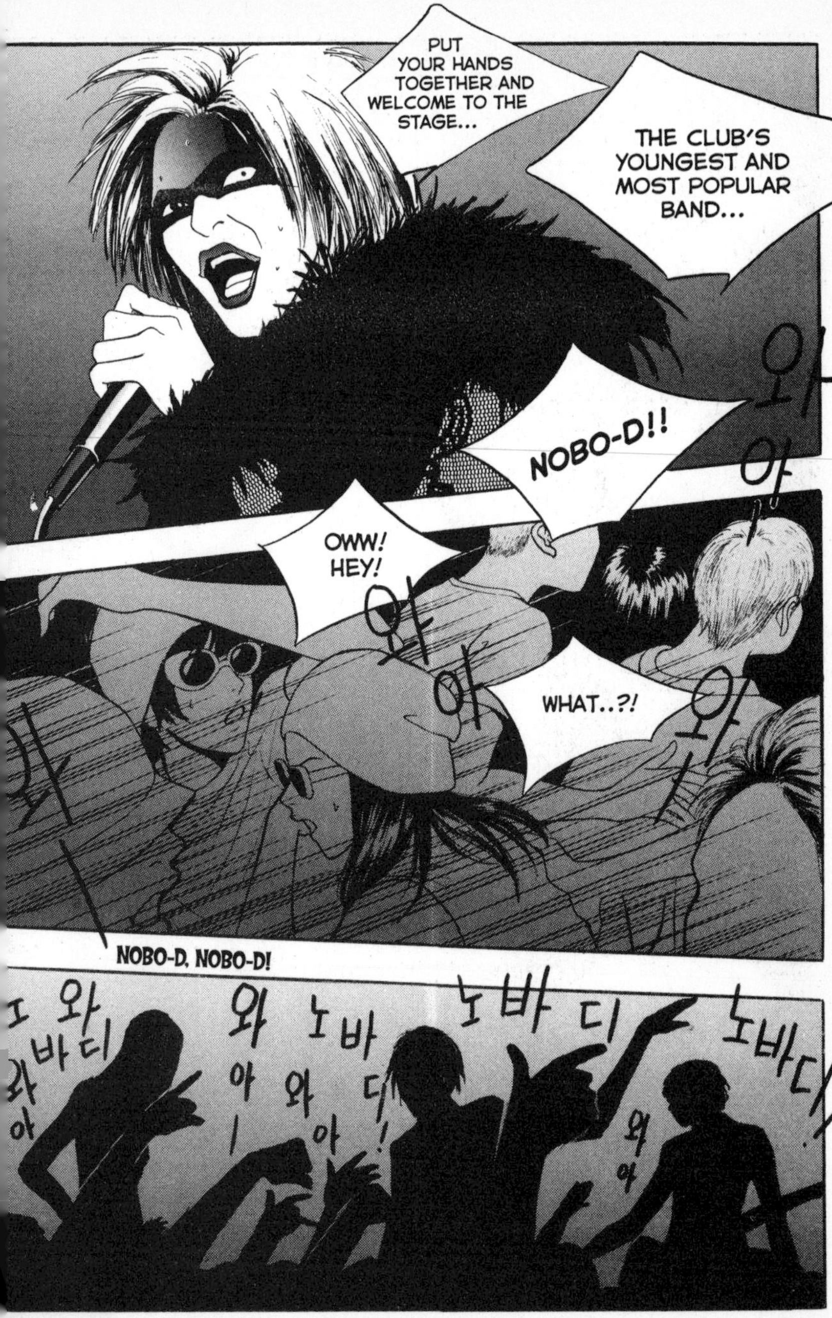
PUT YOUR HANDS TOGETHER AND WELCOME TO THE STAGE...
THE CLUB'S YOUNGEST AND MOST POPULAR BAND...
NOBO-D!!
와아
OWW! HEY!
와아
WHAT..?!
와아
와아
NOBO-D, NOBO-D!
와아 노바디
노바디
노바디!
와아

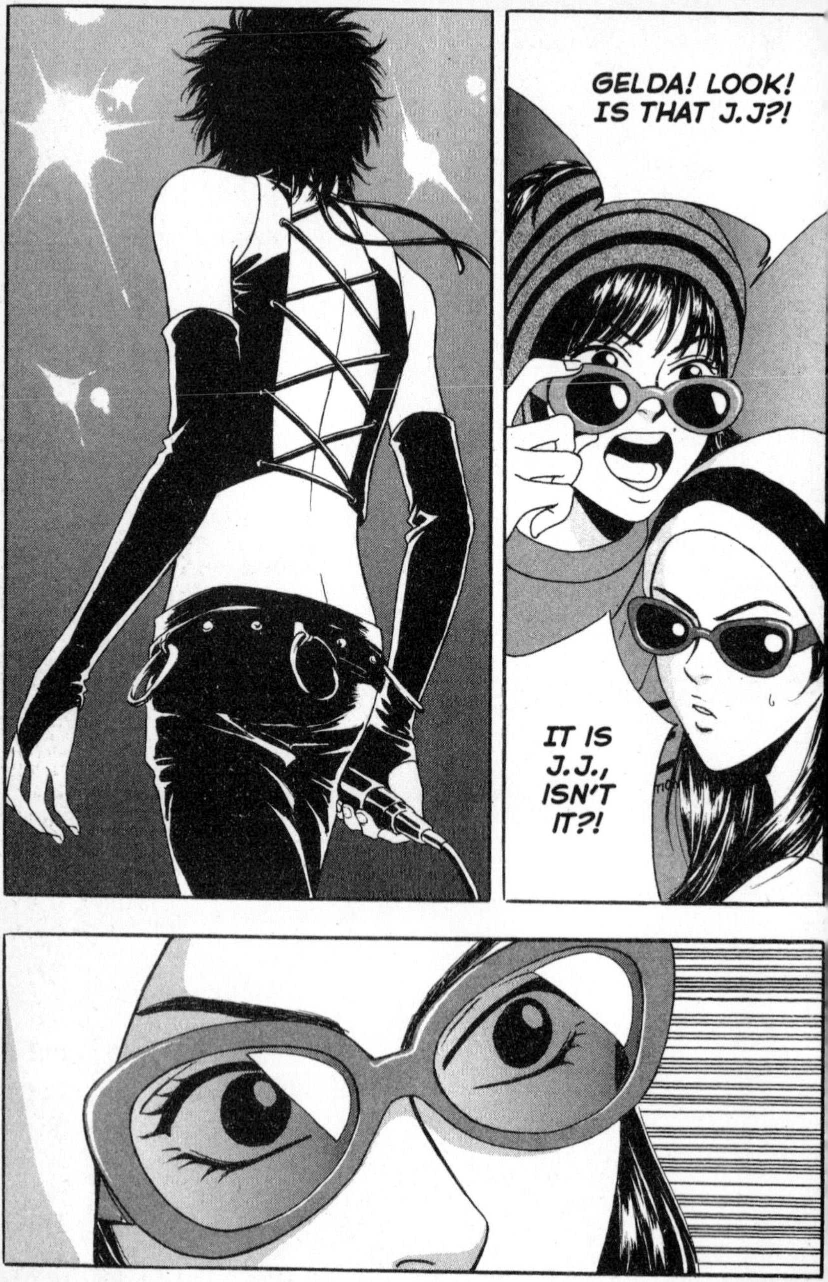
GELDA! LOOK! IS THAT J.J?!
IT IS J.J., ISN'T IT?!

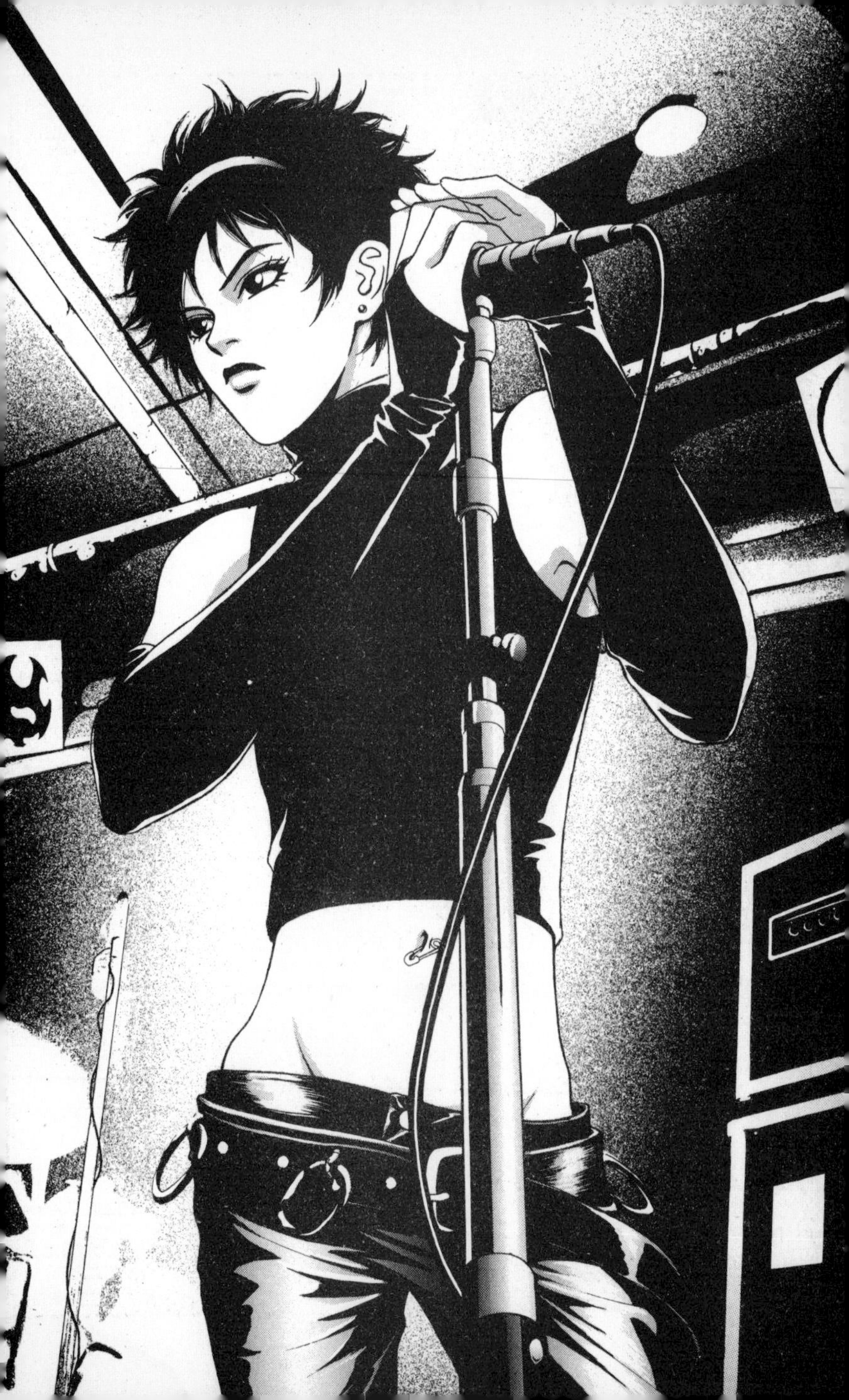

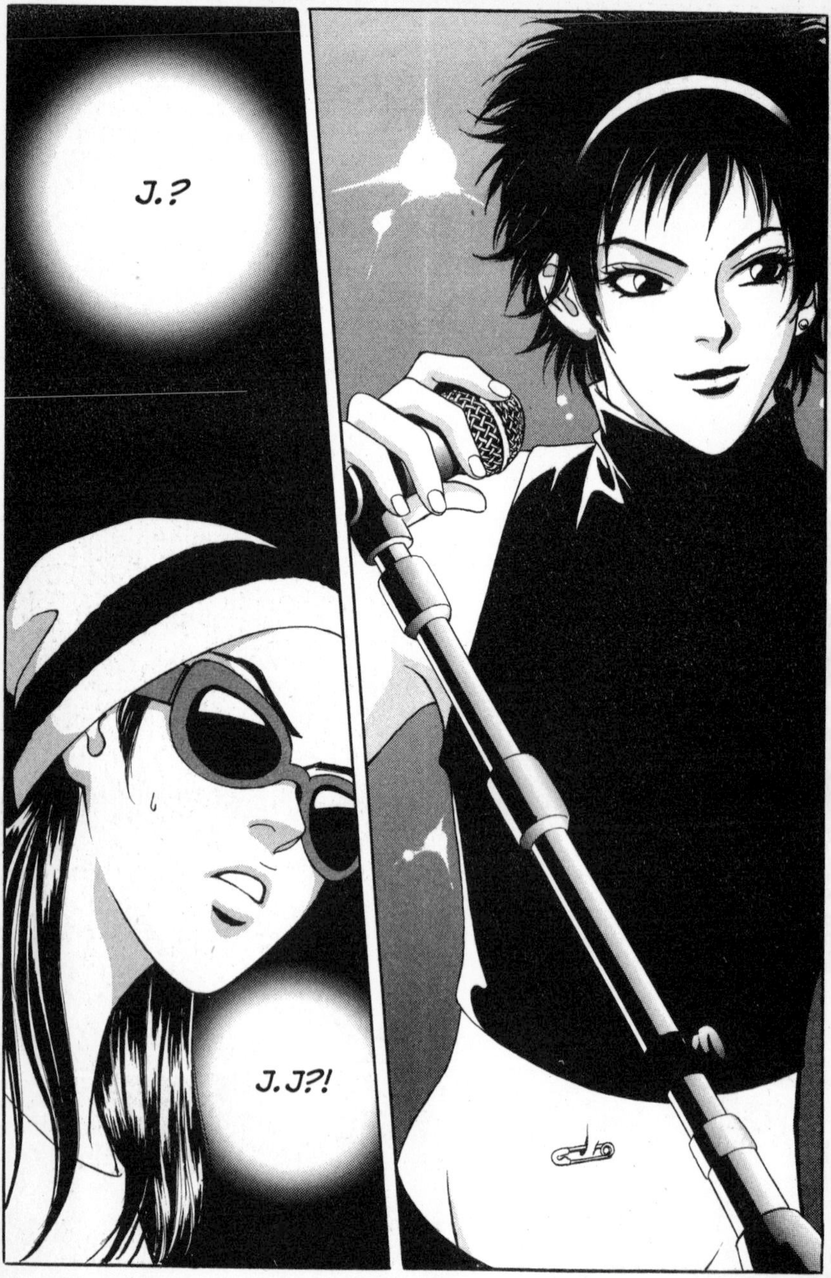
J.?
J.J?!

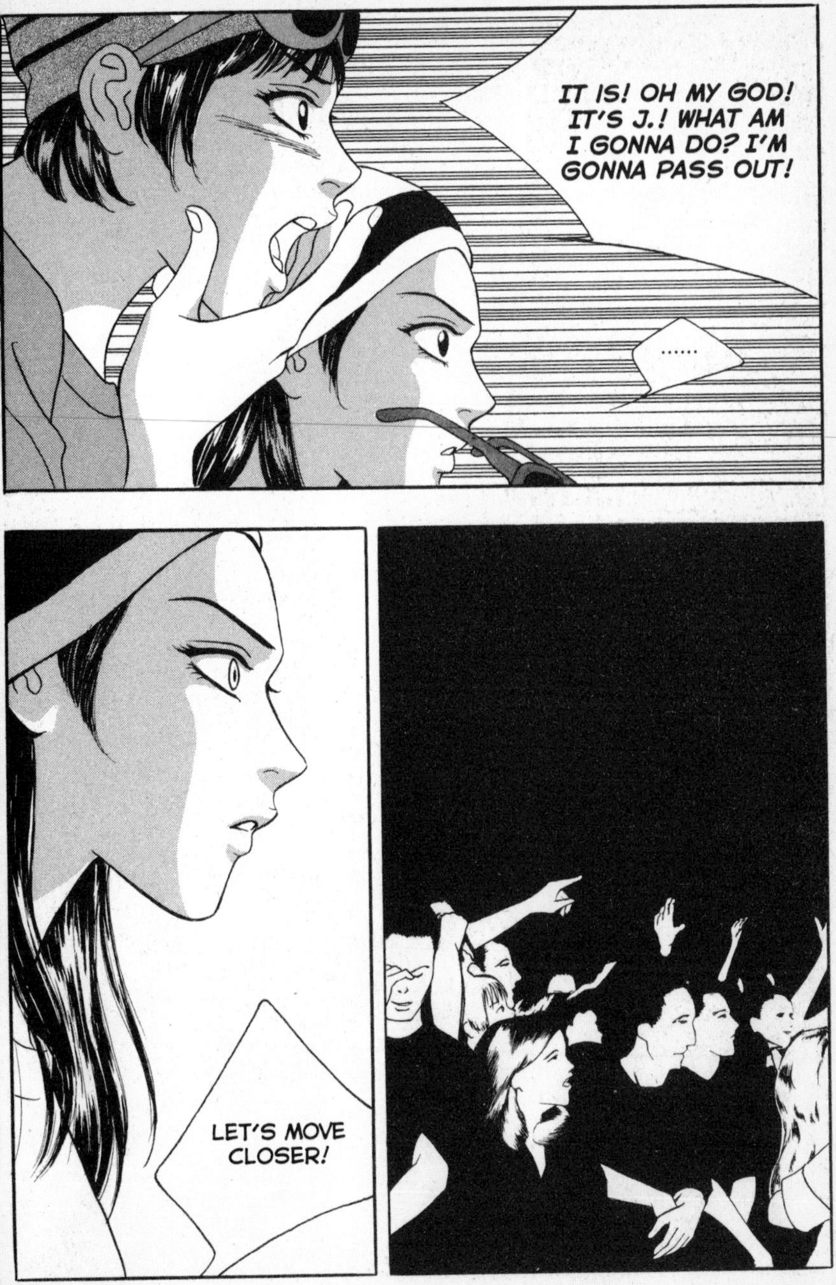
IT IS! OH MY GOD! IT'S J.! WHAT AM I GONNA DO? I'M GONNA PASS OUT!
......
LET'S MOVE CLOSER!

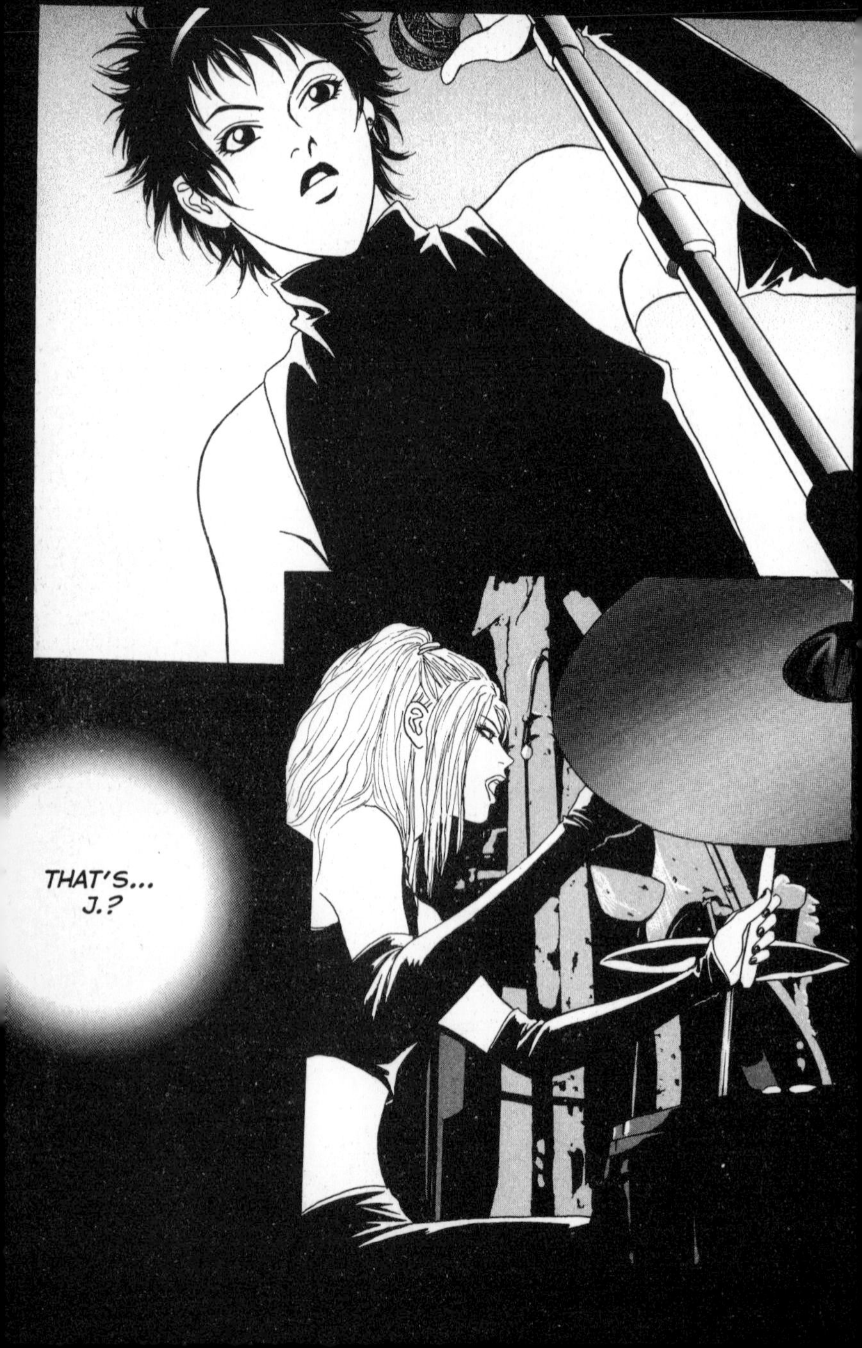
THAT'S... J.?

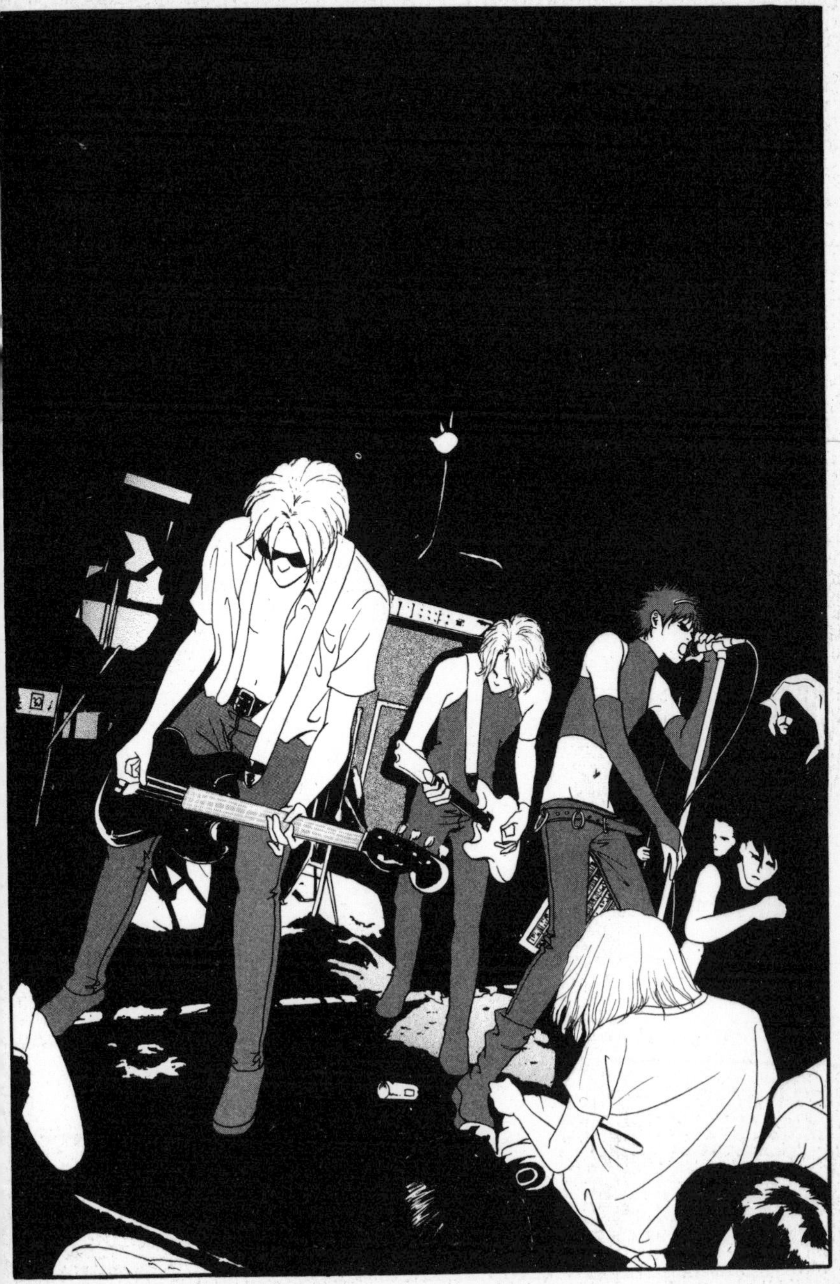

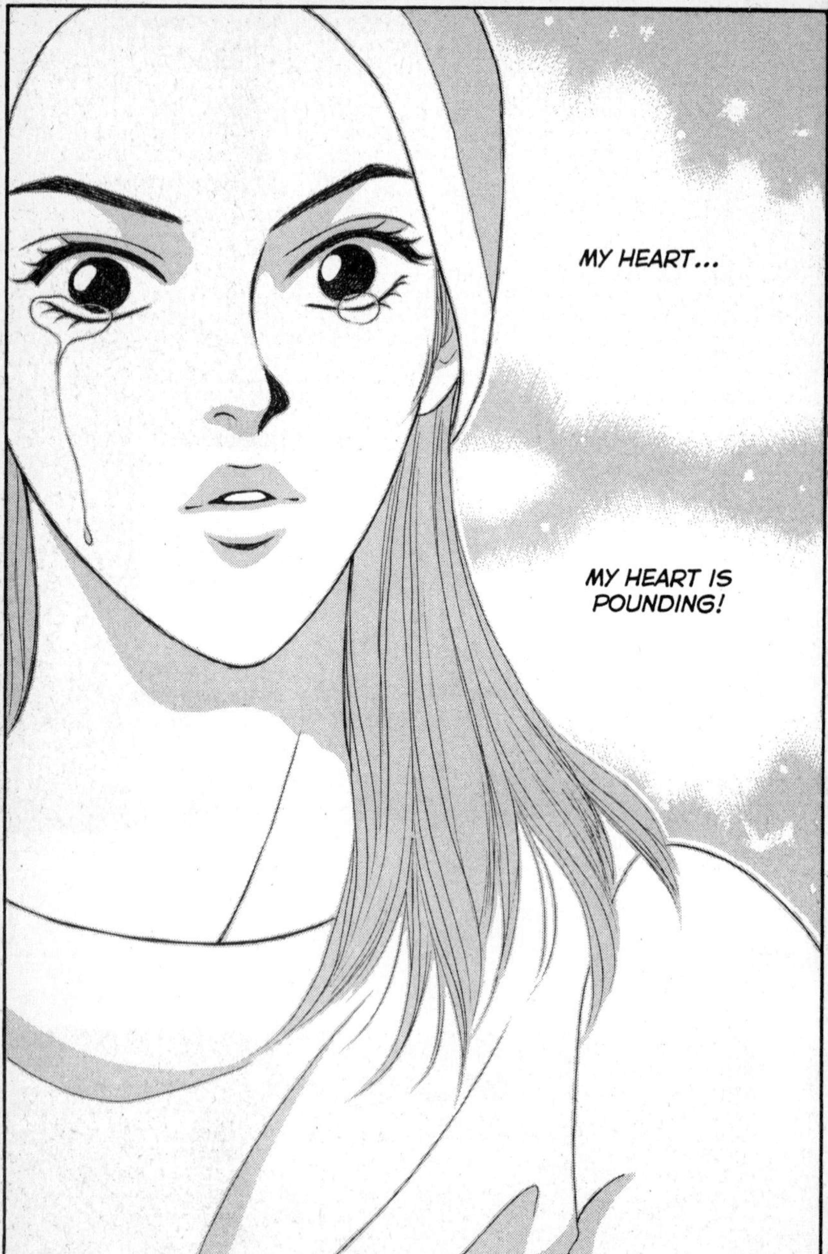
MY HEART...
MY HEART IS POUNDING!

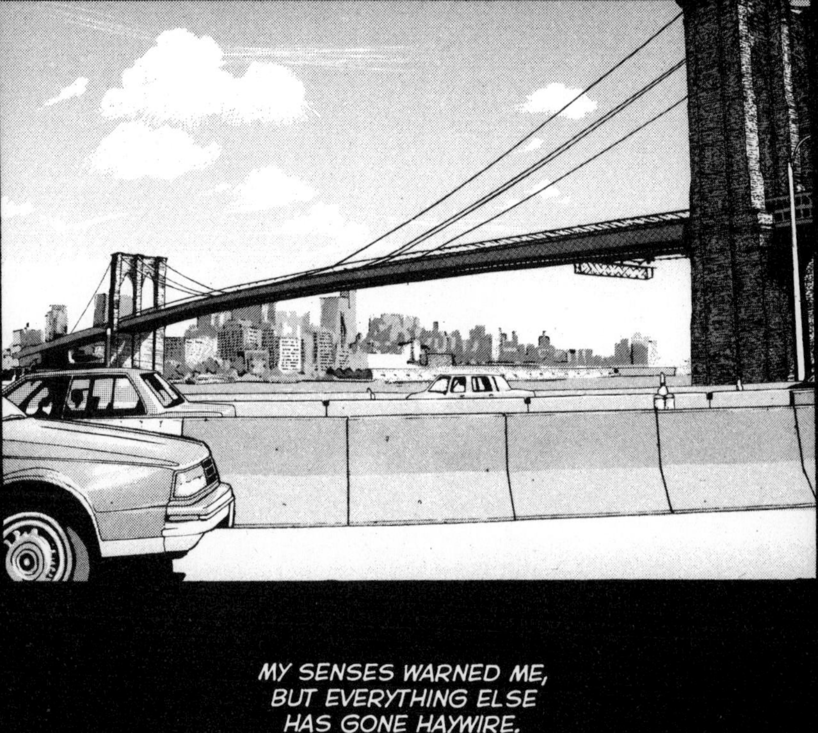
MY SENSES WARNED ME, BUT EVERYTHING ELSE HAS GONE HAYWIRE.

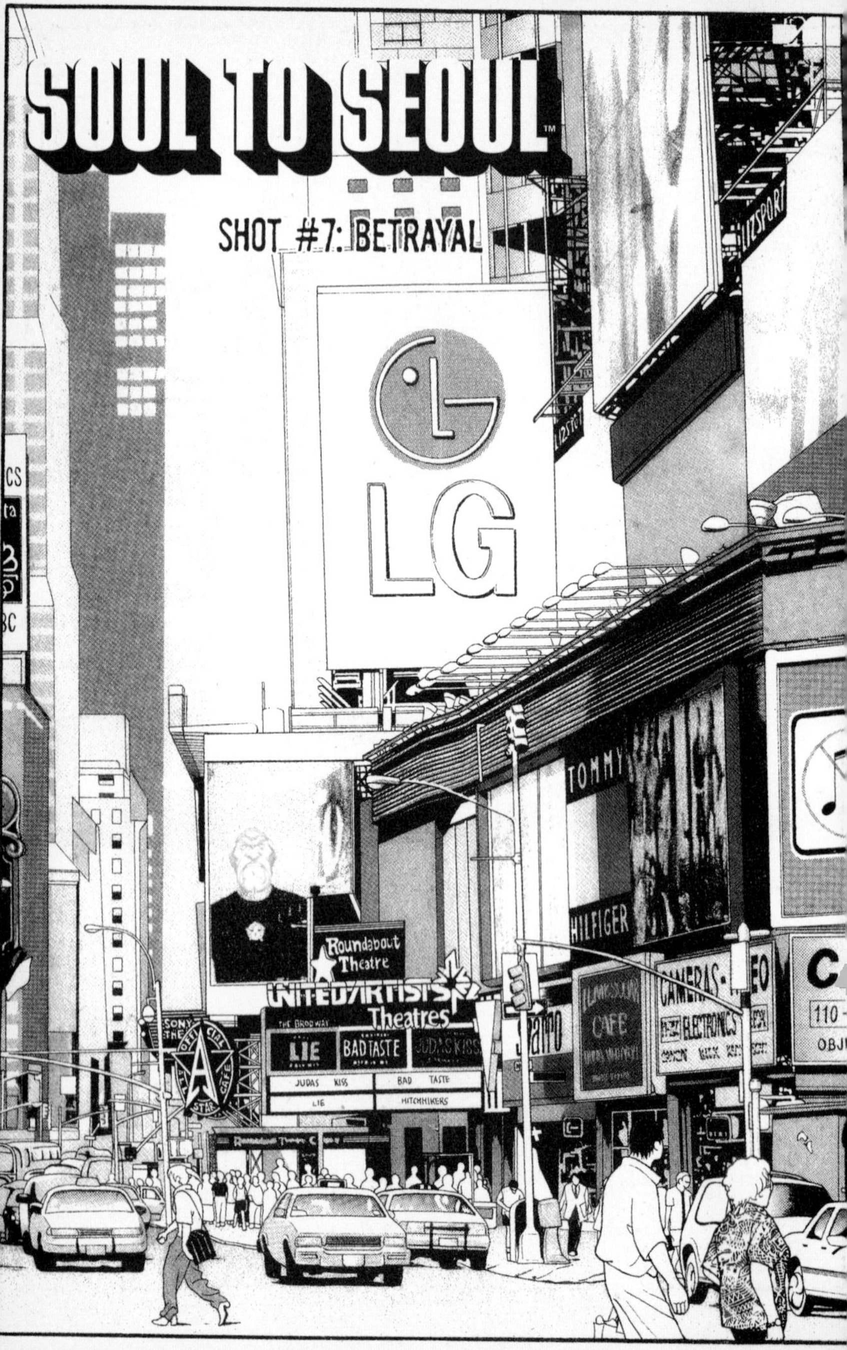
SOUL TO SEOUL™
SHOT #7: BETRAYAL
LIZSPORT
LG
TOMMY
HILFIGER
Roundabout Theatre
UNITED ARTISTS Theatres
LIE
BAD TASTE
JUDAS KISS
BAD TASTE
LIE
HITCHHIKERS
CAMERAS
ELECTRONICS

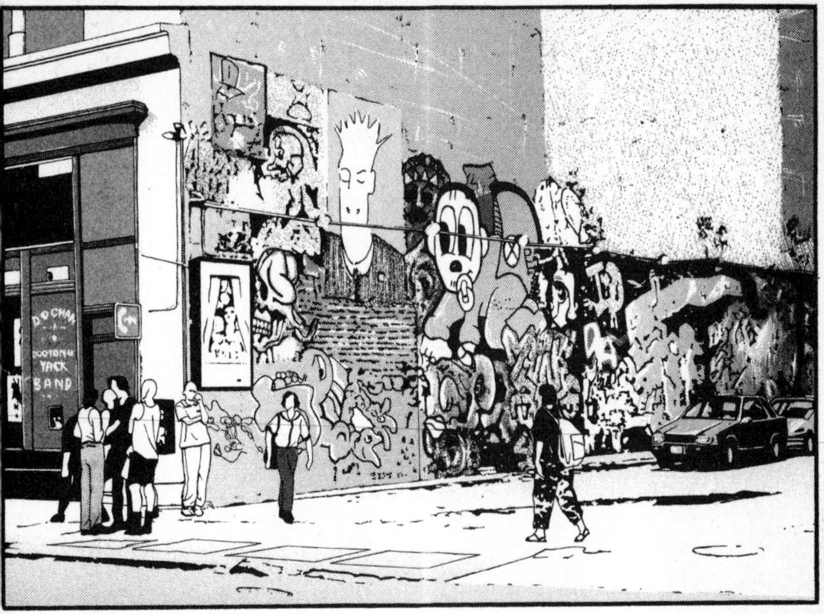

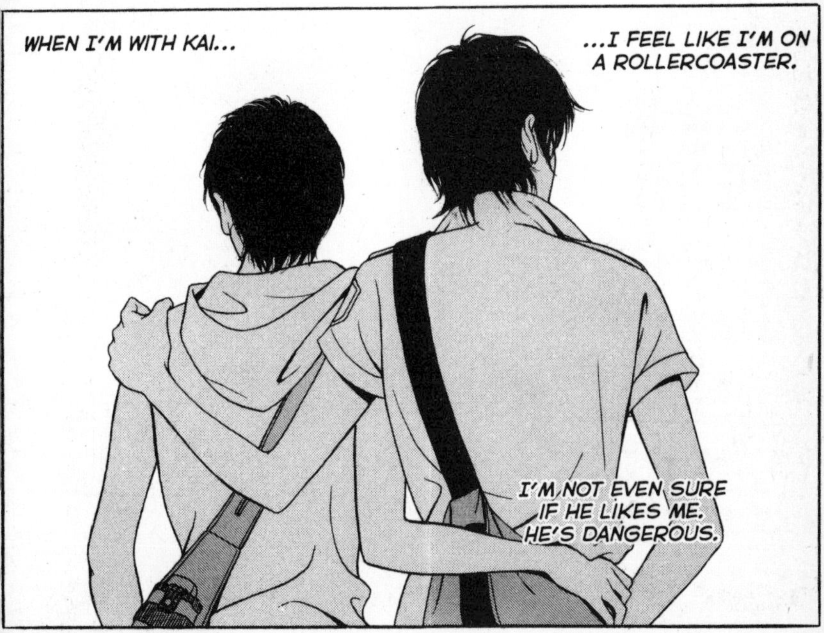
WHEN I'M WITH KAI...
...I FEEL LIKE I'M ON A ROLLERCOASTER.
I'M NOT EVEN SURE IF HE LIKES ME. HE'S DANGEROUS.

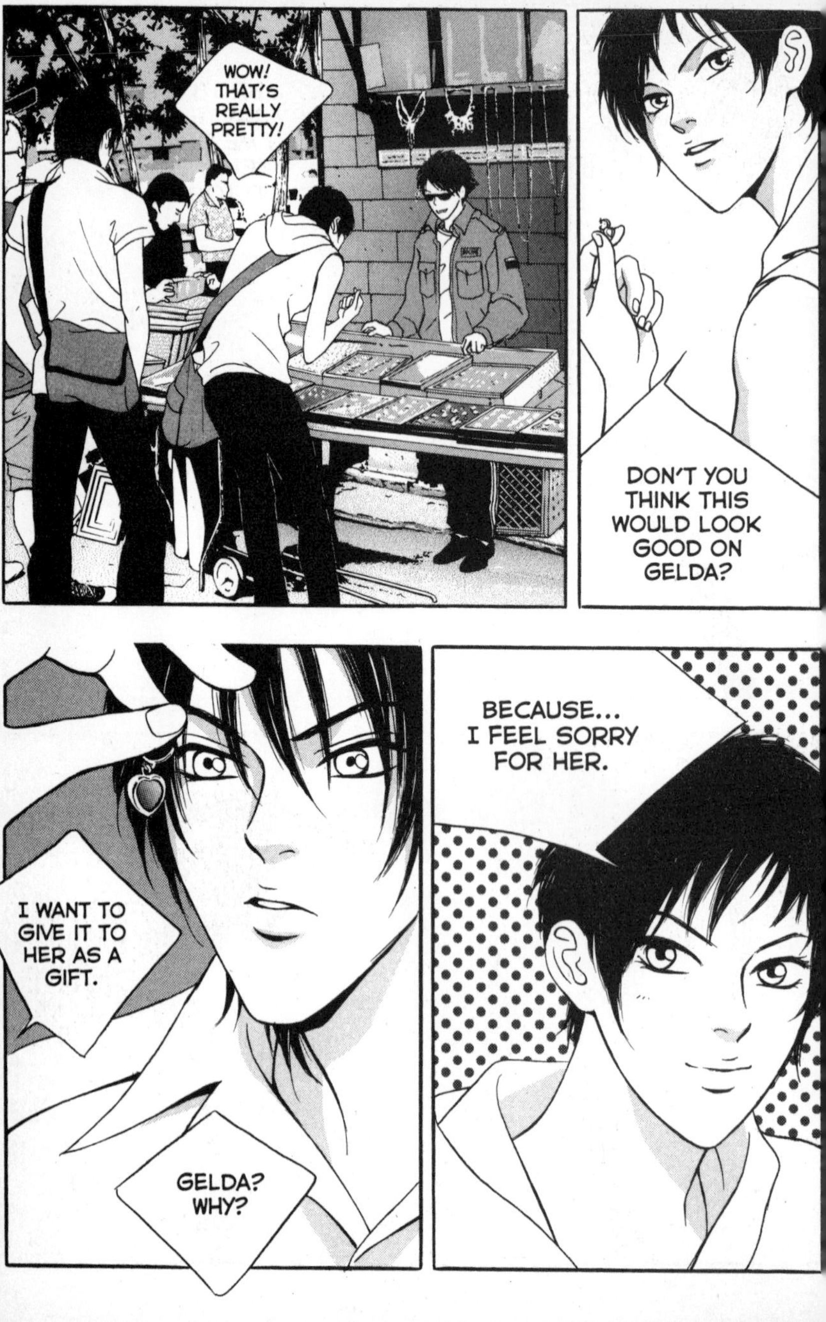
WOW! THAT'S REALLY PRETTY!
DON'T YOU THINK THIS WOULD LOOK GOOD ON GELDA?
I WANT TO GIVE IT TO HER AS A GIFT.
GELDA? WHY?
BECAUSE... I FEEL SORRY FOR HER.

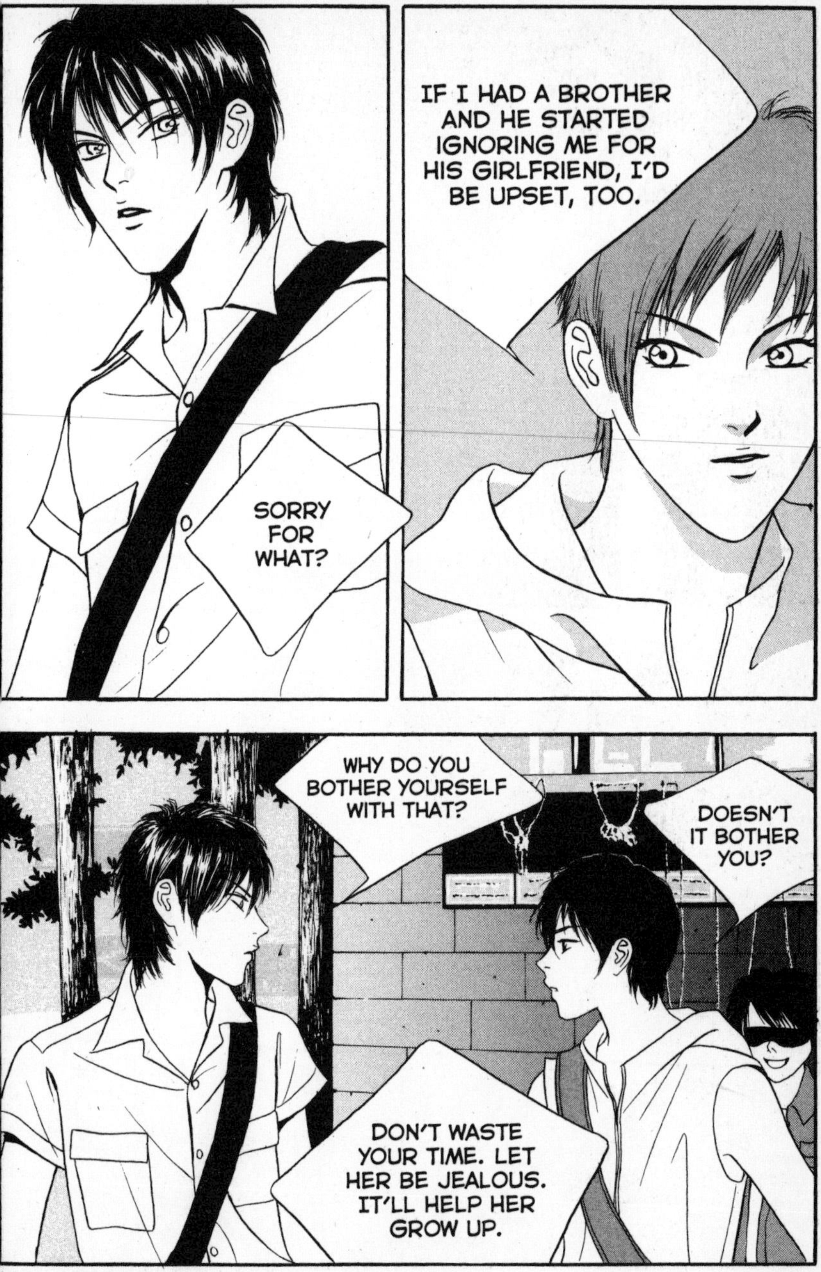
SORRY FOR WHAT?
IF I HAD A BROTHER AND HE STARTED IGNORING ME FOR HIS GIRLFRIEND, I'D BE UPSET, TOO.
WHY DO YOU BOTHER YOURSELF WITH THAT?
DOESN'T IT BOTHER YOU?
DON'T WASTE YOUR TIME. LET HER BE JEALOUS. IT'LL HELP HER GROW UP.

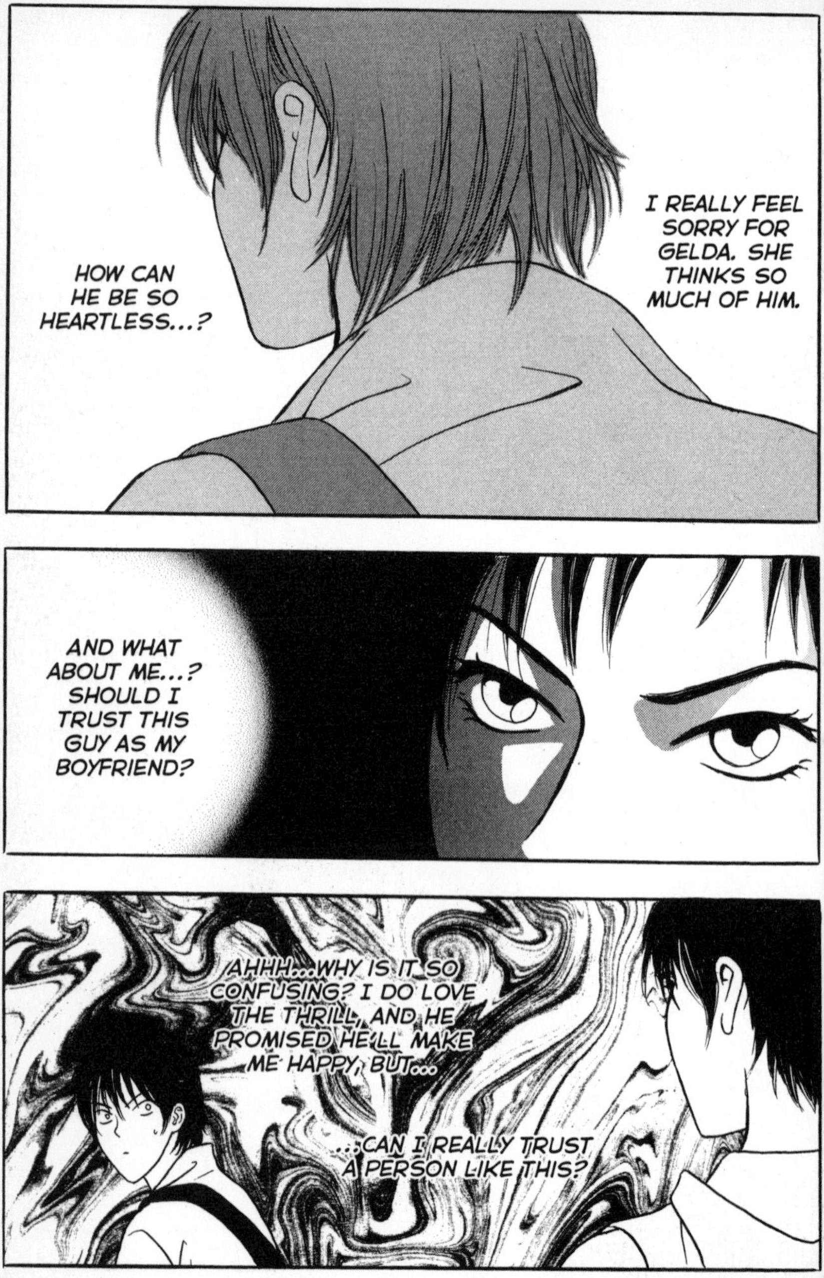
HOW CAN HE BE SO HEARTLESS...?
I REALLY FEEL SORRY FOR GELDA. SHE THINKS SO MUCH OF HIM.
AND WHAT ABOUT ME...? SHOULD I TRUST THIS GUY AS MY BOYFRIEND?
AHHH...WHY IS IT SO CONFUSING? I DO LOVE THE THRILL, AND HE PROMISED HE'LL MAKE ME HAPPY, BUT...
...CAN I REALLY TRUST A PERSON LIKE THIS?

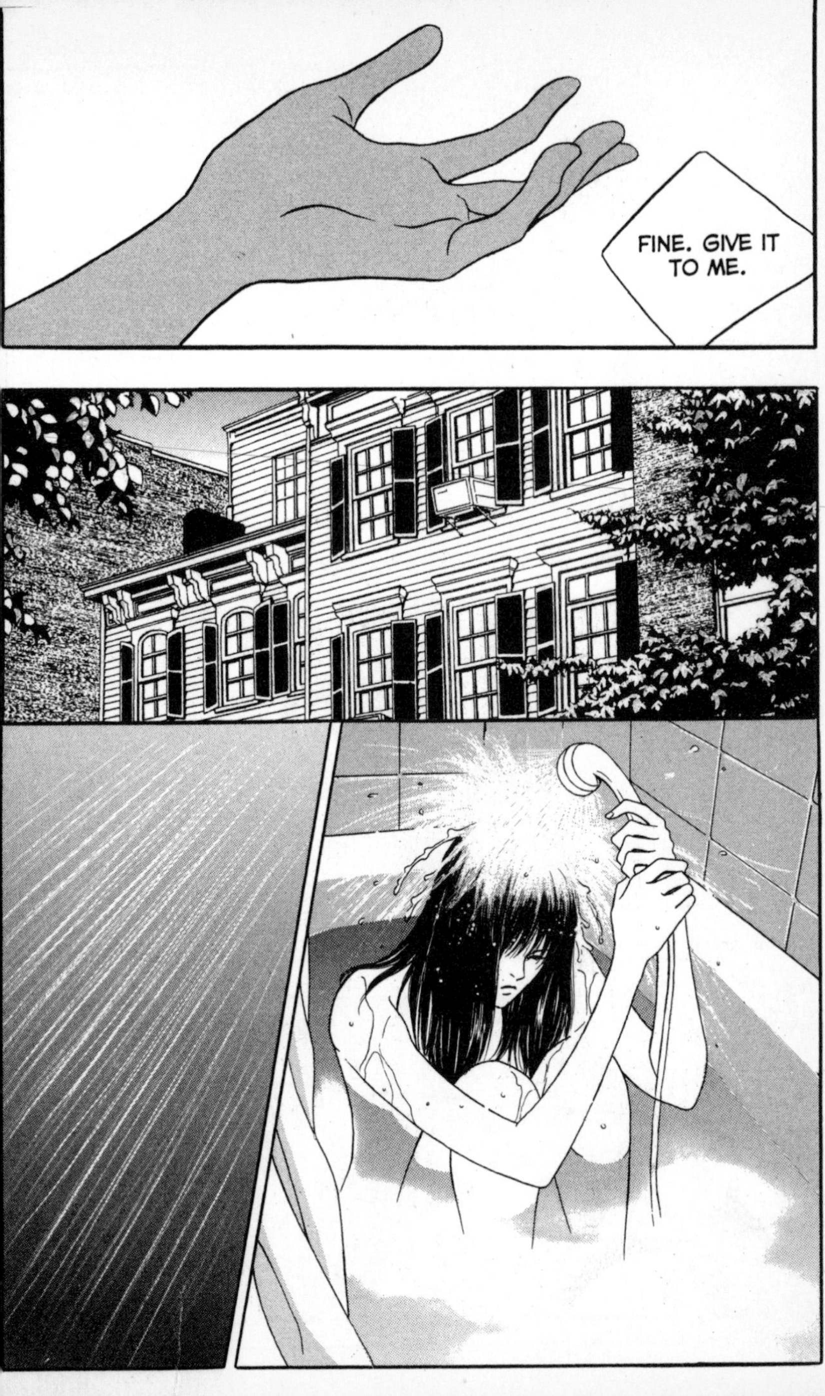
FINE. GIVE IT TO ME.

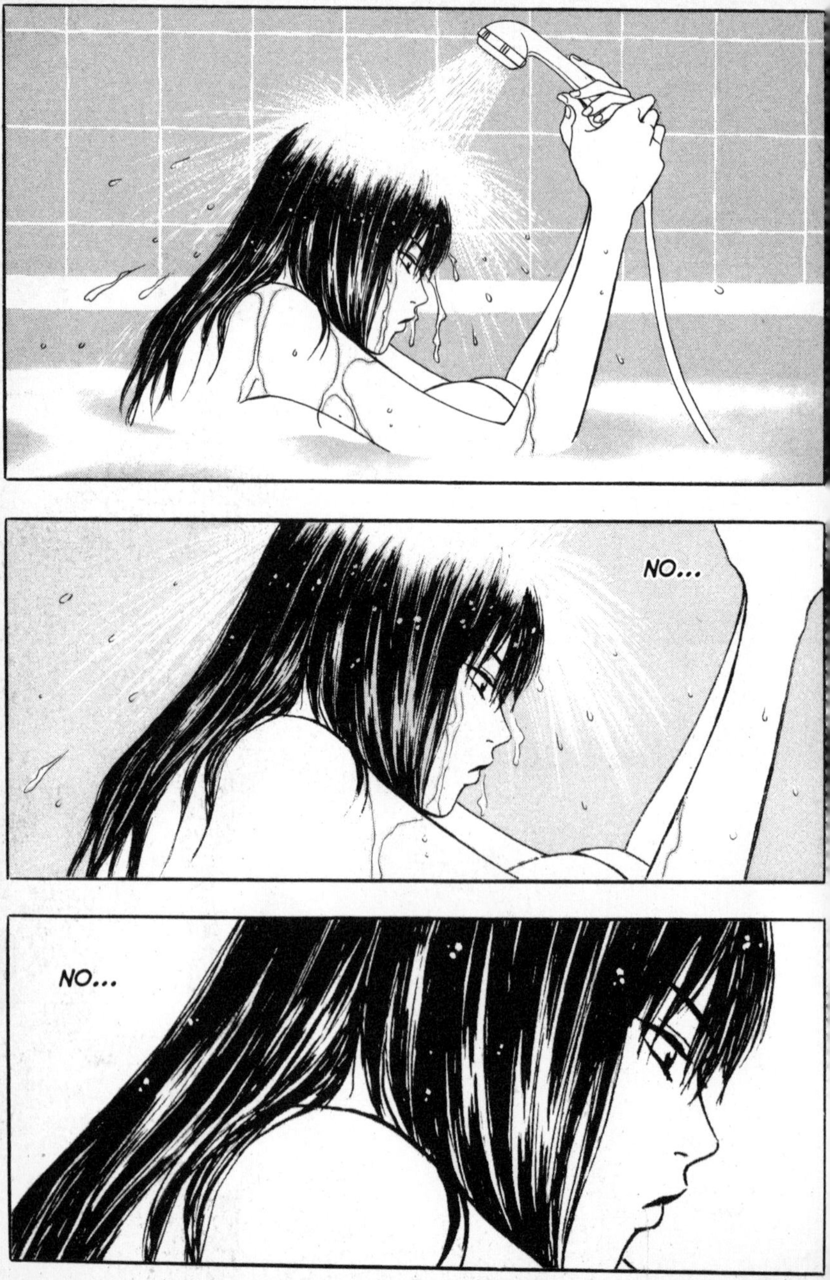
NO...
NO...

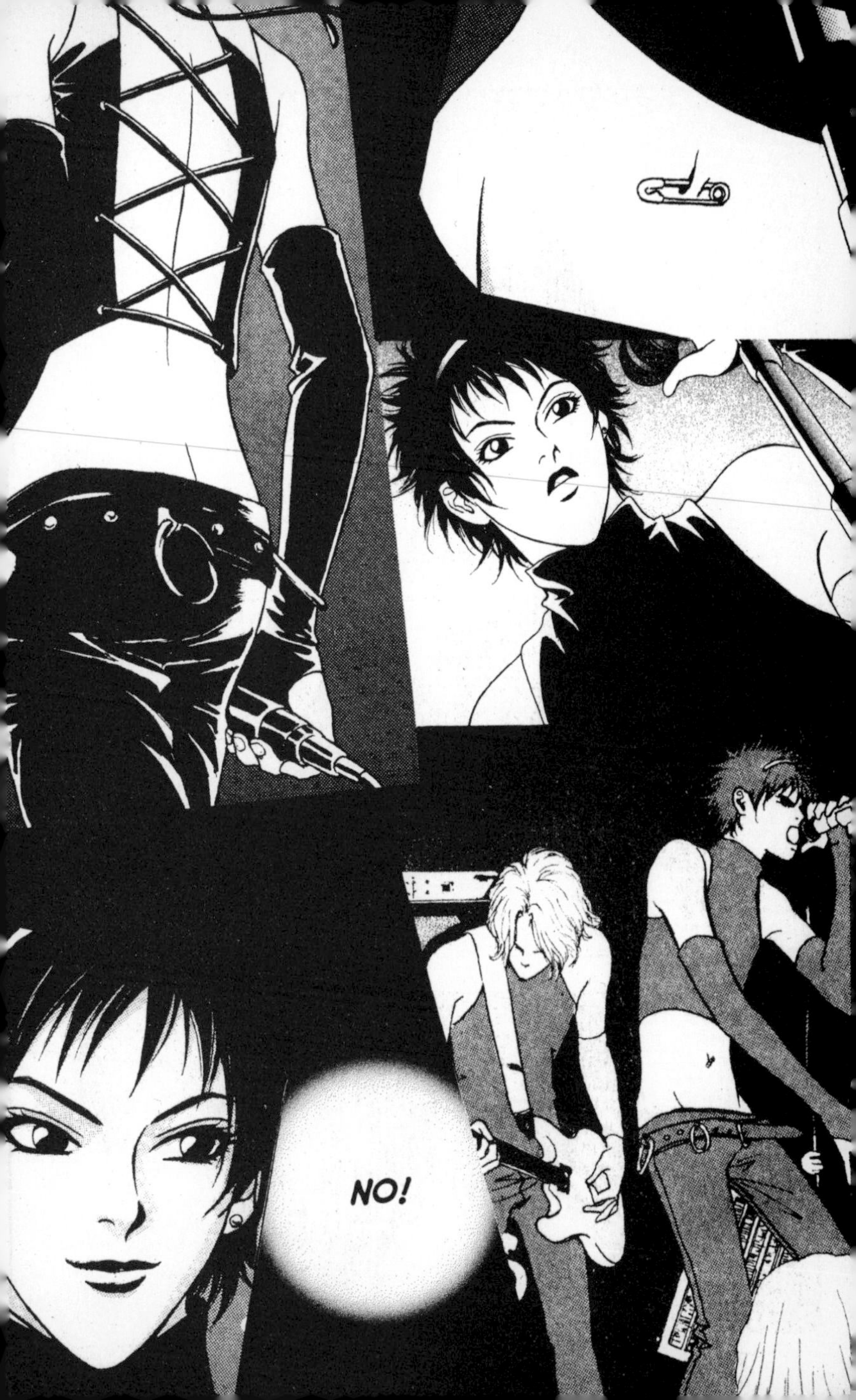
NO!

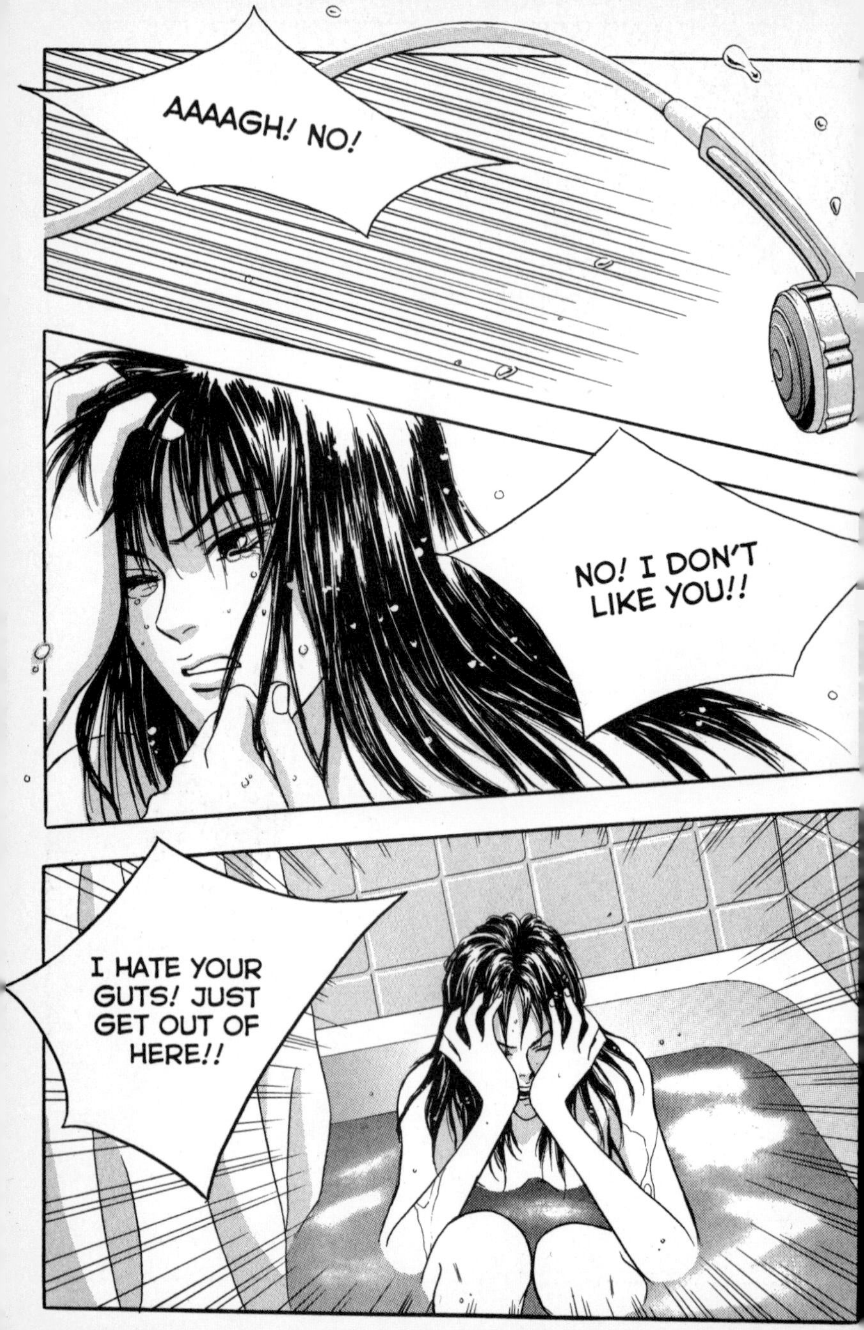
AAAAGH! NO!
NO! I DON'T LIKE YOU!!
I HATE YOUR GUTS! JUST GET OUT OF HERE!!

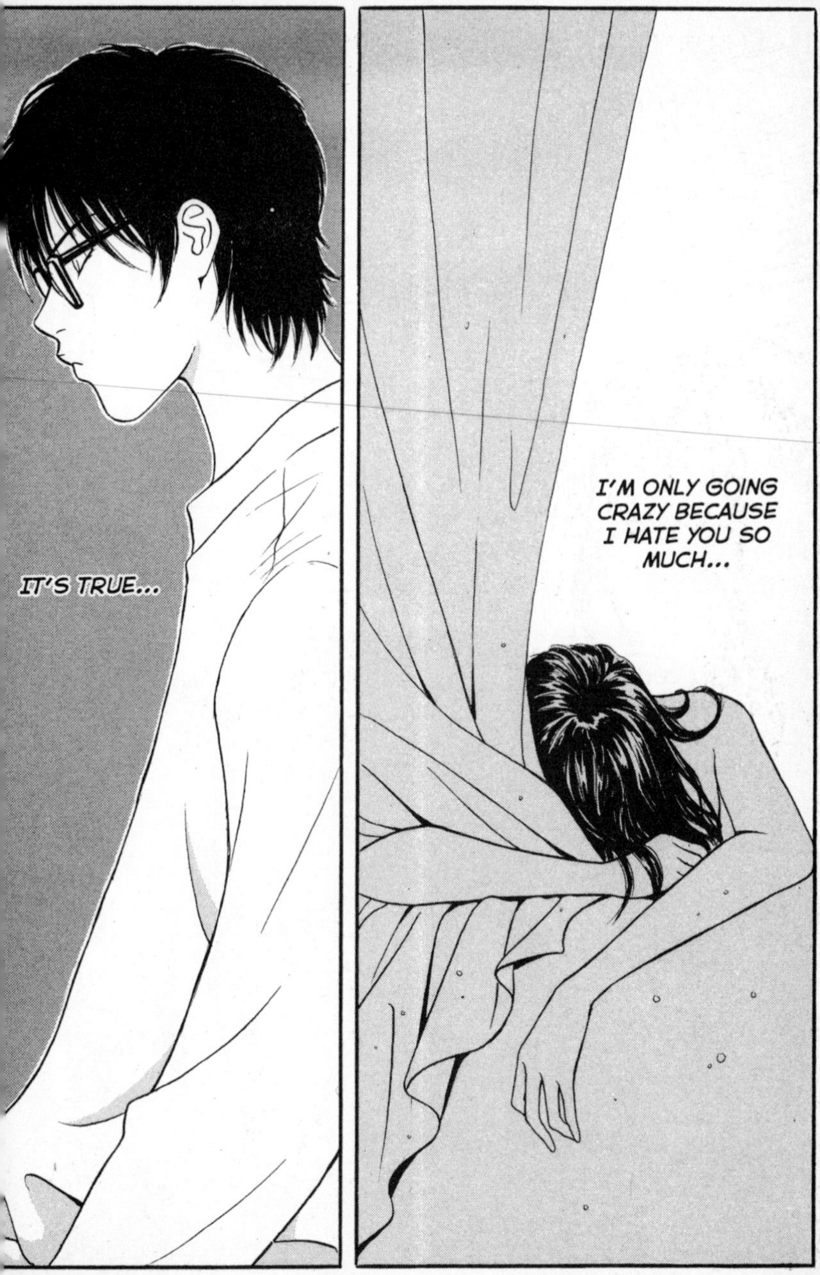
IT'S TRUE...
I'M ONLY GOING CRAZY BECAUSE I HATE YOU SO MUCH...

FEEL SORRY FOR GELDA...?

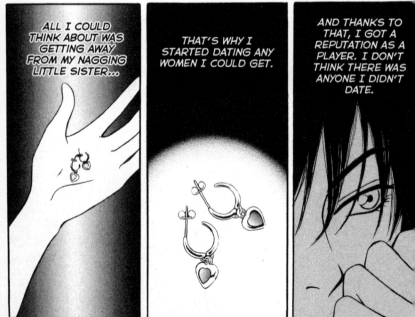

ALL I COULD THINK ABOUT WAS GETTING AWAY FROM MY NAGGING LITTLE SISTER...

THAT'S WHY I STARTED DATING ANY WOMEN I COULD GET.

AND THANKS TO THAT, I GOT A REPUTATION AS A PLAYER. I DON'T THINK THERE WAS ANYONE I DIDN'T DATE.

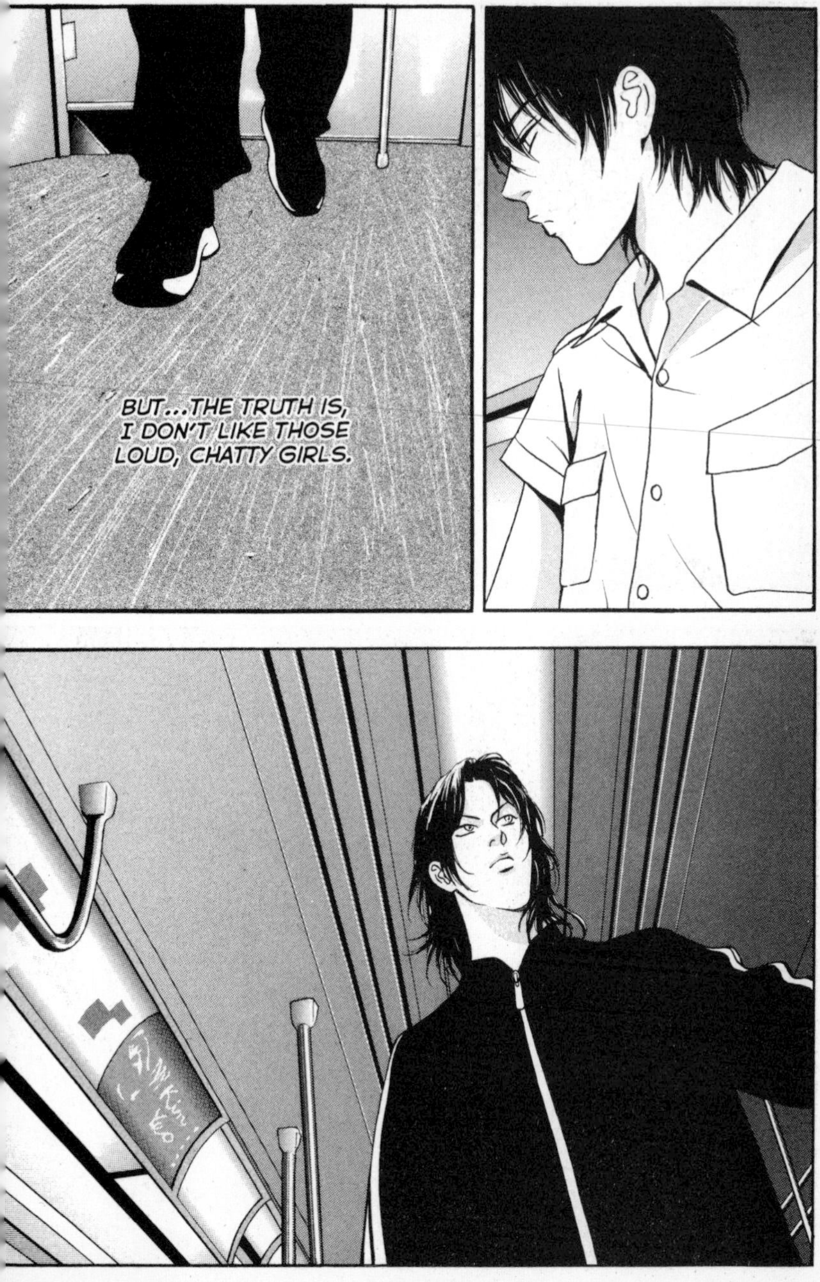
BUT...THE TRUTH IS, I DON'T LIKE THOSE LOUD, CHATTY GIRLS.

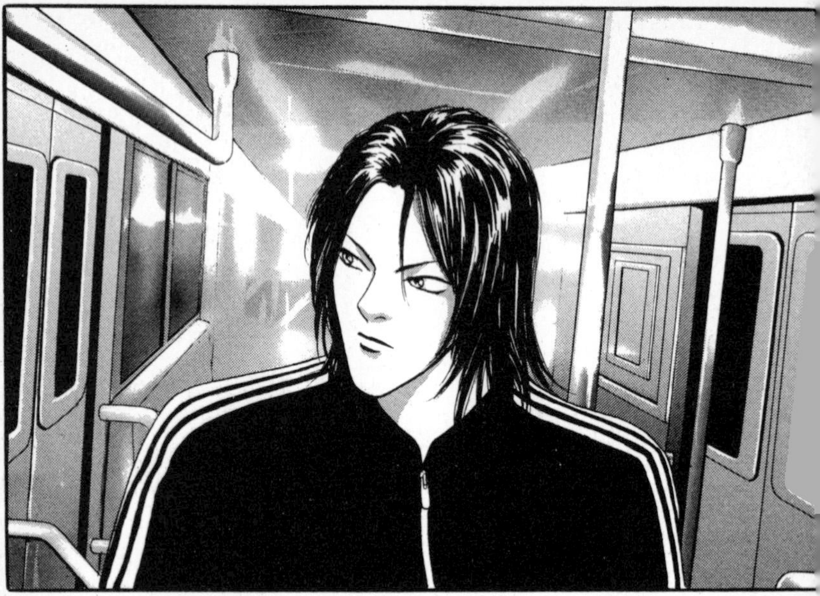
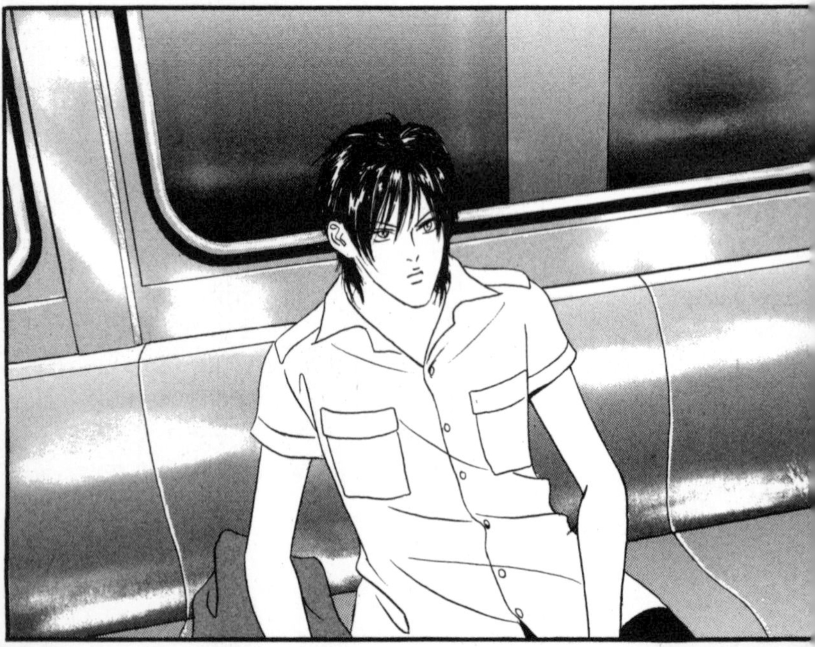

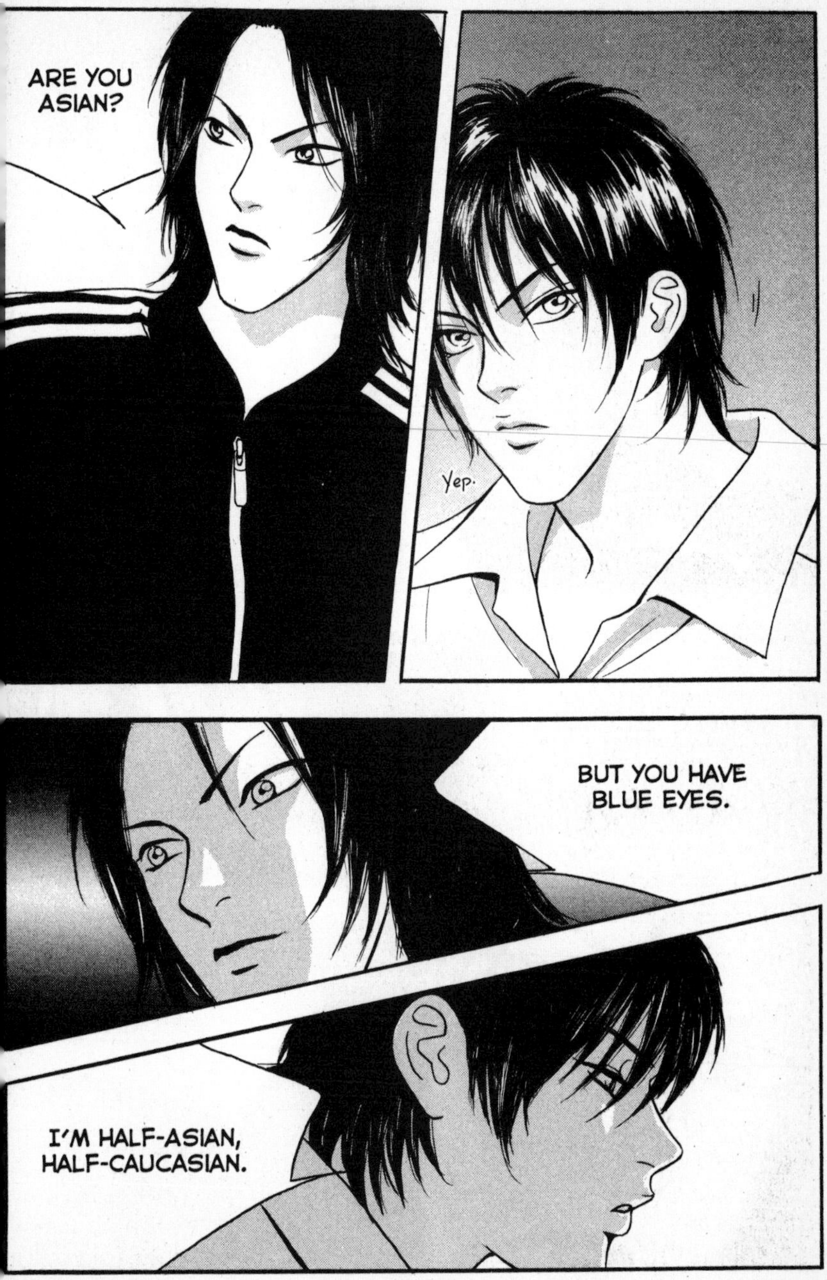
ARE YOU ASIAN?
Yep.
BUT YOU HAVE BLUE EYES.
I'M HALF-ASIAN, HALF-CAUCASIAN.

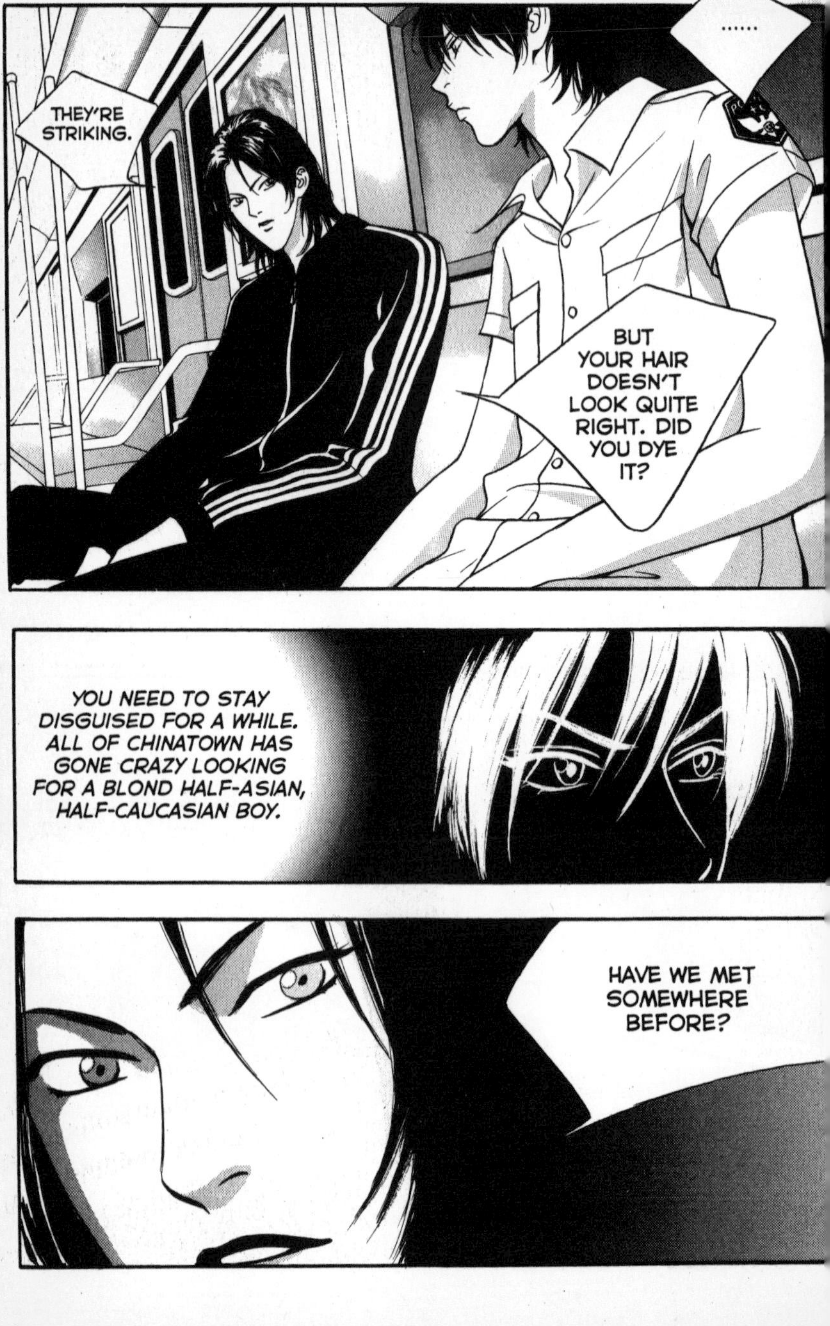
THEY'RE STRIKING.
......
BUT YOUR HAIR DOESN'T LOOK QUITE RIGHT. DID YOU DYE IT?
YOU NEED TO STAY DISGUISED FOR A WHILE. ALL OF CHINATOWN HAS GONE CRAZY LOOKING FOR A BLOND HALF-ASIAN, HALF-CAUCASIAN BOY.
HAVE WE MET SOMEWHERE BEFORE?

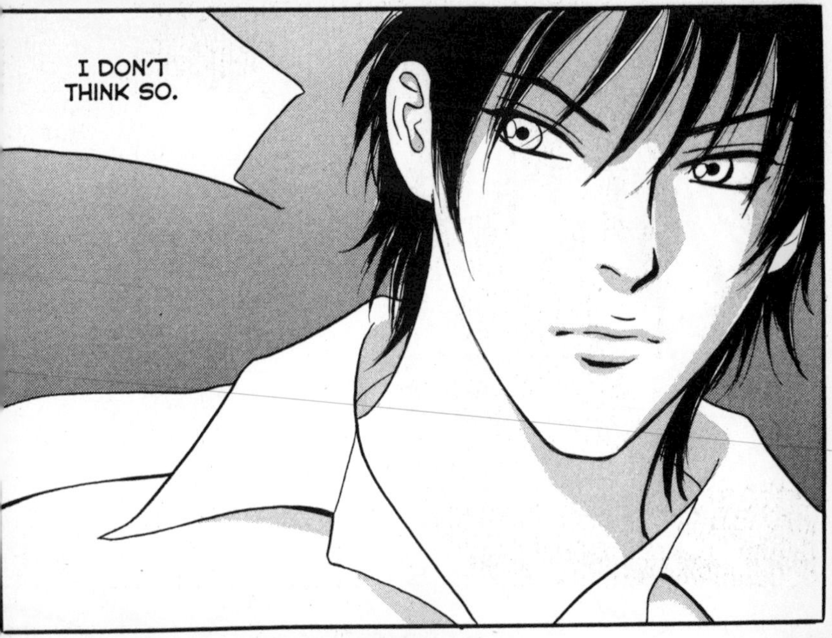
I DON'T THINK SO.

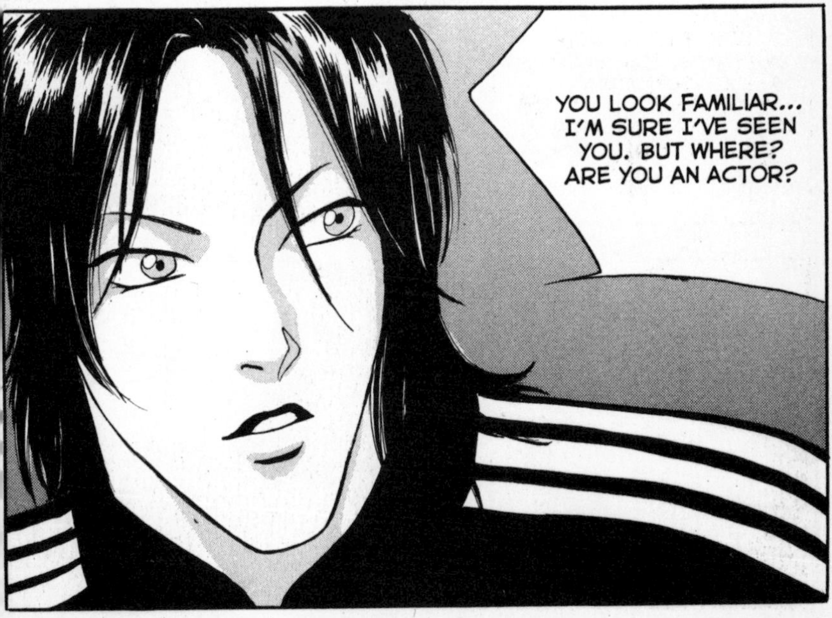
YOU LOOK FAMILIAR... I'M SURE I'VE SEEN YOU. BUT WHERE? ARE YOU AN ACTOR?

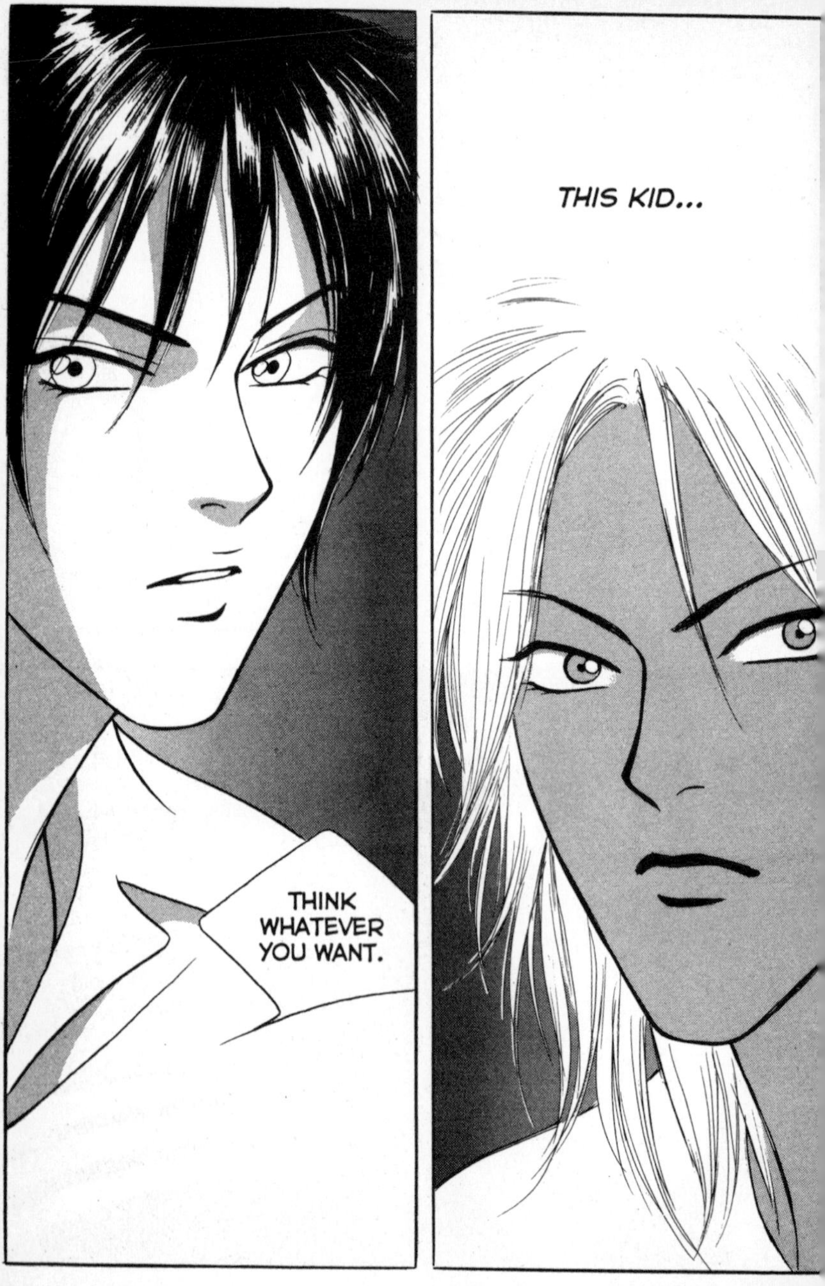
THINK WHATEVER YOU WANT.
THIS KID...

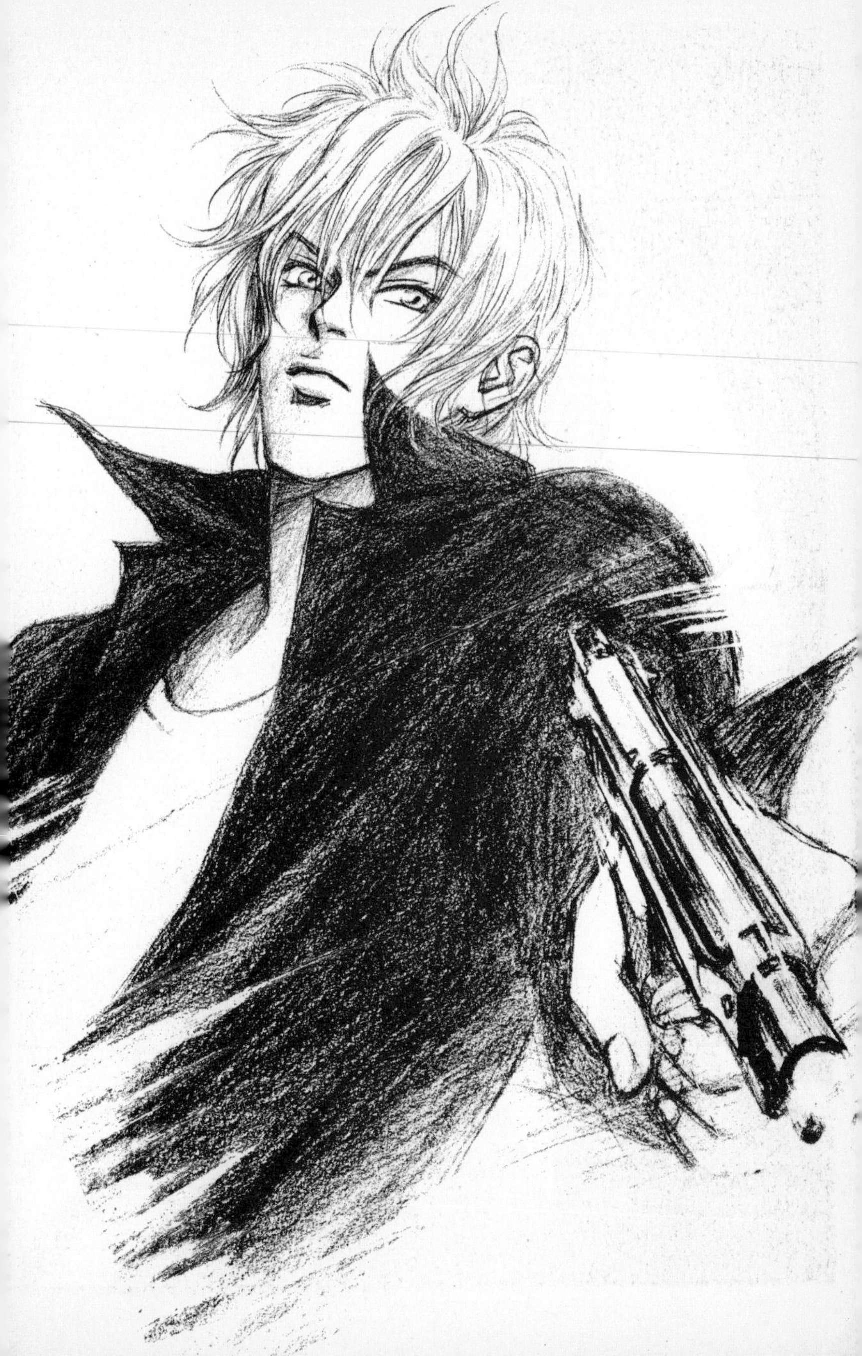

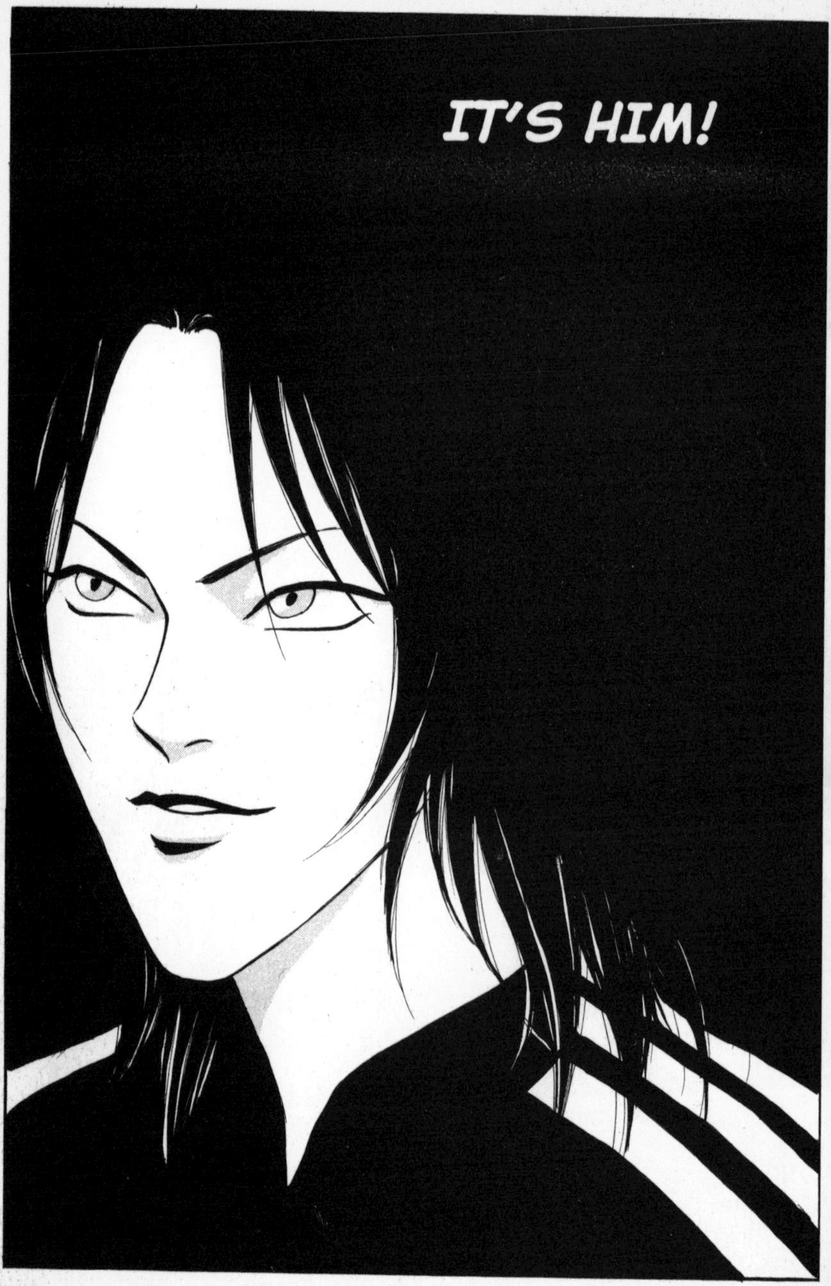
IT'S HIM!

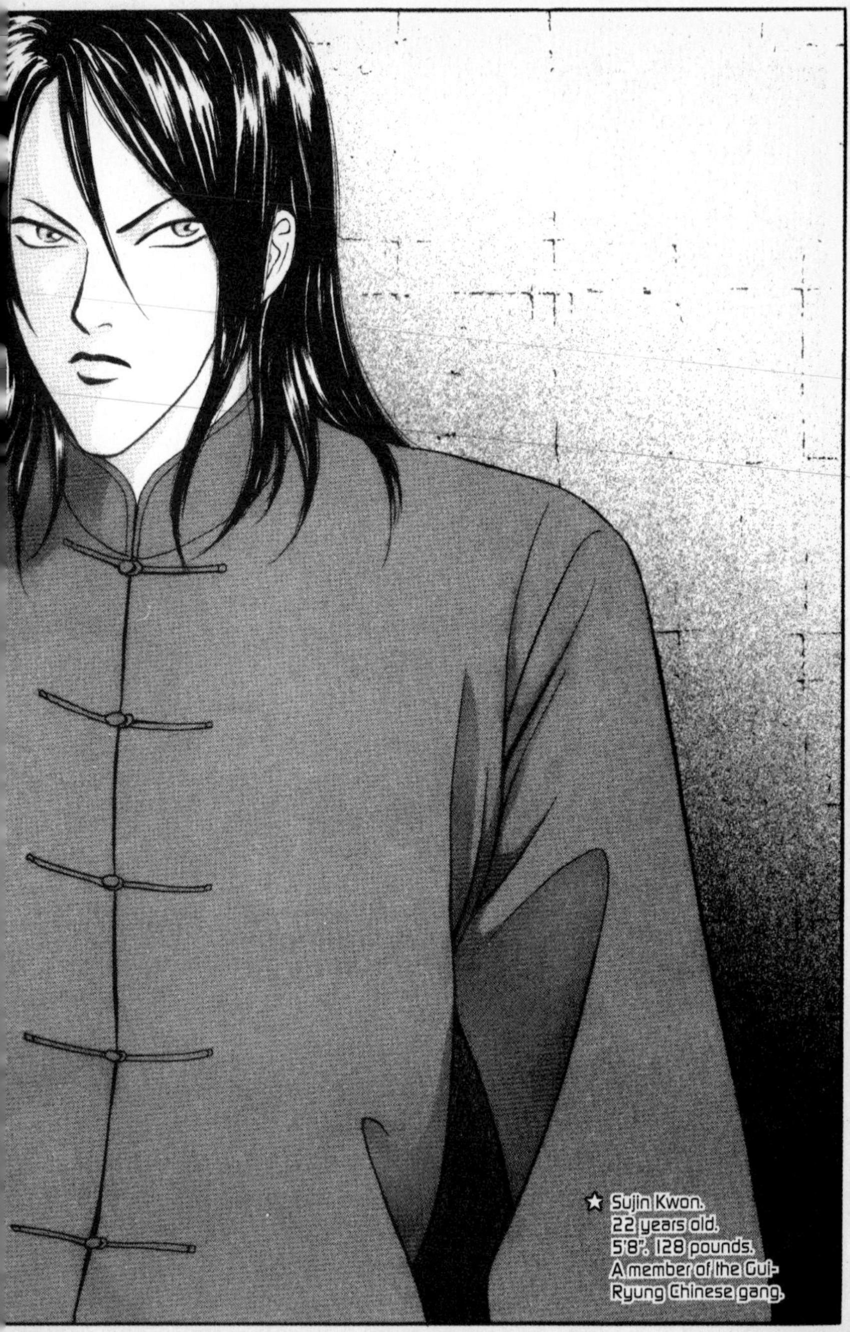
☆ Sujin Kwon.
22 years old.
5'8". 128 pounds.
A member of the Gui-
Ryung Chinese gang.

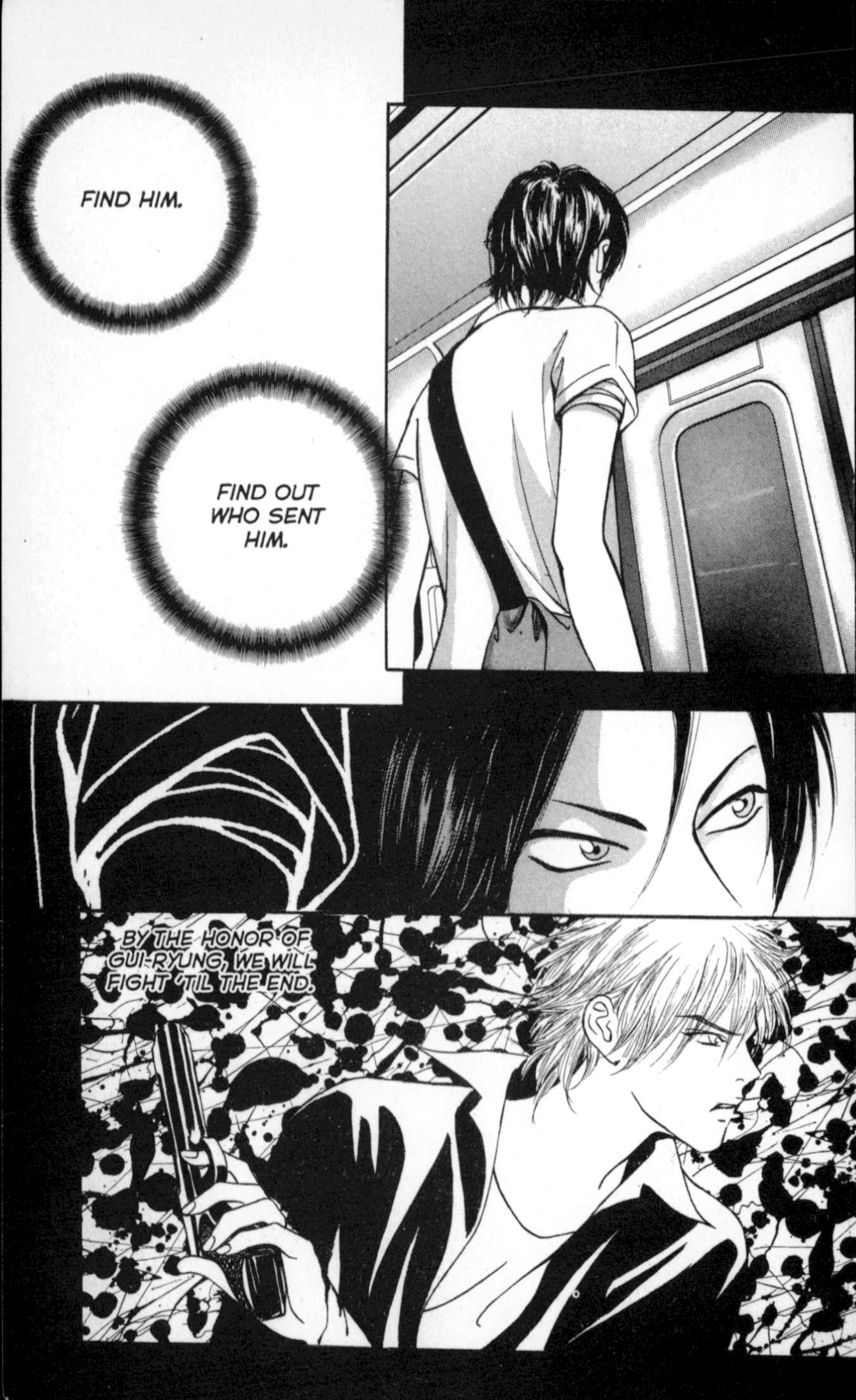
FIND HIM.
FIND OUT WHO SENT HIM.
BY THE HONOR OF GUI-RYUNG, WE WILL FIGHT 'TIL THE END.

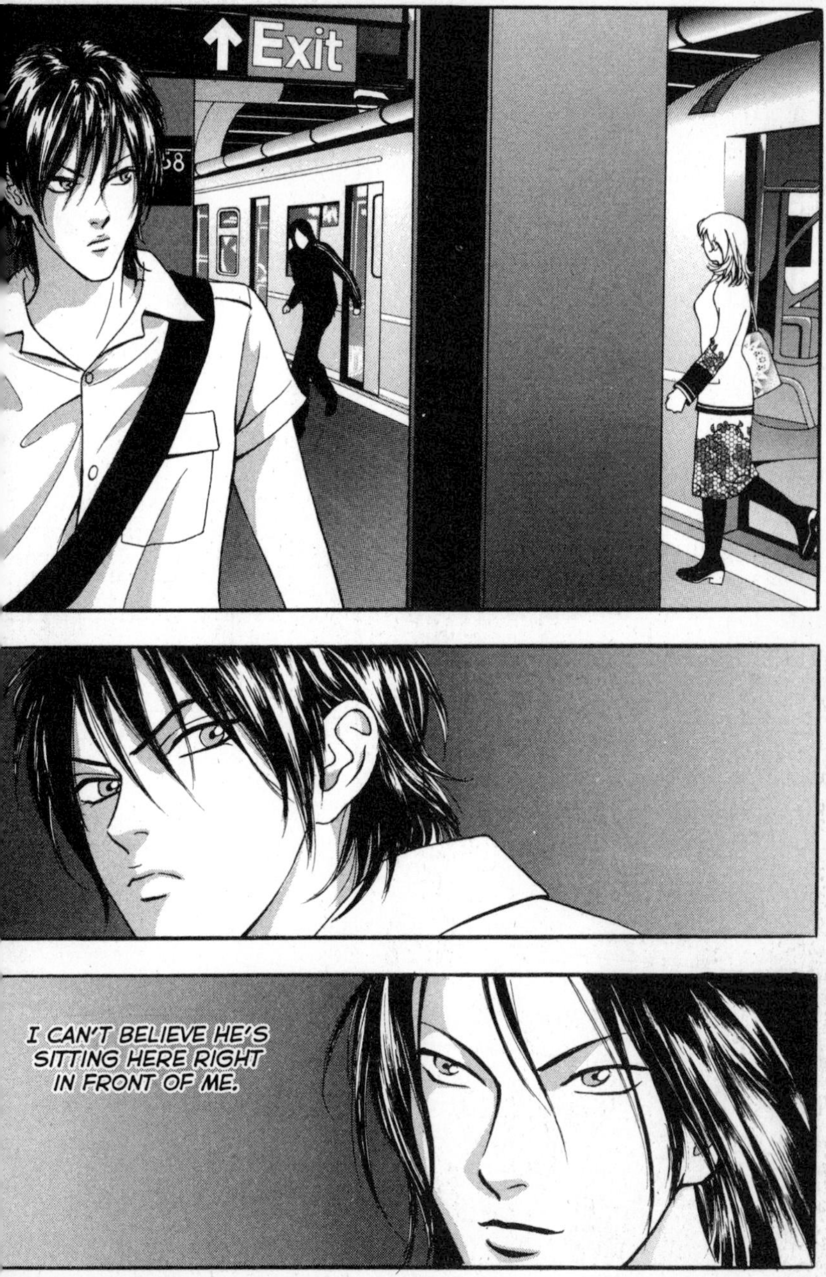
Exit
58
I CAN'T BELIEVE HE'S SITTING HERE RIGHT IN FRONT OF ME.

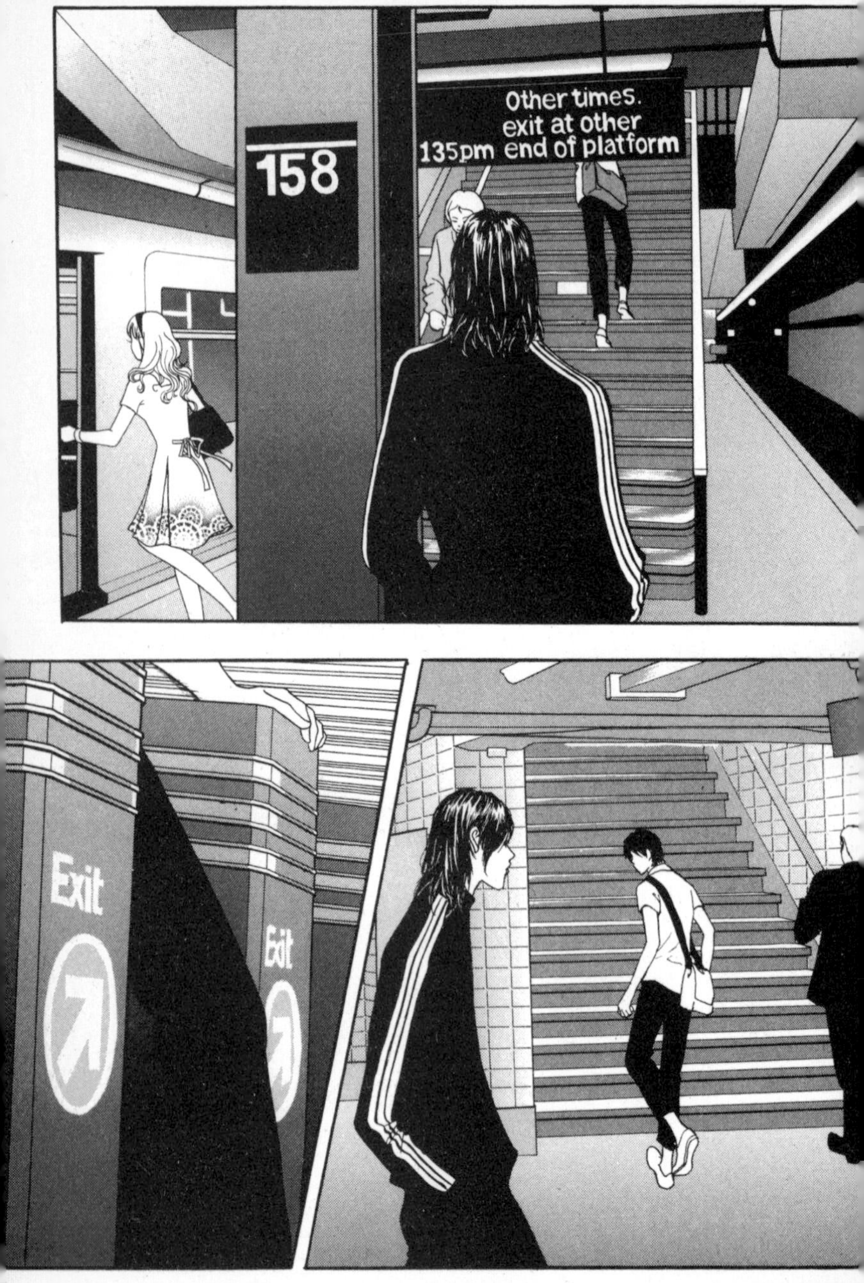
158
Other times.
exit at other
135pm end of platform
Exit
Exit

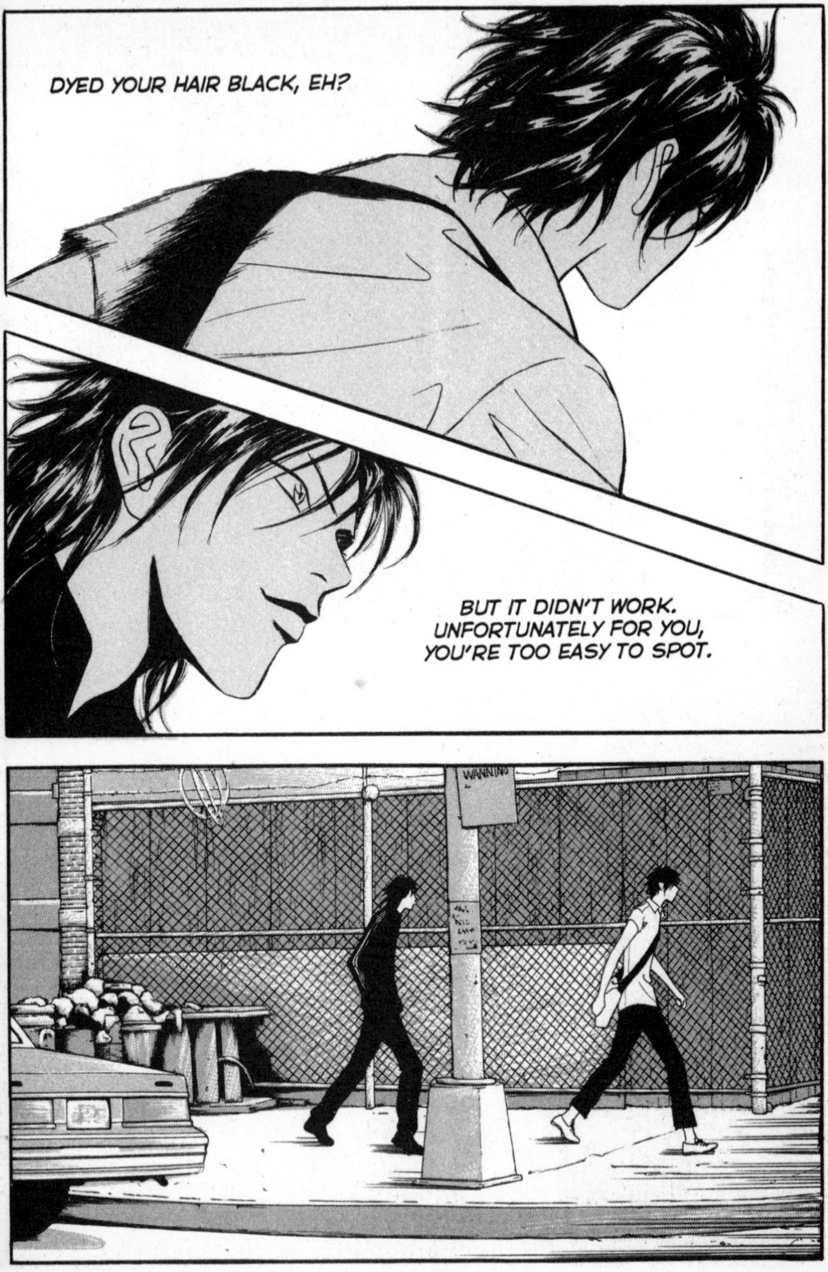
DYED YOUR HAIR BLACK, EH?
BUT IT DIDN'T WORK. UNFORTUNATELY FOR YOU, YOU'RE TOO EASY TO SPOT.

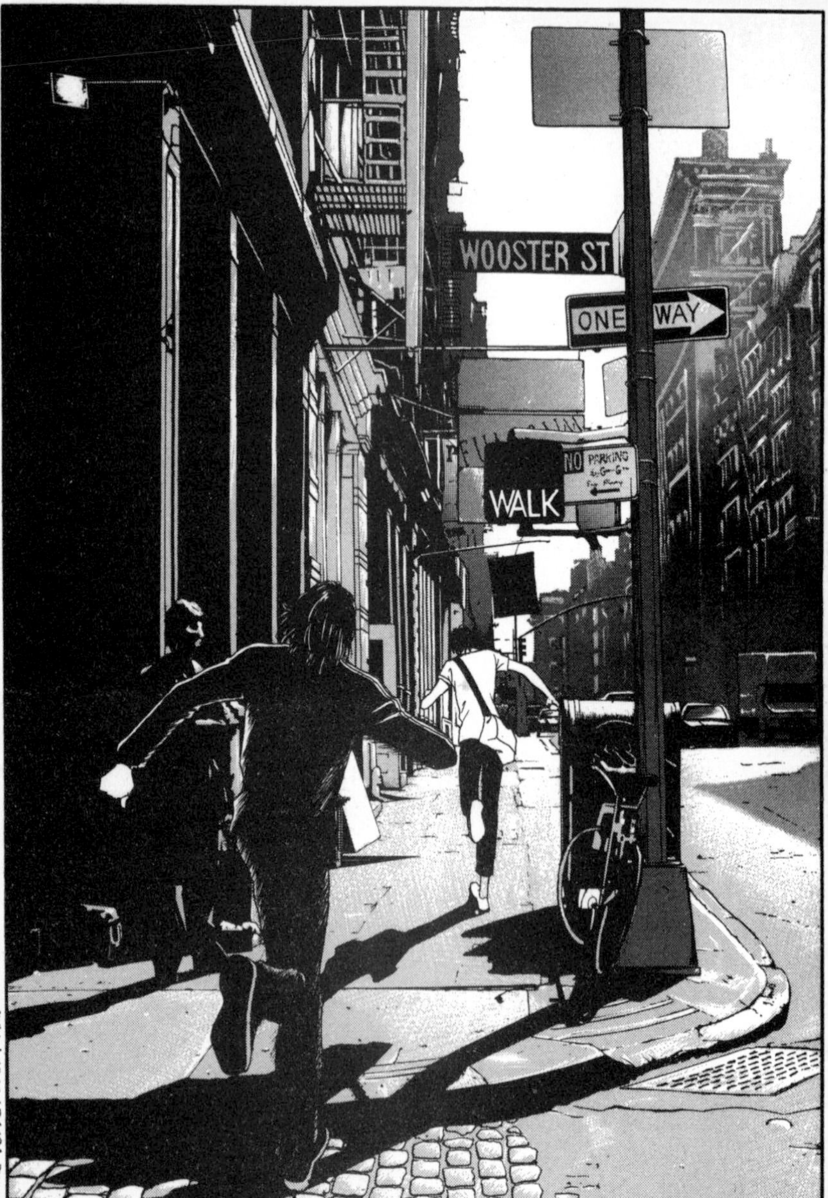
WOOSTER ST
ONE WAY
WALK
NO PARKING

B·G·M: The Verve / LUCKY MAN

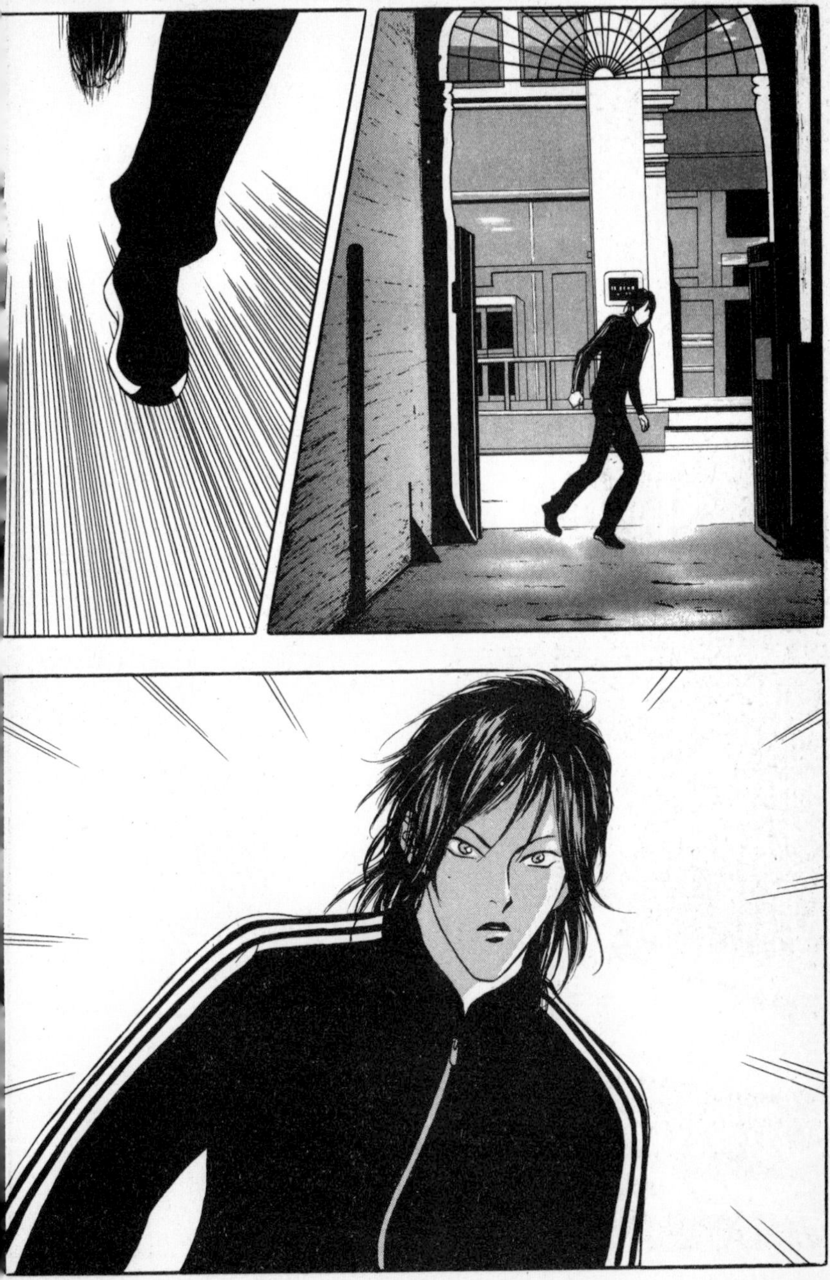

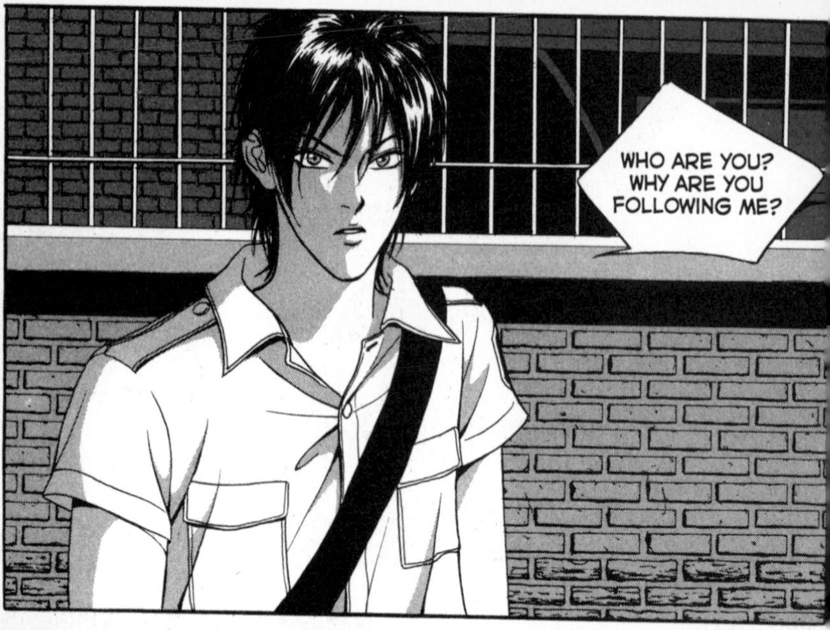
WHO ARE YOU? WHY ARE YOU FOLLOWING ME?

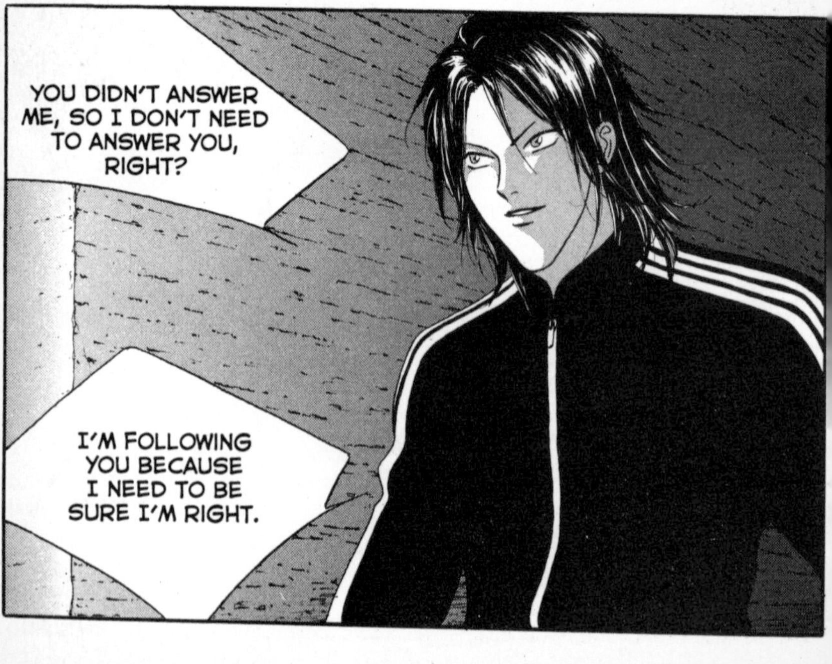
YOU DIDN'T ANSWER ME, SO I DON'T NEED TO ANSWER YOU, RIGHT?
I'M FOLLOWING YOU BECAUSE I NEED TO BE SURE I'M RIGHT.

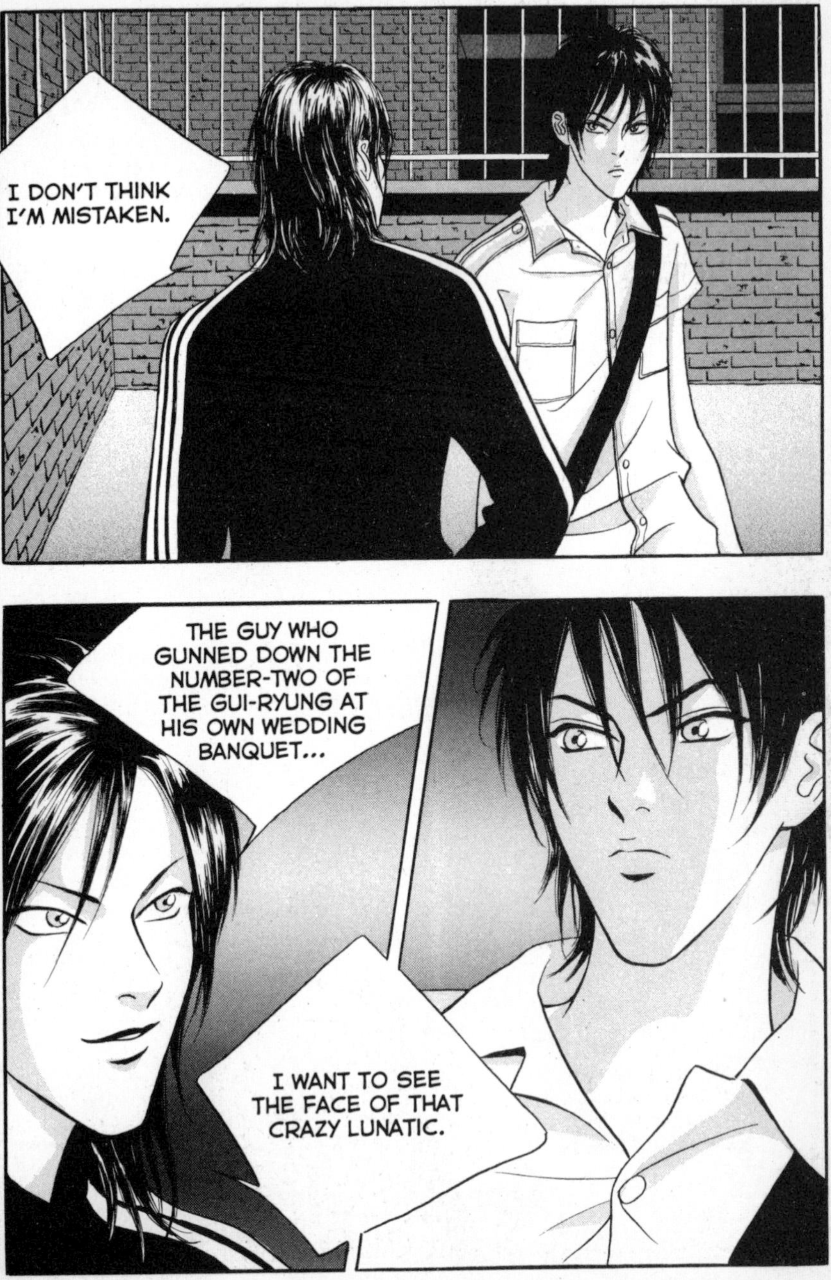
I DON'T THINK I'M MISTAKEN.
THE GUY WHO GUNNED DOWN THE NUMBER-TWO OF THE GUI-RYUNG AT HIS OWN WEDDING BANQUET...
I WANT TO SEE THE FACE OF THAT CRAZY LUNATIC.

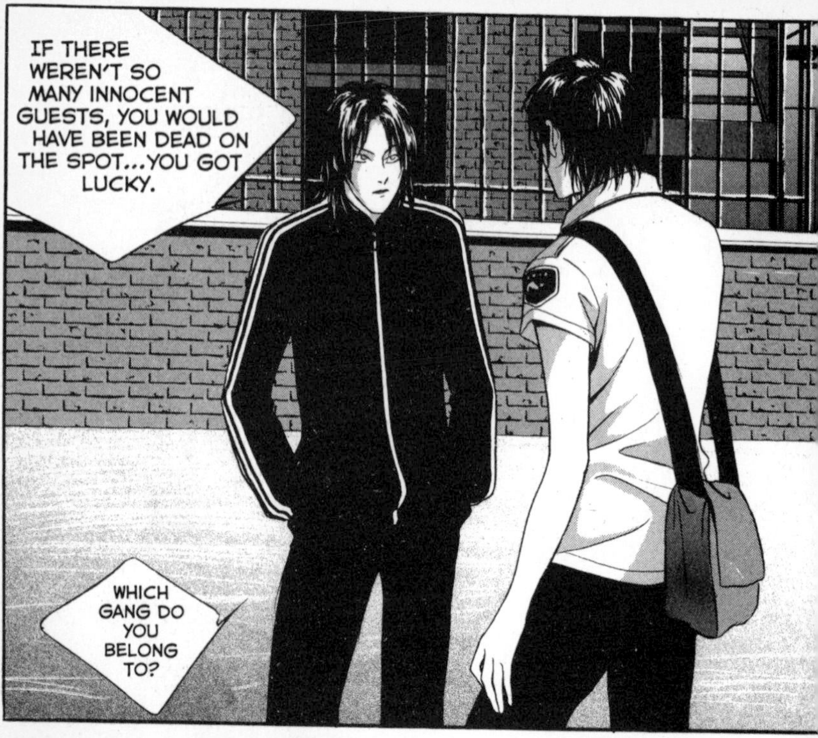
IF THERE WEREN'T SO MANY INNOCENT GUESTS, YOU WOULD HAVE BEEN DEAD ON THE SPOT...YOU GOT LUCKY.
WHICH GANG DO YOU BELONG TO?
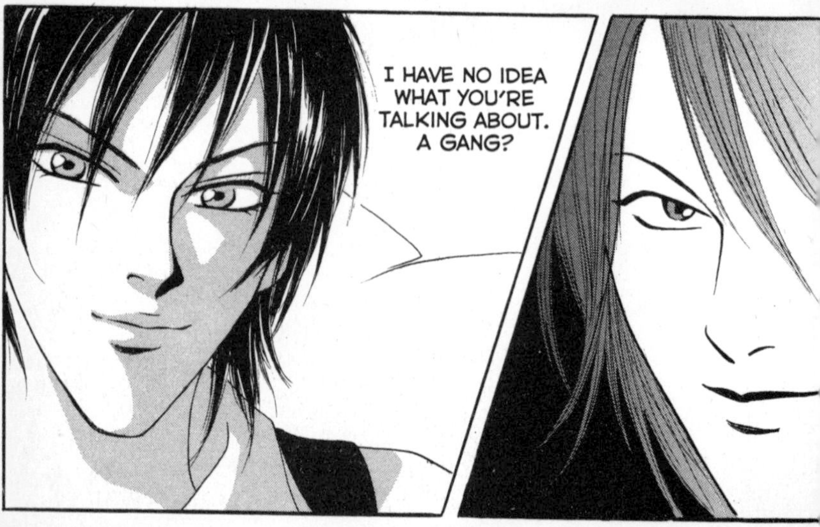
I HAVE NO IDEA WHAT YOU'RE TALKING ABOUT. A GANG?

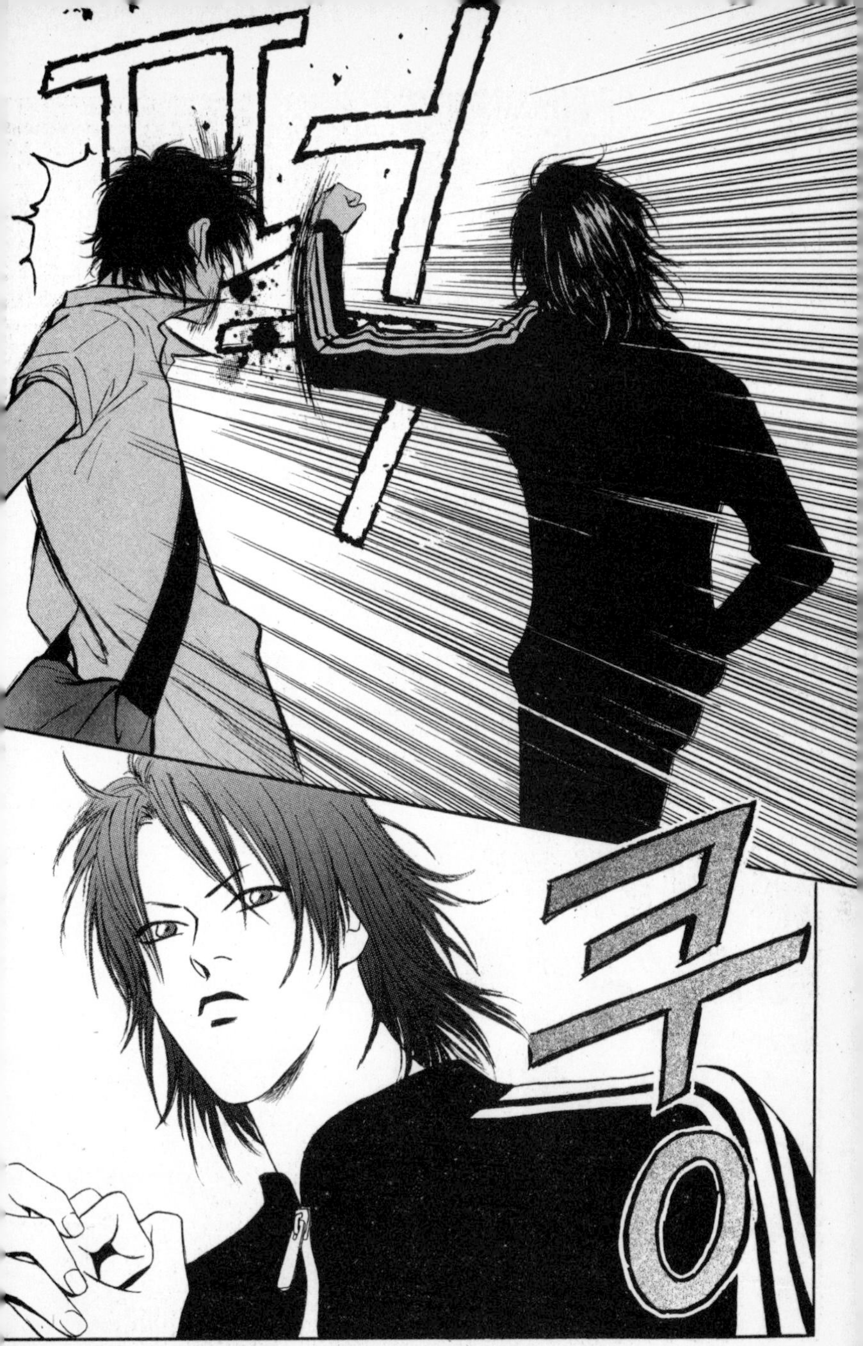

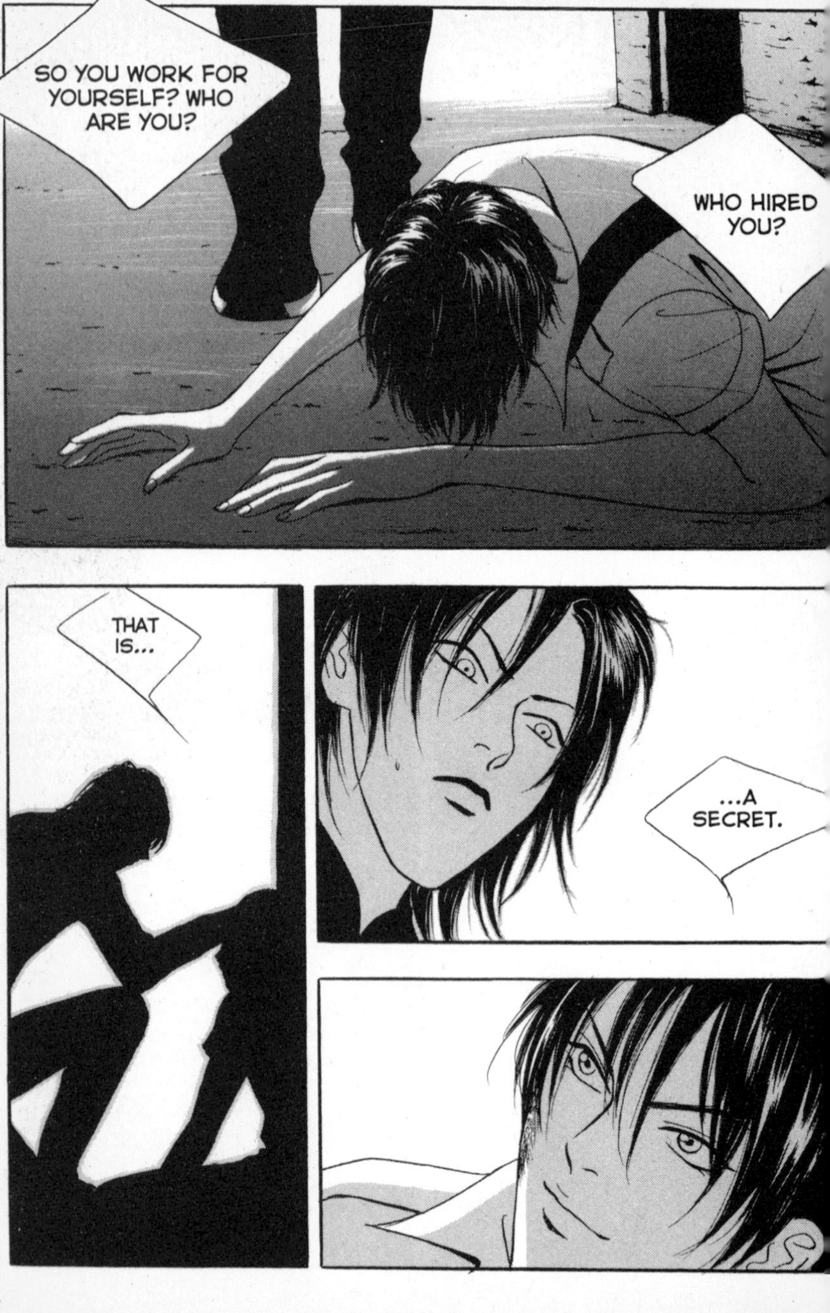
SO YOU WORK FOR YOURSELF? WHO ARE YOU?
WHO HIRED YOU?
THAT IS...
...A SECRET.

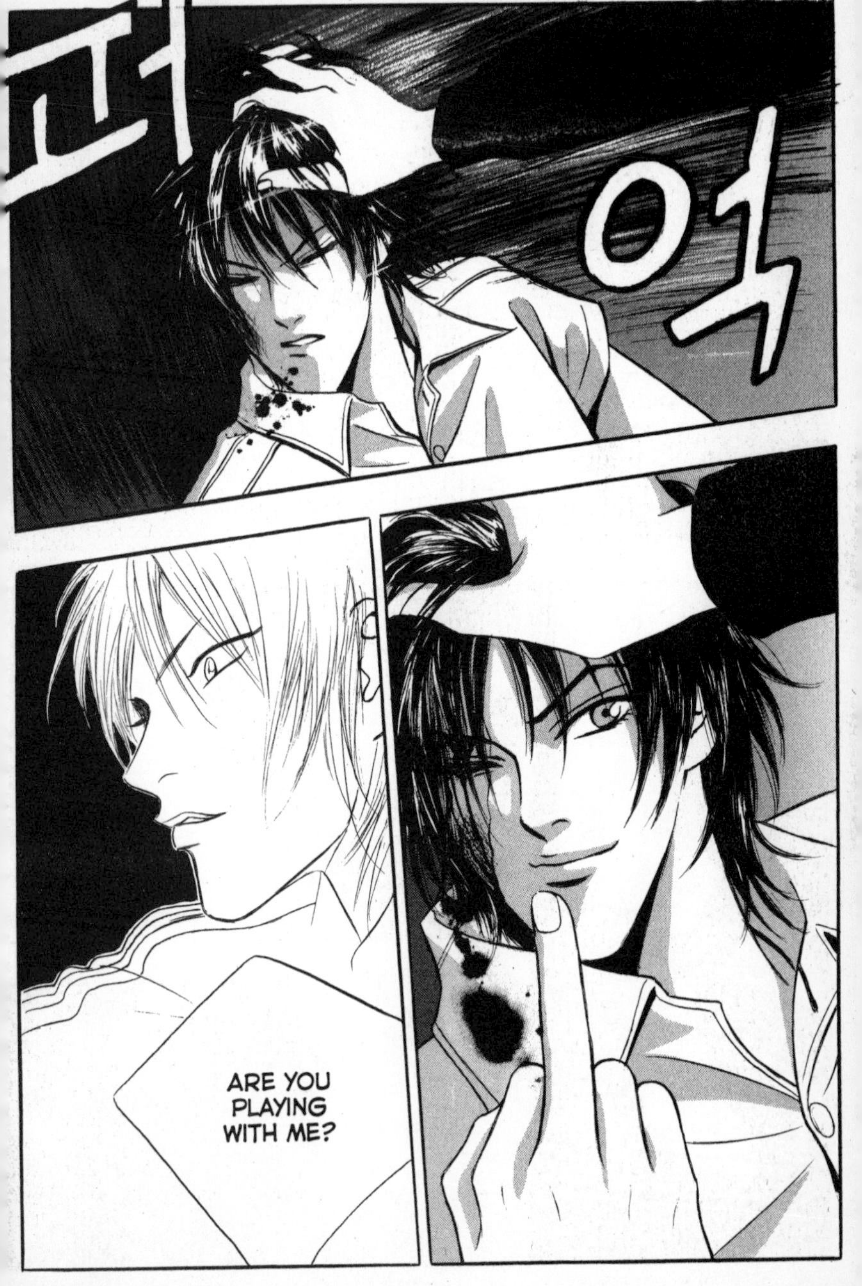
퍼억
ARE YOU PLAYING WITH ME?

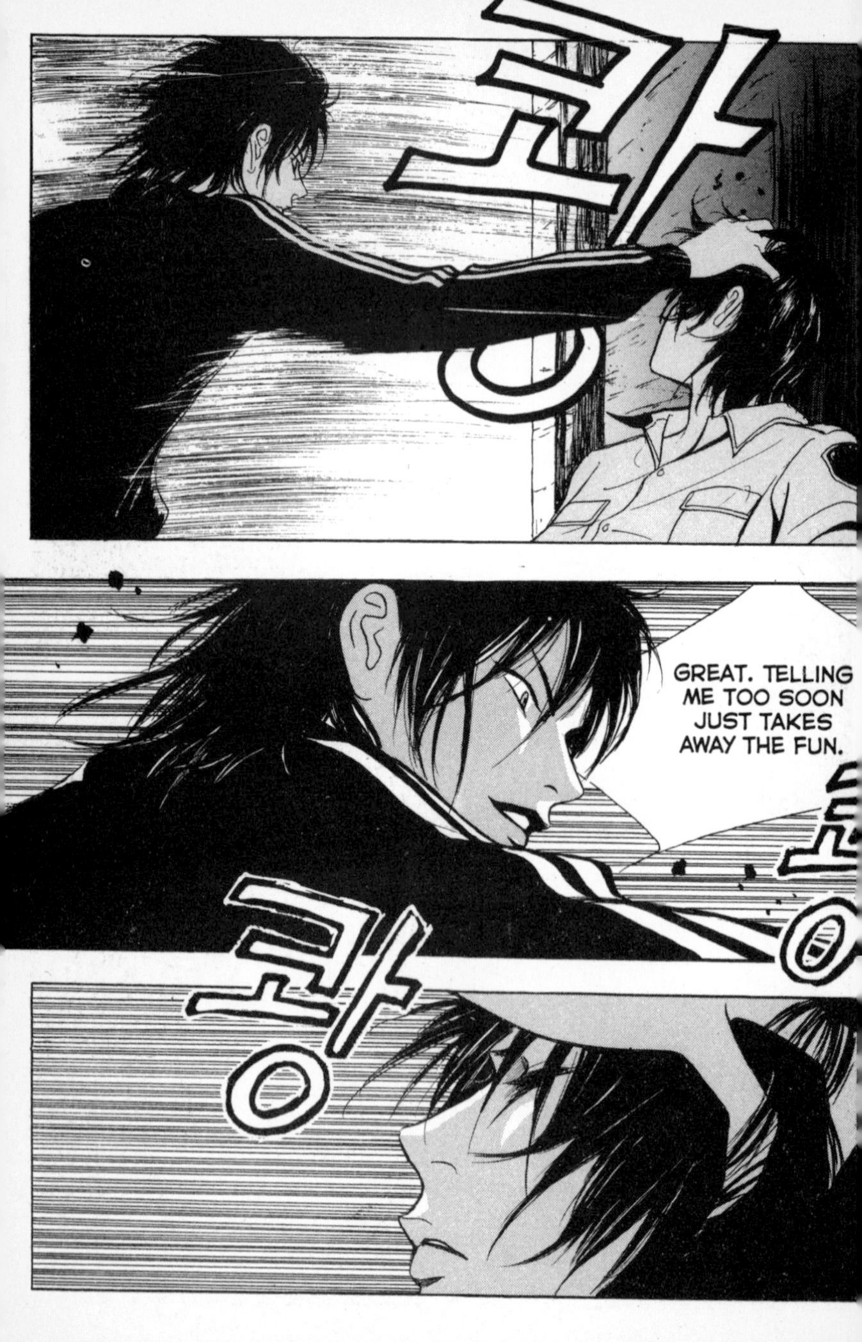
쾅
GREAT. TELLING ME TOO SOON JUST TAKES AWAY THE FUN.
쾅

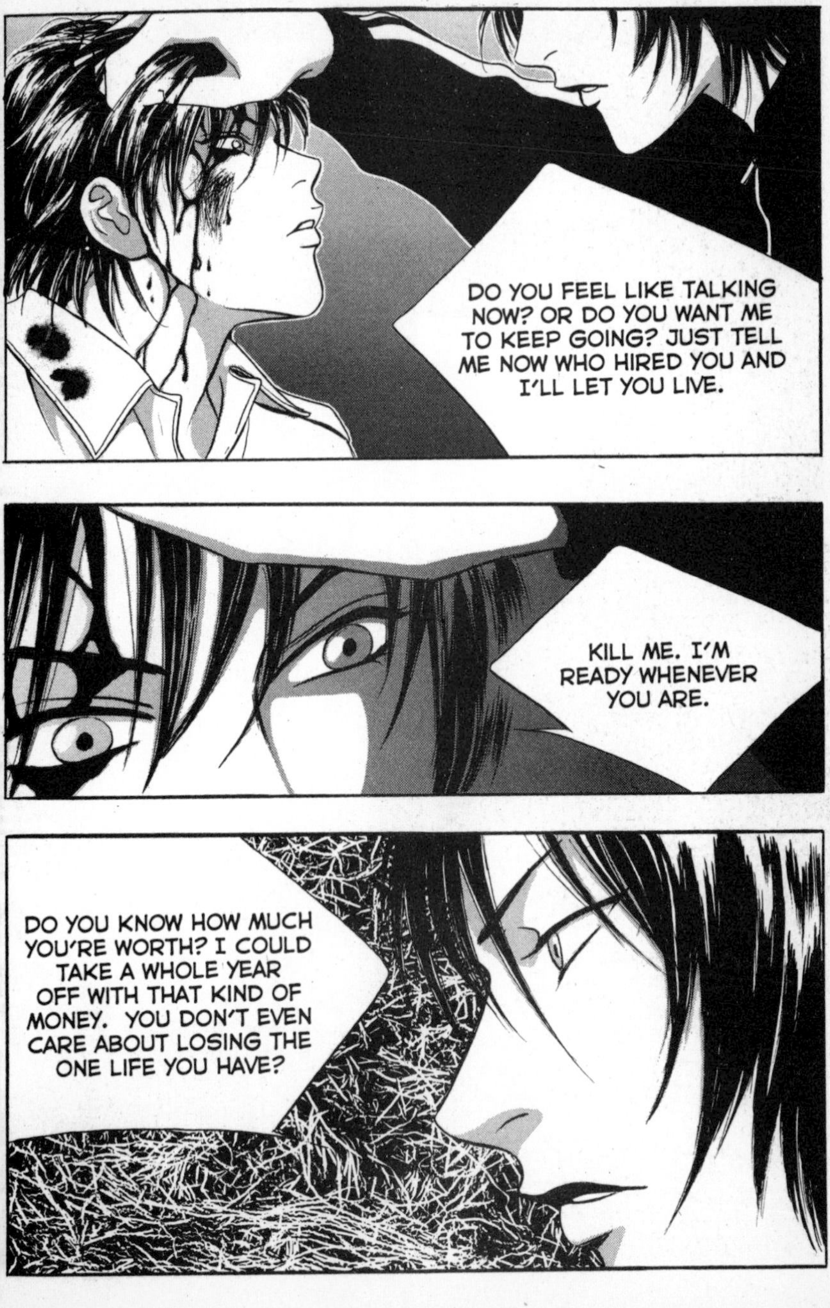
DO YOU FEEL LIKE TALKING NOW? OR DO YOU WANT ME TO KEEP GOING? JUST TELL ME NOW WHO HIRED YOU AND I'LL LET YOU LIVE.
KILL ME. I'M READY WHENEVER YOU ARE.
DO YOU KNOW HOW MUCH YOU'RE WORTH? I COULD TAKE A WHOLE YEAR OFF WITH THAT KIND OF MONEY. YOU DON'T EVEN CARE ABOUT LOSING THE ONE LIFE YOU HAVE?

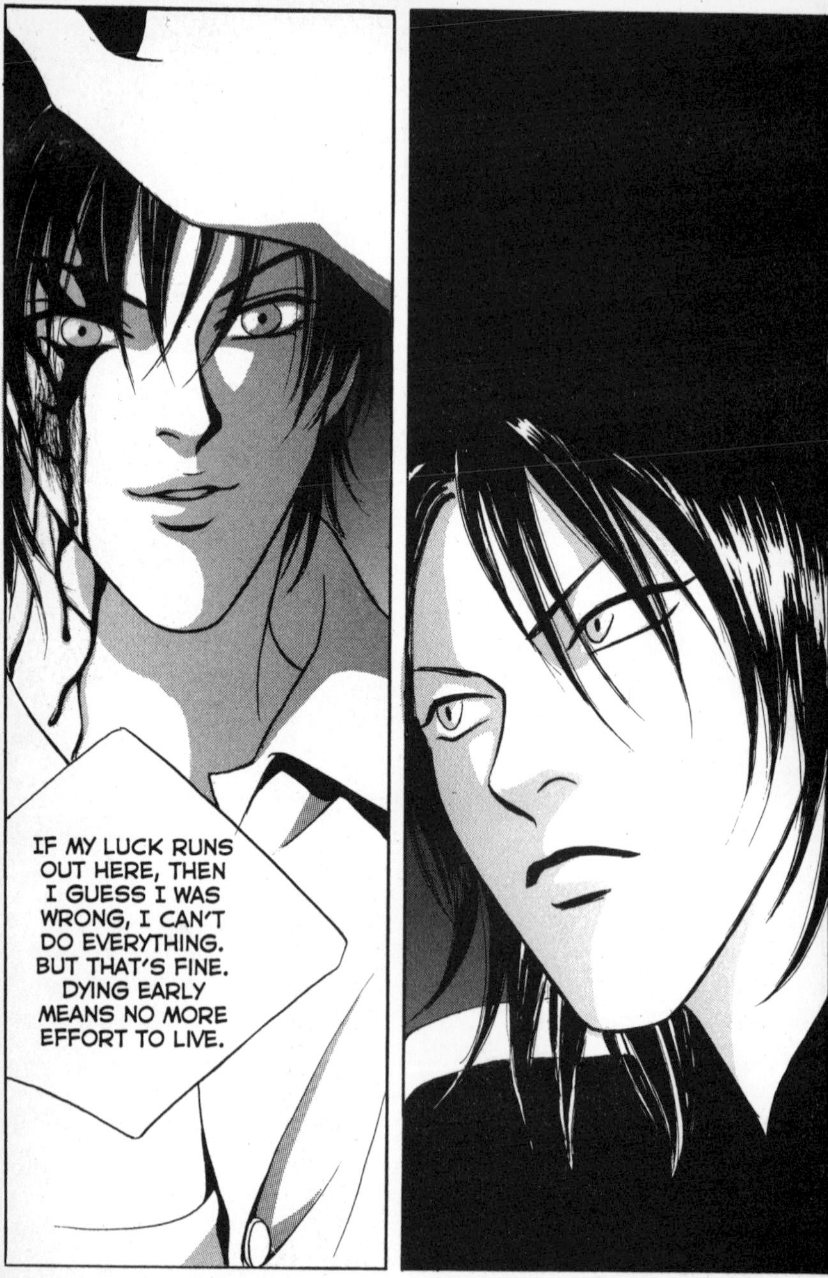
IF MY LUCK RUNS OUT HERE, THEN I GUESS I WAS WRONG, I CAN'T DO EVERYTHING. BUT THAT'S FINE. DYING EARLY MEANS NO MORE EFFORT TO LIVE.

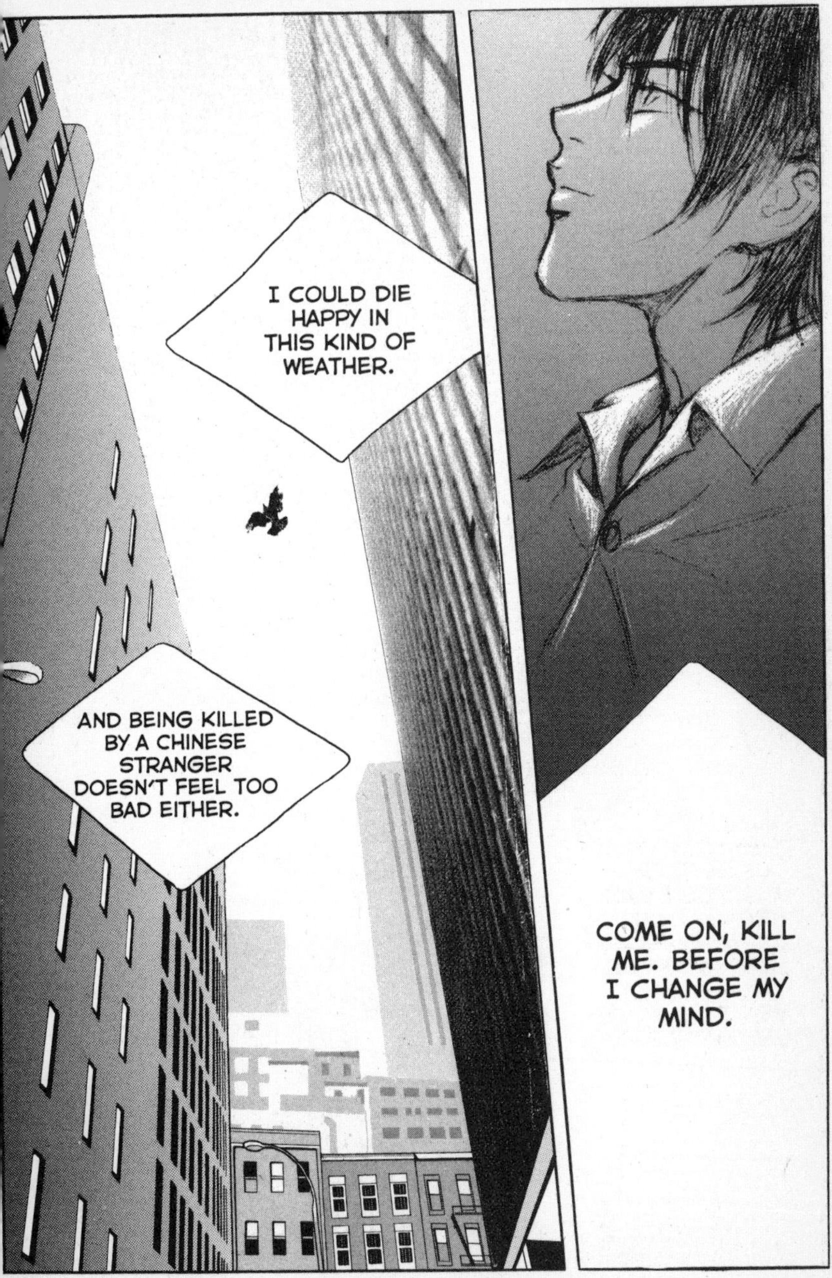
I COULD DIE HAPPY IN THIS KIND OF WEATHER.
AND BEING KILLED BY A CHINESE STRANGER DOESN'T FEEL TOO BAD EITHER.
COME ON, KILL ME. BEFORE I CHANGE MY MIND.

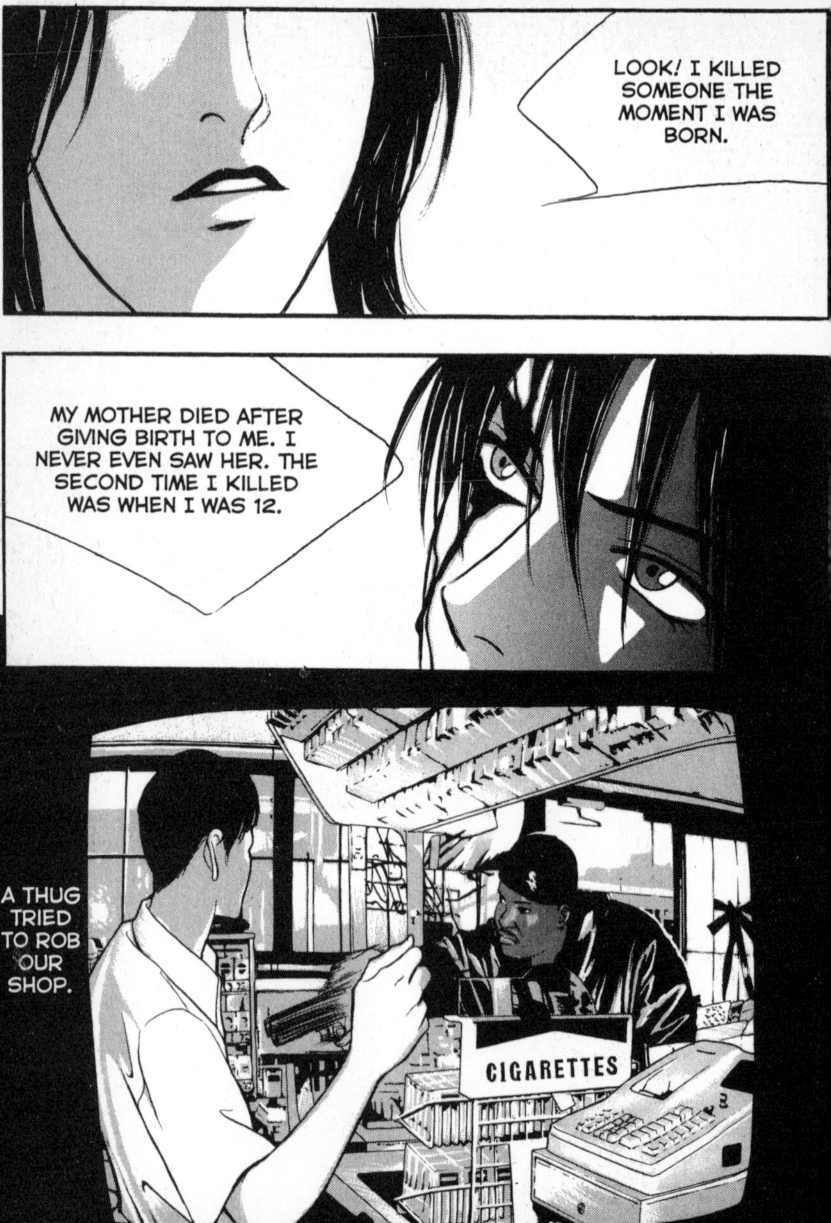
LOOK! I KILLED SOMEONE THE MOMENT I WAS BORN.
MY MOTHER DIED AFTER GIVING BIRTH TO ME. I NEVER EVEN SAW HER. THE SECOND TIME I KILLED WAS WHEN I WAS 12.
A THUG TRIED TO ROB OUR SHOP.
CIGARETTES

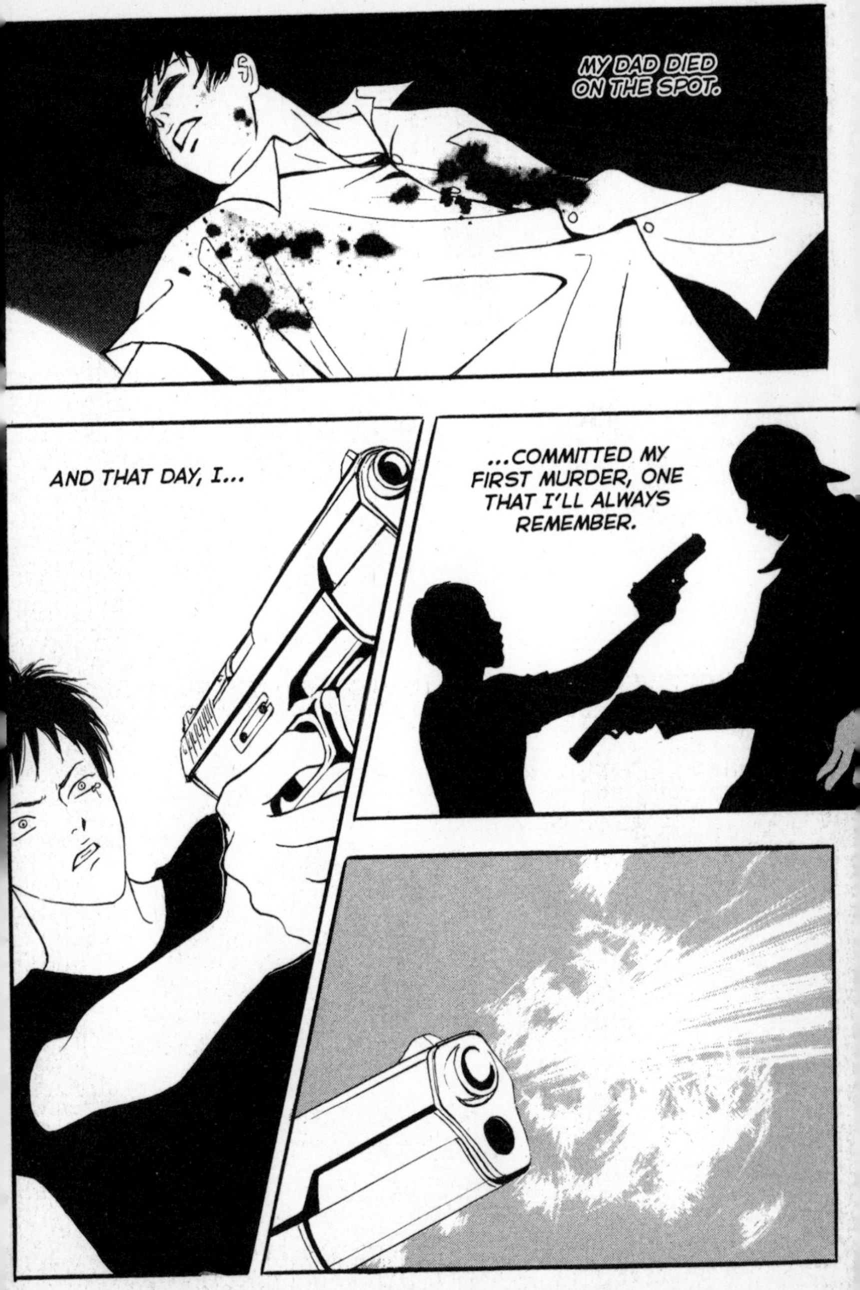
MY DAD DIED ON THE SPOT.
AND THAT DAY, I...
...COMMITTED MY FIRST MURDER, ONE THAT I'LL ALWAYS REMEMBER.

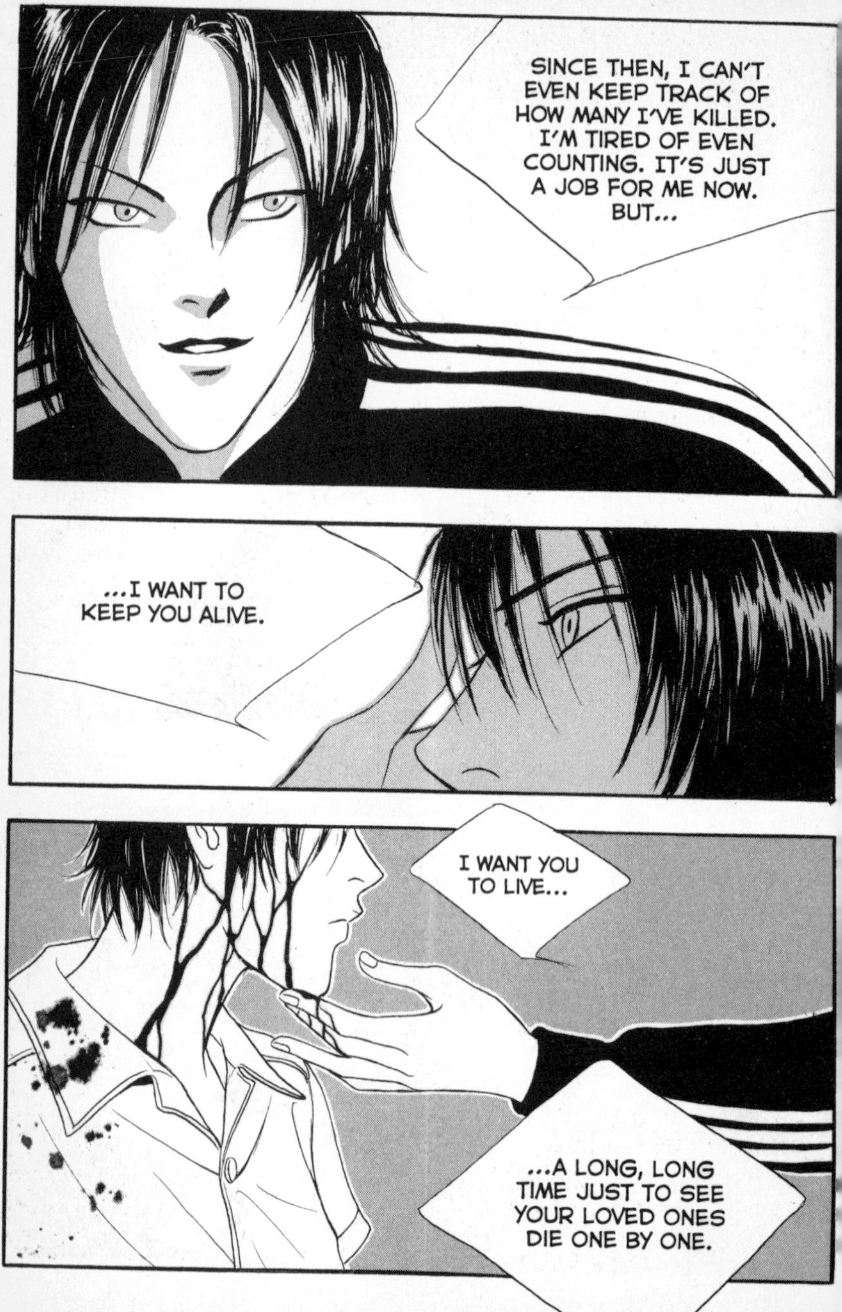
SINCE THEN, I CAN'T EVEN KEEP TRACK OF HOW MANY I'VE KILLED. I'M TIRED OF EVEN COUNTING. IT'S JUST A JOB FOR ME NOW. BUT...
...I WANT TO KEEP YOU ALIVE.
I WANT YOU TO LIVE...
...A LONG, LONG TIME JUST TO SEE YOUR LOVED ONES DIE ONE BY ONE.

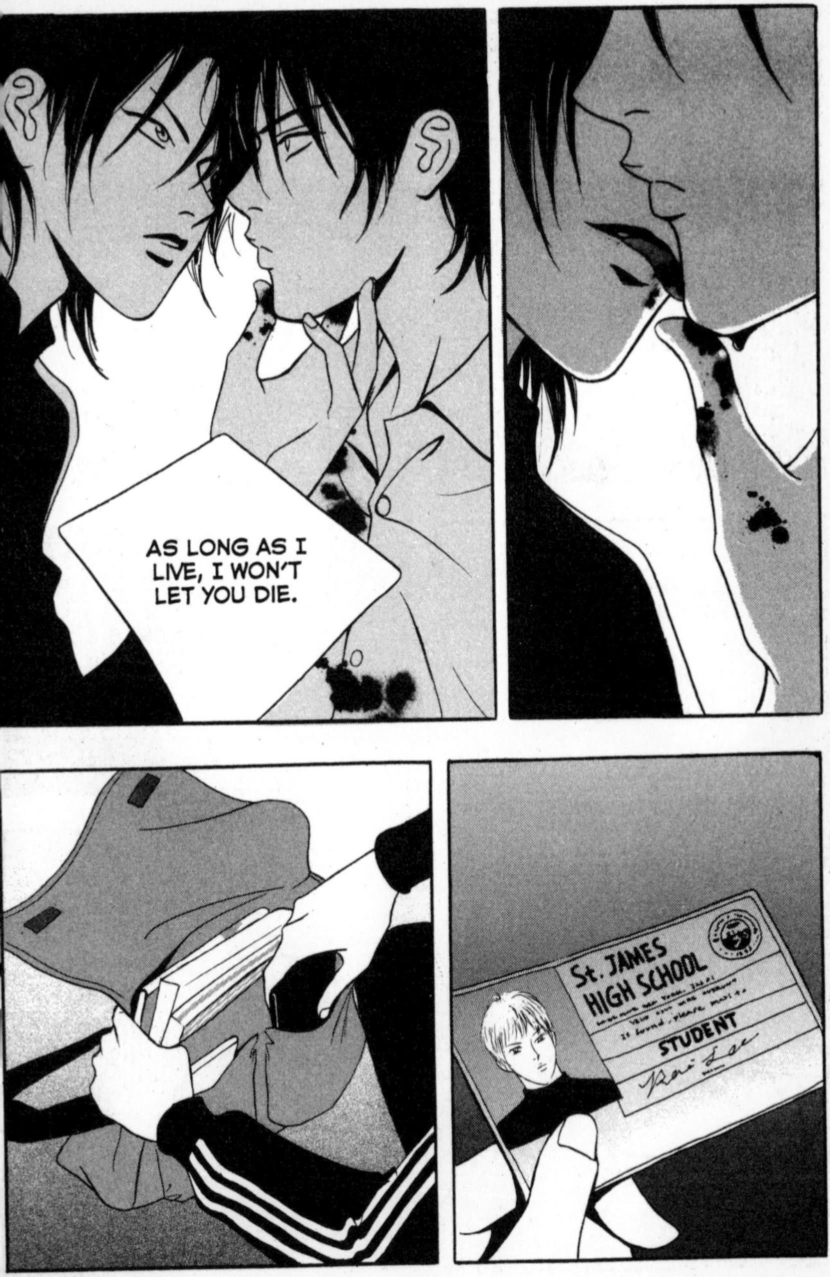
AS LONG AS I LIVE, I WON'T LET YOU DIE.
St. JAMES HIGH SCHOOL
STUDENT

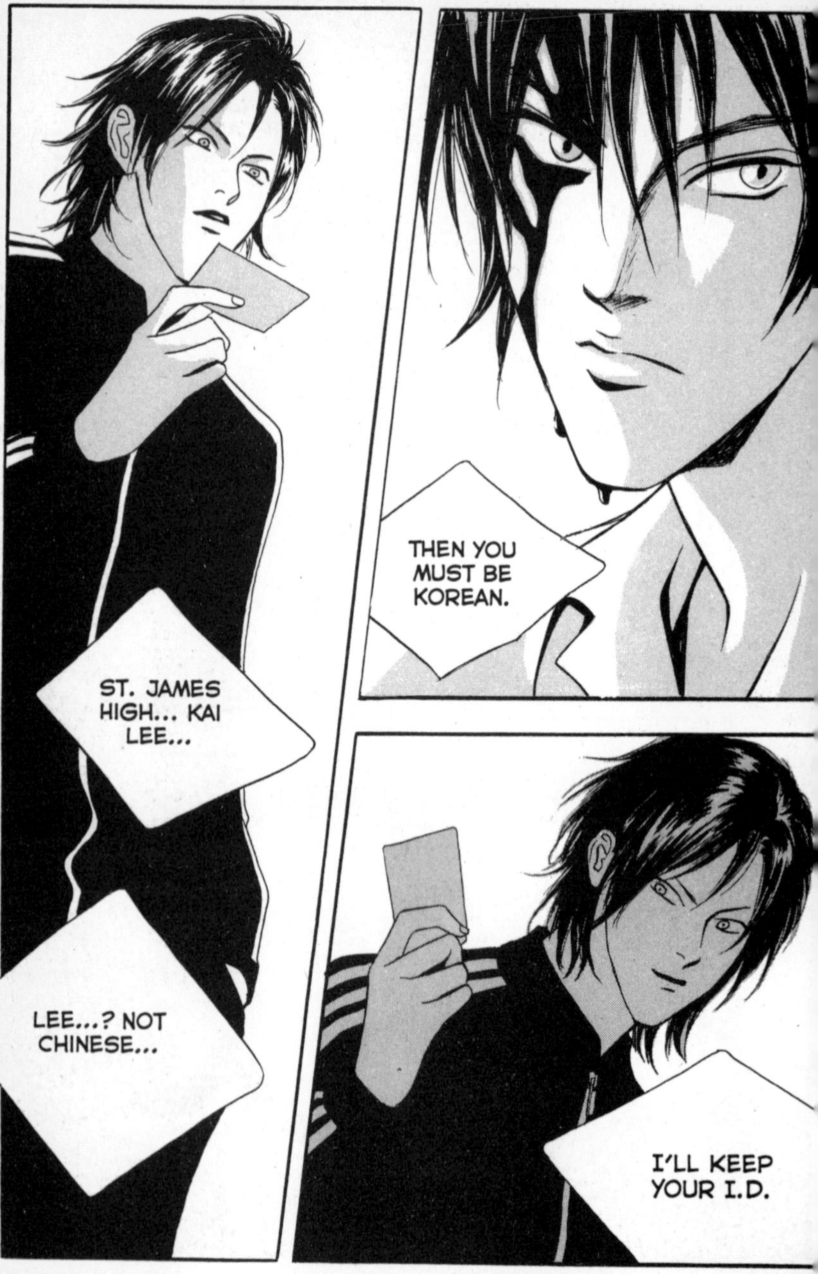
ST. JAMES HIGH... KAI LEE...
LEE...? NOT CHINESE...
THEN YOU MUST BE KOREAN.
I'LL KEEP YOUR I.D.

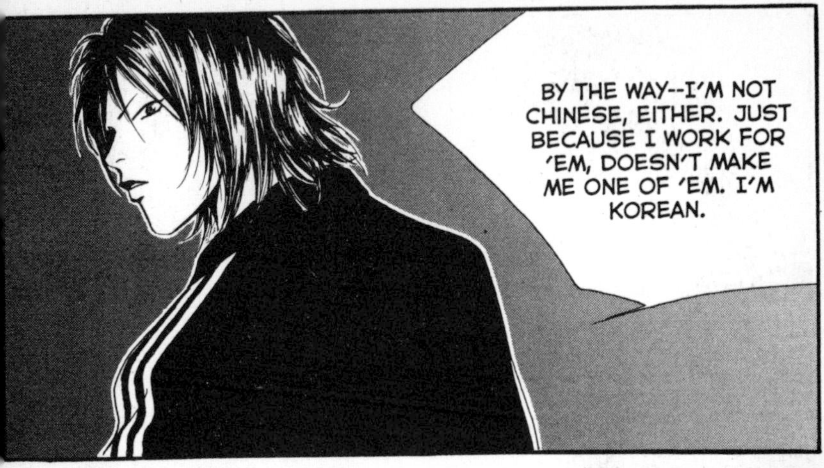
BY THE WAY--I'M NOT CHINESE, EITHER. JUST BECAUSE I WORK FOR 'EM, DOESN'T MAKE ME ONE OF 'EM. I'M KOREAN.

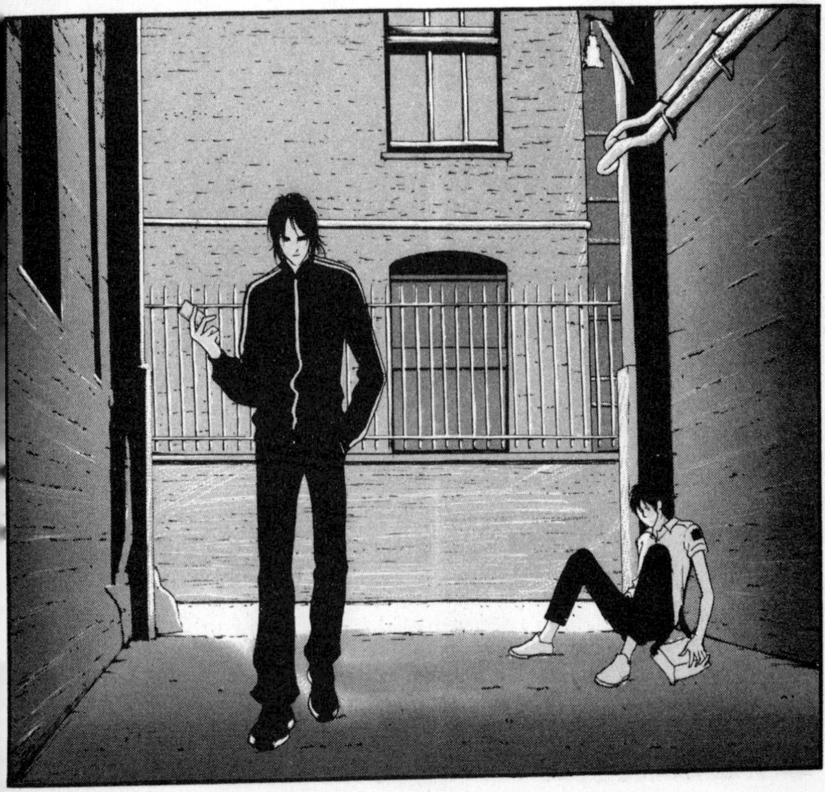

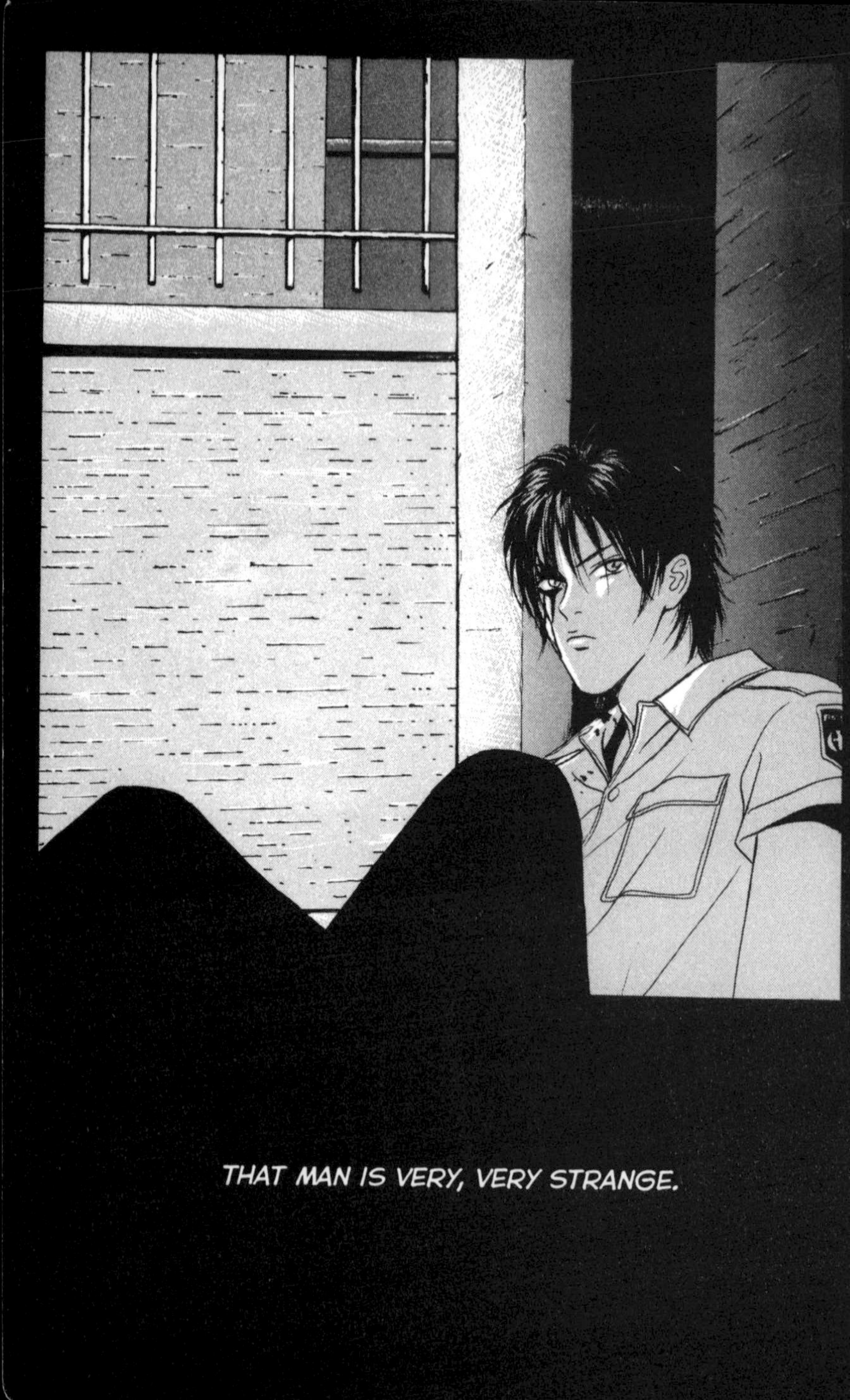
THAT MAN IS VERY, VERY STRANGE.

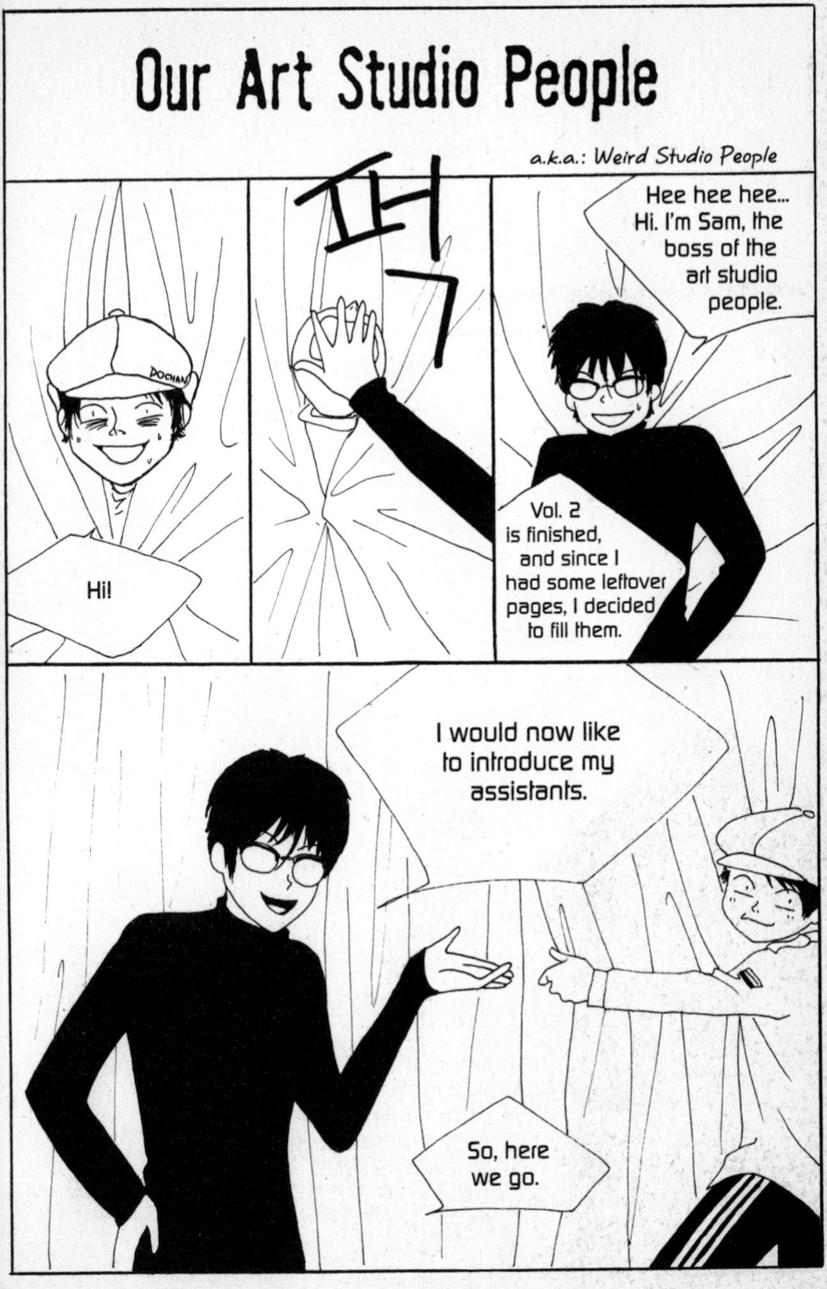
Our Art Studio People
a.k.a.: Weird Studio People
Hi!
Hee hee hee... Hi. I'm Sam, the boss of the art studio people.
Vol. 2 is finished, and since I had some leftover pages, I decided to fill them.
I would now like to introduce my assistants.
So, here we go.

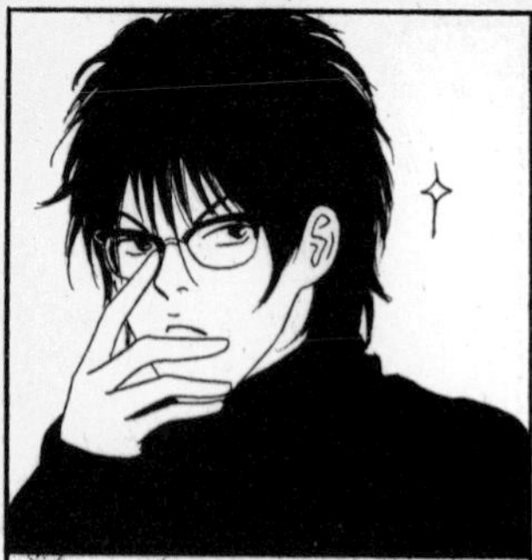

The Boss, "Sam"

An alien from the Pleiades.
Favorite music: Punk, Hardcore, Psychedelic, etc.
Least favorite music: Ballads
Hobby: To scare the assistants with his eyes (it doesn't work on Yeojin)

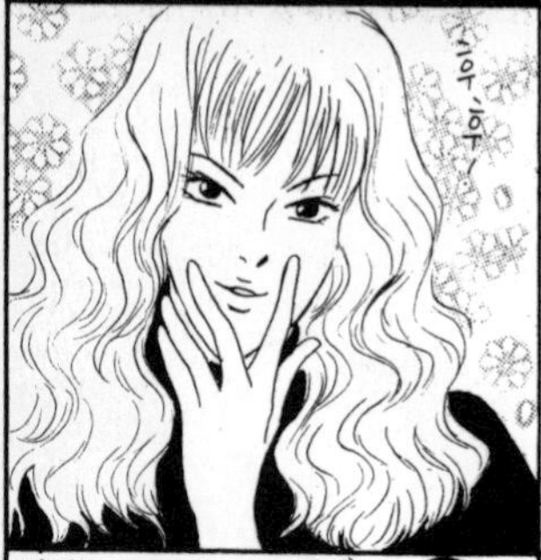

The Head Assistant, "Yeojin"

Lives 10 minutes from the studio, so he has no worries about transportation expenses.
Favorite music: Korean pop (especially pretty female singers)
Least favorite music: Anything with a husky man's voice
Hobby: To change the guys in the background pictures to girls. Looking at girls' bodies in magazines. Talking to himself.
Specialty: Being girly
**Married!

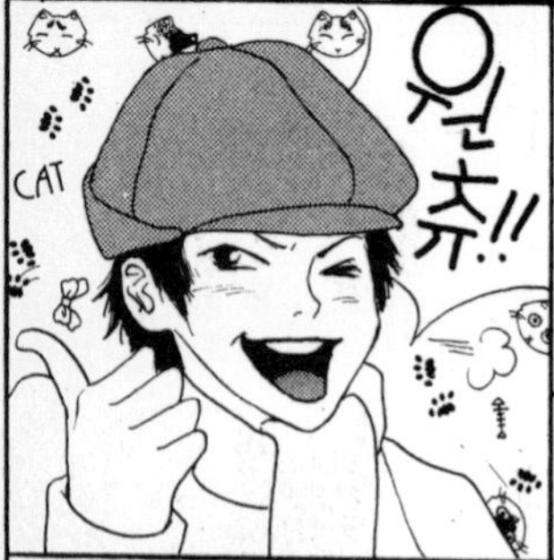
윈츄!!
CAT

The Rookie, "Do-Chan"

Transportation fee: 3,000 won* roundtrip (He's afraid to go home)
Favorite music: J-Rock, Traditional Korean music
Least Favorite music: Latin music (Especially Ricky Martin!)
Hobby: Destroying things around the studio
Specialty: Being exciting
**Single

*won is Korean currency

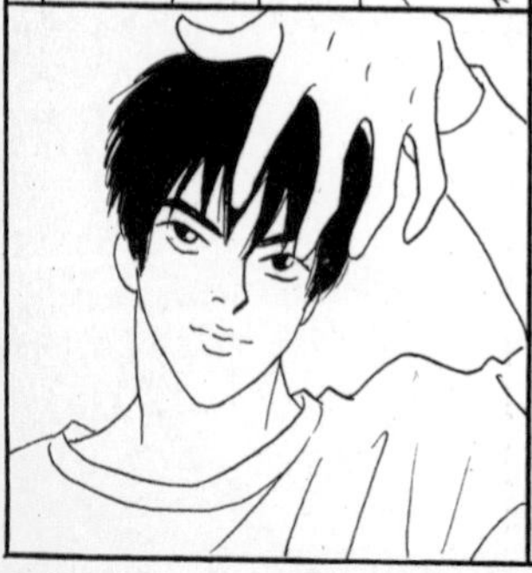

The Former Head Assistant, "Sangyul"

Model for the character "Sangyul" in *Soul to Seoul.*
He had to leave the studio to fulfill his army duty .
He is currently working part-time.
Favorite music: Anything good
Least favorite music: Doesn't exist
Hobby: Self-directing
Specialty: Falling asleep while pretending to work. Smiling in a gross way to freak out the studio people.

The Former Assistant, "Inho"

6'2". He was used frequently as a model for Spike. He also left the studio to fulfill his army duty.
Favorite music: Anime soundtracks
Least favorite music: ?
Hobby: Remembering the dialogue from games
Specialty: Talking in his sleep and memorizing the dialogue by doing that
**Currently going out with a girl who is eight years older than him.

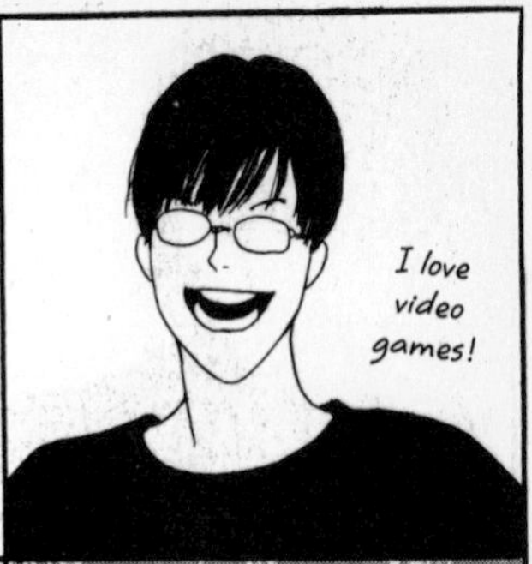
I love video games!

The Friend, "Zoo"

My longtime friend, who was also my very first assistant. Currently lives in Australia.
Favorite music: J-pop, Jazz
Least favorite music: ?
Hobby: Threatening friends and dragging them to PC rooms.
Specialty: ?
**Currently going out with someone who is eight years younger.

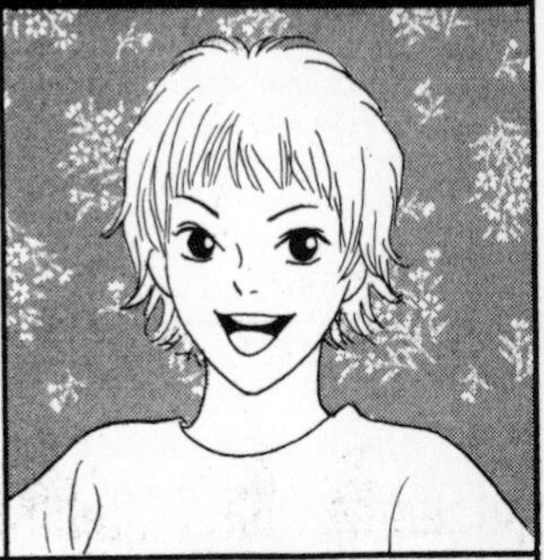

The Side Assistant, "Chiho"

Survival Game maniac. Heavily into military fashion, but only tough-looking stuff.
Favorite music: ?
Least favorite music: Anything sung by a female
Hobby: Collecting guns
Specialty: Being cutesy
**Married

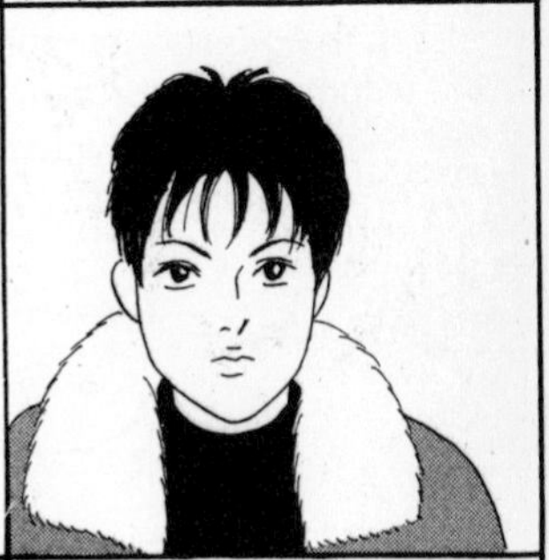

My Pet, "Yaongs"

We had to amputate her leg in December of 1998. She currently has three legs.
Hobby: Hunting with her master
Specialty: Imitating people's voices. (She can almost imitate things like "Yaong" "no eat" "not me.")
She is so loved by the studio people that she's spoiled rotten.
**Has been neutered.

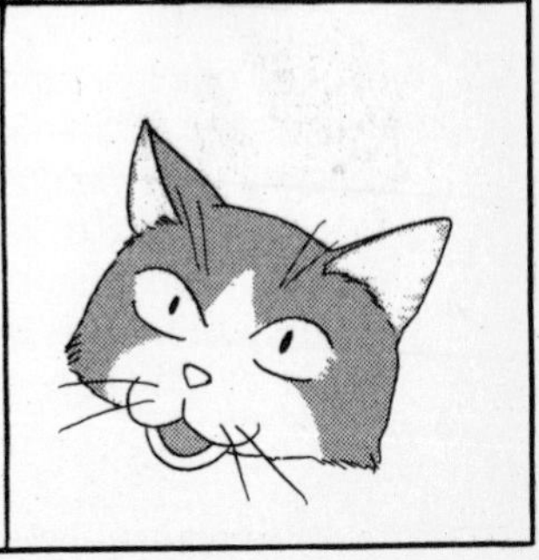

Semi Studio People...

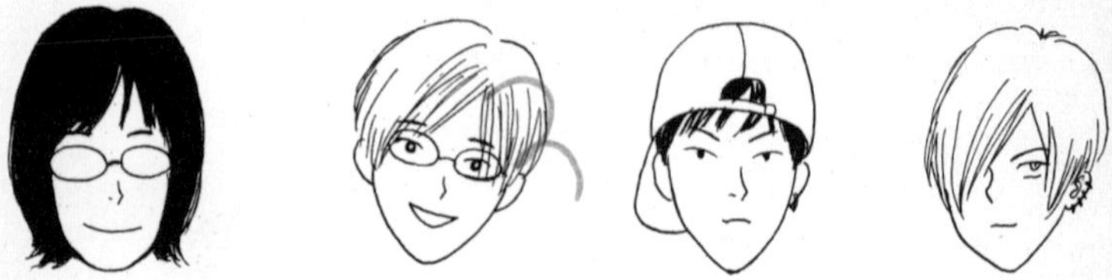

Rookie Rocker *Taejun*

Has long hair, a wide forehead and a great sense of humor. Great to be around.

Byungchul
(who wants to be a singer)

Started joining our meetings without anyone noticing.

Techno DJ Sujin

The model for *Soul to Seoul's* "Sujin." It is rumored he would kill for food.

Shinwoo
(the flaky college student.)

He doesn't come out that often anymore, but he was the motivator for many of us getting together in the beginning.

Oh...and for those of you who frequently send me pictures, and want to be assistants...I'm so sorry for not responding quickly enough... All the assistants and their team leader, Mr. Lee, are very sorry for being so late all the time...

Oh! And one last thing... please send any fan letters to my e-mail address. It's yachak@unitel.co.kr. Or send correspondence to editor@TOKYOPOP.com. Thank you for all your support.

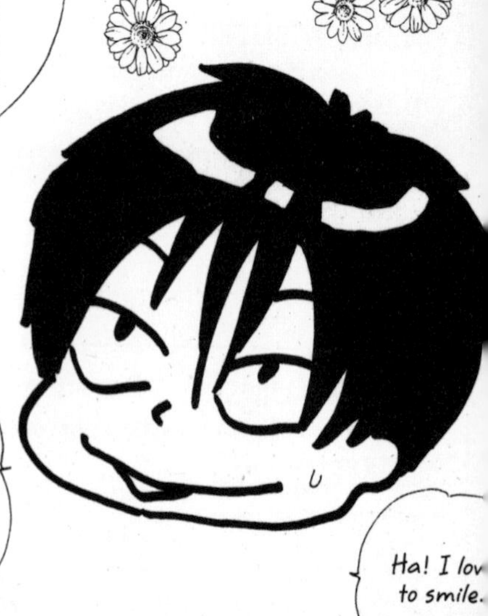
Ha! I lov
to smile.

The End

In the next volume of...

SOUL TO SEOUL™

Spike, one of the only constants in Kai's life, disappears from the neighborhood for a while. When he returns, it is as a bodyguard--and he and the girl he protects enroll in the same high school as Kai and Sunil! Although Kai and Sunil spend more time together, she wants to know everything about him--including his hidden life. But living dangerously is no laughing matter; to keep Sunil safe when a fight breaks out with rival Gui-Ryung gang members, Kai might pay with his life!

Check it out!

VAN VON HUNTER

EVIL NEVER DIES...
BUT EVIL STUFF DOES!

FROM THE WINNERS OF TOKYOPOP'S FIRST RISING STARS OF MANGA COMPETITION

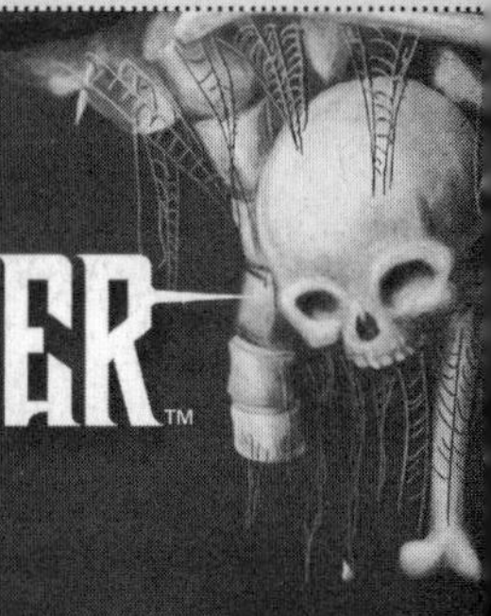

VAN VON HUNTER™

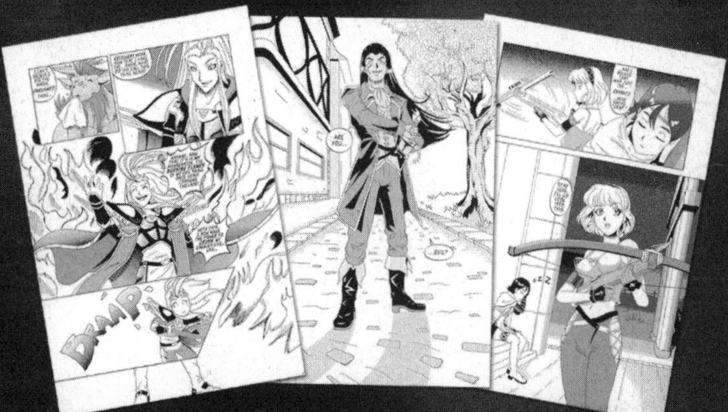

In the dark ages long ago, in a war-torn land where tranquility and harmony once blossomed, tyranny ruled with a flaming fist! At last, a hero arose to defeat the evildoers and returned hope to the people and peace to the countryside. Now...the sinister forces are back with a vengeance, and in their hour of direst-est need, the commoners once again seek a champion to right wrongs and triumph over villainy! Unfortunately, they could only get the mighty warrior Van Von Hunter, Hunter of Evil...Stuff!

Together with his loyal, memory-challenged sidekick, Van Von Hunter is on a never-ending quest to smite the bad guys—and believe us, they're real bad!

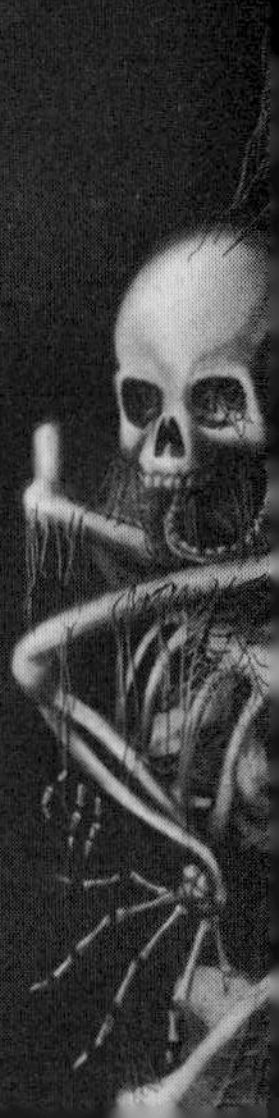

Preview the manga at:

www.TOKYOPOP.com/vanvonhunter
www.VanVonHunter.com

T
TEEN
AGE 13+